Genealogy of the Tragic

Genealogy of the Tragic

GREEK TRAGEDY AND GERMAN
PHILOSOPHY

Joshua Billings

PRINCETON UNIVERSITY PRESS

PRINCETON AND OXFORD

Copyright © 2014 by Princeton University Press
Published by Princeton University Press, 41 William Street, Princeton, New Jersey 08540
In the United Kingdom: Princeton University Press, 6 Oxford Street, Woodstock, Oxfordshire
OX20 1TR

press.princeton.edu

Cover art: *Oedipus at Colonus*, Fulchran-Jean Harriet, 1798. Courtesy of the Cleveland
Museum of Art, Mr. and Mrs. William H. Marlatt Fund 2002.3.

First paperback printing, 2017

Cloth ISBN 978-0-691-15923-2

Paperback ISBN: 978-0-691-17636-9

British Library Cataloging-in-Publication Data is available

This book has been composed in Sabon Next LT Pro

Printed on acid-free paper. ∞

Printed in the United States of America

For my parents, Susan and Andy, and my brother, Gabe

Σοφοκλέους Οἰδίπους ἐπὶ Κολωνῷ.
εὗρες Σοφόκλεις ἐν σοφοῖς μέγα κλέος·
ἀλλοτρίας γὰρ συμπλέκων θρηνῳδίας,
ἅπαντας ἡμᾶς πενθίμους ἀπειργάσω.

The *Oedipus at Colonus* of Sophocles.
You found, Sophocles, great renown [*kleos*] among wise people [*sophois*].
For entwining the lamentations of others,
You made us all sorrowful.

—Scholiastic epigram to Oedipus at Colonus

Viele versuchten umsonst das Freudigste freudig zu sagen
    Hier spricht endlich es mir, hier in der Trauer sich aus.

Many tried in vain to say the most joyous joyously,
    Here finally it reveals itself to me, here in mourning.

—Hölderlin, "Sophocles"

Contents

Preface

TRAGEDY, PLATO TELLS US (*LAWS* 658D), is a subject for young men. Since middle school, I have continually been drawn to tragedy in performance and on the page, and in the ten years since entering university, Greek tragedy has been the center of my intellectual life. Most of all, I have wondered what it is about these works that makes them speak so profoundly to my own experience and sense of the world. In figures like Hölderlin, Nietzsche, and Benjamin, I found young men who had answered these questions with staggering brilliance and insight, and enriched my own appreciation and understanding. This book arose out of my effort to see tragedy through their eyes. As an investigation of an investigation, it has led far astray from the phenomenon itself, but it may be, as Hölderlin writes, that it is only "aus linkischem Gesichtspunkt" ("from an awkward point of view") that we can hope to grasp the most important questions of meaning. Reading tragedy through Idealism may not make us "more Greek" readers (whatever that would mean), but it can make us more authentically modern ones, in the sense of reflecting on the timeliness and untimeliness of Greek tragedy for us. And I believe we *need* tragedy—not only as scholars and teachers, but as beings thrown into existence and one another.

I have had extraordinary good fortune in mentors, colleagues, and institutional homes, and the generosity with which I have been treated makes the flaws of the work presented here all the more glaring. This project began as a dissertation in Classics at Oxford, where Oliver Taplin and Fiona Macintosh supervised my work. Despite the unconventionality of the project, they welcomed me warmly and advised my research with extraordinary perceptiveness. Oliver asked me, at a number of crucial moments, vital and unexpected questions, while Fiona showed an uncanny ability to foresee where my research was going long before I did. During a year in the Oxford German department, and for some time after, Manfred Engel guided my halting steps in German intellectual history and offered me a standard of rigor that I can only hope to have satisfied. At intermediate stages, Gregory Hutchinson, Tim Whitmarsh, and Patrick Finglass all served as assessors, and I benefited from their feedback on early drafts. The dissertation was examined by Glenn Most and Felix Budelmann, and their thoughtful comments directed the revisions in which the book assumed its current form. To Glenn especially, I owe special thanks for his continued guidance, and for the model his scholarship has provided me.

Four colleagues endured the entire dissertation-cum-book at different stages, and offered me crucial advice. Miriam Leonard has been a mentor and friend from early on in the project, and I have continually learned from her scholarship, conversation, and penetrating comments on written work. Constanze Güthenke read and listened to too many stages of this work to count, and offered thoughtful suggestions, probing questions, and warm encouragement. Jim Porter was a formative influence in print long before I found him to be a generous colleague, and his reading of the full manuscript was pivotal in clarifying and honing the central argument. Most recently, Allen Speight kindly agreed to read the entire manuscript, and offered extraordinarily perceptive comments, which have greatly improved the rigor of my interpretations and argument.

This project was in many ways inspired by my undergraduate mentors, Albert Henrichs and John Hamilton. In different ways, their approaches to scholarship have been lodestars for my own—Albert's for the warmth and open-mindedness with which he approaches questions of meaning, ancient and modern, and John's for the imagination and rigor he brings to philology. Renate Schlesier has welcomed me to Berlin numerous times over the past six years, and I have learned from her in every exchange. Michael Silk has been a wise counselor and good angel at several important moments. Since my time in Cambridge, I have benefited from the good friendship and extraordinary intellectual energy of Simon Goldhill.

I have been further lucky to find stimulating interlocutors in Matthew Bell, Angus Bowie, Jessica Blum, Rüdiger Campe, Roger Dawe, William Fitzgerald, Renaud Gagné, Susanne Gödde, Nora Goldschmidt, Emily Gowers, Edith Hall, Katherine Harloe, Richard Hunter, Daniel King, Oliver Leege, Pauline LeVen, Charlie Louth, Roger Paulin, Andrei Pesic, Peter Pesic, Martin Ruehl, Anette Schwarz, Scott Scullion, Richard Seaford, Amia Srinivasan, Oliver Thomas, Anna Uhlig, Marie-Christin Wilm, and Larry Wolff. Lucas Zwirner served as much more than a last pair of eyes before print, and I benefited greatly from his comments on the near-final manuscript. Finally, though they were not directly involved in this project, I wish to record my gratitude to four undergraduate teachers, from whom I learned many of the skills that went into this work, and whose kindness has buoyed me at important moments: Jim Engell guided me through my first effort at producing scholarship; Greg Nagy opened my eyes to possibilities for thinking imaginatively about Greek literature; Hugo van der Velden showed me a way of looking; and Helen Vendler taught me to read poetry.

Of the institutions that have facilitated this work, my first thanks goes to the Rhodes Trust, to which I owe the opportunity to study at Oxford. Merton College and the Oxford Faculties of Classics and Medieval and Modern Languages proved stimulating environments in which to live and work, and offered financial assistance for research travel (including grants from the Craven Committee, the Zaharoff Fund, and the Simms Fund). A semester exchange at the Maximilianeum in Munich was particularly fruitful, in large part because Friedrich Vollhardt, Arne Zerbst, and the Schelling-Kommission of the Bayerische Akademie der Wissenschaften welcomed me into their midst and provided an exciting ferment for work on German Idealism. St. John's College, Cambridge offered beautiful surroundings and warm interactions for a year while I turned the dissertation into a book as a Research Fellow, and has continued to be generous and flexible. At Yale, I have found a welcoming home in the Department of Classics and the Humanities Program, and I am especially grateful to Howard Bloch, Kirk Freudenburg, Bryan Garsten, and Chris Kraus, for their goodwill and wise guidance in the transition. A research grant from the Griswold Fund and a publication grant from the Hilles Fund helped me complete final work on the manuscript. Joshua Katz brought this project and me to Princeton University Press and has guided me through the process with warmth and insight, and Rob Tempio and Ryan Mulligan deftly oversaw its publication. Eva Jaunzems provided thorough copyediting, and Jill Harris was a pleasure to work with as production editor. Finally, Dylan Kenny was a careful proofreader.

Trying to thank the people who have enriched life outside of the library in a scholarly preface seems to me at once superfluous and inadequate, but this book is dedicated to my family, my first and best teachers.

Note on Translations, Citations, and Abbreviations

ALL TRANSLATIONS FROM Greek, Latin, French, and German are my own, and aim for transparency at the expense of elegance. For major works, in addition, citations of English translations are given, and I have often referred to these for assistance. I have given the original language in brackets where it seemed particularly important, and I felt it essential to give all quotations from Hegel's *Phenomenology* and Hölderlin's *Sophocles* in the original German, as these two texts constitute a major focus of the entire book and are so intricate as to render translation particularly perilous.

Modern editions of major texts are cited parenthetically in text, using the abbreviations below, while older editions and secondary literature are cited in footnotes. In choosing editions, I have prioritized ease of reference over philological exactness, which has led to relying in the first instance on the editions of the Deutscher Klassiker Verlag (and for Hegel, the Suhrkamp *Werke in zwanzig Bänden*), and using other editions only as necessary. Despite the DKV editions' modernized orthography and selective coverage, the accessibility of the texts and their up-to-date supplementary materials recommended them. When citing from older editions, I have not modernized any spelling, which leads to an occasionally jarring coexistence of original and modernized orthography. Greek accents and breathings have not been added where absent from the source text. Standard citations are given for classical texts and refer to the *Oxford Classical Text* (OCT) edition.

The amount of secondary literature on any one of the major figures discussed in the book is intimidating. I believe I have taken into account the major references as of submission (summer 2013), but I have sought not to burden the book with endless citations of helpful but inessential literature, or to engage in the kind of esoteric debates important only to scholars of a single figure. Citations of secondary literature are therefore limited to those works that have directly informed my reading, or which provide avenues for further thought. Since I recognize that some of the material in the book will be new to almost all readers, I have provided bibliographical notes at the beginning of each chapter that orient my discussion within (mainly) English-language secondary literature.

ABBREVIATIONS

Goethe

Sämtliche Werke, Briefe, Tagebücher und Gespräche, ed. Frankfurt: Deutscher Klassiker Verlag, 1985–99. (*FA*)

Hegel

Werke in zwanzig Bänden. Frankfurt: Suhrkamp, 1970. (*WZB*)
Briefe von und an Hegel. Hamburg: Meiner, 1969–81. (*Briefe*)
    Aesthetics: Lectures on Fine Art, trans. T. M. Knox. Oxford: Clarendon, 1975. (*Aesthetics*)
    Early Theological Writings, trans. T. M. Knox. Chicago: University of Chicago Press, 1948. (*ETW*)
    Natural Law, trans. T. M. Knox. Philadelphia: University of Pennsylvania Press, 1975. (*NL*)
    Phenomenology of Spirit, trans. Terry Pinkard. Online at: http://web.mac.com/titpaul/Site/Phenomenology_of_Spirit_page.html. (*Phenomenology*)
    "Oldest System Program of German Idealism," trans. H. S. Harris, in *Hegel's Development: toward the Sunlight, 1770–1801*, 510–12. Oxford: Clarendon, 1972. (*SP*)

Herder

Werke. Frankfurt: Deutscher Klassiker Verlag, 1985–2000. (*HW*)
    Selected Writings on Aesthetics, trans. Gregory Moore. Princeton: Princeton University Press (*Aesthetics*)

Hölderlin

Sämtliche Werke und Briefe. Frankfurt: Deutscher Klassiker Verlag, 1992–94. (*SWB*)
    Essays and Letters, trans. Jeremy Adler and Charlie Louth. London: Penguin, 2008. (*E&L*)
    The Death of Empedocles, trans. David Farrell Krell. Albany: SUNY Press, 2008. (*DoE*)

Kant

Gesammelte Schriften (Akademie-Ausgabe). Berlin: Preussische Akademie der Wissenschaften (et seq.), 1900–. (*AA*)
    Critique of Pure Reason, trans. Paul Guyer and Allen W. Wood. Cambridge: Cambridge University Press, 1998. (*CPR*, cited according to B text)
    Critique of the Power of Judgment, trans. Paul Guyer and Eric Matthews. Cambridge: Cambridge University Press, 2000. (*CPJ*)

Lessing

Werke und Briefe in zwölf Bänden. Frankfurt: Deutscher Klassiker Verlag, 1985–2003. (*WBZB*)

Nietzsche

Kritische Studienausgabe. Berlin: de Gruyter, 1988. (*KSA*)
Werke: kritische Gesamtausgabe. Berlin: de Gruyter, 1967–. (*KGW*)
    The Birth of Tragedy and Other Writings, trans. Ronald Speirs. Cambridge: Cambridge University Press, 1999. (*Birth*)

Schelling

Historisch-kritische Ausgabe. Stuttgart: Frommann-Holzboog, 1976–. (*AA*)
Sämtliche Werke. 14 vols. Stuttgart: Cotta, 1856–61. (*SW*)
    "Philosophical letters on dogmatism and criticism" in *The Unconditional in Human Knowledge: Four Early Essays,* trans. Fritz Marti, 156–96. London: Associated University Presses, 1980. (*LDC*)
    Philosophy of Art, trans. Douglas W. Stott. Minneapolis: Minnesota University Press, 1989. (*Philosophy*)

Schiller

Werke und Briefe in zwölf Bänden. Frankfurt: Deutscher Klassiker Verlag, 1992–2004. (*FA*)
Schillers Werke: Nationalausgabe. Weimar: Böhlhaus, 1943–. (*NA*)
    Essays, ed. Walter Hinderer and Daniel O. Dahlstrom. New York: Continuum, 1993. (*Essays*)

A. W. Schlegel

Kritische Ausgabe der Vorlesungen. Paderborn: Schöningh, 1989–. (*KAV*)
Kritische Schriften und Briefe. Stuttgart: Kohlhammer, 1962–74. (*KSB*)
    A Course of Lectures on Dramatic Art and Literature, trans. John Black; rev. A.J.W. Morrison. London: Bohn, 1846. (*Lectures*)

Friedrich Schlegel

Kritische Friedrich-Schlegel-Ausgabe. Paderborn: Schöningh, 1958–. (*KFSA*)
    On the Study of Greek Poetry, trans. Stuart Barnett. Albany: SUNY Press, 2001. (*Study*)

Genealogy of the Tragic

Tragedy and Philosophy around 1800

TRAGEDY IS THE MOST PHILOSOPHICAL of art forms. The reasons may be historically contingent, but the consequences have been profound. No form of art has inspired as much theoretical reflection, or been as important to the development of philosophy. This interrelation of text and theory, which reaches from Greek antiquity to the present, results largely from the survival of Aristotle's *Poetics*. Aristotle, writing in the mid-fourth century BC, gave an account of tragedy's constitution and effect that has influenced nearly all philosophical understandings of the genre—and of poetry in general—since. Tragedy is the only form to arrive in modernity with a more or less comprehensive theory (despite its fragmentariness and occasional obscurity) from so authoritative a source. The *Poetics* is the origin of the notions that have turned the Greek form τραγῳδία, which flourished in Athens in the fifth century BC, into the modern genre of tragedy, which has effloresced in various times and places throughout Western cultures of the last half millennium.

The link between ancient Greek and modern tragedy is, in a historical sense, tenuous in the extreme. It is only through an act of will or imagination that we can speak of Sophocles and Shakespeare in the same breath. Yet, though there is no continuous tradition of creation linking fifth century Athens to the present, there is a rich tradition of reading and commentary. This is true for all of "canonical" classical literature, but tragedy is unique in that it has consistently been understood through the lens of a more or less systematic theory. This theory, much more than the Greek plays themselves, made possible the "revival" of tragedy in the Renaissance, and allows us to speak of a continuity in the genre from antiquity to the present (notwithstanding its variously diagnosed "deaths"). No modern genre has been defined by such an intimate relation between theory and practice, nor does any other form of art have such a substantial body of philosophical reflection surrounding it. Tragedy for moderns is uniquely philosophical.

But tragedy has not always been philosophical in the same way. Around 1800, tragedy's way of meaning underwent a major shift, with broad consequences for thought on literature and philosophy. This shift was not unique to tragedy—it was part of the intellectual currents associated with the romantic period broadly—but tragedy held a privileged place for some of the most important figures of the era, those associated with German idealist thought: Schiller, the Schlegel brothers, Schelling, Hölderlin, and

Hegel.[1] Among these extraordinarily talented, closely interconnected thinkers, Greek tragedy acquired a philosophical importance different in kind from any envisioned previously. Through the eighteenth century, tragedy had been considered primarily in rhetorical terms (as a way of producing a certain emotional effect), but since 1800 it has more often been considered in speculative terms (as a way of making sense of the human world). This new way of meaning has had wide-ranging consequences for notions of tragedy and antiquity, and also for understandings of artistic value, of the project of philosophy, and of the character of modernity.[2] It is only since around 1800 that works of art have been considered in such philosophical and often metaphysical terms. Greek tragedy played a leading role in this development, as the foundation for elaborating a concept of "the tragic" that extended far beyond an aesthetic context, encompassing history, politics, religion, and ontology.[3]

This book tries to grasp the turn to tragedy around 1800 as both a historical phenomenon and a theoretical paradigm. Historically, it asks how the significance of tragedy changed so radically in such a short period and, especially, how the theories of Hegel and Hölderlin emerged as and when they did. Theoretically, it tries to understand the consequences of this shift for understandings of tragedy, philosophy, and antiquity, and to describe the most important legacies of idealist thought. These aims place the concerns of the book, perhaps somewhat uneasily, between the methods of positive, "scientific" inquiry and disciplinary history; and between the objects of literary criticism and philosophical aesthetics. Though these pursuits are usually separated in academic discourse—into classical philology and classical reception on the one hand, and philosophy and intellectual history on the other—I maintain that they are crucially interdependent, and that a continuous dialogue between them makes us more reflective and more insightful historians, philosophers, and literary critics. Imperfect as my attempt at integrating these perspectives is, I hope it will demonstrate the

[1] Throughout, I use "idealist" in a general sense to describe the tendency to employ forms of speculative thought in reaction to the critical philosophy of Kant, indicating a broad swath of philosophers from the 1780s forward (some, though not all of whom, considered themselves "idealists"). "Idealism" (as a proper noun) refers, in a more specialized sense, to the philosophers Fichte, Schelling, and Hegel and their immediate circles (with Hölderlin important in the early development).

[2] "Modernity" in this sense is a philosophical category more than an epochal distinction, and is defined especially by the consciousness of historical rupture that characterizes the postrevolutionary age.

[3] On the relationship between tragedy and the tragic, see M. S. Silk, ed. *Tragedy and the tragic: Greek theatre and beyond* (Oxford: Oxford University Press, 1996); Glenn W. Most, "Generating genres: the idea of the tragic," in *Matrices of genre: authors, canons, and society*, ed. Mary Depew and Dirk Obbink (Cambridge, MA: Harvard University Press, 2000); Simon Goldhill, *Sophocles and the language of tragedy* (New York: Oxford University Press, 2012), 137–65.

value of bringing together positivist and historicist approaches, and critical and theoretical inquiries—and encourage others to do the same.

The idealist concept of the tragic is particularly in need of an integrative approach, as it is at once a major concern of critical theory, and a foundation, consciously or not, for many historical treatments of Greek tragedy. The list of twentieth- and twenty-first-century thinkers who have engaged with tragedy is extensive: Freud, Benjamin, Heidegger, Schmitt, Camus, Lacan, Foucault, Derrida, Irigaray, Žižek, and Butler would be only a start.[4] Many of these theorists directly confront Idealism (though Nietzsche is a more direct influence on some), yet very often the mode of dialogue is appropriative or polemical, and fails to do justice to the complexity of the original theories. Such engagements are undoubtedly legitimate in their own terms, but they have often led to a severely attenuated understanding of idealist thought, and an overlooking of some of the most interesting and provocative elements of these theories.

If Idealism is rhetorically present and substantively absent in much philosophical discourse, for classical scholarship, the situation is the reverse. The influence of Idealism is profoundly and widely felt, but very seldom acknowledged.[5] Though idealist theories substantially define the possibilities for reading tragedy in the present, they are often vaguely understood, ignored, or explicitly disavowed. This is particularly striking since the "political turn" in classical scholarship, which has often taken the form of a historicism that rejects the supposed universalism of idealist readings, while practicing a mode of historical interpretation that is profoundly indebted to Idealism. Only through a direct engagement with Idealism, though, can classical scholars genuinely question or appropriate its legacy. For both theorists of the tragic and historians of tragedy, a fresh approach to idealist thought holds the potential to enrich contemporary approaches and provoke new directions in scholarship.

The objections are well known: Idealism is ahistorical in its understanding of literature, willful and appropriative in its readings, selective in its canon, alternatively naive or reactionary in its politics, and fatally imbued with idiosyncratic Christian theologies. None of these reproaches is false, though most are less true than is usually assumed. The reason for taking Idealism seriously, though, is not that its readings of tragedy are convincing as historical scholarship, but that its readings of tragedy make profound sense of the texts of Greek tragedy. Even if the particulars of its sense would not be

---

[4]Though it appeared too late to be taken fully into account, there is an illuminating treatment of the twentieth century in Julian Young, *The philosophy of tragedy: from Plato to Žižek* (Cambridge: Cambridge University Press, 2013).

[5]On the conflicted place of the philosophy of the tragic in classical scholarship, see Miriam Leonard, "Tragedy and the seductions of philosophy," *Cambridge Classical Journal* 58 (2012): 147–54.

upheld today, the *possibilities of meaning* it discovers can be a guide for us.[6] These possibilities are importantly different from (though related to) the possibilities we actualize in reading ancient literature. Reading tragedy with idealist thinkers pushes us to reconsider our own approaches and to entertain other, no less significant, ways that Greek tragedy might be meaningful.

This aim is different from the "feeding back" often cited in studies of classical reception. The significance of reception studies, I propose, does not lie in their ability to offer answers to the questions typically posed by classical scholars, but in suggesting different questions to put to the classics. For the present purposes, the most significant result of reception theory and scholarship is the recognition that the traces of past readings are active in every interpretation, that there is no "immediate" access to a text—no more today than in 458 BC.[7] In recent years, it has become clear that German Idealism remains the most powerful mediation of Greek tragedy for the present, and this inquiry seeks to vindicate and extend this importance.[8] The aim of excavating the idealist roots of our understanding of tragedy is at once to increase our reflective consciousness of its influence, and, more importantly, to suggest ways in which our own frames of interpretation might be broadened by engagement with past mediations. We should not only look to receptions of the classics for their congruence with contemporary concerns (which can lead only to reinforcing our own critical orientations, with their inevitable blind spots), but for their difference, their untimeliness.

• • • • •

The central historical argument of this book is that concepts of the tragic around 1800 are fundamentally conditioned by reflections on history, and particularly by a questioning of the place of ancient literature in modernity. The importance of historical thought for theories of tragedy has often been noticed, but its significance has not adequately been explored. The problems of historical thought, I argue, are formative for modern approaches to tragedy, and establish a crucial continuity between pre- and post-Kantian understandings of the genre. Concentrating on thought on tragedy through the long eighteenth century brings into focus the most important consequence of idealist thought on art: its reformulation of the possibilities of artistic meaning. This reformulation is crucially motivated by the question of

---

[6] For Idealism as a form of "making sense," see Pierre Judet de la Combe, *Les tragédies grecques sont-elles tragiques? Théâtre et théorie* (Montrouge: Bayard, 2010), 46–56.

[7] There are productive discussions of such processes of mediation in Charles Martindale and Richard F. Thomas, eds., *Classics and the uses of reception* (Malden: Blackwell, 2006). For the current state of discussion, see *Classical Receptions Journal* 5.2 (2013).

[8] Especially important are Miriam Leonard, *Athens in Paris: ancient Greece and the political in postwar French thought* (Oxford: Oxford University Press, 2005); Judet de la Combe, *Les tragédies grecques sont-elles tragiques?*; Goldhill, *Sophocles and the language of tragedy*.

how to account for the significance of works of art across time. Greek tragedy is the central ground for idealist inquiries into the historical nature of artworks and their philosophical significance, and an increasing knowledge of Greek tragedy is an important catalyst in its own right for these theories.

The roots of idealist thought on tragedy, I argue, reach back well before the romantic era. Idealism is crucially shaped by a change in the status of history that took place in the latter half of the eighteenth century. For approaches to tragedy, the salient feature of this shift was that a sense of historical difference entered into an understanding of genre that had previously been essentially ahistorical. The history of tragedy could no longer be treated as continuous from ancient Greece to modern times, and the Aristotelian theory that had guided creation and reflection appeared radically limited in its ability to explain the experience of tragedy in the present. Without the assumption of continuity that grounded earlier critical approaches, the meaning of Greek works was refounded on the basis of a new philosophy of art that took its formative impulses from Kantian philosophy and the French Revolution. The conceptions of tragedy that emerged in the 1790s are animated by the question of the place of ancient literature in a philosophical modernity that saw itself as radically different from previous moments in time.

This might seem a rather narrow way of approaching idealist theories of tragedy. The importance of tragedy to post-Kantian thought reaches into many domains that are not ostensibly historical, and is not always elaborated in reflections on the difference between antiquity and modernity. Yet I argue that the engagement with historical thought is not simply one of many contexts for tragedy's meaning, but the foundation of tragedy's possibility of meaning for idealist thinkers. The importance of historical thought to theories of the tragic emerges particularly strongly when contrasted with previous understandings of the genre. For the early eighteenth century, the significance of Greek tragedy was essentially ahistorical, accessible to anyone with the proper rational faculties and a dose of imagination. This mode of thought ensured the continuing value of Greek tragedies, but it saw nothing especially meaningful about them, in comparison to Homeric epic, Latin lyric, or modern French dramatic poetry. The mid-eighteenth century, though, brought with it two important changes, which together raised Greek tragedy above other forms in its meaningfulness for modernity: first, a growing body of aesthetic thought sought to place different forms of art into more or less hierarchical relations, ultimately finding tragedy distinct in its representation of human action in general (a much broader sense than previous moralizing readings); and second, an explosion of philhellenic discourse elevated Greek above Roman culture in European (especially German) thought, and located the height of Greek culture in Athenian civic freedom. Tragedy's content, as a representation of meaningful action, and its form, as a product of the Athenian golden age, gave the genre a privileged role as both *depiction of* and *object within* historical processes.

The historical perspective adopted here sheds new light on why idealist thinkers turn to tragedy in particular. Appropriations of tragedy around 1800 are efforts to grapple with the question of human freedom, a problem of central importance to post-Kantian thought.[9] Idealist thinkers understand Greek tragedy to represent a distinctive form of human freedom, and to crystallize issues of agency and subjectivity that are central to their own philosophical inquiries. Oedipus' discovery of his own past, Antigone's struggle against the edict of Creon, Orestes' submission to the judgment of the Areopagus—all are seen in terms of a concept of freedom that is ontological, political, social, and religious at once.

Yet Greek tragedy's representation of freedom is also importantly alien to modernity, and this foreignness explains a great deal of the urgency of idealist theories. The questions of freedom that draw idealist thinkers to ancient tragedy do not find immediate answers, and force these thinkers to elaborate relations of distance and proximity in grappling with tragic freedom. This imbrication of historical and philosophical thought can only be adequately understood against the background of previous regimes of historical reflection. Theories of tragedy are not simply alternate means of philosophical inquiry, but represent a particular, and crucially important, perspective on a central problem: *the historical nature of human freedom*. The freedom at issue in Greek tragedy is and is not the freedom of idealist philosophy, and this tension makes Greek tragedy "the closest other" for philosophical thought around 1800.[10] Grappling with tragedy's representation of human freedom becomes a means through which modernity seeks to understand itself by engagement with the alterity of antiquity.

Tracing the nexus of tragedy and history in idealist thought illuminates connections and continuities that previous scholars have neglected, and gives broader definition to a formative intellectual moment that is often studied atomistically.[11] Research into tragedy in the idealist period has been widely

[9] Robert Pippin has argued that the problem of freedom is the distinctive question of modern philosophy from Idealism forward: Robert B. Pippin, *Idealism as modernism: Hegelian variations* (Cambridge: Cambridge University Press, 1997); Robert B. Pippin, *Modernism as a philosophical problem: on the dissatisfactions of European high culture*, 2nd ed. (Malden: Blackwell, 1999).

[10] The concept comes from the work of Uvo Hölscher, who describes the Greeks as the "closest other" ("das nächste Fremde") of modernity. See Uvo Hölscher, "Selbstgespräch über den Humanismus," in *Das nächste Fremde: von Texten der griechischen Frühzeit und ihrem Reflex in der Moderne* (Munich: Beck, 1994).

[11] I follow, loosely, the method of *Konstellationsforschung* pioneered by Dieter Henrich. Henrich showed the extent to which early Idealism developed as a corporate project, with many different and contradictory strands. Much the same could be said of idealist thought on tragedy. See the essays in Martin Mulsow and Marcelo Stamm, eds., *Konstellationsforschung* (Frankfurt: Suhrkamp, 2005).

dispersed between the disciplines of history of philosophy, German studies, and classical reception, with individual studies usually concentrating on single thinkers or small groups, without giving a broader picture of their interactions and disputes. The idealist moment, I show, is united by common questions (though not shared answers), which make tragedy important to the development of quite disparate philosophical approaches. For all of the major theories, though, historical reflection is an integral aspect of thinking about tragedy. Charting this interplay as it emerges from the Enlightenment and becomes central to post-Kantian aesthetics yields a picture of Idealism as substantially engaged with the particularities of Greek tragedy and reflective on the limits of its own aesthetic theories. For idealist thinkers, elaborating a historical way of meaning for ancient literature seemed to demand, on the one hand, a contextual understanding of Greek tragedy, and on the other, an account of tragedy's place in modernity. The concept of the tragic is defined by a dual imperative: to understand both the Greekness of Greek tragedy and its modernity.

From the central nexus of idealist thought, other concerns and contexts radiate: textual scholarship and commentary, translation and adaptation, performance (especially operatic), other literatures with substantial bodies of tragedy (especially French, Spanish, and English), and philosophical idealism in its Platonic and Neoplatonic forms. Constructing this picture draws on various national literatures and social domains, and illuminates interactions and parallels that have not been noticed before. Such a broad-based inquiry is potentially endless and inevitably imperfect, but it is intended to serve as a corrective to the widespread tendency among historians of philosophy to concentrate only on more or less systematic theories, instead of accepting a broader diversity of reflection as relevant to theoretical understanding. Looking at philosophical developments in the context of a broader cultural change in attitudes to tragedy and antiquity, the perspective adopted here brings out the multiplicity of perspectives on a single, widely important topic.

In concentrating on historical thought, I draw attention to an area in which idealist theories could be especially valuable for contemporary approaches to antiquity. Idealism is highly—perhaps uniquely—reflective about the way that meaning is constructed through an interplay of past and present contexts. Poised between the universalizing assumptions of the eighteenth century and the historicizing currents that would dominate the nineteenth, idealist thinkers struggle to define a way of recognizing both the singularity of Athenian culture and its value for the present. The period around 1800 is a liminal moment in thinking about antiquity, and idealist theories show historical thought at a moment of particularly fruitful tension. Idealism understands the very process of reading ancient literature as a problem, considering the texts of tragedy in relation to a vision of what it is to be modern. This endeavor is historical and philosophical at once, and entails a reflection on the processes of mediation that condition the meaning of ancient literature in the present. Such reflection may be even more important today, when the universalist humanism that had ensured the central place of the Western classics is increasingly in question. In this moment of doubt about the educative value of antiquity, idealist theories of the tragic offer a rich ground for inquiry into the way that history conditions meaning in literature.

• • • • •

Since Peter Szondi's 1961 "An Essay on the Tragic," it has been proverbial that "since Aristotle, there has been a poetics of tragedy. Only since Schelling has there been a philosophy of the tragic."[12] Szondi diagnoses a symptom of a larger change in attitudes towards tragedy and antiquity generally, but he substantially misrepresents the causes of this shift and its continuity with earlier thought.[13] Though the meanings attributed to tragedy do change as radically as Szondi suggests, I argue that the questions remain deeply Aristotelian, and develop reflections on antiquity and modernity that have a significant history in eighteenth-century, mainly French, thought. These contexts are important to any understanding of theories of tragedy around 1800. Moreover, the "philosophy of the tragic" inaugurated by Schelling and carried forward by Schopenhauer, Kierkegaard, and Nietzsche in the nineteenth century, and Max Scheler and Walter Benjamin in the early twentieth century describes only one of many consequences of the broader shift in the understanding of tragedy at this moment. The significance of idealist thought on tragedy is not only that it establishes "the tragic" as a philosophical concern for an important (though limited) strand of German philosophy, but that the meaning that it finds in tragedy substantially alters ways of reading well beyond philosophy—that it establishes a possibility for Greek tragedy's meaning that did not exist before, which informs philosophical, literary, and historical discussions to this day. It is in creating these possibilities, rather than in discovering the essential tragic content, that Idealism has been and remains essential to thinking about tragedy.

The genealogical perspective adopted here is a direct response to Szondi's essay and the many accounts of the era that follow its basic narrative of rup-

---

[12]Peter Szondi, *An essay on the tragic*, trans. Paul Fleming (Stanford: Stanford University Press, 2002), 1. Szondi's historical narrative is broadly followed, though with a glance at earlier material, by Vassilis Lambropoulos, *The tragic idea* (London: Duckworth, 2006).

[13]Szondi's work is teleological in two ways: its historical account is, as he himself acknowledges, dominated by the thought of Hegel, which provides a lens through which all other thinkers are understood; and he then seeks to vindicate the Hegelian pattern of thought on tragedy through readings of tragedies in the second half of the book.

ture.[14] Without disputing that there is something radically new in what Szondi calls the "philosophy of the tragic," I argue that questions of history, which have been central for thinking about tragedy since the *Querelle des Anciens et des Modernes*, persist through the idealist era and continue to define modern approaches to tragedy. This necessitates a methodology that is developmental, or in Foucault's Nietzschean terminology, "genealogical."[15] Rather than jumping from one more or less fully developed theory to the next, I attempt to bring out the historical conditions, influences, and tensions that define thought on tragedy in this period.[16] The scope of thought treated is therefore much broader than has previously been considered relevant to the tragic. The account begins with the *Querelle des Anciens et des Modernes* in France at the end of the seventeenth century, and passes through eighteenth-century translations and commentaries on Greek tragedy to focus on the crucial period of idealist thought from 1792 onward. The account of this period pays far greater attention to the interaction of thinkers than any previous discussion, and describes the collective and farreaching development of a broadly idealist approach to tragic meaning. Finally, I turn to a close study of two major tragic texts of the early nineteenth century, Hegel's *Phenomenology of Spirit* (1807) and Hölderlin's "Notes" to his translations of Sophocles (1804), extraordinarily dense and fruitful discussions, which represent the strongest and today the most influential idealist theories. Though this story is teleological, privileging two texts over others of the period, it is also importantly aporetic in that it sees the significance of these texts in their formulation of tensions and paradoxes in the modern understanding of tragedy and antiquity, which define thought to

[14]Michael Lurie (Lurje) describes the history of reading Sophocles, *contra* Szondi, as essentially continuous: Michael Lurie, "Facing up to tragedy: toward an intellectual history of Sophocles in Europe from Camerarius to Nietzsche," in *A companion to Sophocles*, ed. Kirk Ormand (Chichester: Blackwell, 2012). See also Michael Lurje, *Die Suche nach der Schuld: Sophokles' Oedipus Rex, Aristoteles' Poetik und das Tragödienverständnis der Neuzeit* (Munich: Saur, 2004). I agree with certain aspects of Lurie's narrative, but it fails to do justice to the impact of the idealist philosophy of art. Though the nineteenth century's interpretive questions are substantially continuous with the eighteenth century's, the speculative theory of art changes the consequences of these concerns substantially, and in turn the way that tragedy is meaningful.

[15]See Michel Foucault, "Nietzsche, genealogy, history," in *Essential works of Michel Foucault, 1954–84. Vol. 2: Aesthetics, method, and epistemology*, ed. James D. Faubion (New York: New Press, 1998). I should make clear, though, that my adherence to Foucault's methodology is quite approximate, and would be fatally flawed (to a dogmatic genealogist) for its focus on "great thinkers" and the implicit—though self-conscious—teleologies of the discussion.

[16]This focus on the historical conditions of thought on tragedy distinguishes my study from most English-language literature on the topic: Dennis J. Schmidt, *On Germans and other Greeks: tragedy and ethical life* (Bloomington: Indiana University Press, 2001); Terry Eagleton, *Sweet violence: the idea of the tragic* (Oxford: Blackwell, 2003); David Farrell Krell, *The tragic absolute: German Idealism and the languishing of God* (Bloomington: Indiana University Press, 2005); Young, *The philosophy of tragedy*.

the present. It seeks neither to vindicate nor to apologize for idealist theories, but to show how idealist approaches have redefined the meaning of Greek tragedy and still pose urgent questions.

A genealogical perspective on German philosophy around 1800 allows for continuities with previous thought to emerge as they have not previously. These form a background—nearly always neglected—to the tragic philosophy of idealist thinkers. Two continuities are particularly striking, and are emphasized throughout the book. The first is the engagement with Aristotle's *Poetics*, and especially the notion of *catharsis*.[17] This may be surprising, as the generation following Herder is usually thought to be the first to see Aristotle's importance as primarily historical, describing conditions and goals that were valid for a single point in time, but which are not necessarily transferable to other ages. That picture needs nuance—even "arch-Aristotelians" like Dacier invoke reason as well as ancient authority, and "anti-Aristotelians" like Herder see elements of the *Poetics* as valid in all times and places—but the change in Aristotle's prestige is real. Despite the diminished centrality of the *Poetics*, however, Aristotle's terminology and his preference for the *Oedipus the King* (*Oedipus Tyrannus*) remain powerful for idealist thinkers. This is particularly evident in descriptions of the ends or aim of tragedy, which inevitably center on moments of cognitive revelation and recur to cathartic models in one way or another. Amid the variety in understandings of tragedy, an interpretation of *catharsis*, implicit or explicit, lies at the heart of every major theory around 1800.

The second major area of continuity is a sense of Greek tragedy's political valences. The turn to tragedy around 1800 is in many ways a response to the French Revolution, but it is not a turn away from politics. Theories of tragedy continue the questioning of authority and social constitution that had become urgent with the events in France. Consciously or unconsciously, tragedy came to be seen as a figure for the aporias of social transformation that the Revolution had revealed. This is well-documented and much-debated in the case of Hegel and Hölderlin, but frequently overlooked with respect to other idealist thinkers. It has not been noted, moreover, that the connection between Greek tragedy and contemporary political organization emerges directly from Enlightenment thought and establishes itself as the dominant approach to tragedy well before the 1790s. English and French approaches to tragedy from early in the century placed political issues at the heart of the genre, and sought to harmonize the social world of

---

[17] Aristotle's continuing influence through the idealist period is discussed brilliantly and provocatively in the work of Philippe Lacoue-Labarthe, especially: Philippe Lacoue-Labarthe, "The caesura of the speculative," in *Typography: mimesis, philosophy, politics*, ed. Christopher Fynsk (Cambridge, MA: Harvard University Press, 1989); Philippe Lacoue-Labarthe, *Métaphrasis, suivi de le théâtre de Hölderlin* (Paris: Presses universitaires de France, 1998).

tragedy with modern notions of authority.[18] These impulses gained new resonance in Germany with the fashion for Greek freedom inspired by Winckelmann, and led to readings that emphasized the kinship of Greek and German (or Swiss) political organizations and saw tragedy as an essentially patriotic (*vaterländisch*) form of art. The belief that Greek tragedy was fundamentally about political events transformed the early modern trope of history-as-tragedy into the modern notion of tragedy as a meaningful representation of historical process.

• • • • •

The genealogical viewpoint on idealist thought reveals that what is often thought of as a single movement is actually composed of two distinct (though interrelated) strands: the first centers around the *Oedipus Tyrannus* (*OT*) and is elaborated mainly by Schiller, Schelling, and A. W. Schlegel from 1793 onward, then canonized in Schelling's *Philosophy of Art* and Schlegel's *Lectures on Dramatic Art and Literature*; the second is centered on the *Antigone* and seems to emerge from almost nowhere in the writings of Hölderlin and Hegel in 1804 and 1807, respectively, and is canonized by Hegel's posthumously edited and published *Lectures on Aesthetics*. To be sure, the strands are related. Schelling and Schlegel do not ignore the *Antigone*, and Hölderlin and Hegel both write prominently about the *OT*, but their respective generic understandings of tragedy are substantially based on a single play. Hölderlin is unusual in giving equal prominence to the two works, but he is at pains to distinguish between their differing models of the tragic.

Though idealist interest in the *OT* was quite importantly rooted in thinking on tragedy going back to Aristotle, and spoke in important respects to the concerns of previous generations of critics, the interest in the *Antigone* did not arise from any substantial critical tradition. The *Antigone* had only been moderately popular with previous translators and adaptors, and Hölderlin and Hegel were among the first philosophers to take the work seriously. The central models of Sophoclean tragedy, from antiquity onward, were the *OT* and the *Electra*; both were included in the "Byzantine triad," the three plays that were most intensively studied and commented in late antiquity, and the revenge plot of the *Electra* exerted great influence on seventeenth- and eighteenth-century drama. The *Antigone*, by contrast, was largely absent from discussions of the generations before Idealism, and was not thought a particularly seminal work—though, to be sure, as one

---

[18] Political contexts for Greek tragedy are emphasized in Christian Biet, *Œdipe en monarchie: tragédie et théorie juridique à l'âge classique* (Paris: Klincksieck, 1994); Edith Hall and Fiona Macintosh, *Greek tragedy and the British theatre, 1660–1914* (Oxford: Oxford University Press, 2005). My discussion of the eighteenth century in France and England builds on their studies.

of Sophocles' seven surviving plays, it did receive sporadic treatment and translation. (It had in fact been translated into German by Martin Opitz in 1636—though that version seems to have been forgotten by the eighteenth century).[19]

One can find only scattered hints of interest in the *Antigone* before 1800, and it definitely belonged to the second tier of extant Greek tragedy. From around 1800 to the present, though, it is the *OT* and *Antigone* that have been the touchstones of tragedy. The rise of the *Antigone* in critical esteem is both a symptom and a cause of changing conceptions of genre: its central ethical conflict, political context, and foregrounding of gender relations (to say nothing of the power of its poetry and drama) have given it a special role in modern thought about tragedy. The play's importance has only increased since the idealist period, and today it is one of the most frequently translated, adapted, and appropriated of all Greek tragedies.[20] The *Antigone*, as much or even more than the *OT*, poses the questions of meaning that have been central to thinking about tragedy over the past two hundred years. The idealist canon has powerfully defined later interests and placed questions of freedom and identity at the heart of modern approaches to tragedy.

Changes in taste and aesthetics brought about a broad reorganization of the canon of classical works in the late eighteenth century. Aeschylus' presence grew, while Seneca's, and then Euripides', waned. Sophocles, whose importance in the *Poetics* had ensured his prestige previously (though it was occasionally challenged by a love for Euripides, especially in France), became the undisputed pinnacle of tragedy. Until the 1770s, Aeschylus had largely been absent from popular discussions of Greek tragedy, and was considered primitive, obscure, and impossibly difficult to translate (Aristotle's neglect of his plays in the *Poetics* did not help either). Complete translations into French and English only appeared in the 1770s, and Germany had to wait until the 1780s for translations of individual plays (and until 1808 for a complete translation). Still, Germany seems to have taken the most readily to Aeschylean drama. This is visible in an attention to the chorus, which had been quite marginal in earlier discussions but became vitally important for German thinkers.[21] Aeschylus also brought (or cemented) a new model of tragedy that became particularly central for Idealism: the *Eumenides*, so unusual a work in the ancient context, came to represent the possibility of

---

[19] On the baroque *Antigone*, see Anastasia Daskarolis, *Die Wiedergeburt des Sophokles aus dem Geist des Humanismus: Studien zur Sophokles-Rezeption in Deutschland vom Beginn des 16. bis zur Mitte des 17. Jahrhunderts* (Tübingen: Niemeyer, 2000).

[20] See, most recently, S. E. Wilmer and Audronė Žukauskaitė, eds., *Interrogating Antigone in postmodern philosophy and criticism* (Oxford: Oxford University Press, 2010); Erin B. Mee and Helene P. Foley, eds., *Antigone on the contemporary world stage* (Oxford: Oxford University Press, 2011); Bonnie Honig, *Antigone, interrupted* (Cambridge: Cambridge University Press, 2013).

[21] See Joshua Billings, "'An alien body?' Choral autonomy around 1800," in *Choruses, ancient and modern*, ed. Joshua Billings, Felix Budelmann, and Fiona Macintosh (Oxford: Oxford University Press, 2013).

an affirmative tragedy. The influence of the *Eumenides*, along with that of Sophocles' *Oedipus at Colonus* (*OC*), suggested that reconciliation could be an essential element of Greek tragedy, and that it might have been the aim of the greatest dramatists to provide a sense of redemption after suffering (often with Christian overtones). These affirmative conclusions provided a way of understanding *catharsis* as a form of spiritual reconciliation, and established the *Eumenides* and *OC* firmly within idealist thought.

The disappearance of Seneca from the canon of tragedy is another striking feature of the late eighteenth century in contrast to the early modern period, when Senecan practice was by and large more influential than Greek works. The change in taste is difficult to date, but Gotthold Ephraim Lessing was particularly influential. After advocating for the Roman tragedian in his youth, Lessing turned against Seneca, launching an influential broadside in the *Laocoön* (1766) and generally disparaging his works as poor imitations of Greek tragedy. The growing sense of ancient Greece's historical distinctiveness and the philhellenism of the time continued to marginalize and demonize Seneca within major discussions of tragedy. Though not forgotten, he was no longer a touchstone of the genre, as he had been for earlier dramatists. Seneca's visceral, bloody dramas seem to have offended the aesthetic of distance and idealization that was often invoked to justify Greek tragedy. His works can seem to deny any comfort to the reader, focusing on bitter hatred and acts of vengeance that are more shocking than calming or uplifting.

Euripides fell along with Seneca, losing the prestige that he had enjoyed in the Renaissance and French classical era. In the earlier eighteenth century it would have been rare to find someone who preferred Euripides to Sophocles, but the younger tragedian's works were broadly considered more approachable, somehow more "modern." Racine's Euripidean adaptations (*Phaedra*, *Iphigenia*, and *Andromache*) shed reflected light on the Greek tragedian and made his works the more fruitful for adaptation in French (notwithstanding important adaptations of the *OT* by Corneille and Voltaire and of *Electra* by Crébillon and Voltaire). Through the eighteenth century, Euripides was also better edited and more widely discussed in scholarly circles than the other Greek tragedians, with Joshua Barnes' bilingual Greek-Latin edition of 1694 setting a standard of accessibility. German tastes, though, always ran more to Sophocles than Euripides, in part because Sophocles was thought, on evidence from his ancient *Life*, to be the more patriotic. It was, however, on aesthetic grounds, that the Schlegel brothers influentially attacked Euripides, and the poet's reputation would not recover until the age of Wilamowitz.[22] Like Seneca, Euripides seemed to transgress idealist

[22] See Glenn W. Most, "Schlegel, Schlegel und die Geburt eines Tragödienparadigmas," *Poetica* 25 (1993); Ernst Behler, "A. W. Schlegel and the nineteenth-century *damnatio* of Euripides," *Greek, Roman, and Byzantine Studies* 27 (1986); Albert Henrichs, "The last of the detractors: Friedrich Nietzsche's condemnation of Euripides," *Greek, Roman, and Byzantine Studies* 27 (1986).

aesthetic norms and to deny the emotional and philosophical reconciliation that works like the *Eumenides* and even the *Antigone* (for its apparent symmetry of punishment) offered.

A subtle shift in vocabulary underlines the broad transformation of notions of Greek tragedy. For the German eighteenth century, the word for "tragedy," ancient and modern, is *Trauerspiel* (literally, "mourning play"), a word coined in the Renaissance as a German equivalent to the Greek term and a counterpart to the word for comedy, *Lustspiel* ("pleasure play"). Before 1800, *Tragödie* and its derivatives are in occasional use, but they are never consistently preferred and have a faintly exotic air about them.[23] The first translation of Greek works to place *Tragödie* in the title comes only in 1802, and the word is used throughout K.W.F. Solger's important 1808 *Tragedies of Sophocles (Des Sophokles Tragödien).*[24] Without ever being discussed, the change in vocabulary seems to have taken hold, for it is visible almost immediately in translations of Greek texts and works describing themselves as *Tragödien*. From Greek tragedy, the word spread to describe modern works in elevated style, establishing a continuity founded on the ancient genre. This is only a symptom, but a significant one, of the growing recognition of Greek tragedy's historical singularity, and, often, of the desire to emulate the ancient form. *Tragödie* came to have a distinct connotation as Greek works established themselves as the generic standard.[25] "Tragedy" and "tragic" acquired a normative force that remains with the genre, marking it out for its profundity and universality.

• • • • •

Making the case for continuities, and giving definition to discontinuities requires a form of presentation that takes into account the variety of contexts in which Greek tragedy was important to the eighteenth century. The methodological weight is laid differently in the three parts of the book, first on broadly cultural developments, then on intellectual-historical constellations, and finally on textual exegesis. The focus is resolutely on Idealism, and earlier material is introduced primarily in so far as it gives background to the idealist turn in thinking about tragedy. The first two chapters form the first section of the book ("Tragic modernities") and construct this background by ranging across scholarship, translation, literature, and philosophy, and across French, English, and German-speaking contexts from the

---

[23] For example, Steinbrüchel in his 1763 *Das tragische Theater der Griechen* uses the word *Trauerspiel* throughout his preface. Generally, *tragisch* is often used where *Tragödie* is not, reflecting the lack of an adjectival form of *Trauerspiel*.

[24] Friedrich Leopold zu Stolberg's 1802 *Vier Tragödien des Aeschylos* is the first prominent usage of the term in a translation, and Solger's extensive preface uses *Tragödie* exclusively.

[25] This forms the (unconscious) background to Walter Benjamin's distinction between the two forms in the *Ursprung des deutschen Trauerspiels*.

late seventeenth century to 1790. Over this period, Greek tragedy went from being a relatively obscure form, little translated and discussed, to being the touchstone ancient genre, considered a distillation of the ancient Greek spirit. Crucial to this change in prestige is the development of historical thought, which was given particular impetus by the *Querelle des Anciens et des Modernes* in France. Especially in the wake of the *Querelle*, tragedy was an important ground for comparisons of antiquity and modernity, and such juxtapositions increasingly revealed fundamental differences between the ages. Changing conceptions of history resituated debates about tragedy, and introduced a sense of distance and idealization into the relation to ancient Greek literature and culture. Tragedy was the central literary touchstone for this growing historical consciousness, because it, more than any other ancient genre, seemed to have a modern canon of comparable achievement. Thinking about ancient and modern tragedy together became a particularly pressing task for literary criticism, and led to the development of radical historicisms in Germany and France, as well as to a flourishing of interest in Greek tragedy generally.

The second section of the book ("Tragic themes") investigates, in three roughly chronological chapters, major topics in idealist thought on tragedy: freedom and necessity, the relation of ancient and modern culture, and theology. These issues are reconceived in the wake of Kantian critique and the French Revolution, which form the immediate catalysts for idealist thought. A pervasive consciousness of rupture made tragedy, as the genre of *peripeteia*, newly important as a means of representing and grasping historical chaos. The chapters trace dialogues between major thinkers in detail—a notable lacuna in previous studies, which have tended to isolate and privilege certain strands. The picture that emerges brings out the pivotal role of Friedrich Schiller, along with the continuing importance of questions of tragic poetics and politics. By looking carefully at the variety of approaches to each issue, new continuities as well as divergences emerge, suggesting a much more dynamic and contradictory intellectual field than has ever been acknowledged. There is no unified idealist theory or approach, but all the thinkers are united by a conviction that Greek tragedy has an urgent contemporary importance. The paradox of an ancient form that offers a unique insight into modern existence is the defining feature of post-romantic understandings of Greek tragedy.

The final two chapters look in depth at the most complex idealist works dealing with tragedy, Hegel's *Phenomenology* and Hölderlin's translation of and "Notes" to Sophocles. Both chapters emphasize close engagement with the texts of Greek tragedy, grounding broader understandings of the tragic in specific acts of interpretation. Hegel and Hölderlin developed their thought on tragedy in conversations of the late 1790s, and for both tragedy is essentially historical and progressive, not only depicting but contributing to moments of revolutionary change in ancient Greece. Though Hegel's text was published three years after Hölderlin's, it is discussed first, both to challenge accepted teleologies of Idealism, and because Hegel's concerns are more easily framed by the previous discussions. Hölderlin's *Sophocles*, though it draws on all the major strands of idealist thought, nevertheless resists the dominant tendency towards reconciliation, understanding tragedy as a catastrophic and transformative meeting of god and man.

Hegel and Hölderlin suggest different paths for thinking the place of Greek tragedy in modernity: for Hegel, the social role that tragedy played in ancient Greece has been superseded in modernity by Christian religion and philosophy, leaving the form of tragedy valuable only for its crystallization of a past stage of spirit; for Hölderlin, on the contrary, Greek tragedy remains radically alien to the present, and its value lies in its historical perspective on timeless questions of meaning. For both, the question of Greek tragedy's role in modernity presents a profound philosophical and aesthetic challenge. Though their understandings are highly individual, Hegel and Hölderlin are both foundational for, and exemplary of, the importance of Greek tragedy to modern thought. If, like them, we today think of tragedy both as central to our understanding of Attic culture and as profoundly meaningful to our own lives, then in some way we remain idealists.

TRAGIC MODERNITIES

CHAPTER 1

Quarreling over Tragedy

ANTIQUITY OR MODERNITY? Today, the question seems incoherent. Even if "antiquity" and "modernity" were clearly defined, the notion of comparing the merits of one age to another seems both pointless and perilous. Antiquity was one thing; modernity is another. There is no general method of evaluating ages or cultures. If we speak of ancients and moderns in the same breath, it may be with an eye to understanding their differences and similarities, but never to declaring the absolute superiority of one over the other. Evaluating entire epochs is not the work of serious thinkers, any more than debating the relative merits of coffee and tea.

Yet this way of thinking is a recent development. From the Renaissance until around 1800, evaluative comparison of antiquity and modernity was an important mode of thought throughout Western Europe. These inquiries are often grouped under the name of the *Querelle des Anciens et des Modernes*. The term refers specifically to a virulent dispute that arose in France at the end of the seventeenth century, but quarrels over the value of antiquity were widespread for centuries before, and tenacious even for some time after the *Querelle* proper.[1] Indeed, comparisons of antiquity and modernity were one of the major forms of literary-critical thought in the seventeenth and eighteenth centuries, and the positions of the *Anciens* and *Modernes* (the proper nouns referring to partisans of the two camps) are discernible well beyond the temporal bounds of the *Querelle*. Towards the end of the

---

*The *Querelle des Anciens et des Modernes* and its consequences are well discussed by Dan Edelstein, *The Enlightenment: a genealogy* (Chicago: University of Chicago Press, 2010); Larry F. Norman, *The shock of the ancient: literature & history in early modern France* (Chicago: University of Chicago Press, 2011). On antiquity in the eighteenth century generally, foundational are Chantal Grell, *Le dix-huitième siècle et l'antiquité en France, 1680–1789* (Oxford: Voltaire Foundation, 1995); Suzanne L. Marchand, *Down from Olympus: archaeology and philhellenism in Germany, 1750–1970* (Princeton: Princeton University Press, 1996). On Greek tragedy: Biet, *Œdipe en monarchie*; Lurje, *Die Suche nach der Schuld*; Hall and Macintosh, *Greek tragedy and the British theatre*; Christopher Meid, *Die griechische Tragödie im Drama der Aufklärung: "Bei den Alten in die Schule gehen"* (Tübingen: Narr, 2008). On Brumoy's *Theater*, see further the essays collected in *Anabases* 14 (2011), some cited here. There has, however, been little effort at comparison across national traditions, as I attempt here. There is much more to be done.

[1] For a long perspective on these debates see: Levent Yilmaz, *Le temps moderne: variations sur les Anciens et les contemporains* (Paris: Gallimard, 2004); Marc Fumaroli, "Les abeilles et les araignées," in *La querelle des anciens et des modernes: XVIIe–XVIIIe siècles*, ed. Anne-Marie Lecoq (Paris: Gallimard, 2001).

eighteenth century, though, these comparisons began to disappear.[2] They were replaced by an understanding of cultural difference and relativism that is recognizably modern.

We know this change as historicization, the assumption that past societies have their own unique modes of existence, which are not necessarily comparable to one another or immediately comprehensible in contemporary terms.[3] Antiquity can no longer be measured against modernity; there are no firm grounds for evaluation. Though this attitude to the products of the past is by no means new around 1800 (historicization is at least as old as history), it takes on a new prevalence and explanatory prestige. Origins, contexts, and idiosyncrasies become the defining features of thought about the past, and historicized understanding the *sine qua non* of sound inquiry. As Reinhart Koselleck influentially argues, the final third of the eighteenth century sees "the temporalization [Verzeitlichung] of history": temporality is no longer a neutral container for events, but exerts its own force on agents and actions.[4] The temporalization of history grounds the familiar concept of the "spirit of the time" (*Zeitgeist*, a word that first enters the German language in this period), which describes the particularity of a given culture as a result of its unique historical character. With each age defined by a characteristic rhythm and shape, it becomes impossible to judge the products of different historical moments against one another.

This chapter and the next will trace the rise of historicization and its consequences for thinking about Greek tragedy. These chapters argue that tragedy was a crucial ground for thinking about history in the eighteenth century, and, reciprocally, that historical thinking fundamentally shifted the terms in which tragedy was understood, with consequences that persist to the present. The notion of history that informs most contemporary approaches to antiquity was largely formed in this period, as modernity came to define itself as categorically different from previous ages—effectively ending the *Querelle*. From the other side of this conceptual shift, it is easy to read the texts of the *Querelle* with condescension, as the silly answer to a silly

[2] See François Hartog, *Anciens, modernes, sauvages* (Paris: Galaade, 2005). Hartog draws attention to the disappearance of the parallel form, seeing its epitaph as Benjamin Constant's 1819 "De la liberté des Anciens comparée à celle des Modernes" (251). For tragedy, the final binary parallel of importance would have to be A. W. Schlegel's 1807 *Comparaison entre la Phèdre de Racine et celle d'Euripide*, which was quickly eclipsed by the wide scope of his *Vorlesungen über dramatische Kunst und Literatur*.

[3] I adopt Glenn Most's distinction between historicism (a self-conscious academic method, which emerges in the nineteenth century) and historicization, which is possible in all times and places, but becomes particularly important for thinkers at the end of the eighteenth century. See the "Preface" in Glenn W. Most, ed. *Historicization—Historisierung* (Göttingen: Vandenhoeck & Ruprecht, 2001).

[4] See Reinhart Koselleck, *Futures past: on the semantics of historical time*, trans. Keith Tribe (New York: Columbia University Press, 2004).

question, or (the prevalent scholarly approach until recently) as the platform for a largely ulterior struggle to define authority under the absolute monarchy.[5] Historians seems to be moving away from ideological readings, towards seeing the *Querelle* as a formative moment in the self-consciousness of modernity, and as a rich and dynamic debate in its own right.[6] For the partisans of the *Querelle*, the question of antiquity's role in modern culture was a live one in a way it has rarely been since. Answering it entailed defining a way of living within history, of understanding the present in relation to a series of pasts.

Ancients and Moderns on Tragedy

The exemplary discursive form of the *Querelle* is the "parallel" (the French term *parallèle* is often used to designate this subgenre of criticism).[7] The parallel could draw on classical roots, most importantly Plutarch's *Lives*, which examined Greek and Roman lives in *synkrisis*, the rhetorical mode of comparison.[8] More explicitly evaluative were the ancient contests of poets: the *Certamen* of Homer and Hesiod and the competition of Aeschylus and Euripides in Aristophanes' *Frogs*. Such works drew on the agonistic contexts in which epic and tragedy were performed in ancient Greece in order to stage competitions between the great poets. Antithesis and evaluation were major features of ancient literary culture, and this tendency seems to have authorized or inspired the parallels and comparisons that pervaded discussions of ancient literature from the Renaissance. Tragedy, as a genre that had flourished in antiquity and modernity, was one of the most popular grounds for thinking the ages in parallel. But it could also be problematic, as critics found profound differences beneath the apparent similarities of ancient and modern works. From the *Querelle* onward, understandings of Greek tragedy were formed by divergent ways of thinking about the play of similarity and difference in history.

In parallels of the *Querelle*, the achievements of ancients and moderns in practically any area could be compared. Most important was Charles Perrault's *Parallel of ancients and moderns, in regard to the arts and sciences* (*Parallèle des Anciens et des Modernes, en ce qui régarde les arts et les sciences*, 1688–97),

---

[5] The most important, and still valuable, study is Bernard Magne, *Crise de la littérature française sous Louis XIV: humanisme et nationalisme* (Toulouse: Université de Toulouse Le Mirail, 1976).

[6] Most recently, Edelstein, *The Enlightenment*; Norman, *Shock of the ancient*.

[7] See Grell, *Le dix-huitième siècle et l'antiquité*, 359–60. Grell places the first phase of the *Querelle* in arguments about the superiority of French over classical languages, dating to the publication in 1670 of Desmarets' *Comparaison de langue & de la poësie françoises avec la grecque & la latine, & des poëtes grecs, latins & françois*.

[8] On Plutarch and the *Querelle*, see Hartog, *Anciens, modernes, sauvages*: 125–88.

which attempts a systematic evaluation of the ages. His aim throughout is to prove that "the ancients were extremely inferior to the moderns for this general reason, that there is nothing that time does not perfect."[9] The doctrine of progress—applied equally to the arts and sciences—became a rallying cry of the *Modernes*.[10] The *Anciens*, though accepting elements of the narrative of progress (especially those concerned with science), denied its universal applicability, pointing out that societies develop in different domains and at different paces, undermining the possibility of a comprehensive, binary parallel.[11] Over the course of the eighteenth century, this latter strand would acquire a firmer theoretical basis as thinkers explicitly questioned the possibility of comparing ancients and moderns.[12] An important part of this thinking took place around tragedy, which came to be understood as the genre that represented the height of both Greek and modern literary achievement, and so became a testing ground for the question of progress in the arts.

Greek tragedy was decidedly less important to the *Querelle* (and to early modern culture generally) than Greek epic.[13] Yet drama was by no means absent from the *Querelle*; indeed, it was in a parallel of tragedies that Charles Perrault first articulated some crucial historical and aesthetic priorities. More than ten years before delivering his opening salvo to the Académie française, Perrault published an anonymous defense of Lully and Quinault's controversial opera *Alcestis*, kindling some of the passions and debates that would flare up in the *Querelle* proper. The short piece stages a dialogue between a partisan of Quinault's libretto and a skeptical friend. Though it is ostensibly the opera that is at issue, the discussion takes the form of a parallel of Euripides' and Quinault's treatments of the story of Alcestis. Considering the major changes to the Greek original, Perrault finds in favor of the modern author on every count.[14] In Euripides' play, Perrault is particularly

---

[9] Charles Perrault, *Parallèle des anciens et des modernes en ce qui régarde les arts et les sciences*, 4 vols. (Paris: Coignard, 1688–97; repr., Munich: Eidos, 1964), 4, 285.

[10] But progress for the *Modernes* is always in the past; that is, they have no model of progress beyond the present, and so are in no way "progressives." See Grell, *Le dix-huitième siècle et l'antiquité*, 429; Joan E. DeJean, *Ancients against moderns: culture wars and the making of a fin de siècle* (Chicago: University of Chicago Press, 1997), 18.

[11] See Norman, *Shock of the ancient*: 51–62.

[12] See Hans Robert Jauß, "Ästhetische Normen und geschichtliche Reflexion in der 'Querelle des anciens et des modernes,'" in *Charles Perrault, Parallèle des anciens et des modernes en ce qui regarde les arts et les sciences* (Munich: Eidos, 1964), 60–64.

[13] DeJean, *Ancients against moderns*, 56. DeJean shows the importance of epic and its modern counterpart, the novel, but is too quick to exclude tragedy as a major force. On the *Querelle d'Homère*, see Geneviève Commagre, "De l'avenir des Anciens: la polemique entre Mme Dacier et Houdar de La Motte," *Littératures classiques* 72 (2010); Noémi Hepp, *Homère en France au XVIIe siècle* (Paris: Klincksieck, 1968).

[14] In general, though, Perrault is rather more conciliatory in the *Critique* than he would be later, framing his argument as a critique of the authority accorded to the ancients, rather than

scandalized by the scene in which Admetus reproaches his father for refusing to die in his stead, which renders Admetus "so contemptible and worthy of hatred that one has no pleasure in seeing him escape death."[15]

The heroes of tragedy, for Perrault, should be exemplary, providing models of conduct that will guide the audience—as he finds in Quinault's portrayal of the noble, self-sacrificing Hercules (a stark contrast to Euripides' riotous drunk). Perrault's critic opines, "If these kinds of works do not contain some kind of morality, they are vain amusements not worthy of claiming the attention of a rational spirit."[16] The attacks made on Greek literature in the late seventeenth century often followed such a moralizing line. They could invoke Plato as their forebear in rebuking epic and tragedy for the morals of the characters portrayed.[17] In contrast, the defenders of Greek tragedy, such as René Rapin and Racine, sought to argue that the improving power of tragedy did not lie in its presentation of exemplary characters, but in allegorical situations from which the audience could draw instructive morals.[18] This way of reading goes back to Greek antiquity, when epic allegoresis was well-known by the classical period, and likewise responded to those, like Xenophanes, who sought to evaluate heroes' conduct by rational and moral standards.[19] In reading archaic literature, the difference from contemporary conduct and values was unmistakable (even in antiquity). The *Anciens* sought to explain these differences as constructive, while the *Modernes* viewed them as reprehensible and even dangerous. Both sides of the debate, though, essentially agreed on the moral aim of the arts. They differed only on the mechanism for improvement, and on whether ancient or modern works better achieved a salutary effect.

When André Dacier published his translations of Aristotle and Sophocles in 1692, he was joining the *Querelle* with a defense of the neoclassical aesthetic. These volumes were the first translations into French of Aristotle's *Poetics* and of any Greek tragedy since the Renaissance. It is significant that the *Poetics* was translated first, followed by *OT* and *Electra* (as Dacier mentions in his introduction to the Sophocles). There could be no doubt as to the

---

denigrating them absolutely: Charles Perrault, "Critique de l'Opera, ou Examen de la tragédie intitulée Alceste," in *Alceste, suivi de La querelle d'Alceste: anciens et modernes avant 1680*, ed. William Brooks, Buford Norman, and Jeanne Morgan Zarucchi (Genève: Droz, 1994), 97–98.

[15]Ibid., 90–91.

[16]Ibid., 97.

[17]Norman, *Shock of the ancient*: 118.

[18]René Rapin, *Reflexions sur la Poetique d'Aristote, et sur les ouvrages des Poetes anciens & modernes* (Paris: Muguet, 1674), 21.

[19]On allegory in antiquity, see Andrew Ford, *The origins of criticism: literary culture and poetic theory in classical Greece* (Princeton: Princeton University Press, 2002), 67–89. On the seventeenth and eighteenth century, see Glenn W. Most, "The second Homeric Renaissance: allegoresis and genius in early modern poetics," in *Genius: the history of an idea*, ed. Penelope Murray (Oxford: Blackwell, 1989).

relative importance of the two: the "rules" found in Aristotle are of the essence, with the examples of Sophocles serving as illustrations of their validity. Dacier writes that his aim in translating Aristotle is "to establish not merely that poetry is an art, but that this art is solved [cet art est trouvé], and that the rules are certainly those which Aristotle gives us, and that it is impossible to succeed by another way."[20] Dacier's understanding of poetry is rhetorical and universalizing: it is a means of producing an effect in its readers and audiences, which does not change through time. Echoing Racine's famous preface to *Iphigenia*, he writes that "the same subjects that have caused so many tears to fall in the theater of Athens and in that of Rome, again make them fall today in our own."[21] In 1692, in the middle of the *Querelle*, these words assumed a combative stance in favor of ancient literature and against the *Modernes'* notion of progress. Dacier does not deny that modern authors can reach the same heights as the Greeks, but he insists that ancient poetry and—even more—ancient *poetics* is the standard against which modern works should be evaluated.

Aristotle's treatise is at the very least ambiguous as to the moral effect of tragedy. The key term *catharsis* can be interpreted in many ways, with the main division between those who see it as a morally improving effect and those who see it as a purely emotional discharge. Dacier's interpretation of *catharsis* as an educative, moderating influence on the spectator is paradigmatic of the period's defenses of Greek tragedy: "Tragedy is therefore a true medicine [une véritable médecine], which purges the passions in that it teaches the ambitious one to moderate his ambition, the impious one to fear the gods, the impulsive one to hold back his anger, etc."[22] Dacier adapts the allegorizing strategy to the defense of tragedy: the poet intends for the reader to discover a deeper, moral meaning in the conduct of the characters. Oddly (though not uniquely), Dacier understands the passions purged by *catharsis* not only as those relating to the audience's experience in viewing the drama, but also as the passions that cause the protagonists to meet unhappiness.[23] Likewise, in his preface to Sophocles, Dacier writes that the character of Oedipus shows "that curiosity, arrogance, violence, and impulsivity precipitate men who otherwise have quite good qualities into inevitable misfortunes, and these are the passions that he [Aristotle] wishes the example of Oedipus to purge in us."[24]

Dacier sees the characters of tragedy as negative exemplars, whose weaknesses are a reminder of the destructive influence of certain passions. This

---

[20] André Dacier, *La Poëtique d'Aristote* (Paris: Barbin, 1692), iii.

[21] Ibid., vii. Racine's preface was itself partly a response to the *Critique d'Alceste*.

[22] Ibid., 81.

[23] See ibid., 70–71. On Dacier's reading of the notion of *catharsis*, see Lurje, *Die Suche nach der Schuld*: 128–37.

[24] André Dacier, *L'Oedipe et l'Electre de Sophocle : tragédies grecques* (Paris: Barbin, 1692), Preface: 8.

understanding of the flawed heroes of tragedy is directed against Corneille, whose works and theory had advocated a drama of exemplary characters falling through no fault of their own. Dacier adduces Aristotle to refute Corneille's dramaturgy, arguing that such a plot, though it may be enjoyable and involving, is not properly tragic, giving the audience nothing from which to draw instruction.[25] The means of improvement Dacier puts forward is not based on admiration and emulation, but on reflection and self-determination. Yet for all the divergence between Dacier and his opponents, they agree that tragedy should be morally improving and that it can be evaluated on the basis of universal criteria. Both of these consensuses will break down in the century following, as comparisons of ancient and modern tragedy find profound differences in what had been assumed to be a unified genre.

Comparisons of tragedy are essential to the most important publication on tragedy of the early eighteenth century, the Jesuit Pierre Brumoy's 1730 *The Theater of the Greeks* (*Le Théâtre des Grecs*).[26] Translating three works of Sophocles (*OT, Electra, Philoctetes*) and four of Euripides (*Hippolytus, Iphigenia in Aulis, Iphigenia among the Taurians, Alcestis*) into French prose, and summarizing the rest of the extant tragedies, comedies, and the *Cyclops, The Theater of the Greeks* quickly became the primary reference work on Greek drama for much of Western Europe. The work was reprinted immediately in Amsterdam, revised in 1749 and 1763, and completely reedited in 1785–89.[27] Brumoy's *Theater* built on the popularity and influence of Dacier's translations, but sought to extend the acquaintance with Greek drama beyond a few canonical works and the purported rules for creation. In comparison with his predecessor, Brumoy is notable for his more nuanced historicism and less normative viewpoint. Both of these qualities appealed to readers weary of the partisan quarrels of previous decades and interested to discover for themselves the much-disputed qualities of Greek theater. Brumoy's ecumenical discussion and clear translation made his *Theater* an extremely durable work, which influenced many of the major thinkers and artists of the French Enlightenment.[28]

Brumoy's understanding of Greek tragedy is laid out in three prefatory essays, "On the Theater of the Greeks," "On the Origin of Tragedy," and

[25] Dacier, *Poëtique*: 177.

[26] The 1730 edition does not print the circumflex in 'théâtre' (the 1785 edition, though, does).

[27] On the various editions, see Vanessa de Senarclens, "Éditer le théâtre antique grec au siècle des Lumières: *Le Théâtre des Grecs* de Pierre Brumoy (1730) et ses nombreuses rééditions au cours du dix-huitième siècle," in *Die Antike in der Moderne: vom Umgang mit der Antike im Europa des 18. Jahrhunderts*, ed. Veit Elm, Günther Lottes, and Vanessa de Senarclens (Hanover: Wehrhahn, 2009); Jean-Noël Pascal, "De la somme à l'encyclopédie: parcours à travers un siècle d'éditions du *Théâtre des Grecs* (1730–1826)," *Anabases* 14 (2011).

[28] On its influence, see Raymond Trousson, "Le Théâtre tragique grec au siècle des Lumières," *Studies on Voltaire and the Eighteenth Century* 155 (1976).

"On the Parallel of Theaters." The last essay is particularly important as the most substantial general comparison of ancient and modern drama to date. Throughout, Brumoy is quite sensitive to the differences between ancient Greek and modern French theater, and accordingly does not try to set down or abstract timeless rules for creation. His avowed aim is to educate his readers in this still-obscure area of literature, so that they may form more accurate judgments. Though comparisons of ancient and modern pervade the edition, polemic is almost entirely absent.[29] Brumoy situates himself between *Anciens* and *Modernes*, noting repeatedly that his advocacy for Greek works does not preclude recognizing their flaws, or prevent him from praising the glories of French theater.

Brumoy's understanding of tragic *catharsis* is, like Dacier's, moral. In the essay "On the Origin of Tragedy," Brumoy describes *catharsis* as a purely homeopathic effect, a strengthening through artificial exposure: "As one accustoms oneself to the idea of misfortunes, one fortifies oneself against them, and one undertakes more energetically to ease them in another, through the hope for the return."[30] Tragic *catharsis* has a social as well as an individual benefit, based on its emotional power. This is characteristic of Brumoy's discussion, which is generally more oriented to affect than Dacier's and frequently employs the category of the sublime to describe the experience of tragedy. Aligning himself with Boileau, who famously translated the *Treatise on the Sublime* (*Traité du sublime*) in 1674, Brumoy advocates an affective universalism with respect to tragedy:

> Every beautiful and true thought, every sentiment that passes for sublime in a place and during a time, is the same everywhere and always. Such is the "That he had died" of Corneille. So one cannot say that the thoughts, sentiments, and turns that explain them are like fashions and manners that change with the climate, or the passing of the years [... qu'on ne dise pas qu'il en est des pensées, des sentimens, & des tours qui les expriment, comme des modes & des manieres qui changent en changeant de climat, ou par la révolution des années].[31]

The concept of the sublime had been a major source of conflict in the *Querelle*. Its irrational, ecstatic nature (as understood by Boileau and his followers) provided a powerful legitimation for the *Anciens*, as a poetic quality that would shift the field of discussion from the perceived flaws of ancient literature.[32] Brumoy similarly understands the sublime as a quality that transcends history, making its emotional impact felt without regard to circumstance. Yet at the same time, his reference reflects the compromise

---

[29] See further Charalampos Orfanos, "La critique suspendue: le P. Brumoy et l'histoire," *Anabases* 14 (2011).

[30] Pierre Brumoy, *Le théatre des Grecs*, 3 vols. (Paris: Rollin, 1730), 1, liii.

[31] Ibid., 1, viii.

[32] See Norman, *Shock of the ancient*: 185–92.

reached between Boileau and Perrault, in that it cites a modern author, Corneille, as the exemplary instance.[33] Brumoy's universalism is founded on emotional effect rather than on the rational construction central to Dacier's understanding of tragedy, but it is nevertheless a means of grounding a continuity between ancient and modern works and the possibility of critical judgment. Only once such a continuity is established do comparison and evaluation become possible.

Though he assumes a fundamental similarity between ancient and modern tragedies, Brumoy recognizes the difficulties of comparison. Much of Greek theater would appear ridiculous if judged by the standards of French drama. In order to fully appreciate the beauties of Greek tragedy, one must set oneself "in the point of view where the authors wished to place us."[34] Brumoy demonstrates this in relation to the most controversial Greek tragedy of the time, the *Alcestis*. Brumoy imagines himself as an Athenian at a performance of Euripides' *Alcestis* and finds that

> If I become Athenian, like those whom the poet intended to please, despite some faults that I perceive along with the parterre, I cannot restrain myself from joining my applause to the acclamations of assembled Greece, because, being a man like the Greeks, I am necessarily touched by the same truths and the same beauties that struck their spirits so powerfully.[35]

For Brumoy, temporal difference can be surmounted by an act of imagination. Because of common humanity, the modern reader, having "become Athenian," can experience the same emotions that the ancients did.[36] In his parallels and notes to the tragedies, Brumoy returns to the imaginative effort necessary to comprehend and judge Greek literature. Failing to do so, the reader, like Perrault, "finds all of it risible."[37] It is from such a failure that Greek theater is often condemned unfairly, "as if one judged a foreigner by French law."[38] Brumoy shifts the criterion of judgment from the rational construction of the author (implicitly rejecting allegorical readings) to the imagination and emotions of the reader. Without thinking oneself into the position of the Greeks, no emotional response and therefore no evaluation of Greek tragedy is possible.

Brumoy's description of the imaginative leap necessary to experience Greek tragedy confronts the objection of the *Modernes* that some elements

---

[33] The Corneille citation (from *Horace*) comes directly from Boileau, who added it to his 1701 preface as a reflection of his partial reconciliation with the *Modernes*: Nicolas Boileau Despréaux, *Oeuvres diverses du Sr Boileau Despreaux*, 2 vols. (Paris: Thierry, 1701), 2, 15.

[34] Brumoy, *Théatre* (1730): 1, xii.

[35] Ibid., 1, ix.

[36] See further Claire Lechevalier, "L'imaginaire de la représentation dans *Le Théâtre des Grecs* de Brumoy (1730)," *Anabases* 14 (2011).

[37] Brumoy, *Théatre* (1730): 1, x.

[38] Ibid., 1, xiii.

of ancient works are simply incomprehensible in modern terms. In his essay "On the Parallel of Theaters," Brumoy introduces a distinction between universal and particular elements of taste, which allows him to distinguish between those aspects of ancient works that transcend time and those that do not. In any body of people, he writes, each individual has "something of the general that extends to everyone, and something of the personal that distinguishes each from one another."[39] The latter, particular character of Greek tragedy is for Brumoy an obstacle to appreciating the general character of the works as tragedy. Brumoy recognizes that particular differences exist, but imagines himself and fifth-century Athenians as linked by the universality of emotional response. Thus he insists, as the "principle of the parallel [principe du parallèle]" that ancient and modern tragedies are created by the same means and to the same ends:

> The same goal, same subjects, same economy for their basis. That is to say, an attempt to create an agreeable sadness, great and noble subjects throughout, a regular economy according to the idea of regularity by which each is created.[40]

Brumoy understands the goal (*but*) of tragedy in rhetorical terms, as the production of a sublime effect on its viewer, which establishes a continuity across time. Having posited the essential similarity of ancient and modern tragedies, Brumoy continues in the essay to define their differences. Such differences, though, are seen merely as contingent variations, to be transcended through an effort of imagination. At the heart of the parallel is the assumption that two phenomena have a common essence, a general similarity upon which particular differences can be discerned and judged.

Tentatively, Brumoy also expresses doubts about the possibilities of parallel thinking. "The comparison of the modern with the ancient," Brumoy writes, "appears obnoxious to some, reckless to many, and bold to those who, without being idolatrous of antiquity, still do not cease to respect it."[41] In previous years, the form of the parallel had often been used polemically, to denigrate one age and exalt the other, and so had inevitably offended one party. Brumoy, though, suggests that his parallel will have a more constructive and reflective aim, "to mark the extent and the limits that taste gives to this parallel."[42] Most striking among these limits is politics. Greek tragedy was performed in a democracy, often depicted the downfall of kings, and brought on stage members of the polity in the chorus. The French tragedy of Brumoy's time, on the other hand, took place under an absolute monarchy, and with rare exceptions, portrayed only members of the nobility. These political worlds could hardly have been more opposed, and advocating for

---

[39] Ibid., 1, cxxxiii.
[40] Ibid., 1, cxxxv.
[41] Ibid., 1, xcix.
[42] Ibid., 1, c.

Greek tragedy in 1730 may have carried a whiff of subversion—especially for a member of the Jesuits, who were already suspect for their use of theatrical texts in instruction.[43] In his attempt to rehabilitate Greek tragedy, Brumoy had to avoid any hint that he was advocating for its political outlook to be revived in modernity.

The form of the parallel allows Brumoy to distinguish firmly between those political elements that moderns can accept and those they must resist. In comparison to Dacier's thoroughly formal view, Brumoy places substantial weight on the politics of Greek tragedy.[44] He emphasizes the importance of republican sentiments to ancient drama, yet seeks to distance them as much as possible from the present, arguing that such passages are no longer comprehensible to modern audiences.[45] Though both ancient and modern tragedy concern kings, their notions of kingship have nothing in common: "The first did not want their kings on stage except to rejoice at their abasement, out of their implacable hatred of supreme dignity; the second cannot see them humiliated except to emphasize their majesty."[46] The tragedies of the two nations reflect their opposed views of political authority. The Greek hatred for kings makes them enjoy the *peripeteiai* of plays like *OT* or *Hercules*, while the French respect for monarchy leads to plays concerning more admirable characters who meet with happier ends, obvious in Racine's Euripides adaptations. Brumoy's historical viewpoint leads him to recognize the political character of Greek tragedy—indeed, to emphasize it—while simultaneously using the parallel to place that political character outside the essence of the genre. The form of the parallel, by isolating the historical, and therefore inessential elements of tragedy, enables Brumoy's striking consideration of politics in Greek works.

In other realms as well, Brumoy stresses the difference between ancient and modern tragedy. The essay "On the Parallel of Theaters" begins with a detailed sketch of the Athenians and their history, deducing the character of tragedy from that of the people for whom it was created. This leads Brumoy, in the parallel proper, to a systematic opposition of the characteristics of Greek and French tragedy. The Greeks excel in representing single, timeless nature, the French in depicting the world's multiplicity.[47] French theater introduces a diversity of plots, characters, and themes that would have been impossible for the Greeks, and does so without a strict adherence to

---

[43] In the years leading up to their suppression in 1762, the Jesuits were accused of subversion with increasing fervor, and Brumoy himself would briefly be exiled in 1739 for having approved publication of a work that allegedly cast aspersions on the monarchy. See Catherine M. Northeast, *The Parisian Jesuits and the Enlightenment, 1700–1762* (Oxford: Voltaire Foundation, 1991), 23–27, 45.

[44] See Biet, *Œdipe en monarchie*: 61–63.

[45] Brumoy, *Théâtre* (1730): 1, cxxi–cxxiii.

[46] Ibid., 1, cxl.

[47] Ibid., 1, clix.

the Aristotelian "rules." Brumoy seems almost baffled by the differences he discovers, writing in his conclusion that the genres are "entirely differing in certain respects, and as a consequence, hardly susceptible to a very exact comparison."[48] This doubt about the viability of the parallel makes clear an inherent ambiguity of the form: though all parallels assume that the elements being compared have something in common, at the same time, they tend to draw more attention to differences than to similarities. Brumoy seems acutely conscious of this difficulty, but his insistence on the two levels of comparison—universal effect and particular form—allows for the parallel to go forward, distinguishing a panoply of historical difference against a ground of similarity.

The assumption of comparability also allows Brumoy to make a series of secondary parallels throughout the work. After treating each Greek tragedy, he appends a short essay, where applicable, on other treatments of the same subject. Indeed, Brumoy's choice of tragedies to translate, which might seem strange to modern tastes, suggests that he is seeking out parallels with other works, ancient and modern: for the *OT*, he has Seneca and Corneille; for *Hippolytus* and *Iphigenia in Aulis*, tragedies by Racine; for *Electra*, the two other Greek works on the same subject.[49] This comparative tendency may explain the inclusion of the Taurian *Iphigenia*, which had been adapted by François Joseph Lagrange-Chancel as *Oreste et Pylade* in 1697, and became quite popular for its idealized depiction of friendship. *Alcestis* was well-known from the opera by Lully and Quinault, and the story of *Philoctetes* from François Fénelon's hugely popular 1699 novel *Télémaque*. The obscurity of Greek tragedy at the time made these modern parallels particularly important, as a way of legitimizing ancient theater and understanding its effect.[50] It is important to remember that public performance of Greek drama was rare until well into the nineteenth century, so the only way of forming any idea of ancient works onstage was through their modern adaptations. The kinds of distinctions often drawn today between translations, adaptations, versions, etc., were not operative for most of the seventeenth and eighteenth centuries—a manifestation of the same relatively fluid historical consciousness as finds a common ground for comparison between ancient and modern works.

In each parallel, Brumoy notes and evaluates the essential points of departure from the Greek original. Without exempting any work from criticism, he is at pains to point out what is most difficult for moderns to comprehend in ancient tragedies. The comparison of ancient and modern, as

---

[48] Ibid., 1, clviii.

[49] Brumoy does not mention them, on the principal that living authors should not be considered, but Voltaire's 1718 *Oedipe* and Crébillon's 1708 *Électre* would have reinforced those subjects' popularity (as of course did Dacier's advocacy).

[50] Trousson, "Le Théâtre tragique grec au siècle des Lumières," 2117.

he writes in remarks preferring Racine's *Phaedra* to Euripides' *Hippolytus*, should reflect well on both, "since the inventor always has a good part of the glory of the one who perfects it after him."[51] Just as a judgment in favor of the modern poet reflects well on the ancient, so too, when preferring Euripides' *Iphigenia in Aulis* to Racine's *Iphigenia*, Brumoy reflects that "one could not better understand the beauties of Euripides than in setting them beside those of Racine."[52] Brumoy, though usually declaring the priority of one or the other work, does not intend the parallel to be destructive or polemical; it seems rather a means of education and reconciliation after the polemics of the *Querelle*.

Following Brumoy's *Theater*, parallels pervaded the discussion of tragedy in France. They were furnished with seemingly inexhaustible material by the classic works of Corneille and Racine on ancient subjects. Parallels of Racine's and Euripides' tragedies on the same theme were particularly frequent, occasionally delivered by Racine's son to the Académie Royale des Inscriptions et Belles-lettres, France's elite group of scholars of antiquity.[53] Though Brumoy had sought to tame the partisan passions of the *Querelle*, his attempts to be evenhanded often incensed the *Modernes*. The most substantial parallel after Brumoy was Louis Jacquet's 1760 *Parallel of Greek and French Tragedians* (*Parallèle des tragiques Grecs et François*), which sought to "open our eyes to our advantages" over antiquity. Jacquet accuses Brumoy of being too timorous in rendering a final verdict on the parallel of theaters, "in order to avoid a judgment which he well foresaw could not be favorable to the ancients."[54] Likewise, Voltaire, in his 1754 *The Age of Louis XIV* (*Le Siècle de Louis XIV*), deplores Brumoy's blindness to the "superiority of French theater to Greek."[55] Far from being forgotten, the *Querelle* continued in the parallels of the eighteenth century, with tragedy one of the most frequent objects of dispute. Distinguishing between ancient and modern literary works was a means of articulating an understanding of one's historical place and the particular character of one's modernity. These modernities were manifold: Perrault's was the culmination of centuries of progress,

---

[51] Brumoy, *Théatre* (1730): 1, 390: A similar idea is found in Louis Racine, "Comparaison de l'Iphigénie d'Euripide avec l'Iphigénie de Racine," *Mémoires de la littérature, tirez des registres de l'Académie Royale des inscriptions et belles lettres* 8 (1733): 299.

[52] Brumoy, *Théatre* (1730): 1, ciii.

[53] On the Académie, see Grell, *Le dix-huitième siècle et l'antiquité*: 110–23. Examples of parallels are Racine, "Comparaison de l'Iphigénie d'Euripide avec l'Iphigénie de Racine," Louis Racine, "Reflexions sur l'Andromaque d'Euripide et sur l'Andromaque de Racine," *Mémoires de la littérature, tirez des registres de l'Académie Royale des inscriptions et belles lettres* 10 (1736); Charles Batteux, "Observations sur l'Hippolyte d'Euripide et sur la Phèdre de Racine," *Mémoires de la littérature, tirez des registres de l'Académie Royale des inscriptions et belles lettres* 42 (1786).

[54] Louis Jacquet, *Parallèle des tragiques Grecs et François* (Lyon: Duplain, 1760), 138.

[55] François Marie Arouet de Voltaire, *Le siècle de Louis XIV*, 2 vols. (Leipzig: Francheville, 1754), 2, 176.

effortlessly superior to any other moment in history; Dacier's, on the contrary, was subject to the essentially ahistorical dictates of reason; Brumoy's modernity was again different, a moment of enlightened moderation that could imaginatively assimilate other historical epochs and participate in them emotionally. Over the course of the eighteenth century, Greek tragedy became a privileged ground for answering the *Querelle*'s question of what it means to be modern.

NACH ATHEN: LITERARY MODELS IN GERMANY

Turning from France to Germany, one finds the field of literary thought in a very different state in the first half of the eighteenth century. If for France the major questions concerned hierarchy (of reason or imagination, antiquity or modernity), in Germany the major questions concerned autonomy: Did Germany have a literature to speak of? How could German artists create works that would stand comparison with other nations? Part of this difference is the result of geopolitics: unlike highly centralized France, Germany (*Deutschland*) did not exist in any meaningful way, but was a loose confederation of states of different sizes, with varying forms of government and religion. There was no clear center, and a great deal of regional diversity. German elites tended to Francophilia and had relatively little interest in the rich native artistic traditions of the middle ages and early modern period. (It is astonishing how little discussion of German baroque tragedy one finds in the eighteenth century.) This background explains part of the vigor with which philhellenism arose among German thinkers. Styling themselves heirs to the legacy of ancient Greece was an attractive alternative to being belated followers of their neighbors across the Rhine. Appropriating Greek achievement seemed the way to realizing an authentically German culture, as expressed in Winckelmann's famous dictum that "the only way for us to become great, indeed, if it is possible, inimitable, is the imitation of the ancients [Der einzige Weg für uns, groß, ja, wenn es möglich ist, unnachahmlich zu werden, ist die Nachahmung der Alten]."[56]

German thought on literature in the first half of the eighteenth century is dominated by the figure of Johann Christoph Gottsched. His most important work on poetry, the *Attempt at a Critical Art of Poetry* (*Versuch einer critischen Dichtkunst*, first edition 1730), set out a normative poetics aimed at the construction of a tragedy based on a "moral precept [Lehrsatz]," which would be illustrated, allegorically, by the flaws of the protagonist.[57] Gott-

[56] Johann Joachim Winckelmann, *Gedanken über die Nachahmung der Griechischen Werke in der Malerey und Bildhauerkunst*, 2nd ed. (Dresden: Walther, 1756), 3.

[57] Johann Christoph Gottsched, *Versuch einer critischen Dichtkunst*, 4th ed. (Leipzig: Breitkopf, 1751), 611. See Frederick C. Beiser, *Diotima's children: German aesthetic rationalism from Leibniz to Lessing* (Oxford: Oxford University Press, 2009), 80–82.

sched was an enthusiastic reader of Dacier's translations, similarly seeing the *Poetics* as a timeless source of rules derived by reason alone.[58] Gottsched's frequent appeals to the wisdom of the ancients serve as a means of legitimizing his own program of theater reform, which sought to banish popular travelling entertainments from the stage and establish a permanent company performing drama in the more elevated French style.[59] Greek tragedy, for Gottsched, was useful as a rhetorical instrument, but his actual engagement with Greek texts seems to have been quite limited. A promised translation, following in Dacier's footsteps, of the *Poetics* and Sophocles never materialized—either because Gottsched's Greek was not equal to the task or because he preferred to concentrate on modern thinkers and artists. His knowledge and appreciation of French works was far more vital, as he himself seems to have recognized:

> What the Greeks were for the Romans, so the French are now for us. They have given us very good models in all the great genres of poetry, and have written moreover many discourses, censures, critiques and other guides from which we can draw many rules.[60]

For the next generation, these words would be anathema. Gottsched's critical orientation was overturned within his lifetime, as the English replaced the French as German thinkers' modern reference, and the Greeks eclipsed the Romans among ancient cultures. Gottsched's words make clear the state of German literary thought in the early part of the eighteenth century, however, as a field struggling to define its place with respect to the classical tradition. Greek literature at this point was still largely the dusty province of the erudite and did not seem to demand a direct engagement.[61] Though this was not a universal position, it was a widespread one, and forms the background for Winckelmann's radical exhortation to the imitation of Greek works.

Far from Gottsched's perch in Leipzig, another learned group, led by J. J. Breitinger and J. J. Bodmer in Zurich, put forth a different vision for the development of German literature. Though both camps agreed on the need for a normative poetics (Breitinger published his own *Critical Art of Poetry* in 1740), they disagreed on some of the fundamental aims of poetry.[62] The Zurich circle advanced a sensualistic aesthetic that owed a great deal

[58] On Gottsched's reading of French criticism, see Catherine Julliard, *Gottsched et l'esthétique théâtrale française: la réception allemande des théories françaises* (Bern: Lang, 1998).

[59] Christopher Wild, "Geburt der Theaterreform aus dem Geist der Theaterfeindlichkeit: Der Fall Gottsched," *Lessing Yearbook / Jahrbuch* 34 (2002).

[60] Gottsched, *Versuch einer critischen Dichtkunst*: 41.

[61] For an example of indirect engagement, see Johann Heinrich Steffens, *Oedipus: ein Trauerspiel in Versen nach den Sophocles eingerichtet* (Zelle: Gsellius, 1746). Despite its title, it owes as much to Corneille as to Sophocles. See Meid, *Die griechische Tragödie im Drama der Aufklärung*: 77–81.

[62] The best account of the debate is now Beiser, *Diotima's children*: 112–7.

to Boileau's advocacy of the sublime, which oriented criticism more to the reader's affective experience than to the author's rational creation.[63] Bodmer rejected the view of Gottsched and Dacier that tragedy teaches by example or precept, arguing rather that it instills "moral, virtuous and useful sentiment [Empfindung]" in the viewers: "The affects have a far stronger power over them [the mass of men] than the power of understanding."[64] The Leipzig-Zurich debate centers on the question of whether philosophical reason or emotional response is the final ground for evaluating a work of art. While Gottsched insisted that rational principles circumscribed the realm of aesthetics, the Swiss critics suggested that there were aspects of aesthetic pleasure that lay beyond the bounds of reason (though, usually, such nonrational pleasures served reason in one way or another). Both positions, it is important to remember, could find support in Aristotle's *Poetics*: discussions of the constituent elements and proper construction of tragedy could suggest a purely rational deduction, while references to tragic emotions and the enigmatic notion of *catharsis* could suggest a more experiential framework.

For all their disagreements, the Leipzig and Zurich circles were both committed to the growth of German literature on ancient models, and to the development of German dramatic poetry. As early as the late 1730s, the young Johann Elias Schlegel (uncle of the famous brothers) attempted to fill the vacuum of a German Sophocles with a free translation of the *Electra*, but deemed the work unsuccessful and only published it somewhat later.[65] While still a student at Schulpforta, Schlegel wrote a *Hecuba* (1737; later titled *The Trojan Women*), which was a popular success and mixed elements from various ancient texts (Euripides' *Trojan Women* and *Hecuba* along with Seneca's *Troades*)—all of which he would have read in the original.[66] Particularly interesting for the history of the parallel, though little remarked, is Schlegel's "Critical Notes on the Tragedies of the Ancients and Moderns" ("Kritische Anmerkungen über die Trauerspiele der Alten und Neuern"). Originally written as a letter to his brother around 1740, the essay shows Schlegel's increasing disillusionment with Gottsched's Francophilia and the tradition of normative poetics. Like Brumoy, whom he may have read, Schlegel points to the political differences between Greek and modern states as an important cause of their aesthetic divergence. Schlegel, though, sees this as a clear advantage for the ancients: "The ancients had one more advantage, which cannot be imitated in our times. The Greeks were a free

---

[63] See Marilyn K. Torbruegge, "Bodmer and Longinus," *Monatshefte* 63(1971).

[64] Johann Jakob Bodmer, *Kritische Betrachtungen über die poetischen Gemälde der Dichter* (Zürich: Orell, 1741), 432.

[65] Eugen Wolff, *Johann Elias Schlegel* (Berlin: Oppenheim, 1889), 29–31.

[66] See Meid, *Die griechische Tragödie im Drama der Aufklärung*: 36–42.

people. They did not have the high estimation of kings that we have."[67] For this reason, Schlegel argues, their tragedies could portray more realistic protagonists and more harrowing reversals. Though Schlegel's text was not widely read, it shows the potent political valences of Greek tragedy in Germany, even before the first translations were published. When the first wave of philhellenism arrived shortly afterwards, it met with a culture already in search of a new aesthetic and political model.

The 1750s mark the beginning of widespread engagement in Germany with Greek tragedy and with Greek culture generally. In 1753, Michael Conrad Curtius's translation of the *Poetics* was published; in 1755 Winckelmann's *Thoughts on the Imitation of Greek Works in Painting and Sculpture* (*Gedanken über die Nachahmung der griechischen Werke in der Malerey und Bildhauerkunst*) created a sensation; and in 1759, Johann Jacob Steinbrüchel's translations of Sophocles began to appear anonymously in Zurich. The two translations would provide the German language with equivalents to Dacier and Brumoy, and Winckelmann's essay would lay the foundation for the imagination of ancient Greece for the rest of the century.[68] As in France, translation of the *Poetics* preceded translation of the plays (discounting Opitz's forgotten baroque *Antigone*). The two endeavors spoke to importantly different notions of how to build literary culture: translation of the *Poetics* was a means of regulating taste and practice by making accessible the apparently timeless dictates of reason; translation of the plays themselves often carried a more emotional and explicitly exhortatory aim, seeking to inspire contemporaries through the example of the ancients. Both tendencies, the rational and the emotional, were importantly adumbrated in Winckelmann's aesthetics of imitation, which argued that the way to discern the ideal of creation was through the experience of viewing ancient artworks. There, Winckelmann argues, one finds "even more than nature— that is, certain ideal beauties of nature [noch mehr als Natur, das ist, gewisse idealische Schönheiten derselben], which, as an ancient commentator on Plato teaches, are made from images sketched only in the mind."[69] Part of the power of Winckelmann's program was its suggestion that a rational understanding of creation could be obtained through (nonrational) experience.

Curtius's translation of the *Poetics* reads as a contribution to academic philosophy rather than a manifesto for any form of practice. In this respect, it is quite different from Dacier's edition, which, in responding to the

[67] Johann Elias Schlegel, *Werke*, ed. J. H. Schlegel, 5 vols. (Leipzig: Mumm, 1764–73), 3, 212.
[68] The bibliography on Winckelmann's influence is vast. For a start, see Marchand, *Down from Olympus*; Alex Potts, *Flesh and the ideal: Winckelmann and the origins of art history* (New Haven: Yale University Press, 1994); Katherine Harloe, *Winckelmann and the invention of antiquity* (Oxford: Oxford University Press, 2013).
[69] Winckelmann, *Gedanken*: 4.

burning issues of the *Querelle*, aimed at accessibility and persuasion. Curtius is conscious of his predecessors at each step, carefully weighing previous viewpoints before coming to his own conclusions. Though Curtius thanks Gottsched in his introduction, the dominant intellectual influence is Alexander Baumgarten, who in his 1735 *Meditations on Poetry* coined the term "aesthetics" and defined poetry as a "perfected sensible discourse [oratio sensitiva perfecta]."[70] The early decades of the eighteenth century saw a theoretical development in which the "fine arts" were set off in a separate domain of thinking and opposed to the products of craft, to rhetoric, and to the sciences broadly.[71] This went hand in hand with the elaboration of philosophical aesthetics as the investigation of a particular kind of experience, defined by rules proper to it ("autonomous" in at least a limited sense). From Baumgarten, Curtius took an understanding of aesthetics as a serious philosophical project, which was not to be sullied with practical advice to the poet or critic (and thus quite far from Aristotle's project). Though generations of readers of Aristotle had appealed to reason as their guide in thinking about poetry, Curtius's edition differs in its systematic presentation, which borrows more from scholarly philosophical discourses than from popular poetics.

On the issue of *catharsis*, Curtius's viewpoint is eclectic and brings together a number of different justifications for a moral interpretation, equating "purification" (*Reinigung*) with "improvement" (*Verbesserung*) of the passions.[72] His understanding of this process of improvement combines Brumoy's notion of the social character of *catharsis* (as an increased sensitivity to the suffering of others) with Dacier's individual, allegorical interpretation (as a negative example of passions to avoid). "Through the arousal of the passions," Curtius writes, "the drives of humanity [Triebe der Menschlichkeit] are planted, awakened, and maintained."[73] The experience of watching unhappiness onstage, Curtius argues, makes the spectator into

[70] Alexander Baumgarten, *Meditationes philosophicae de nonnullis ad poema pertinentibus* (Halle: Grunert, 1735), 7. Curtius's debt is acknowledged at Michael Conrad Curtius, *Aristoteles Dichtkunst* (Hanover: Richter, 1753), 372. The decision to write in German is significant and suggests that Curtius conceives of his audience as broader than Baumgarten's.

[71] See the canonical, but recently disputed, Paul Oskar Kristeller, "The modern system of the arts: a study in the history of aesthetics," *Journal of the History of Ideas* 12–13 (1951–52). There is a sharp critique and sensible rebuttal, respectively, in James I. Porter, "Is art modern? Kristeller's 'modern system of the arts' reconsidered," *British Journal of Aesthetics* 49 (2009); Peter Kivy, "What *really* happened in the eighteenth century: The 'modern system' re-examined (again)," *British Journal of Aesthetics* 52 (2012). For my purposes, the question of the "system" of the arts and the extent of their autonomy in the eighteenth century is less important than the simple fact of the possibility of a system, and the theorization of the aesthetic as a particular domain of experience, whether more or less autonomous.

[72] Curtius, *Aristoteles Dichtkunst*: 394.

[73] Ibid., 390.

a "friend to man [Menschenfreund]," capable of sympathy for those in real misfortune. This notion of *catharsis* as a social education constitutes a link between Brumoy's *Theater* and Lessing's influential discussions, with Curtius as the probable mediator.

The second part of Curtius's explanation of *catharsis* is much like Dacier's, seeing the aim of tragedy as instilling moral attitudes in the viewer. Curtius's translation of the relevant passage goes even further than Dacier in its interpretive liberty: tragedy "purifies us, by means of terror and compassion, from the errors of the passions represented [uns, vermittelst des Schreckens und Mitleidens, von den Fehlern der vorgestellten Leidenschaften reiniget]."[74] This is a willful translation, making the passions of the characters on stage (rather than those of the audience) the objects of *catharsis*, and giving this an explicitly moralizing aim. Like Dacier, Curtius sees the characters on stage as negative examples, and *catharsis* as a moment of reflective moral improvement. Curtius thus combines, without apparent conflict, affective and cognitive understandings of tragedy's effect.[75] Yet this confused and derivative discussion should not obscure the importance of the edition. As the young Lessing gleefully pointed out, it for the first time allowed German readers to bypass Dacier and Gottsched alike and go straight to the Greek text.[76]

Steinbrüchel's project, unlike Curtius's, is explicitly popularizing, presenting itself as a step towards creating the conditions for a national literature (though the nation was Switzerland rather than Germany). This entailed first of all supplanting Brumoy as the primary reference on Greek tragedy for Germanophones. The need for a more accessible edition of Greek tragedy was felt in England as well, and Steinbrüchel's first translations are contemporaneous with a complete English edition of Brumoy's *Theater*.[77] Steinbrüchel's translations of Sophocles were initially released individually, beginning in 1759 with *Electra* and *OT*—still the exemplary works of ancient tragedy—and continuing with *Antigone* and *Philoctetes* the following year. The choices replicate Brumoy's, with the addition of *Antigone*, which might have seemed necessary as a replacement for Opitz's baroque version. Each is translated in prose throughout (as in Brumoy) and

---

[74] Ibid., 12.

[75] See Peter-André Alt, *Tragödie der Aufklärung: eine Einführung* (Tübingen: Francke, 1994), 100–107. Alt points out the tensions within Curtius's description, but places it in a development of German thought on tragedy from Gottsched to Lessing that obscures the French roots of the discussion.

[76] See Lessing's review in *WBZB* 2, 532.

[77] Charlotte Lennox, *The Greek theatre of Father Brumoy*, 3 vols. (London: Millar et al., 1759). It is tempting to see them both as influenced by Winckelmann, but there is no trace of this in the English edition, and Steinbrüchel is not explicit in the 1759–60 releases. The 1763 collection, as demonstrated below, does show the indelible mark of the *Nachahmung* essay.

prefaced with a Pindaric ode. The logic of this juxtaposition is nowhere explicit (and does not seem to have anything to do with the contents of either play or poem), but it may seek to align the two authors in creating the sublime effect that was widely associated with Pindar at the time.[78] At any rate, the translations seem to have been a success (as evidenced by the series' continuation), and were noted as much for the translations of Pindar as they were for Sophocles.

The Tragic Theater of the Greeks (*Das tragische Theater der Griechen*), published in 1763, expands Steinbrüchel's project with an outspoken didactic intention. Collecting the four previous Sophocles translations, and adding a volume of Euripides, the work competes with Brumoy's translation (which was revised in the same year) in format and name alike. In choosing works of Euripides, again, Steinbrüchel shows the influence of Brumoy, translating *Iphigenia in Aulis* and *Hippolytus* (as Brumoy had), along with the *Phoenician Women* (probably for its background to the *Antigone* and parallels with Racine's *Enemy Brothers*), and *Hecuba* (capitalizing on Schlegel's success with the story). One notices, as with Brumoy, the effort to translate those works that have been most successfully adapted, and Steinbrüchel's notes are full of quotations from modern plays on the same subjects (particularly Racine's *Iphigenia*, *The Enemy Brothers*, and *Phaedra*). It seems from the volume subtitles (*First Volume of Sophocles/Euripides*) that a complete translation was intended, but did not come to fruition—probably a result of the lukewarm reviews the translations received.[79]

The influence of Winckelmann's program is evident both in Steinbrüchel's nationalistic aim, and more subtly, in a notion of holistic creation that seems inspired by the exhortation to *Nachahmung*. Steinbrüchel tells the story, adapted from Plato's *Phaedrus* (268c), of a young man in ancient Greece who has learned to create by a set of rules and asks Euripides and Sophocles for advice: "I can arouse pity, I can arouse fear," he says, "and now I want to write tragedies." The poets respond derisively to the young man's ambition to create through a recipe:

> "Not so fast!" reply both poets laughing. Tragedy is not what you imagine. It is a whole consisting of varied parts carefully fitted together [ein aus mannigfaltigen und geschikt in einander passenden Theilen bestehendes Ganze]. If they are

[78] Cf. Johann Jakob Breitinger, *Critische Dichtkunst*, 2 vols. (Zürich: Orell, 1740), 1, 359. Breitinger also draws attention to Pindar's patriotic qualities—another possible point of comparison. On Pindar in the eighteenth century, see Martin Völher, *Pindarrezeptionen: sechs Studien zum Wandel des Pindarverständnisses von Erasmus bis Herder* (Heidelberg: Winter, 2005), 117–43.

[79] See Klaus Heydemann, "Literarische Fingerübungen—oder mehr? Zur Geschichte der Sophokles-Übersetzungen im deutschen Sprachraum im 18. Jahrhundert," in *Übersetzung als Vermittlerin antiker Literatur*, ed. Wolfgang Kofler, Florian Schaffenrath, and Karlheinz Töchterle (Innsbruck: StudienVerlag, 2009), 124–6.

brought together incorrectly, the result is a monstrosity [Ungeheuer]. You know what one must know before one wishes to study the art of tragedy; art itself, though, you do not yet understand.[80]

Steinbrüchel hopes to educate his readers, schooled in the normative and Francophile poetics of Gottsched, in "art itself." The concept of wholeness, which will be central to romantic aesthetics, links the analytical creation of neoclassical theory with the Winckelmannian concept of imitation. The rules of art must be learned, but they are not enough for Steinbrüchel: one must have an intuition, gained from the study of great works, which would fit together the various elements into a harmonious whole. This is precisely the kind of intuition Winckelmann recommended to his readers in sending them *nach Athen*.

Steinbrüchel is attracted most of all to the political elements of Greek tragedy, which his teachers had also emphasized.[81] The aim of tragedy, for the Swiss critics, was not just moral, but civic, intended to inspire "love of virtue and the fatherland, hatred of vice and tyranny."[82] Switzerland at the time was a loose confederacy of mostly democratic cantons, which could easily have suggested Greek city-states. Here the translation of Greek tragedy could speak to a desired correspondence between the social and political organizations of the two nations that was not possible in France. Steinbrüchel's preface closes with the hope that, through the acquaintance with ancient tragedy, a modern author will be inspired to create patriotic dramas:

> Should this project, as one hopes, go some way to check the course of these prejudices that are so detrimental to good taste, then the translator would consider himself richly rewarded for his work. But even more so if it could give occasion for a genius, animated by the true spirit of freedom [. . .], following the footsteps of the Greeks, through the glorious examples of the supporters and benefactors of our state, to inflame us with a love of the fatherland and the law, with self-sacrifice, courage, and hatred of partisan spirit and oppression.[83]

Steinbrüchel sees his work more as a political exhortation than an artistic education. He envisions a tragedy that will be based on national history, and will use Greek forms to resolutely contemporary, and political, ends. Political and aesthetic goals are inseparable for Steinbrüchel and lead him to

---

[80]Johann Jacob Steinbrüchel, *Das tragische Theater der Griechen*, 2 vols. (Zürich: Gessner, 1763): 1, ix.

[81]Anton Weilenmann, *Das aufgeklärte Zürich in seinem Verhältnis zur Antike* (Winterthur: Keller, 1961), 110.

[82]Steinbrüchel, *Das tragische Theater der Griechen*: 1, vi. This is a variation on the formula of Dacier and Curtius.

[83]Ibid., 1, xi.

celebrate Greek tragedy as a patriotic art form. His translation, in Winckel-mannian spirit, is an effort to inspire his countrymen through the example of the Greeks.

An interest in the political valences of Sophocles, and particularly of the *Antigone* (which has little precedent in France) is evident in Steinbrüchel's translation. The chorus is listed in the *dramatis personae* as consisting of "the senate of Thebes," when the Greek describes them simply as a group of old men.[84] In a crucial passage of the first stasimon, Steinbrüchel increases their patriotic fervor: for χθονός (368: "land, country") he gives *Vaterland*, for ὑψίπολις (370: "high in the city"), he translates *Patriot*, and ἄπολις (370: "city-less") becomes "kein Bürger mehr" ("no longer a citizen").[85] Where Sophocles' chorus speaks quite generally of belonging to a *polis*, Stein-brüchel's describes citizenship in the *Vaterland*, emphasizing patriotic duty. A similar intensification is present in the conflict between Creon and Haimon, where Steinbrüchel translates Creon's νοσός (732), describing An-tigone's influence as a "disease" as *Aufruhr* ("uproar," or even "revolution," a word that Hölderlin will use prominently in discussing the text).[86] These tendencies, though fairly subtle, serve to make Sophocles' text more eas-ily comprehensible in contemporary political terms, strengthening Stein-brüchel's political program for the translations. In the first modern transla-tion of *Antigone* into German, then, one already sees the seeds of so much of later interest in the text.[87]

The road to ancient Greece often led through Renaissance England. The story of Germany's discovery of Shakespeare runs in parallel to the story of the reception of Greek tragedy.[88] The first volume of Christoph Martin Wieland's translation of Shakespeare was published in 1762, and eventually ran to eight volumes and twenty-two plays—the most extensive translation of Shakespeare into any modern language at the time. Wieland's edition suf-

---

[84]Ibid., 1, 330. Johnson lists the chorus as ἐκ Θηβαίων γερόντων, which gives the idea of old age (*senum* in Latin), but not that of an organized, decision-making body. Likewise, in the *OT*, Steinbrüchel intervenes in the debate between Dacier and Boivin about the identity of the chorus to argue, with Boivin, that it is primarily a political rather than religious body (125).

[85]Ibid., 1, 357. This is part of the prehistory to Heidegger's notorious reading of the passage in the 1935/53 *Einführung in die Metaphysik*.

[86]Ibid., 1, 379. A footnote justifies the translation with a passage from Aelian in which the word can mean "Empörung und Partey-Geist."

[87]See George Steiner, *Antigones* (Oxford: Clarendon, 1984). It is worth noting, against Stein-er's universalism, that interest in the *Antigone* story is far stronger in Germany than in France, where it never gained a foothold in the eighteenth century.

[88]The history of Shakespearean reception in Germany has been far better told than that of Greek tragedy: see Roger Paulin, *The critical reception of Shakespeare in Germany, 1682–1914: native literature and foreign genius* (Hildesheim: Olms, 2003); Renata Häublein, *Die Entdeckung Shakespeares auf der deutschen Bühne des 18. Jahrhunderts* (Tübingen: Niemeyer, 2005).

fered a fate similar to Steinbrüchel's: though recognized by contemporaries as an important moment in German literature, neither survived the change in literary taste associated with the *Sturm und Drang* of the 1770s. Though the translations in both cases were undeniably flawed (Wieland's knowledge of English was faulty and he tended to excise whatever seemed indecorous), perhaps more significant for their reception was that they were both oriented to standards of normative poetics, and sought to harmonize their object with Enlightenment notions of poetic propriety that would soon be rejected. Both Steinbrüchel and Wieland took the French to be their guides in approaching their respective texts.[89] Even in the 1760s, this orientation was not unquestioned; in the 1770s it would be even more problematic. Instead of seeing Racine and Voltaire as the standards of modern tragedy, the *Sturm und Drang* would make Shakespeare the essential modern dramatist and banish the French to ignominy. This change in literary models, though it had been brewing since the debates between Gottsched and Bodmer, is due most of all to Gotthold Ephraim Lessing.

1759, the year of Steinbrüchel's first translations, is often considered a milestone in German poetics for another reason: Lessing launched an influential attack on Gottsched and French tragedy in the seventeenth of his *Letters Concerning Recent Literature* (*Briefe, die neueste Literatur betreffend*). He decries the "frenchifying [französierende]" theater introduced by Gottsched and the cold formalism associated with neoclassical poetics. His goal remains normative and Aristotelian, but he advocates using the *Poetics* as a guide to tragedy's end rather than a prescription of its means. More important than the unities, *vraisemblance*, and *bienséance* is the affective goal of tragedy: *catharsis* through pity (*Mitleid*) and fear (*Furcht*).[90] Comparing Shakespeare and Corneille, Lessing writes that "the Englishman almost always reaches the aim of tragedy, whatever unusual and idiosyncratic paths he chooses; the Frenchman almost never reaches it, even though he treads the cleared paths of the ancients" (*WBZB* 4, 501). Lessing turns the authority of Greek theater against its ostensible defenders, arguing that their understanding of poetics has been superficial and that their works have therefore failed to attain the aim of tragedy. By reorienting criticism to an affective goal, Lessing makes way for Shakespeare to achieve the same tragic aim as the Greeks, even in a radically different form.

---

[89] Steinbrüchel seems to have been conscious of the Shakespeare translation, as he disparages the taste for "the plays of an English poet, whose faults are as immense as his beauties are extraordinary" (1, xi).

[90] Lessing revises Curtius' translation of *Schrecken* to make it a reflective response rather than a sudden shock. For Lessing, *Furcht* is the transfer of pity for the characters on stage to the spectator's themselves (*WBZB* 3, 716 and, in more detail, 6, 551–70). See Max Kommerell, *Lessing und Aristoteles: Untersuchung über die Theorie der Tragödie* (Frankfurt: Klostermann, 1957), 73–77.

Lessing's practice as a creative artist was different again from the Greeks and Shakespeare. From the 1750s, he was the most important German practitioner of bourgeois tragedy (*bürgerliches Trauerspiel*), which depicted (relatively) everyday people in situations of passion and danger. Though the genre had been established first in England, Lessing's inspiration was Denis Diderot, who elaborated a theory of the *tragédie bourgeoise* in his 1757 "Conversations on *The Natural Son*" ("Entretiens sur *Le fils naturel*," published alongside his play of the same name)—a work Lessing translated shortly afterwards. For Diderot, the way forward for drama did not lie in the high tragedy associated with Racine and Voltaire, but in a genre that would appeal directly to the emotions of the audience and speak to common concerns. Such immediacy, he believed, existed in Greek tragedy, and could be recreated through a drama of natural expression and raw emotions. In the anguished screams of the wounded Philoctetes, Diderot believed he had recognized an emotional power that modern drama's *sangfroid* had abandoned. Diderot's excitable mouthpiece declares, "I will not cease to cry to our French: Truth! Nature! The ancients! Sophocles! Philoctetes!"[91] This was, no less than the neoclassicism of Dacier, a way of claiming the authority of antiquity. Likewise, Lessing, though a considerable philological talent, was primarily interested in the elements of ancient drama that could be appropriated to his own ends.[92] By isolating what they believed to be the emotional essence of Greek tragedy, Lessing and Diderot justified their own modernizing practices. The way to be more Greek was, paradoxically, to be more modern.

Lessing formalizes an influential division between the essence of tragedy, now seen in its emotional effect, and the genre's formal qualities. By separating the two, he could argue for the conformity of Sophocles and Shakespeare (and his own works) to the same normative canon. Not coincidentally, it is around this period that *das Tragische* and *le tragique* come into usage in French and German as independent nouns. The concept can be deployed neutrally, simply to describe the qualities of tragedy as opposed to other genres.[93] But it can also be used with greater pregnancy, as when Christoph Friedrich Nicolai writes to Lessing that "the tragic in the characters lies in that they arouse strong passions, not that they improve morals" (*WBZB* 3, 666). For Steinbrüchel, *das Tragische* is occasionally connected to the fall of an apparently great man. His notes apply the quality equally to Aegisthus' self-confidence in the *Electra* (just before he is murdered), and to Oedipus'

---

[91] Denis Diderot, *Le fils naturel, ou les epreuves de la vertu* (Amsterdam 1757), 205. This forms a background to Lessing's famous dispute with Winckelmann in the *Laokoön*. See *WBZB* 5/2, 17–22.

[92] See Uta Korzeniewski, *"Sophokles! Die Alten! Philoktet!" Lessing und die antiken Dramatiker* (Konstanz: Universitätsverlag Konstanz, 2003), 472–75.

[93] As in *WBZB* 1, 914.

virtue in the *OT*.[94] "The tragic," in both cases is "raised" [erhoben] by the audience's perception of the disconnect between how each appears at first and their wretchedness by the end of the play, suggesting something like the concept of Sophoclean irony that would be developed in the nineteenth century: "So full of his greatness, so close to his fall!"[95]

Most concepts of "the tragic" in the 1750s and 60s, though, are narrowly rhetorical, connected to tragic emotions. The *Encyclopédie*, for example, defines *le tragique* as "that which forms the essence of tragedy. It contains the terrible and the pitiable, or, if one pleases, terror and pity."[96] The article, by Louis Jaucourt, is an index of the importance of rhetorical explanations of tragedy's generic characteristics, similar to what Lessing and Diderot had offered. It also reflects the same normative aim that Lessing's discussion had, using affective criteria to distinguish between "the true tragic" and works such as Racine's *Esther* and *Mithridate*, which depict virtue rewarded and vice punished.[97] Notably absent from the *Encyclopédie* article is any mention of the unities, which had so long dominated French poetics. With the essence of tragedy no longer defined by the social status of its characters, the setting of its plots, or the economy of its presentation, emotional effect could be seen as the criterion for establishing what is and is not tragedy.

Lessing shows an extreme of affective normative criticism, rejecting an entire tradition of tragedy for failing to move its audience in the appropriate way. This can lead his argumentation into contortions no less ponderous than moralizing readings of the *OT*, as when he struggles to define Shakespeare's *Richard III*, which does not raise the sympathetic emotions his theory aims at, yet nevertheless remains an utterly compelling work: "Even if *Richard* were not a tragedy, it would remain a dramatic poem [dramatisches Gedicht]; if it lacked the beauties of tragedy, it could nevertheless have other beauties" (*WBZB* 6, 578). Despite Lessing's advocacy, Shakespeare still seems unclassifiable in the classical dramatic categories. The challenge for the younger generation will be to formulate Shakespeare's difference from the ancients while still seeing him as a part of a continuous tradition of tragedy—or, perhaps better, of the tragic. The focus on defining tragedy's essence, which has been incipient throughout many of the texts so far discussed, will distinguish German discussions from the 1770s onward.[98] It

---

[94] Steinbrüchel, *Das tragische Theater der Griechen*: 1, 102, 15.

[95] Ibid., 1, 102.

[96] Louis Jaucourt, "Tragique," in *Encyclopédie ou dictionnaire raisonné des sciences, des arts et des métiers*, vol. 16, ed. Denis Diderot and Jean le Rond d'Alembert (Paris: Briasson, 1765).

[97] Similarly, Lessing writes that "the tragic consists of something more than the simple shedding of blood" (*WBZB* 2, 466). Such distinctions can be traced to the discussion of tragic heroes in the *Poetics* (1453a).

[98] See further Thomas Martinec, "Von der Tragödientheorie zur Philosophie des Tragischen: poetikgeschichtliche Skizze eines Umschwungs," *Jahrbuch der deutschen Schillergesellschaft* 49 (2005).

can no longer be assumed that Euripides and Racine, Sophocles and Shakespeare belong to the same genre; the concept of the tragic responds to this increasing sense of difference by positing an essential similarity. Accordingly, the *Querelle*'s question of superiority becomes a question of identity: Can ancient and modern tragedies be compared? Is the tragic possible in modernity?

CHAPTER 2

The Antiquity of Tragedy

HISTORICIZATION, IN SOMETHING LIKE ITS MODERN FORM, enters discussions of Greek tragedy around 1770. Historicizing elements have been important in discussions of tragedy throughout the eighteenth century—especially in Brumoy and his readers—but they become newly self-conscious in the latter third. Though the conclusions drawn are often not radically new, they are articulated more systematically than previously. Thought about tragedy feeds on ulterior discussions of ancient political systems (most importantly, that of Montesquieu) and of ancient epic (especially those of Robert Wood and John Brown), but the most significant factor may be a change in the status of poetics, and a diminution of Aristotle's authority. Though the *Poetics* continues to provide the framework for all discussions of Greek tragedy, its universal applicability is often questioned. This development is associated in Germany with the *Sturm und Drang*, and receives much of its impetus from discussions in England. In important and often unnoticed ways, however, it is parallel to discussions in France, where normative Aristotelianism was similarly being criticized as inadequate to the task of grasping changes in the genre of tragedy. Across Western Europe, then, one can discern a broad shift away from the foundations of neoclassicism, and towards a philhellenism that emphasizes the singularity of antiquity. Within the academy, the 1770s and 1780s see the first stirrings of the critical editorial practices that will transform the discipline and lay new foundations for the philology of tragedy. Taken together, these new ways of conceiving Greek literature within history represent a fundamental shift in thought about antiquity, which has tragedy as an important focal point.

A holistic view of Greek culture, though it had been suggested by some of the thinkers examined previously (Brumoy and Steinbrüchel especially), was most influentially formulated by Winckelmann in his *History of the Art of Antiquity* (*Geschichte der Kunst des Altertums*, 1764). From the time of the *Imitation* essay, Winckelmann had argued that it was the conditions

---

*On Herder and the growth of historicization see: Robert E. Norton, *Herder's aesthetics and the European Enlightenment* (Ithaca: Cornell University Press, 1991); Robert S. Leventhal, *The disciplines of interpretation: Lessing, Herder, Schlegel and hermeneutics in Germany, 1750–1800* (Berlin: de Gruyter, 1994); Maike Oergel, *Culture and identity: historicity in German literature and thought, 1770–1815* (Berlin: de Gruyter, 2006). There are stimulating essays on the topic in Most, *Historicization—Historisierung*. Literature on antiquity and tragedy in the eighteenth century is given in the previous chapter.

of ancient Athenian life, both cultural (its political freedom) and natural (its climate), that created the glories of classical art. In the *History* he
elaborated this into a historical method of interpretation, which aligned
developments in art with broader developments in culture (though, from
today's perspective, his historical narrative appears deeply flawed). Following Winckelmann, European philhellenism became far more sensitive to
the particularities of Greek culture and to its various periods and internal
tensions. Yet at the same time, neither Winckelmann nor most of his readers
were willing to give up the postulate that ancient Greece had achieved the
ideal of aesthetic perfection.[1] The generation immediately following Winckelmann took from his work a dual legacy: on the one hand, the imperative
to historicize; on the other, the conviction that the history of ancient Greece
had a privileged value—it was not just one culture among many, but had a
unique closeness to the highest aesthetic and social achievement. Thought
on Greek tragedy reflected both impulses, seeing the genre increasingly as
a product of its time while investing it with exceptional status as the bearer
of timeless insight.

It is relatively easy to date the historicization of tragedy: 1773 has long
been considered a milestone in German thought for Johann Gottfried
Herder's essay "Shakespeare," which rejected Aristotelian poetics as inappli-
cable to the literature of other places and times. Less well known (indeed,
all but forgotten) is a contemporaneous debate in Paris, which erupted in
the Académie des Inscriptions and pitted a normative Aristotelian perspective on Greek tragedy against a radically historicizing one. Though little remarked in itself, the minor quarrel contains the germs of the monumental
1785–89 reedition of the *Theater of the Greeks*, which is notable for its historicizing tendencies. The parallel became increasingly suspect as thinkers in
France and Germany argued that there was little or no common ground for
comparing ancient and modern tragedy. Between the first edition of Brumoy's *Theater* in 1730 and the revised edition of the 1780s, one can read the
changes in the parallel form: where earlier the parallel assumed similarity
and sought difference; by 1790, it assumed difference and sought similarity.

Guillaume Dubois de Rochefort: Tragedy and Cultural Difference

The comparison of ancient and modern tragedies relies on an assumption of continuity, a presumed genealogy that places the roots of modern
forms in Greco-Roman antiquity. This genealogy was broadly accepted by

---

[1] On the tensions between Winckelmann's universalization of beauty and his historicization of art in Greece, see Luca Giuliani, "Naturalisierung der Kunst versus Historisierung der
Kunst," in *Historicization—Historisierung*, ed. Glenn W. Most (Göttingen: Vandenhoeck & Ruprecht, 2001).

both *Anciens* and *Modernes*, though it could be conceived in quite different ways—as a cyclical variation of cultural highs and lows, as a fall from prehistoric innocence, as a progress from barbarism. Depending on which narrative one subscribed to, the results of comparison could be diametrically opposed. Around 1770, though, we find a new possibility: ancients and moderns are not connected by any kind of continuity, but are divided by a temporal rift that renders comparisons empty. This position is taken up by a nearly forgotten French scholar, Guillaume Dubois de Rochefort, in an extraordinary debate that took place in 1772 at the Académie des Inscriptions. Rochefort vigorously contests the assumption that ancient and modern arts have enough in common for comparison, setting a narrative of rupture against the prevailing assumption of continuity. His account of difference reveals a gradual but far-reaching change in the terms of historical thought, as the debate shifts from divergent forms of the classical genealogy to the genealogy itself. Though Rochefort is by no means the most influential or eloquent exponent of this latter inquiry, he is one of the first to see the question of tragedy's modernity as a question of the genre's continuity with antiquity.

Rochefort's antagonist was the philosopher Charles Batteux, who had gained fame throughout Europe for applying the doctrine of *mimesis* to the whole spectrum of the arts in his 1746 *The Fine Arts Reduced to a Single Principle* (*Les beaux arts réduits à un même principe*). Batteux's rationalist and universalist aesthetic found Aristotle's dictates to be proven by the laws of reason, and applicable across time. The way to understand all the arts, ancient and modern, he argued, was simply to understand Aristotle. Batteux's edition of the *Poetics* in facing-page translation (along with texts of Horace, Vida, and Boileau) appeared in 1771, the first French version since Dacier. The publication of the translation formed the occasion for a series of "Notes [*Mémoires*] on the *Poetics* of Aristotle" delivered to the Académie in June 1771. Rochefort answered in a "Note on the Object of Tragedy among the Greeks," delivered in January 1772, which was followed almost immediately by Batteux's response eleven days later, and then Rochefort's final rebuttal in May (all of which were published in the Académie's regular publication, *Mémoires de littérature*, of 1777). The debate has been almost completely ignored by scholars, but illuminates the changing currents of thought of the period and lingering debates about the universal validity of ancient poetics.

Batteux's viewpoint considers tragedy in formal and rhetorical terms, with respect to the kinds of plots it depicts and their effects on the audience.[2] He advances a reading of *catharsis* as a strictly emotional effect, without relation to cognition or morality. The goal of tragedy is straightforward: the thrill of having one's emotions moved and ultimately calmed. Tragedy is pleasurable,

---

[2]On Batteux's theory of tragedy, see Lurje, *Die Suche nach der Schuld*: 198–217.

Batteux insists, only in so far as it is set off from any real effects: "It is a pure pleasure, of emotion without sadness, of fear without danger, of compassion without unhappy ones. [C'est un plaisir pur, de l'émotion sans douleur, de la crainte sans danger, de la compassion sans malheureux.]"[3] By emphasizing the distance between imitation and reality, Batteux avoids any sense of Greek tragedy as politically problematic or morally questionable. He strenuously opposes any suggestion that tragedy has a moral aim—that it is constructed allegorically, inspires its viewers with admiration, or satisfies their moral sense. In particular, he denigrates the many tragedies that end happily for failing to create the properly tragic pleasures of vicarious pity and fear.[4] The best tragedies, ancient or modern (Batteux names, in addition to the *OT*, Corneille's *Polyeucte*, Racine's *Phaedra*, and Voltaire's *Zaïre*), are those that "end in unhappiness, their heroes are good, or good more than bad, the enterprise attains that goal, and morality does not enter at all."[5]

Rochefort objected to two elements of Batteux's argument. Most vocally, he argued against a reading of the *Poetics* that denied tragedy a moral aim. Implicit, though just as fundamental, was a disagreement as to whether the experience of tragedy in ancient Greece could be compared to the experience of tragedy in his own time. Throughout his life, Rochefort argued for a holistic view of Greek literature, which emphasized the links between all the forms of art in ancient Greece and their social and political contexts. The spheres of life in ancient Athens formed a unity for Rochefort, in which all cultural products were directed to the public good. This led him to the conviction, repeated throughout his writings, that ancient and modern cultures were fundamentally different and incomparable. In making this consciousness of difference the starting-point for the discussion of ancient cultural products, Rochefort's thought shows parallels to Herder's more famous writings. Obviously, they were not the first to note these differences, but they were among the first to use historical variation as a hermeneutic principle. For Rochefort, there is an epistemological gulf separating antiquity and modernity, which renders efforts at understanding through comparison inherently suspect.

Batteux's discourse moved the relatively unknown Rochefort to disagree publicly with one of the most eminent members of the Académie. In his re-

[3] Charles Batteux, "Second mémoire sur la tragédie," *Mémoires de la littérature, tirez des registres de l'Académie Royale des inscriptions et belles lettres* 39 (1777): 60. This is a well-worn *topos* of eighteenth-century discussions of tragedy, which often refer to Lucretius' description of a shipwreck at the beginning of *De rerum natura* 2: "suave, mari magno turbantibus aequora ventis / e terra magnum alterius spectare laborem." Cf. ibid., 87. On the topos, see Carsten Zelle, "Erhabene Weltuntergänge im Kleinen: Über Schiffbrüche und Schlachten vor Zuschauer," in *Il gesto, il bello, il sublime: Arte e letteratura in Germania '700 e '800*, ed. Emilio Bonfatti (Rome: Artemide, 1997); Hans Blumenberg, *Shipwreck with spectator: paradigm of a metaphor for existence*, trans. Steven Rendall (Cambridge, MA: MIT Press, 1997).

[4] Batteux, "Second mémoire," 64.

[5] Ibid.

sponse, Rochefort sets out a principle of holistic interpretation that denies Batteux's assumption of continuity within the genre of tragedy:

> If I wanted to speak of the object of an art among the ancients, I would consider the character of the people among whom the art was in use, the effect it produced, the occasion that caused it to be born, the changes that it underwent; [...] I would not assume that I could compare the tragedy of the Greeks to our own because of external resemblances, which constitute its sensible effect and not its moral object.[6]

For Rochefort, interpretation of works of art is not a question of rules or emotional effects, but of the historical circumstances and purposes of a form. Within the complex social organism of ancient Athenian culture, tragedy "entered better into the general plan of the institutions of this democracy, where all the arts, like those of music, of dance, of gymnastics, were directed towards public utility."[7] Though this viewpoint is undeniably idealized, its subordination of tragedy's formal qualities to its specific cultural circumstances is an important moment in the historicization of the genre.

Rochefort's holistic view of the arts in ancient Athens leads to the most radical feature of his discussion: an absolute refusal of the analogy of ancient and modern tragedies. It is here that he differs most from previous thinking on ancient literature, which so often conceived of it through analogy with modern forms. Against Batteux, Brumoy, and most of the commentators of his time, Rochefort argues that a parallel of ancient and modern tragedies is impossible:

> In summing up all we have just said, as much about the history as about the essence of Greek tragedy, it appears impossible to compare it to our own. When we go to a performance, we do not seek there anything but the pleasure of a passing emotion. The poet, on his side, has no other aim than to give us that emotion. Each of the spectators may enjoy his own pleasure independent of the rest of the assembly. One could be there alone and amuse oneself, just as one does in solitude by the sound of an instrument, a beautiful painting, or an interesting reading. But among the Greeks, a performance was a national assembly, occasioned by some solemnity. It was the fatherland that called together its children, it was a single and common spirit than animated the spectators, directed their thoughts and their attention.[8]

The fundamental difference between ancient and modern tragedies, for Rochefort, does not consist in any internal characteristics, but in the relation

---

[6] Guillaume Dubois de Rochefort, "Premier mémoire sur l'objet de la tragédie chez les Grecs," *Mémoires de la littérature, tirez des registres de l'Académie Royale des inscriptions et belles lettres* 39 (1777): 128–29.

[7] Ibid., 126.

[8] Ibid., 146. Cf. Guillaume Dubois de Rochefort, "Discours sur l'objet et l'art de la tragédie grecque," in *Le théâtre des Grecs*, ed. Pierre Brumoy et al. (Paris Cussac, 1785), 234.

of the genre to its culture. Greek culture made tragedy one thing; modern culture has made of it something entirely different. Rochefort's emphasis on the political context of tragedy is even stronger than Brumoy's, yet at the same time the implications are even more remote, because set in an alien past.[9] Tragedy in modernity not only treats politics differently, as Brumoy argued, but is inherently apolitical. Rochefort's emphasis on the cultural significance of Greek tragedy is double-edged, as the affirmation of the importance of politics for ancient works brings with it a denial of this same significance in modernity.

Rochefort's viewpoint on ancient Greece seems to have developed largely from his reading of Homer.[10] Homeric epics, for Rochefort, are the mirror of the age in which they were created, and reflect its simple but firm sense of morality and reason. English Homeric scholarship had for many years investigated the cultural circumstances that gave rise to the epic poems, and so suggested a more contextualized approach to the products of the past. The "primitivists," centered in Scotland, elaborated a kind of anthropology of artistic production, emphasizing the originality and simplicity of Greek epic and its organic growth from society.[11] The notion of poetry as a reflection of the customs of its time suggested that the Homeric poems should be admired as documents of a prelapsarian moment and not judged as highly wrought poetic artifices. Homer's "original genius," to the primitivists, lay in his ability to represent the natural world as it appeared to man. Seeing Homer as the embodiment of a natural state that is forever lost, the primitivists had a tendency to nostalgia for the past and disdain for the present.[12] This would prove one of the points of difference between the discussions of epic and tragedy: where epic, it often seemed, had reached its height in antiquity, tragedy could obviously flourish in modern cultures—as the examples of Shakespeare and Racine, among others, proved. The nostalgia for prehistory that informs Rochefort's approach to ancient epic is importantly modified when it comes to tragedy: without denying the achievement of the great French tragedians, he insists that they have excelled in fundamentally different ways. His approach to all works of art is based on an attention

[9] Biet, Œdipe en monarchie: 63.

[10] Rochefort translated the *Iliad* and *Odyssey* in 1766 and 1777, to notably poor reception. His image of Homer is fleshed out in Guillaume Dubois de Rochefort, "Mémoires sur les moeurs des siècles heroïques," *Mémoires de la littérature, tirez des registres de l'Académie Royale des inscriptions et belles lettres* 36 (1774).

[11] See Kirsti Simonsuuri, *Homer's original genius: eighteenth-century notions of the early Greek epic (1688–1798)* (Cambridge: Cambridge University Press, 1979), 119–32.

[12] Most, "The second Homeric Renaissance," 71. One of the most interesting figures is John Brown, whose 1763 *Dissertation* created a sensation for its anthropological approach to ancient Greek culture and critical attitude towards the present: John Brown, *A dissertation on the rise, union, and power, the progressions, separations, and corruptions, of poetry and music* (London: Davis and Reymers, 1763). On Brown, see Michael Sonenscher, *Sans-culottes: an eighteenth-century emblem in the French Revolution* (Princeton: Princeton University Press, 2008), 178–95.

(however imperfectly informed) to the interplay of art and society, and a refusal to judge antiquity by the standards of the present.

The 1785–89 *Theater of the Greeks* announces its historicizing perspective with Rochefort's "Discourse on the Origin and the Art of Greek Tragedy," which is largely a revision of his Académie address. The essay aimed, as the front matter declares, to establish "a sort of doctrine, which will then have its proofs in the notes and examinations that accompany the tragedies."[13] As a program for the edition, the essay is striking for its rejection of Brumoy's universalism and insistence on the fundamental difference of antiquity and modernity. Though Rochefort's interest in tragedy as a cultural product derives from Brumoy, he pursues the implications of the historicizing viewpoint further. Where Brumoy argued that Greek and French tragedy, for all their divergences, have enough common characteristics for comparison, Rochefort finds that the two are far more opposed than alike:

> The more one examines the art of tragedy among the Greeks according to its nature, according to the principles of Aristotle, according to the character of the people where it was born, the more it is easy to recognize that tragedy was not what it is today [la tragédie n'étoit point ce qu'elle est aujourd'hui.].[14]

Printed just following Brumoy's "Discourse on the Parallel of Theaters," Rochefort's declaration reveals an edition in which old and new viewpoints coexist uneasily. Knowledge of Greek tragedy in 1785 does not lead to a recognition of a similarity, as Brumoy had suggested, but to an impression of difference. Though the edition retains all of Brumoy's original material (including his outdated translations), it is guided by a radical spirit. The assumption of similarity that grounded Brumoy's rehabilitation of ancient tragedy no longer holds. The taste of Paris and the taste of Athens no longer seem to agree.[15]

When Brumoy published his *Theater* in 1730, he wrote that tragedy was the least respected genre of Greek literature.[16] Yet in 1785 Brumoy's apologetic attitude towards the Greeks no longer appeared necessary to the editors, as modern readers had become more used to Greek drama's idiosyncrasies.[17] The increasing knowledge of Greek tragedy paved the way for an edition of impressive scope. Translating the entire corpus of Greek drama, the 1785 *Theater* expands Brumoy's original three volumes (or six in octavo)

---

[13] Pierre Brumoy et al., ed. *Le théâtre des Grecs*, 13 vols. (Paris: Cussac, 1785–89), 1, viii.

[14] Rochefort, "Discours," 240.

[15] Rochefort is not the only one to feel this; his co-editor Prévost writes in his 1782 Euripides translations that "the performances that in our times are the pleasures of civilized nations cannot give us an accurate idea [of the Greek theater]." See Pierre Prévost, *Les tragédies d'Euripide*, 3 vols. (Paris: Pissot, 1782), 1, xix.

[16] Brumoy, *Théatre* (1730): 1, 2.

[17] Brumoy, *Théâtre* (1785–89), 4, 309–10 (footnote).

to thirteen. The project was undertaken by a group of scholars led by André-Charles Brotier, with major contributions from Rochefort, Gabriel de La Porte du Theil, and Pierre Prévost.[18] All of Brumoy's original material is retained, with new essays on each work added, as well as parallels with more recent drama (including a particularly tart one on Voltaire's *Oedipus*). There is often a dissonance between Brumoy's viewpoint and that of the later editors, which is particularly clear in a number of footnotes disagreeing with aspects of the original text.

Beyond Rochefort's programmatic account of Greek theater, the historicizing bent of the 1785 *Theater* is visible in a new attitude to accuracy in translation.[19] Footnotes are often appended to Brumoy's translations, correcting mistranslations or outdated readings. Most of these notes simply read "not in the Greek" or "Greek: [. . .]," and restore ancient phrasing where Brumoy had adopted more idiomatic renderings or elaborated the text for rhetorical effect.[20] Rochefort's essay "On the Difficulty of Translating the Greek Tragic Poets" draws attention to Greek particles, which are, he writes "in the Greek language that which the joints are in the arrangements of the bodies of animals."[21] They are "the principles of life and of movement of their poetry [les principes de la vie & du mouvement de leur poésie]."[22] Such an organic metaphor had occurred also in Rochefort's "Discourse," where Greek tragedy without its musical accompaniment represented no more than "the exterior and the body of these ancient tragedies [l'extérieur & le corps de ces tragédies anciennes]. But that melody, these energetic songs which gave it, so to speak, a new soul, we do not know."[23] This consciousness of what is inaccessible to the modern translator or performer is a consequence of Rochefort's historical ethos. The deeper one immerses oneself in antiquity, the stranger and more distant it appears.

Rochefort's 1788 *Theater of Sophocles* (*Théâtre de Sophocle*) was the first complete translation of Sophocles by a single author (Dupuis had translated those excluded from Brumoy's edition in 1761), and pulls together the distinctive strands of his criticism. In comparison to Brumoy, Rochefort is far more sensitive to the distinctive expressions of ancient Greek. In the *Philoctetes*, for example, much of what Brumoy had smoothed or adapted

---

[18]On the editors, see Claire Lechevalier, *L'invention d'une origine: traduire Eschyle en France de Lefranc de Pompignan à Mazon: le Prométhée enchaîné* (Paris: Champion, 2007), 142–43.

[19]Christian Biet and Susanne Saïd, "L'enjeu des notes: les traductions de l'Antigone de Sophocle au XVIIIe siècle," *Poétique* 58(1984). This is one of the few recognitions of the radical nature of Rochefort's program in modern scholarship.

[20]For example, at *OT* line 369, Brumoy's "Telle est la force de la vérité" receives the correction "Tirésias dans le grec ne réplique que par ces mots: "la verité me remplit de confiance": for εἴπερ τί γ᾽ ἐστὶ τῆς ἀληθείας σθένος ("if there is any strength in truth"). Many of the notes, though assuming the mantle of accuracy, are not notable improvements.

[21]Brumoy, *Théâtre* (1785–89), 1, 336.

[22]Ibid., 1, 338.

[23]Ibid., 1, 225.

for readers used to French drama is given a more literal rendering. Rochefort draws attention to his preservation of paradox[24] and repetition[25] in the original, and does away with the scene and act divisions used in all editions of Brumoy's *Theater*. Rochefort is aided by the new edition of Brunck (1786), which for the first time since the Renaissance critically examined the surviving manuscripts, and removed many of the interpolations of Demetrius Triclinius. Though Rochefort's skill as a translator was middling, he presents a text substantially more accurate and informed than existed previously.

Most striking in Rochefort's translation is its didactic bent. The notes and commentaries appended to the end of each play consistently seek to show that Greek tragedy did have a moral aim, and that Sophocles was seeking "to offer them [the citizens of Athens] the picture of great revolutions of human life and teach them to expect them and to bear them [leur offrir le tableau des grandes revolutions de la vie humaine, & leur apprendre à les prévoir & à les supporter]."[26] At the heart of Sophocles' art, he finds, lies the lesson of the closing words of the *OT*: "Call no man happy before he reaches the end of life having endured no suffering."[27] Rochefort's insistence on the power of Greek tragedy to strengthen its audiences against catastrophe is particularly poignant at a time when real revolution was brewing in France. Despite his emphasis on cultural difference and the difficulties in accessing the power of ancient works, Rochefort is visionary in recognizing the urgent contemporary force that Greek tragedy would take on in an age of "such terrible revolutions": "Who is the man so little philosopher as not to see that the moral effect, which the ancients made the principal object of their tragedy, would not be more out of place in our time than it was in theirs?"[28]

Johann Gottfried Herder: Tragedy for the *Volk*

The year after Rochefort delivered his address to the Académie, Johann Gottfried Herder took up the comparison of ancient and modern tragedy in his essay "Shakespeare." Herder, like Rochefort, was powerfully influenced by English reflections on epic, which led him to see Homer as the

---

[24] Rochefort draws attention to his translation of ὕπνος ἄυπνος (847) as "le sommeil [...] inquiet & vigilant," and notes it is the best he can do for the expression: Guillaume Dubois de Rochefort, *Théatre de Sophocle*, 2 vols. (Paris: Nyon, 1788), 2, 244.

[25] πάλιν πάλιν παλαιὸν ἄλγημ' ὑπέμνασας (1169–70) is (almost) preserved as "C'est rappeler éternellement mes éternelles peines," and Rochefort notes that the duplication of the words "has a great energy." Ibid., 2, 265.

[26] Ibid., 2, v.

[27] Cf. ibid., 1, 133.

[28] Ibid., 1, viii.

bard of an entire *Volk*, expressing a people's character and values in educative, accessible form.[29] He emphasizes the organic connection between the social organization and the artistic products of a culture. Interpretation for Herder is a thoroughly historical endeavor and must be based on knowledge of the circumstances surrounding any work of art. In this sense, his thought is a precursor to the historical hermeneutics that would transform classical philology at the end of the century.[30] Herder makes context not only the starting point of criticism, but very often its explanatory goal as well: artistic works are seen as documents of cultural process as much as aesthetic products. When he turns to Greek tragedy, it is with the most thoroughly historicizing viewpoint of any thinker considered so far.

Herder's understanding of Greek tragedy, like Lessing's, is often articulated through the comparison with Shakespeare. The difference between their two viewpoints, though, shows the generational gap that divided the German Enlightenment from the *Sturm und Drang*: in 1768, Lessing was measuring, with increasing difficulty, Shakespeare's works against his Aristotelian standard of *Mitleid*; in 1773, Herder would deny Aristotle's applicability to modern works and call for a new poetics in order to understand Shakespeare. Where Lessing had been resigned to describing *Richard III* as "a dramatic poem" and not a tragedy, Herder calls for new definitions altogether. In rejecting the rationalizing strands of Enlightenment aesthetics, Herder and his friend Johann Wolfgang Goethe found a new program for German art and culture. Their thought is animated by a concept taken primarily from English aesthetics: the genius. Though the notion of genius had existed since Roman antiquity (and even longer, if one considers Socrates' *daimonion* as a prototype), its theorization substantially dates to the eighteenth century. The most important text for German thinkers was Edward Young's *Conjectures on Original Composition*, published in 1759 and translated into German twice the following year.[31] Young elaborates a theory of the "Original," whose creation "rises spontaneously from the vital root of Genius."[32] The original genius has no need of knowledge or rules, but creates instinctively, following internal impulses to create an original work of art. Young draws encouragement from the progress of culture, seeing modernity as providing materials equal to and even more fertile than those of antiquity. The great example of such a modern genius is Shakespeare, who,

---

[29] See particularly the 1778 "Vorrede" to *Volkslieder* II (HW 3, 230–48) and two essays of 1795: "Homer und Ossian" and "Homer, ein Gunstling der Zeit" (*HW* 8, 71–87, 89–115). On Herder and Homer, see Ernst-Richard Schwinge, *"Ich bin nicht Goethe": Johann Gottfried Herder und die Antike* (Hamburg: Joachim Jungius-Gesellschaft der Wissenschaften, 1999).

[30] See Leventhal, *Disciplines of interpretation*: 235–42.

[31] See Jochen Schmidt, *Die Geschichte des Genie-Gedankens in der deutschen Literatur, Philosophie und Politik, 1750–1945*, 3rd ed. (Heidelberg: Winter, 2004), 150–58.

[32] Edward Young, *Conjectures on original composition: in a letter to the author of Sir Charles Grandison* (London: Millar and Dodsley, 1759), 12.

Young writes, "is not their [the ancients'] Son, but Brother; their Equal."[33] Out of different roots, Shakespeare has created an equally estimable flower. The concept of genius, as an innate ability that can arise in any time and place, levels the playing field between ancients and moderns.

By the time of Herder's essay, Shakespeare was already a favorite of the *Sturm und Drang*. The first major advocate, and the first to draw consequences for contemporary poetics from Shakespearean works, was Heinrich Wilhelm Gerstenberg.[34] In his 1766–67 *Letters on Curiosities of Literature* (*Briefe über Merkwürdigkeiten der Litteratur*), Gerstenberg devoted a series of letters to Shakespeare. He points to a problem that has prejudiced the reception of Shakespeare: "the wrongly applied concept that we have from the drama of the Greeks."[35] Gerstenberg understands the aim of Greek drama as "the arousal of passions or laughter" and finds, on this definition, "that Shakespeare's tragedies are not tragedies, his comedies not comedies, nor could they be."[36] The ancient definitions as Gerstenberg understands them appear too limited for Shakespeare's capacious genius. Shakespearean drama, for Gerstenberg, comprehends all possibilities of experience, and thus transcends distinctions of genre and comparisons with ancient works. This rejection of comparison brings with it a rejection of normative Aristotelianism. Similarly, in his 1771 "Address for Shakespeare's Name Day" ("Rede zum Shakespears Tag"), Goethe describes reading Shakespeare as an epiphany, an experience so transformative that "I did not for a moment question abandoning the rule-governed theater" (*FA* 18, 10). The *Sturm und Drang* discovered an affinity between its own ends and what it took to be Shakespeare's means, and made his name a rallying cry for a new freedom and expressiveness in literature.

Herder's "Shakespeare" was published in 1773 in *On German Custom and Art* (*Von deutscher Art und Kunst*), a volume coedited with Goethe. Against the taste for French and classical art, Herder and Goethe assert the rights of German styles and folk forms in a democratizing, nationalist gesture.[37] The collection begins with two essays by Herder, both of them seeking to appropriate British works as models of closeness to nature and originality: the first celebrates Ossian as an example of folk poetry's sublime simplicity, while "Shakespeare" rhapsodizes on the dramas for their world-encompassing power. The original essays by Herder and Goethe depict creation as an act of genius, with the power to unite the disparate elements of experience into a unified artistic whole. The genius, Goethe writes in his essay on the Strassburg

---

[33] Ibid., 78.

[34] Paulin, *Shakespeare in Germany*: 140–43.

[35] Heinrich Wilhelm von Gerstenberg, *Briefe über Merkwürdigkeiten der Litteratur*, reprint ed. (Hildesheim: Olms, 1971), 219.

[36] Ibid., 220.

[37] Oergel, *Culture and identity*: 52.

Cathedral, "is the first from whose soul the parts, grown together into one eternal whole, come forth [ist der erste aus dessen Seele die Theile, in Ein ewiges Ganze zusammen gewachsen, hervortreten]" (*FA* 18, 12). The concept of wholeness here has a Spinozistic overtone, which will become even stronger in Herder's essay.[38] For the *Stürmer und Dränger*, genius is the power of integrating the wholeness of existence into a work of art, a quasi-divine second creation.

Herder's "Shakespeare" follows Goethe's "Address" in exalting the natural, passionate, and sublime in Shakespeare. The perceived faults that continued to trouble English critics and had served as ammunition for the French are, for Herder and Goethe, the necessary consequences of Shakespeare's originality. Goethe writes, transferring Diderot's and Lessing's eulogy of Sophocles to Shakespeare, "I cry Nature! Nature! Nothing so natural as Shakespeare's people [Ich rufe Natur! Natur! nichts so Natur als Schäkespears Menschen]" (*FA* 18, 11). Herder follows Goethe and Gerstenberg in seeking to distance Shakespeare from Aristotelian poetics by an appeal to nature, but takes the critical step of grounding this polemic in historical circumstances.

Like Rochefort, Herder calls for a criticism that does not simply judge works, but explains how they arise from their culture. In comparing Shakespeare's plays to the dramas of other times and places, he writes, "This alone will be the first and last question: How is the soil? For what has it been prepared? What has been sown in it? What should it be able to produce? (*Aesthetics* 297; *HW* 2, 507). Aesthetics and anthropology are inextricable for Herder, and lead to a criticism that rejects typical comparisons of ancient and modern.[39] "Sophocles' drama and Shakespeare's drama," he writes, "are two things, that in a certain respect have hardly the name in common [Sophokles Drama und Shakespears Drama sind zwei Dinge, die in gewissem Betracht kaum den Namen gemein haben]" (*Aesthetics* 292; *HW* 2, 499). At the outset, Herder denies the possibility of a parallel of Shakespearean and Sophoclean tragedy: emerging from different cultures, their works appear to have no common ground for comparison.

Herder's rejection of comparison, however, is only a part of the story. Though recognizing the historical singularity of both Sophocles and Shakespeare, he preserves a principle on which their works can be evaluated. This is, for Herder, the work's relation to its historical circumstances.[40] Greek tragedy is not exemplary as an aesthetic product, but as the endpoint of an organic

---

[38] See Michael N. Forster, "Herder and Spinoza," in *Spinoza and German Idealism*, ed. Eckart Förster and Yitzhak Y. Melamed (Cambridge: Cambridge University Press, 2012).

[39] John H. Zammito, *Kant, Herder, and the birth of anthropology* (Chicago: University of Chicago Press, 2002), 342–45.

[40] Norton, *Herder's aesthetics*: 76.

process. Describing how the form of tragedy developed from its origin in choral song, Herder concludes that "the artificial in their rules was—not art! It was nature!" (*Aesthetics* 293; *HW* 2, 502). All the so-called "rules" of tragedy developed, he writes, as responses to particular historical circumstances, not as deductions from immutable laws of reason. French drama, then, in modeling itself on a form that does not respond to the needs of its own time, has become a "puppet of Greek theater." (*Aesthetics* 294; *HW* 2, 503). While seeking to follow Aristotelian rules, French dramatists have failed to take into account the change in historical circumstances, and so have created an artificial, lifeless theater, unsuited to antiquity or modernity: "The puppet lacks spirit, life, nature, truth—that is, all the elements that move us—that is, purpose and the attainment of that purpose" (*Aesthetics* 296; *HW* 2, 505). Though Herder's criticism is essentially the same as Lessing's, his polemic is based on a new normative aesthetic of nature and originality.[41] Herder rejects normative poetics as it had been practiced, but he nevertheless preserves a universal principle for judgment, elevating art's cultural relativity to an imperative.

Shakespeare's achievement, Herder argues, must be understood in relation to his own historical background. Characteristic of Renaissance England, and in direct contrast to ancient Greece, is multiplicity. Shakespeare's genius lies in the ability to distill the heterogeneity of modern experience into a coherent artistic form: "He found no such simple spirit of history, story, and action; he took history as he found it, and brought together with creative spirit the most diverse stuff into a wondrous whole [setzte mit Schöpfergeist das verschiedenartigste Zeug zu einem Wunderganzen zusammen]" (*Aesthetics* 298; *HW* 2, 508). The complexities of existence in Shakespeare's time do not allow for the unified action of antiquity, but demand a god-like act of transformation before they can become drama. Shakespeare's works do not simply portray "the unity of an *action* [das Eine einer *Handlung*]," but rather "the whole of an *event*, an *occurrence* [das Ganze eines *Eräugnisses*, einer *Begebenheit*]" (*Aesthetics* 299; *HW* 2, 509). This makes them better suited to the heterogeneity of modern experience and to Herder's own people: "If [Sophocles] represents and teaches and moves and educates *Greeks*, then Shakespeare teaches, moves, and educates northern *men*!" (*Aesthetics* 299; *HW* 2, 509). The geographical affinity between Germany and England is of course rather tenuous, but it points to an important consequence of Herder's argument: the closer in time and place, the more relevant an organic work of art will be.

Sophocles and Shakespeare fulfill similar roles in their time, creating tragedy that is true to its historical circumstances and cultural origins—

---

[41] Barbara Belhalfaoui, "Johann Gottfried Herder: Shakespeare—ein Vergleich der alten und der modernen Tragödie," *Deutsche Vierteljahrsschrift für Literaturwissenschaft und Geistesgeschichte* 61 (1987): 104.

authentic *Volkspoesie*. Though Herder's concept of *Volkspoesie* is nebulous, it denotes an artwork addressed to a nation in its natural or originary qualities.[42] Taking account of the national difference between the two poets opens the door to a deeper correspondence in their faithfulness to nature:

> Even here then Shakespeare is Sophocles' brother, where he is so unlike in appearance, only to be inwardly just like him. [. . .] Sophocles remained true to nature when he fashioned *one* story of *one* place and *one* time; Shakespeare could remain true to nature only if he followed his world-event and human destiny through all places and times. (*Aesthetics* 303; *HW* 2, 515)

The distinction of outer form and inner essence is crucial to Herder's project. At the beginning of the essay, the metaphor of a seed's growth illustrates this opposition: "The kernel [Kern] would not grow without the husk [Schlaube] and one will never get the kernel without the husk" (*Aesthetics* 292; *HW* 2, 499). In its immediate context, the metaphor suggests that artistic production is bound to its time, that the heart of a work is dependent on historical circumstance. Yet another meaning emerges in the course of the essay. The division of exterior and interior allows for a correspondence between Shakespeare and Sophocles, a similarity in "kernel" that goes beyond the "husk" of a form. The essence of both forms of tragedy, Herder reveals, is one and the same: "So a mortal was endowed with divine powers to summon from completely different material and by quite different means precisely the same effect: *fear* [*Furcht*] and *pity* [*Mitleid*]" (*Aesthetics* 298; *HW* 2, 508). Beneath the external dissimilarities, Sophocles and Shakespeare coincide both in their natural means and in their emotional end. Ultimately, Herder's conclusion is not far from Lessing's, and reveals, despite his insistence on cultural difference, the continuing importance of Aristotle for a definition of tragedy. Ancient or modern, tragedy remains synonymous with pity and fear.

Herder's conception of artistic genius has an ambiguous relation to history: the genius' organic connection to nature has the effect, on the one hand, of historicizing the products of genial creation; the genius' uniqueness and ultimate inexplicability, on the other, could seem to transcend any historical circumstance. The genius aesthetic historicizes Shakespeare's and Sophocles' products, while at the same time allowing for a universalism in their process. This forms one of the differences between Herder's historicism and Rochefort's: Rochefort could not (and did not seek to) account for equal achievement in different ages, but insisted on the incomparability of ancient and modern works. Herder, on the other hand, can compare ancients and moderns for the way they express their moment in history.

---

[42] See Ulrich Gaier, "Volkspoesie, Nationalliterature, Weltliteratur bei Herder," in *Die Europäische République des Lettres in der Zeit der Weimarer Klassik*, ed. Michael Knoche and Lea Ritter-Santini (Göttingen: Wallstein, 2007); Oergel, *Culture and identity*: 52–64.

The appeal to genius helped the theorists of the *Sturm und Drang* both to recognize historical difference and to set it aside when it suited.

A doubt, though, remains in Herder's mind, which will continue to plague historicizing thinkers: If the circumstances of production change so radically, do the possibilities for reception alter as well? Does historical change, which makes ancient forms invalid for modern authors, also make ancient works irrelevant to modern audiences? Herder is well aware of the question his essay raises, noting that he is "closer to Shakespeare than the Greek" (*Aesthetics* 298; *HW* 2, 509). Presumably, future generations will be still further from both. The final paragraph of the essay thinks through the consequences of the historicization Herder has advocated:

> Sadder and more important becomes the thought that even this great creator of history and world-soul constantly grows older! that the words and customs and categories of the ages wither and fall like autumn leaves, [...] and soon perhaps, when everything is so much blurred and tends in other directions, even Shakespeare's drama will become incapable of living performance, and will be a ruin of Colossus, of the pyramids, which everyone marvels at and no one understands [eine Trümmer von Kolossus, von Pyramide sein wird, die jeder anstaunet und keiner begreift]. (*Aesthetics* 307; *HW* 2, 520)

A thorough historicization of the products of the past leads to a problem: if temporality creates works of art, it can also destroy them. Historicization inevitably has to confront the question of the present value of works of the past.[43] Herder's historical thought is truly radical in recognizing its own consequences for the appreciation of works of the past: as cultures change, so too do the demands made on art. Yet this thought, which is for him "sadder and more important," will be utterly unbearable for the still more philhellenic generation after him. Where Herder argued that art should be homogeneous with its audience, later thinkers will find ways of valuing the difference and even the difficulty of Greek tragedy.

RETURNS TO THE GREEK: TRANSLATION, PHILOLOGY, PERFORMANCE

Greek tragedy experienced a kind of renaissance in the 1770s and 80s, which encompassed translation, adaptation, and scholarship. While the plays were being translated at an increasingly rapid pace, academic scholarship was undergoing its own turn to tragedy, as the texts were reedited for the first time

---

[43] Herder will consider this problem directly in the *Adrastea*, where he argues that the comparative primitiveness of earlier tragedy is salutary for its outsized representation of human nature: *HW* 10, 360. On Herder's later thoughts on tragedy, which show some influence of idealist theories, see Wolfgang Düsing, "Die Tragödientheorie des späten Herder," in *Johann Gottfried Herder, 1744–1803*, ed. Gerhard Sauder (Hamburg: Meiner, 1987).

in a century or more. The audiences of these two endeavors were by and large different, and their synchrony testifies to a broad change in attitudes towards the genre (as to Greek antiquity generally). Though performance of the texts in translation remained rare well into the nineteenth century, adaptations of Greek tragedies proliferated in these years, gaining new aesthetic impulses from the Winckelmannian ideal of "noble simplicity and quiet grandeur." Beyond the famous operas of Gluck, performances of spoken and musical dramas on tragic themes in France, Germany, and England made important impacts, coalescing around certain recognizably "Greek" elements. The effect of these developments was paradoxical: Greek tragedy became at once far more accessible, vital, and meaningful to society at large, while at the same time its historical particularity and difference from present drama was increasingly recognized.

Steinbrüchel's translation did not establish itself as a reference work for German speakers to nearly the extent that Brumoy's had for Francophones. There were no further editions of *The Tragic Theater of the Greeks*, and other translators moved to supplant it in the years following. Translators of tragedy were inspired by Johann Heinrich Voss's 1781 translation of the *Odyssey*, which proved the most successful translation from Greek into German to that point (and is still read today). Voss contributed to the growing enthusiasm for Greek literature in Germany, and so set the stage for a revival of interest in tragedy. Yet a lasting translation proved elusive: most of the early efforts were undertaken by private scholars and schoolmasters (academic classical philology still being rare in German universities) and proved unmemorable.[44] The failure of any to establish itself as a standard, combined with the extreme decentralization of German intellectual life, meant that translators tended to return to the same works over and over again.[45] The plays chosen are overwhelmingly Sophoclean, and the 1780s see two complete translations of Sophocles, both in verse, by Georg Christoph Tobler (1781) and Christian Graf zu Stolberg (1787). Tobler, a Swiss pastor and former student of Bodmer, and Stolberg, a German-Danish nobleman and functionary, are representative of the geographical and professional diversity of German letters at a time when there was no one city or institution that brought together the learned.

Besides the unsurprising concentration on Sophocles, early German translations show a notable interest in Aeschylus, who was not translated into French or English at all until the 1770s. Three Aeschylean works were

[44]See Heydemann, "Literarische Fingerübungen—oder mehr? Zur Geschichte der Sophokles-Übersetzungen im deutschen Sprachraum im 18. Jahrhundert"; Richard Stoneman, "'A crazy enterprise': German translators of Sophocles, from Opitz to Boeckh," in *Sophocles revisited: essays presented to Sir Hugh Lloyd-Jones*, ed. Jasper Griffin (Oxford: Oxford University Press, 1999).

[45]Three *Hecubas* are published in succession in 1787–89, and as many *OTs* over the decade.

translated by four translators in the 1780s: the *Prometheus* in 1784 (Schlosser), the *Agamemnon* in 1785 (Halem) and 1786 (Jenisch), and the *Persians* in 1789 (Danz). Though this is hardly a flood, it is a comparatively substantial presence in the trickle of translations, almost on par with Euripides. Both Aeschylus and Euripides, though, would have to wait until 1808 and 1803, respectively, for complete translations.

Examining the field of early translations, one finds a strong sense of tragedy's political role in Athenian culture, which has affinities with the discussions of Rochefort. Steinbrüchel and the Swiss critics had pointed to Greek tragedy's centrality in Athenian life as an ideal for modernity to strive for, and tragedy came to seem the exemplary patriotic art form.[46] Christian Graf zu Stolberg's 1787 *Sophocles*, an important reference for readers around 1800, offers a description of the poet that recalls Steinbrüchel and Rochefort in its celebration of the political nature of Greek tragedy:[47]

> Sophocles, the most patriotic man [der vaterländischste Mann], was also the most patriotic [vaterländischste] of Greek poets. Among his few extant tragedies, there is not a single one which, through its patriotic content, would not awaken the whole nation to participation (even without reference to its poetic beauties), and through its noble sentiments, which are so unique to it, touch every string of this harmonic lyre.[48]

The ideal of a form of poetry that would awaken *vaterländisch* sentiment was particularly compelling in a region bound by language but not by shared political institutions. Early translators of Greek tragedy into German emphasize its patriotic qualities with the hope that modern works will have the same unifying effect.[49] Ancient Greece provided an example of a culture that, though as decentralized as modern Germany, seemed to come together around works of art. The patriotic impact of Greek tragedy,

---

[46] Bodmer's 1771 *Karl von Burgund* is a particularly striking example, transposing the text of Aeschylus' *Persians* to the Battle of Nancy to make a patriotic drama. See Joshua Billings, "Greek tragedy and *vaterländische* Dichtkunst," in *"Das Fremde im Eigensten": Die Funktion von Übersetzungen im Prozess der deutschen Nationenbildung*, ed. Bernd Kortländer and Sikander Singh (Tübingen: Narr, 2011).

[47] This is typical of Stolberg's own relation to the Greeks: see Dirk Hempel, *Friedrich Leopold Graf zu Stolberg (1750–1819): Staatsmann und politischer Schriftsteller* (Weimar: Böhlau, 1997), 70–75.

[48] Christian Graf zu Stolberg, *Sofokles*, 2 vols. (Leipzig: Göschen, 1787), 1, xxi. Similarly, see Christoph Friederich Ammon, *Hekabe und Andromache: zwei Trauerspiele des Euripides* (Erlangen: Palm, 1789), xxv.

[49] Constanze Güthenke points out that many of these early translators—Schlosser, Halem, Stolberg—were simultaneously engaged with events in modern Greece, and that their notions of patriotism would have had a dual modern context (which is seen also in Hölderlin's *Hyperion*). On the dual political context of philhellenism in this period, see Constanze Güthenke, *Placing modern Greece: the dynamics of romantic Hellenism, 1770–1840* (Oxford: Oxford University Press, 2008), 93–139.

which French critics had pointed to as an element of difference from modern works, became for German thinkers a point of fervently desired, though unaccomplished, similarity.

A patriotic or even nationalistic aim could also be reflected in attitudes towards translation. An early translator of Sophocles prides himself on being more accurate than previous French versions, ascribing this "not to myself, but to the happier genius of my fatherland and its language."[50] Fidelity seemed to be one way that German translators could improve on the French standard works, and agonistic discussions are common in prefaces and notes.[51] Though most of these translations would today be considered quite free, an emphasis on accuracy and apologetic tone for alterations suggests a changing mindset. Stolberg's introduction, for example, draws attention to the single passage in Sophocles that he finds objectionable: the moment in *The Women of Trachis* when the dying Hercules asks his son to marry his own consort. Though tempted to leave the passage out, Stolberg translates it because of the "firm principle ... to render Sophocles as he is, wholly unmutilated by modern improvements."[52] It became important to represent Greek tragedy accurately, even if this alienated readers.

The growing recognition of Greek tragedy's alterity meant that the parallel had to proceed differently from the way it had in the past. It was no longer possible to assume the similarity of ancient and modern works and compare them aesthetically. The parallel in the latter half of the eighteenth century tended to reveal more opposition than commonality, and was often used to formulate a critique of the state of modern (especially French) drama. A 1784 *Prometheus* begins with a comparison of ancient and modern works, emphasizing Greek tragedy's social role while deploring modern drama's lack of cultural relevance (much as Rochefort had done). It concludes, "Thus Greek drama stood before the eyes of a noble nation. To them it was a true performance [wahres Schauspiel], for us mere play [blos Spiel]!"[53] A similar play on words crops up in Jenisch's *Agamemnon*, which notes "the borderline [Gränzscheide] between our theater and the Greeks: theirs was a house of teaching [Lehr-Haus], a temple, ours is—a play house [Spiel-Haus]."[54] The parallel remains important to the critical aims of translators, but it often takes the form of a polemic against the debased state of modern theater (a perspective more extreme than that of any of the

---

[50]Eustachius Moritz Goldhagen, *Des Sophokles Trauerspiele* (Mitau: Hinz, 1777), Vorrede.

[51]Köhler's 1778 *Iphigenia in Aulis* is one example: its preface attacks Steinbrüchel and French translators for dividing the works into scenes, and its footnotes wage a withering campaign against Racine's version of the story: Johann Bernhard Köhler, *Iphigenia in Aulis: ein Trauerspiel des Euripides* (Berlin: Nicolai, 1778).

[52]Stolberg, *Sofokles*: 1, xxvii.

[53]Johann Georg Schlosser, *Prometheus in Fesseln, aus dem Griechischen des Aeschylus* (Basel: Thurneysen, 1784), 13.

[54]Daniel Jenisch, *Agamemnon, ein Trauerspiel* (Berlin, 1786), 134.

protagonists of the *Querelle*). There is a strong current of nostalgia running through political approaches to Greek tragedy in Germany, which could be rueful or exhortatory—and often both. Images of ancient Greece were laden with an emotional energy that was at once dehistoricizing, seeing Athenian civic culture as a goal for modern Germany, and painfully aware of the distance separating antiquity from modernity.

Eighteenth-century scholarship on Greek tragedy is not given to displays of pathos or nostalgia, though an increasing interest in Greek texts in the second half of the century surely takes part in the Winckelmannian *retour à l'antique*.[55] Philology of tragedy most often focused on establishing reliable texts, which was a labor demanding considerable time and resources, as manuscripts were scattered widely and travel was slow and expensive. For most of the century, scholars relied on old (and often haphazard) editions of the tragedians—Thomas Stanley's Aeschylus (1663), Thomas Johnson's Sophocles (1705–46), and Joshua Barnes's Euripides (1694). That the names are all English is no accident: Greek was far better represented in English universities than it was on the continent.[56] Until the middle of the eighteenth century, moreover, tragedy rarely ranked as an editorial priority.[57] Concurrent with the increasing attention to the genre in popular circles, though, a similar interest seems to have been felt in the academy, which called for new editions and closer investigation of grammar, meter, and performance. Textual studies and editions grew in number and sophistication, engaging scholars in England, France, the Netherlands, and, increasingly, Germany.

In 1781, a German editor writes (in Latin), "It is the merit and happiness of the time in which we live that, just when the study of Greek letters had nearly died out, their cultivation rises again from meager remains to new life and new vigor."[58] This renaissance forms the background to the truly epochal work of Richard Porson and Gottfried Hermann (the latter discussed in the next chapter) around 1800. Yet the late eighteenth century also contributed importantly to the study of Greek tragedy, not least with improved editions of all the tragedians. Most important was the Alsatian Richard Brunck's 1786 Sophocles (with individual plays published from 1779). Though Brunck was a corresponding member of the Académie des Inscriptions, his interest in textual criticism is unusual among French scholars.[59]

---

[55] This issue is explored by Harloe, *Winckelmann and the invention of antiquity*.

[56] See M. L. Clarke, *Greek studies in England, 1700–1830* (Cambridge: Cambridge University Press, 1945), 48–66.

[57] Grell, *Le dix-huitième siècle et l'antiquité*: 298. Grell tallies editions (including reeditions) of the ancient authors in France; Sophocles is twelfth overall and third in Greek, after Plutarch and Homer.

[58] Friedrich Gedike, *Sophoclis Philoctetes graece* (Berlin: Mylius, 1781), 3.

[59] Grell, *Le dix-huitième siècle et l'antiquité*: 142.

Brunck's most important innovation was to question the text established in the sixteenth century by Adrianus Turnebus, which had informed editions since. Comparing Turnebus's text with a newly discovered manuscript in Paris, Brunck removed many readings that had been introduced from the recension of the late-Byzantine scholar Demetrius Triclinius. Most of the changes introduced are quite small (and many had already been printed in the Aldine *editio princeps*), but together they established a far sounder text of Sophocles than had been widely used previously.

Brunck's preface begins by expressing his surprise that Sophocles, "the most excellent of the poets after Homer, most perfect of all the tragic poets, lies neglected."[60] Worse, he has been known through inadequate texts based on the Triclinian recension and not on a serious examination of the surviving manuscripts. Brunck takes the Aldine edition for his basis, but collates variant readings from a number of other manuscripts, including the details in his notes. His work, he recognizes, is only a first step on the road to an edition in which "no blemishes of the filth gathered from long barbarism remain [longa barbarie concreti squaloris nulla relinquatur macula]."[61] Beyond the text and his notes, Brunck includes the scholia to Sophocles and Latin prose translations. His greatest editorial innovation over previous efforts, though, is to include all the fragments known at the time.[62] Together, the volumes constituted the most substantial edition of Sophocles ever, on par with the older Euripides editions of Barnes and the recent one of Musgrave (1778). In general, Euripides was much better served in the eighteenth century than Sophocles; the scholars Brunck cites in his preface as particularly important (Valckenaer, Tyrwhitt, Musgrave) were all primarily Euripideans. Brunck was at the time virtually alone in working seriously on the text of Sophocles. Though Sophocles was broadly considered the greatest of the tragedians, it was only in 1786 that he received an edition befitting that preeminence.

Reviewing eighteenth-century philology of tragedy, it can be surprising how little interest there is in anything we might recognize as literary history or interpretation. This may best be understood as part of the intellectual division of labor in society at large: literary thought in England and France was largely the province of non-university intellectuals, and textual criticism the work of university philologists. *Lumières* such as Voltaire and Diderot and lesser-known figures like Brumoy and Rochefort all did their work outside of university contexts (Batteux is here the exception, though his chair was in philosophy). In England, figures like Pope and Johnson, the Homerists examined above, and even some of those who did produce

---

[60] Richard Brunck, *Sophoclis quae exstant omnia, cum veterum grammaticorum scholiis*, 2 vols. (Strassburg: Treuttel, 1786), 1, i.

[61] Ibid., 1, ii.

[62] Ibid., 1, vi.

scholarly editions, lived from their popular writings or inherited wealth. It is surprisingly rare to find moments of cross-fertilization between the classical academy and more popular criticism.[63] This was not the case at the beginning of the century (if one thinks of the Daciers's or Bentley's interventions in the *Querelle*) and may be a legacy of the acrimony introduced by the *Querelle*.[64] This broad separation of academic philology and literary discussions explains part of what was revolutionary about the new discipline of *Altertumswissenschaft*, which insisted on the interrelation of these modes of inquiry.

Unlike in France or England, intellectual life in Germany supported quite a close interaction between academic and popular discourses. Gottsched and the Swiss critics were based in universities, but widely read beyond. They could step easily between roles as university professors, popular writers, translators, and theatrical practitioners. It was only in the middle of the century with Winckelmann and Lessing that the essayistic forms of French and English *belles lettres* gained a foothold in the German context. But even later, the interaction between universities and the wider intellectual world was always closer, bolstered particularly by publications like the *Göttingische Gelehrte Anzeigen* and the *Bibliothek der schönen Wissenschaften* that crossed the boundaries between scholarly and popular discourse. German scholarly institutions, to be sure, developed later, but then they found themselves much closer to the center of intellectual life. This forms the institutional background to a unique interplay of philosophy, philology, and literary thought that will be the subject of the next chapter.

On the stage, adaptations of Greek tragedy very often reflected programs of aesthetic or political reform. Gluck's operas of the 1760s and 1770s are the most famous example, but not the only one. Gluck's program for reform, as described in the preface to *Alcestis* (probably written in whole or part by his collaborator, Ranieri de Calzabigi), was directed against the excesses of the *opera seria* of the time, and called for a musical style that would serve and enhance the text—rather than seeing the libretto simply as a vehicle for virtuosic vocal displays.[65] Gluck and Calzabigi claimed the authority of Greek

[63] See Glenn W. Most, "Classical scholarship and literary criticism," in *The Cambridge history of literary criticism. Volume 4: The eighteenth century*, ed. H. B. Nisbet and Claude Rawson (Cambridge: Cambridge University Press, 1997). As Kristine Haugen argues, Richard Bentley was one of the few figures to attempt to bridge this gap (though with limited success): Kristine Louise Haugen, *Richard Bentley: poetry and enlightenment* (Cambridge, MA: Harvard University Press, 2011).

[64] See Blandine Barret-Kriegel, *La défaite de l'érudition* (Paris: Presses Universitaires de France, 1988), 271–80.

[65] See the "Preface to Alceste" translated in Patricia Howard, *Gluck: an eighteenth-century portrait in letters and documents* (Oxford: Clarendon, 1995), 84–85.

tragedy to legitimate their own project: "Reduced to the form of Greek tragedy, the drama has the power to arouse pity and terror, and to act upon the soul to the same degree as spoken tragedy does."[66] The three "reform" operas, first produced in Vienna between 1762 and 1770, all adapted Greek stories, though only *Alcestis* was based on a tragedy, and one that had already been thoroughly assimilated into the operatic canon by Lully and Quinault's version. Beginning in Vienna, but even more explicitly in Paris in the 1770s, Gluck and his collaborators were challenging both the tastes of their own time and the established classics of the operatic stage.[67]

Gluck's arrival in Paris in 1773 had been prepared by a publicity campaign that promised "a simple music, natural, always guided by the most true, the most sensible, expression, by the most agreeable melody."[68] Writing on his own behalf, Gluck promised that his *Iphigenia in Aulis* would "make real the prodigious effects that antiquity attributes to music."[69] Comparisons to Greek tragedy were frequent in responses to Gluck's Paris works, which culminated in the 1779 *Iphigenia in Tauris*.[70] One audience member described the work as "a genuine tragedy, a Greek tragedy," praising Gluck for "having discovered the secret of the ancients. [. . .] One saw the spectators sobbing at it from one end to the other."[71] Though today the neoclassical façade of these pieces can seem almost impenetrable, their emotional impact was immediate and visceral and suggested the power of Greek tragedy to many listeners.[72]

Yet Gluck's aesthetic was not unchallenged. One of the most outspoken Paris critics was Jean-François de la Harpe, a friend and follower of Voltaire whose fierce anticlericalism made him a controversial figure in Paris cultural life of the 1770s.[73] In 1781, he published a *Philoctetes*, the most faithful

---

[66]Calzabigi's letter to Prince Kaunitz (March 6, 1767) in ibid., 78–80.

[67]An even more direct challenge to Lully was Gluck's *Armide*, written for Paris in 1777, and using Quinault's libretto.

[68]Open letter to the *Mercure* (October 1772) in François Lesure, ed. *Querelle des gluckistes et des piccinnistes: texte des pamphlets*, 2 vols. (Geneva: Minkoff, 1984), 1, 5.

[69]Open letter to the *Mercure* (February 1773) in ibid., 1, 10.

[70]See Simon Goldhill, *Victorian culture and classical antiquity: art, opera, fiction, and the proclamation of modernity* (Princeton: Princeton University Press, 2011), 216–17; Edith Hall, *Adventures with Iphigenia in Tauris* (Oxford: Oxford University Press, 2013), 183–95.

[71]*Mémoires secrets* 14, 58 (5.21.1779); translated in Howard, *Gluck*: 199.

[72]Gluck was the most widely received, but by no means the only contemporary composer drawn to Greek themes. Important also are Grétry's *Andromaque* (1780), Piccini's *Iphigénie en Tauride* (1781), Lemoyne's *Électre* (1782) and *Phèdre* (1786), and Sacchini's *Oedipe à Colone* (1787). See Arnold Jacobshagen, *Der Chor in der französischen Oper des späten Ancien Régime* (Frankfurt: Lang, 1997), 119–24.

[73]For La Harpe's criticisms of Gluck, see Lesure, *Querelle des gluckistes et des piccinnistes*, 1, 118–24. On La Harpe's tragedies, which often reflect a political agenda that takes inspiration from ancient Greek works, see Thierry Maligne, "La Harpe et la tragédie politique," *Littératures* 62 (2010).

verse version of a Greek tragèdy to date, which largely retained the structure of the original and a good part of Sophocles' language. Compared to other popular "Greek" works such as Chateaubrun's on the same subject of 1755 and Ducis's recent *Oedipus at the House of Admetus* (*Oedipe chez Admète*, 1778), La Harpe's interventions in the text were minor. Hoping for a production, he writes that "it would at least be the first time that one had seen in the French theater a Greek tragedy, approximately such as it was staged in the theater of Athens."[74] The atmosphere seems to have been favorable to such a project: a stage adaptation of *Electra* by Rochefort (much freer than his 1788 translation would be, and in verse) played briefly in 1782, with choruses set by François-Joseph Gossec.[75] Though Rochefort's piece was not a success, La Harpe's was somewhat more enduring on the stage when finally performed in 1783. Critics were divided on the merits of the piece, but largely agreed that it represented a new insight into ancient theater.[76] Ultimately, though, it was the far more accurate *Theater of the Greeks* and the far less "Greek" operas of Gluck that had the greatest effect in mediating Greek drama in France and beyond.

Another experiment with Greek forms, radical in a different way, was underway in England at around the same time. In 1759, William Mason had published a play entitled *Caractacus, a Dramatic Poem: Written on the Model of the Ancient Greek Tragedy*, which followed, quite loosely, the story of the *OC*. Mason was a political radical, and *Caractacus'* depiction of the struggle for liberty against tyranny has strong Whiggish overtones. In the fashion for all things Celtic that accompanied the publication of works attributed to Ossian, *Caractacus* was performed in 1776, with music by Thomas Arne.[77] The staging of the choruses attracted the most attention, for it was the first time that a singing, dancing chorus had been employed in English spoken drama. Mason's works briefly revived hopes for staging Greek tragedy in translation, though this did not bear further fruit.[78] If little more than an experiment, *Caractacus'* brief popularity testifies to an increasing interest in the forms of Greek tragedy—not only as matters of academic interest, but as possibilities for contemporary drama. Though the eighteenth century in England, as in France, saw many tragedies that adapted Greek stories, it was only towards the end of the century that writers and composers made a serious effort to employ formal elements of ancient drama.

[74] Jean-François La Harpe, *Philoctète* (Paris: Lambert and Baudouin, 1781), 8.

[75] These choruses were limited to a strophe at the end of each act, and so were far from Sophocles'. It was much more in the opera that singing, dancing choruses were at home. See Thomas Betzwieser, "Musical setting and scenic movement: chorus and 'chœur dansé' in eighteenth-century Parisian Opéra," *Cambridge Opera Journal* 12 (2000).

[76] H. Carrington Lancaster, *French tragedy in the reign of Louis XVI and the early years of the French Revolution, 1774–1792* (Baltimore: Johns Hopkins Press, 1953), 39–41.

[77] See Hall and Macintosh, *Greek tragedy and the British theatre*: 184–97.

[78] Ibid., 195.

In Germany, the 1770s and 1780s were dominated by the dramas of the *Sturm und Drang*, which drew more on the traditions of Shakespeare and *bürgerliches Trauerspiel* than on the Greeks. Two works of the 1770s, though, show the stirrings of an interest in Greek drama as an alternative to prevailing tastes. In 1773, Wieland's *Alcestis*, a *Singspiel* with music by Anton Schweitzer, was first performed in Weimar, and was an instant success, with productions soon spreading across Germany. It was accompanied by a campaign of publicity that claimed for *Alcestis* the achievement of being the first serious German opera, and set out a program for a reformed music-drama. Like the preface to Gluck's *Alcestis*, Wieland's promotional writing emphasizes simplicity and emotional directness.[79] The libretto thoroughly simplifies and humanizes Euripides' plot, jettisoning the conflicts and moral ambiguities of the original in favor of static scenes of inner turmoil and noble suffering.[80] Admetus, who in Euripides searches desperately for someone to die in his place, is not aware that Alcestis has chosen to die for him, and his only flaw seems to be an excessively emotional disposition. Hercules shows none of the roguish qualities of Euripides' piece (nor is he, as in Quinault, in love with Alcestis), but appears only as a strong comforter and true friend to Admetus. Out of Euripides' problem drama, Wieland creates a fairly typical work of the Enlightenment sentimentality (*Empfindsamkeit*), a moving hymn to fidelity and friendship. Though the work was successful and Wieland's libretto set by other composers in the years following, its sentimentalism was increasingly out of step with the time—as evidenced by a number of parodies of the piece that followed closely on it.[81]

The most successful of the parodies was the work of the young Goethe. *Gods, Heroes, and Wieland* (*Götter, Helden, und Wieland*, 1774) stages a confrontation in the underworld between Wieland (still wearing his trademark nightcap), Euripides, and the characters Alcestis, Admetus, and Hercules. They are not at all pleased by Wieland's adaptation, and ridicule it for its impossibly noble characters and sentimental tone. Euripides criticizes Wieland's adaptation of the story to modern tastes, his "ability to prune and homogenize nature and truth according to morals, theatrical conventions, and roughly patched-together statutes" (*FA* 4, 433). The work seems to reduce its mythical characters to bourgeois ideals, concerned with virtue (*Tugend*), a concept to which Hercules particularly objects. Moral abstractions do not belong in the heroic world, and the flaw of Wieland's adaptation seems to lie in its uncritical acceptance of contemporary ideals: "If you

[79] See Christoph Martin Wieland, "Versuch über das Teutsche Singspiel und einige dahin einschlagende Gegenstände," *Teutsche Merkur* (1775). It is not certain that Wieland knew the *Alcestis* preface, but he does mention Algarotti's 1755 *Saggio sopra l'opera in musica*, which was a major influence on Gluck and Calzabigi.

[80] Jörg Krämer, *Deutschsprachiges Musiktheater im späten 18. Jahrhundert: Typologie, Dramaturgie und Anthropologie einer populären Gattung* (Tübingen: Niemeyer, 1998), 211–20.

[81] Ibid., 252–60.

had not groaned under the servitude of your ethical teachings for so long," Hercules remarks, "something might have come of you" (*FA* 1.4, 437). The ability to abstract oneself from the reigning *mores* and tastes appears necessary for working with ancient stories. Goethe's parody exhibits a form of implicit historical consciousness, suggesting that Greek works are more than raw material for the contemporary poet to appropriate.

Goethe makes his own effort at adapting a Euripidean drama in 1779 with *Iphigenia in Tauris*, originally written in prose and performed for a small circle, then revised into its final, verse form and published in 1787. It is no accident that the Taurian *Iphigenia*, like the *Alcestis*, had been included in Brumoy's *Theater*, which Goethe seems to have known. Throughout his life, Goethe was particularly attracted to Euripides' works for some of the qualities that would make the tragedian controversial for the next generation: the "untragic" averted catastrophes, the psychological focus, the play with dramatic illusion. Goethe was not, he remarked much later in life, "born to be a tragic poet, since my nature is conciliatory," while the "pure tragic case must from the outset be irreconcilable [der rein-tragische Fall [. . .] von Haus aus Unversöhnliche sein muß]" (to Zelter, 10.31.31: *FA* 38, 482).[82] Beyond the *Alcestis* and the *IT*, Goethe engaged substantially with the *Helen*, another work that would not meet his definition of a "pure tragic case." Goethe's affinity with Euripidean fantasy is by no means anomalous in its time, but it does situate him on the margin of the theoretical discussions of tragedy that were developing, which were heavily oriented to Sophocles, suffering, and sublimity. The Euripidean strand, though, was the dominant one in adaptations into the late eighteenth century, and was especially congenial to attempts to find alternatives to the high tragedy of previous generations. Without too much effort, works like the two *Iphigenia*s and *Alcestis* could be assimilated to the ethos of bourgeois tragedy. Indeed, much of what Goethe had ridiculed in Wieland finds its way into his own dramaturgy in *Iphigenia*.[83]

Goethe's Greek seems to have been patchy, and there is no evidence of reading beyond Brumoy's selection before the 1780s.[84] Equally important as his knowledge of Greek works was probably his study of previous *Iphigenia* adaptations in French and German.[85] Goethe concentrates far more on the

[82] See Erich Heller, "Goethe and the avoidance of tragedy," in *The disinherited mind* (New York: Harcourt Brace Jovanovich, 1975). Nicholas Boyle, "Goethe's theory of tragedy," *Modern Language Review* 105 (2010).

[83] Nicholas Boyle, *Goethe: the poet and the age*. Vol. 1: *The poetry of desire* (Oxford: Oxford University Press, 1992), 322.

[84] Uwe Petersen, *Goethe und Euripides: Untersuchungen zur Euripides-Rezeption in der Goethezeit* (Heidelberg: Winter, 1974), 33.

[85] In particular, those of La Grange Chancel (*Oreste et Pylade ou Iphigénie en Tauride*, 1697); J. E. Schlegel (*Orest und Pylades*, 1742); Derschau (*Orest und Pylades oder Denckmaal der Freundschaft*, 1747); and La Touche (*Iphigénie en Tauride*, 1757).

central character than his predecessors, for whom the story was dominated by the selfless sacrifices of Orestes and Pylades for one another. The major conflict of Goethe's version lies within Iphigenia herself, as she is torn between love for her brother and duty to the king Thoas, who—in the greatest contrast to Euripides—is portrayed as a noble king, in love with Iphigenia. Iphigenia's internal conflict approaches her story to that of Neoptolemus in *Philoctetes*, which Goethe would have come to know from conversations with Herder.[86] The transformation of Thoas into an enlightened ruler makes the planned robbery and escape plot problematic, a dilemma solved only by Iphigenia's confession of the intrigue and Thoas' clemency. Dispensing with the *deus ex machina* of Euripides as well as the bloody confrontations of most predecessors, Goethe stages the denouement as a triumph of good will and forgiveness. Even to its author, this would seem thin in later years; in 1802, he writes to Schiller that, on rereading, the work appears "altogether devilishly humane [ganz verteufelt human]" (*FA* 32, 215).

In 1779, *Iphigenia* had come as a surprise from the author of *Götz* and *Werther* for its dramatic economy, internal rather than external conflicts, and relative lack of pathos. To some it appeared cold and long-winded, while to others it seemed an extraordinarily accurate appropriation of Greek style.[87] The work is dramaturgically anomalous among Goethe's plays of the time, and is appropriately considered a harbinger of his "classical" period. Yet the thematic material is defined by the sentimental impulses of the 1770s, creating an incongruity between Hellenizing form and modern content that would only grow with the revision of the work into verse. This decision was motivated at least in part by Goethe's increasing knowledge of Greek tragedy. In the period between the two *Iphigenias*, he became friendly both with Tobler, the translator of Sophocles, and with the Stolberg brothers, who were then working on translations of Sophocles and Aeschylus. During Tobler's stay in Weimar in 1781–82, he and Goethe seem to have discussed Greek tragedy, with Goethe encouraging Tobler to complete further translations.[88] The changes in Goethe's verse *Iphigenia* are largely linguistic, approximating the freedom in word order of the original and the higher register of diction familiar from translations.[89] The result is the first "Greek" play in the German language to succeed as poetry and the only one of its time to establish itself as a classic.

---

[86] See Lisette Goessler, "Zu Goethes *Iphigenie*," *Antike und Abendland* 18 (1973). Herder adapted scenes from *Philoctetes* in 1774, emphasizing Neoptolemus' dilemma: Petersen, *Goethe und Euripides*: 36.

[87] Reactions are collected in *FA* 5, 1301–1308.

[88] Boyle, *Goethe* 1: 354. The translations (all of Aeschylus, and Euripides' *Hippolytus, Hercules*, and *Ion*) are in the Goethe-Schiller Archive in Weimar, and deserve a more careful study than I have been able to give them.

[89] Petersen, *Goethe und Euripides*: 42–8.

The ending of the play, Thoas' incomplete line "Lebt wohl," remains unchanged from the prose version, but seems even more enigmatic as the conclusion to a formally classicizing work: are they words of reconciliation, resignation, or rejection? Goethe denies the closure afforded formally by Euripides' Greek chorus, creating a reconciliation that seems uneasy with itself. For the close of a work containing some of the most beautiful dramatic verse ever written, Thoas' laconic farewell is unsettling, suggesting an ambivalence within Goethe's classical project.[90] The frustration and fascination of the *Iphigenia* is indicative of a larger dilemma of German philhellenism in this period. The Greek model was as vital and important to Germans at the close of the eighteenth century as it has been to any post-classical culture, yet the understanding of historicity that framed the approach to antiquity was more complex than ever before, and could suggest an unbridgeable gulf separating ancients from moderns. The final lines of the *Iphigenia* enact this gulf, frustrating the wish for clarity and resolution that the work had otherwise so richly fulfilled. They suggest the final words of Winckelmann's *History*, which describe the lover of Greek art as "a ... beloved [who] stands on the seashore and follows with tearful eyes her departing sweetheart, with no hope of seeing him again."[91] Winckelmann's beloved watching the sea could be Thoas at the end of Goethe's play, just as it could be Iphigenia at the beginning. In the prologue, she describes herself in a powerful image that encapsulates a generation's desire and frustration confronted with Greek antiquity:

Denn ach mich trennt das Meer von den Geliebten,
Und an dem Ufer steh' ich lange Tage,
Das Land der Griechen mit der Seele suchend.
Und gegen meine Seufzer bringt die Welle
Nur dumpfe Töne brausend mir herüber.

[But ah, the sea divides me from my loved ones, and I stand on the shore for
   long days, seeking the land of the Greeks with my soul. But in answer to my
   sighs the waves bring me only dull sounds roaring.]

(10–14: *FA* 5, 555)

[90] An ambivalence central also to his understanding of tragedy: Heller, "Goethe and the avoidance of tragedy," 41–47. I take this to be the generic corollary to the dialectical irresolution pointed out by Adorno: "The masterpiece creaks, and by doing so indicts the concept of a masterpiece": Theodor Adorno, "On the classicism of Goethe's Iphigenie," in *Notes to literature* (New York: Columbia University Press, 1992), 166. See further Hall, *Adventures with Iphigenia in Tauris*: 206–15.

[91] Johann Joachim Winckelmann, *History of the art of antiquity*, trans. Harry Francis Mallgrave (Los Angeles: Getty Publications, 2006), 351. On the image, see Constanze Güthenke, "The potter's daughter's sons: German classical scholarship and the language of love circa 1800," *Representations* 109 (2010); Katherine Harloe, "Pausanias as historian in Winckelmann's *History*," *Classical Receptions Journal* 2 (2010).

TRAGIC THEMES

CHAPTER 3

Revolutionary Freedom

Two revolutions, the French and the Kantian, contributed to making the concept of freedom newly tragic for German thinkers of the 1790s. "Freedom" can mean many things, but the sense in which it is used in idealist discussions of tragedy is uniquely post-Revolutionary and post-Kantian, reflecting both the political sense of freedom as liberation from arbitrary hierarchy (as opposed to tyranny) and the metaphysical sense of freedom as lack of external determination, (as opposed to necessity). Both of these strands could be linked with tragedy before the 1790s, but the combination of the two in reflections on the sublime from 1792 onward is unique, and forms the basis for the first major strand of idealist thought on tragedy.

The concept of freedom in the 1790s was contested politically and philosophically, as the French Revolution and Kantian critique prompted new doubts about the desirability and even the very possibility of freedom. Both appeared as radical efforts to remake existence on the basis of reason alone, sweeping away old assumptions and certainties, and leaving a sense of disorientation in their wake. A new experience of existing in history began to emerge in this period, characterized by a sense of acceleration in the present and of radical openness in the future.[1] The sense was crystallized most of all by the French Revolution—in Edmund Burke's words, "the most astonishing that has hitherto happened in the world."[2] The impression of a

---

*Good introductions to the philosophical thought of the period are Frederick C. Beiser, *Enlightenment, revolution and romanticism: the genesis of modern German political thought, 1790–1800* (Cambridge, MA: Harvard University Press, 1992); Frederick C. Beiser, *German Idealism: the struggle against subjectivism, 1781–1801* (Cambridge, MA: Harvard University Press, 2002); Terry Pinkard, *German philosophy, 1750–1860: the legacy of Idealism* (Cambridge: Cambridge University Press, 2002); Andrew Bowie, *Aesthetics and subjectivity: from Kant to Nietzsche*, 2nd ed. (Manchester: Manchester University Press, 2003). Important secondary literature on Schiller in English includes David Pugh, *Dialectic of love: Platonism in Schiller's aesthetics* (Montreal & Kingston: McGill-Queen's University Press, 1996); Frederick Beiser, *Schiller as philosopher: a re-examination* (Oxford: Oxford University Press, 2005). On Schelling, see Andrew Bowie, *Schelling and modern European philosophy: an introduction* (London: Routledge, 1993); Krell, *The tragic absolute*. On Friedrich Schlegel, Elizabeth Millán-Zaibert, *Friedrich Schlegel and the emergence of romantic philosophy* (Albany: State University of New York Press, 2007). Particularly important for the argument presented in this chapter is Jean François Courtine, "Tragedy and sublimity: the speculative interpretation of *Oedipus Rex* on the threshold of German Idealism," in *Of the sublime: presence in question* (Albany: SUNY Press, 1993).

[1] I rely again on the work of Reinhart Koselleck, especially Koselleck, *Futures past*: 26–57.

[2] Edmund Burke, *Reflections on the Revolution in France, and on the proceedings in certain societies in London relative to that event* (London: Dodsley, 1790), 11.

world turned upside down was felt both by the Revolution's detractors (like Burke) and its proponents (including most of the idealists). History itself seemed to take on a tragic character, prone to catastrophic and unpredictable upheaval. In this moment of revolutionary change, theories of tragedy assumed the task of grasping *peripeteia*, historical and dramatic.

This chapter traces the concept of freedom in revolutionary context, and argues that Greek tragedy was a privileged vehicle for the investigation of freedom within history. Following the Revolution, it became impossible to take for granted that any form of experience was constant across time. Far from undermining tragedy's contemporary importance, though, the new sense of historical singularity made tragedy even more necessary to philosophical definitions of modernity. Greek tragedy provided a lens for exploring questions of freedom as they related to the historical basis of individual and collective experience. The writings of F.W.J. Schelling and Friedrich Schiller consider the relation between freedom in ancient tragedy and the modern possibility of freedom with particular tenacity and insight. Their reflections, in turn, are taken up and applied by A. W. Schlegel and Gottfried Hermann, who elaborate ways of reading Greek tragedy as a genre fundamentally concerned with human freedom. The importance of tragedy for the idealists lies in its simultaneous distance and closeness, as an ancient representation of central problems of modern existence. This dual context for tragedy is different from the universalisms that preceded it, since it does not see Greek works as standing outside of time (as Dacier or Perrault, for instance, both did). Instead, it treats these works as uniquely, and paradoxically, close to the present, even in their extreme temporal distance. Because of its representation of freedom in action, Greek tragedy becomes the "closest other" for the revolutionary generation.

From this point forward, the story narrows to Germany. This may seem surprising, especially given the relative lack of sophistication observed in most German writings on antiquity earlier in the eighteenth century. Yet in the 1790s, German writing about tragedy began to diverge significantly from French and English thought. Though the theories of the 1790s did not emerge from nothing, they are very much *sui generis* in the long eighteenth century, as in the whole history of thought on tragedy. The context of idealist thought on Greek tragedy was unique in at least three ways: in its relation to Kantian philosophy, which had a far more immediate and profound reception in Germany than anywhere else; in its relation to classical philology, which was then being institutionalized as an academic discipline with a host of innovative methods and approaches to antiquity; and in its relation to artistic practice, which seemed to many to be at a transformational moment, witnessed in the "classical" works of Goethe and Schiller, the Romanticism of the Schlegel brothers, Novalis, and Tieck, and the unclassifiable writings of Hölderlin and Kleist. In different measure, all the thinkers examined here were touched by these contexts and integrated currents of them into their theories.

Just as important as shared preoccupations may have been a geographical center, which enabled a lively exchange of ideas: Weimar and Jena, neighboring towns in the central-eastern part of the German territories, constituted an intellectual and artistic center, and a home to every major thinker at one point or another. The period around 1800 saw an interchange between thinkers, scholars, and artists, which laid important foundations for German cultural life to this day. With extraordinary regularity, their conversations and disputes turned to tragedy.

Some philosophical background is necessary to appreciate the urgency of the turn to tragedy. If, in Szondi's words, the 1790s see the first elaboration of a "philosophy of the tragic" it is because they also see the beginnings of the philosophy of art, understood in its modern sense. The term *aesthetics* was coined by Alexander Baumgarten in 1735, as the name for a subdiscipline of philosophy that would deal with objects that appeal to the senses. The novelty of the term, though, was slightly misleading, as Baumgarten's basic approach—investigation of what makes objects beautiful—was well established, though not yet institutionalized academically.[3] Baumgarten brought a new rigor to such investigations, but his questions remained essentially defined by the rhetorical tradition, which considered beauty primarily in terms of its effect on the subject. This tradition culminated in—and in Germany substantially ended with—Kant's *Critique of the Power of Judgment* (*Kritik der Urteilskraft*) of 1790. What comes after is better called "philosophy of art" than "aesthetics," since it is no longer directed to the sensible effect of beauty, but to the philosophical significance of the beautiful in art.[4] This is a problem as old as Plato, but the answers proposed in the post-Kantian tradition are unique within the history of philosophy. Before 1790, art could often be seen as philosophically significant, contributing in one way or another to the aims of metaphysics or ethics. Beginning with German Idealism, it becomes possible to see art as a quasi-philosophical form, the locus of a truth different from—and for some, more profound than—the truth of philosophical discourse. Before Kant, art could be considered philosophical; after Kant, art could be more philosophical than philosophy.

Kant's work forms the hinge between the two traditions, bringing certain strands of the first to a close and initiating strands of the second. The rhetorical tradition of aesthetics is largely defined by two lines of inquiry:

[3] See Beiser, *Diotima's children*: 118–23.
[4] The point is made by A.W. Schlegel in his 1801–1802 *Lectures on Beautiful Literature and Art* (*KAV* 1, 182–83) and by Hegel at the beginning of his *Aesthetics* lectures (*Aesthetics* 1; *WZB* 13, 13).

first, what makes an object beautiful? and second, how is beauty recognized by the subject, and what is its effect? Kant effectively rejects the first question, arguing that beauty is not a property of the object, but of the subject's cognition. There is thus no sense in trying to prescribe rules for creation (as Baumgarten, Gottsched, and the other aesthetic rationalists had). Yet, in relation to the subject, Kant also seeks to avoid the pure subjectivism that is one possible consequence of his rejection of an objective standard. He does this by introducing the notion of purposiveness (*Zweckmässigkeit*) as a "transcendental principle of the power of judgment," a reflective judgment made by the subject concerning the conformity of an object with an *a priori* principle (*CPJ* 68–73; *AA* 5, 181–86). In aesthetic judgment, the purposiveness of an object is perceived, and this perception is accompanied by the pleasure of finding one's own cognitive faculties in harmony with the outside world. The particularity of aesthetic judgment is that it is free from desire, distinguishing it from judgments of the good and the agreeable. The pleasure of purposiveness does not depend on any purpose being realized (as does the pleasure of moral goodness) or on the possession of the object (like the pleasure of the agreeable), and so is "without any interest" (*CPJ* 96; *AA* 5, 211). Kant outlines a concept of aesthetic autonomy, which sets out a unique sphere for aesthetic judgments as the realm of "free play [*freies Spiel*]," in which cognition detects purposiveness in the object but does not connect it to a determinate concept (*CPJ* 102; *AA* 5, 217).

Kant ascribes an extraordinary importance to the sphere of aesthetic judgment, seeing it as a means of binding together the theoretical and practical domains of philosophy. This is possible because of the unique character of disinterested judgment: in objects of aesthetic judgment, one recognizes purposiveness by an inherent cognitive power, which, though not purely rational, nevertheless is not purely empirical either. Aesthetic judgment appears therefore as a means of mediating between the domains of pure and practical reason, *Vernunft* and *Verstand*. In aesthetic judgment, the subject looks through the empirical into the rational, making "the beautiful [. . .] the symbol of the morally good" (*CPJ* 227; *AA* 5, 353). Through the perception of beauty, the mind "sees itself [. . .] related to something in the subject itself and outside of it, which is neither nature or freedom, but which is connected with the ground of the latter, namely the supersensible, in which the theoretical faculty is combined with the practical, in a mutual and unknown way, to form a unity" (*CPJ* 227; *AA* 5, 353). Where Kant's previous two *Critiques* had had the effect of rigorously dividing cognitive faculties into the realms of nature (theoretical reason) and freedom (practical reason), in the *Critique of the Power of Judgment* he points, tentatively, to a reconciliation of the two in the perception of beauty. The origins of the speculative philosophy of art lie in the effort to define this reconciliation.

Kant in no way anticipates tragedy as the privileged object of a philosophy of art. Indeed, he is only secondarily interested in artistic beauty generally, and shows no stake in the question of tragic pleasure.[5] The philosophy of tragedy binds together two largely separate strands of Kantian thought, both centering on the question of how the subject experiences the supersensible. Kant's *Critiques* are all concerned with determining the limits of cognition, defining the domains of the sensible and the rational for philosophical thought. This effort problematizes freedom, understood as spontaneous determination without external causality (i.e., by a first mover or God). Freedom in this strong sense is banished from the objects of empirical cognition and assigned to the domain of the supersensible, since every effect, considered empirically, must have a cause. This does not deny the possibility of what Kant calls "cosmological freedom," but demands that it be considered as belonging to the world of the intelligible rather than the world of sense. In effect, Kant suggests that cosmological freedom (and therefore, a divine first cause) is possible, but can never be known by the subject. A subject can and must make decisions *as if* free, but can never know that this apparent freedom is not the effect of a natural cause. Properly understood, there can be no conflict between the two understandings: as Kant argues in the "antinomy of pure reason," freedom and spontaneity belong to the domain of the intellect while nature and causality belong to the realm of the senses (*CPR* 484–89; B472–79). This division forms the basis of Kant's approach to problems of ethics in the *Critique of Practical Reason*, which assumes a limited, sensible freedom (along with an idea of God) as the basis of action. Yet despite this conciliatory tone, Kant's relegation of freedom to the domain of metaphysics seemed to many unsatisfying, or worse: a denial of the possibility of human autonomy.

As often in Kant, the third *Critique* restores some of the comfort that the first had denied. Beyond the description of aesthetic judgment as a supersensible union of the theoretical and practical faculties, Kant also describes a way of experiencing the subject's own freedom, which usually lies beyond the realm of sensible experience, through the sublime (*das Erhabene*). The sublime for Kant is a mixed pleasure, which results from the contrast between the sensible impression of overwhelming magnitude or force and the rational power of grasping such an impression. The subject, initially terrified and awed because of a sensible object (the feeling of displeasure) comes, in recognizing the object as purposive, to appreciate his or her own powers of reason in transcending the initially overwhelming sense-impression

---

[5] In a "pre-critical" essay, "Beobachtungen über das Gefühl des Schönen und Erhabenen" (1764), though, Kant did suggest that tragedy tends towards the sublime—though in a fairly conventional way for the time. See *AA* 2, 212.

(the feeling of pleasure). Kant describes the dual quality of the sublime as that "which even to be able to think of demonstrates a faculty of the mind that surpasses every measure of the senses" (*CPJ* 134; *AA* 5, 250). Where the beautiful suggests the conformity of nature to reason, the sublime stages a disjunction of the two, in which reason ultimately demonstrates its power over nature. "Sublime" for Kant is thus only the mind's power (never an object) in feeling its own supersensible vocation. Sublimity appears as an indirect experience of the intelligible realm to which Kant's philosophy had seemed to deny access.

Though Kant is extremely circumspect about the possibilities his theory of aesthetic judgment opened, the subtlety and frequent ambiguity of the third *Critique* made it easy for his followers to breach some of the theoretical walls he had so carefully constructed. Sometimes consciously, sometimes unconsciously, thinkers in the 1790s and 1800s enlarged the scope of Kant's vague notion of the philosophical significance of the beautiful into a philosophy of art, which could see artistic beauty as the instance of the rational and the divine within the sensible. It was Greek tragedy more than any other art form that provided the ground and inspiration for this aesthetic turn in philosophy.

THE TRAGIC SUBLIME: SCHILLER AND SCHELLING

When Friedrich Schiller began to study Kant in 1791, he was already one of Germany's leading dramatists, and a controversial figure for his outspoken political liberalism. The depiction of anarchic rebellion in his first play, *The Robbers* (*Die Räuber*, 1781), had led to troubles with the ruling regime of Württemberg, which eventually compelled him to flee Stuttgart (later, it also recommended him to the French Republic, which named him an honorary citizen). Further dramas of the 1780s, *The Conspiracy of Fiesco in Genoa* (*Die Verschwörung des Fiesco zu Genoa*, 1783), *Intrigue and Love* (*Kabale und Liebe*, originally titled *Luise Miller*, 1784), and *Don Carlos* (1787) all centered on the possibilities of individual freedom under absolutist rule: *Fiesco*, subtitled "a republican tragedy," concerns the (itself highly ambiguous) revolt of the title character against an overbearing ruling family; *Intrigue and Love* portrays an immoral duke preying on the innocent daughter of one of his subjects; and *Don Carlos* indicts clergy and monarchy alike as venal and politically repressive. Schiller's advocacy of political freedom reaches its dramatic pinnacle in the Marquis of Posa's words in *Don Carlos*, as he seeks to convince the King of Spain to grant religious liberty to the Netherlands: "Sehen Sie sich um / In seiner herrlichen Natur! Auf Freiheit / Ist sie gegründet—und wie reich ist sie / Durch Freiheit!" (3217–20: *FA* 3, 894: "Look around at His majestic nature! It is grounded on freedom—and how rich it is through freedom!"). For the young Schiller, before philosophy became a serious preoccupation, freedom is understood first in a political sense, but then also, somewhat fuzzily, in a metaphysical sense, as the ground of natural flourishing. Schiller's thinking on freedom goes through many different iterations, but it is profoundly influenced by the course of the Revolution in France: the early essays on the tragic sublime (considered here) display an optimistic understanding of the possibilities of human freedom, which reflects both deep-seated political commitments and his hopes for reform in his own time. As the Revolution took a disastrous course, though, Schiller seems to have retreated from his earlier, heroic conception of freedom to a more stoical one, which emphasizes the inoculatory effect of tragedy rather than its triumphant vindication of the powers of the individual (considered later in the chapter).

Schiller's philosophical writings of the 1790s are saturated with the concept of freedom, understood in a roughly—though by no means strictly—Kantian sense.[6] Schiller published three essays on tragedy in the years 1792–93, of which the last, "On the Sublime: Towards the Further Development of Certain Kantian Ideas" ("Vom Erhabenen: zur weitern Ausführung einiger Kantischen Ideen")[7] is the most original, creatively applying concepts gained from the reading of Kant to the theory of tragedy.[8] The sublime for Schiller results from a conflict between the physical and the rational: either because an object is so physically imposing that it is impossible to imagine (which Schiller calls the "theoretical sublime") or because a force is so physically threatening that it is impossible to withstand (the "practical sublime").[9] Within the latter, and for Schiller more important, category, there is an important slippage from Kant's purely subjective description of the sublime to an objective usage that can describe actions themselves as sublime. For Schiller, the most important case of the sublime comes when we view the struggle between sense and reason taking place in a single individual. This is, Schiller argues, the case in tragedy.

[6] See Beiser, *Schiller as philosopher*: 213–37.

[7] It is usually printed in modern editions in two parts: as "Vom Erhabenen" and "Über das Pathetische," but this divides what in Schiller's original conception constitutes a single essay (though published across two issues of the journal *Neue Thalia*). In Schiller's 1801 *Kleinere prosaische Schriften*, he split the essay into two parts, replacing the first half (the part conventionally known as "Vom Erhabenen") with "Über das Erhabene" and retitling the second part "Über das Pathetische." As will be shown in the next chapter, this latter organization reveals important changes in the understanding of the sublime, so the textual history should be observed quite closely.

[8] As there are substantial disagreements and discontinuities between the essays, I treat only the last, which is the most substantial and influential.

[9] These are intended (*Essays* 24; *FA* 8: 396) to correlate with Kant's "mathematical" and "dynamic" sublime, but the correspondence is vaguer than it appears, since Schiller's "practical sublime" results from genuine danger, while Kant's "dynamic" sublime is always purely contemplative.

Schiller's understanding of the action of tragedy makes concrete the purely intellectual conflict of faculties described by Kant, seeing the conflict of reason and sense as characteristic of human action (instead of being internal to cognition). Sublime for Schiller is the individual struggle against an overwhelming physical constraint. Such action demonstrates the power of the will to withstand suffering, and thereby makes the viewers sensible of their own freedom:

> Our *intelligible self*, that in us which is not nature, must in every affect of the drive for self-preservation distinguish itself from the sensible part of our being, and become aware of its autonomy, its independence from all that physical nature can touch—in short, its freedom. (*Essays* 34; *FA* 8, 409–10)

Schiller's heroic vision of the sublime is a mixture of Kantian and previous theories—especially that of Moses Mendelssohn, who had similarly seen the sublime as a quality of human action.[10] By objectifying the conflict of the sublime as a struggle of the individual against the outside world, Schiller gives the sublime dramatic form. In the second part of the essay, he then outlines a poetics of tragedy based on this heroic sublime.

"The final aim of art," Schiller writes, "is the presentation of the supersensible, and tragic art in particular accomplishes this in that it renders sensible our moral independence from laws of nature in the state of affect" (*Essays* 45; *FA* 8, 423). In his emphasis on suffering as an essential component of tragedy, Schiller is profoundly indebted to the Enlightenment tradition of Lessing and Mendelssohn. Through depiction of the heroic struggle against pain, the tragic poet demonstrates the autonomy of the individual negatively, as it comes into conflict with natural powers.[11] There are two essential components of tragedy for Schiller: "presentation of suffering nature" and "presentation of moral resistance against suffering" (*Essays* 48; *FA* 8, 426). The tragic poet stages a conflict between the physical and the moral realms of existence, portraying a conflict against the sensible itself. In the struggle of the tragic hero, the audience recognizes an expression of human freedom, converting the vicarious experience of physical suffering into the triumphant recognition of one's own moral autonomy.

Schiller's understanding of suffering and struggle as the heart of tragedy makes the *Philoctetes* paradigmatic.[12] Schiller shows himself a disciple of the

---

[10] See Paul Barone, *Schiller und die Tradition des Erhabenen* (Berlin: Erich Schmidt, 2004), 164–79.

[11] See Klaus L. Berghahn, "'Das Pathetischerhabene'—Schillers Dramentheorie," in *Schiller: Ansichten eines Idealisten* (Frankfurt: Athenäum, 1986), 31–33.

[12] On the suffering Philoctetes in the period, see Liliane Weissberg, "Language's Wound: Herder, Philoctetes, and the origin of speech," *Modern Language Notes* 104 (1989); Felix Budelmann, "The reception of Sophocles' representation of physical pain," *American Journal of Philology* 128 (2007): 451–57.

German Enlightenment's cult of sensibility when he writes that "the heroes are as sensitive to all the sufferings of humanity as others, and just that makes them heroes, that they feel suffering strongly and deeply, and yet are not overwhelmed by it" (*Essays* 47; *FA* 8, 425). But what distinguishes Schiller from both Lessing and Mendelssohn is his insistence that suffering is not performed for the end of creating sympathy or admiration, but in order to demonstrate the freedom of the subject, affirming individual autonomy against political and philosophical doubts.[13] For the Schiller of 1793, art—and particularly the sublime art of tragedy—is both the objective manifestation of freedom, and a means to reinforcing the freedom of the subject. This conviction will be shaken by Schiller's reaction to the French Revolution, and will lead to a significantly more aporetic concept of tragic freedom, which lies at the heart of Schiller's return to playwriting from 1797.

Schiller is the first thinker of German Idealism to move tragedy from the domain of aesthetics into the domain of ontology. By ascribing the tragic sublime to the conflict of sense and intellect, and seeing it as the proof of humanity's moral determination, he fundamentally shifts the ground on which tragedy (and art in general) is discussed. Though the building blocks of Schiller's theory come from his reading of Kant, the edifice he constructs is original and has been quite influential, often in unacknowledged ways. Schiller's aesthetic ontology—the notion that works of art offer an insight beyond what can be known to reason—goes beyond (arguably too far beyond) Kant's circumspect suggestion that aesthetic judgment constitutes a link between sense and reason.[14] It also decisively transfers the center of aesthetics from natural to artistic beauty, reversing the Kantian hierarchy. These developments will be definitive for the philosophical thought of Schelling, Hegel, and Hölderlin in the younger generation. Schiller is by no means the first to see in tragedy a conflict between fate and free will, but his 1792–93 essays canonize it as tragedy's generic essence, establishing the philosophical framework that will pervade idealist discussions.[15] From Schiller onward, tragedy will be privileged for its unique relation to central concerns of human existence, and its ability to represent a truth that even philosophy cannot.

From Schiller's 1792–93 essays, the step to F.W.J. Schelling's reading of tragedy is relatively short, though Schelling's philosophical concerns are quite

---

[13] See Hans-Jürgen Schings, *Der mitleidigste Mensch ist der beste Mensch: Poetik des Mitleids von Lessing bis Büchner* (Munich: Beck, 1980), 46–53.

[14] Renate Homann, *Erhabenes und Satirisches: zur Grundlegung einer Theorie ästhetischer Literatur bei Kant und Schiller* (Munich: Fink, 1977), 53–60.

[15] Arbogast Schmitt, "Zur Aristoteles-Rezeption in Schillers Theorie des Tragischen," in *Antike Dramentheorien und ihre Rezeption*, ed. Bernhard Zimmermann (Stuttgart: M & P Verlag für Wissenschaft und Forschung, 1992). Courtine, "Tragedy and sublimity," 170–71.

different from Schiller's. Schelling sees tragedy, most of all the *OT*, as a representation of the antinomy of freedom and necessity. Schiller has already suggested this approach, but Schelling's concerns are only secondarily related to works of art—a fact that commentators nearly always overlook when they discuss Schelling as the inauguration of a "philosophy of the tragic." Rather, Schelling is interested mainly in the epistemological question of how and whether individual freedom can be known, the problem of Kant's "Third conflict of the antinomy of pure reason."[16] In his 1795 *Philosophical Letters on Dogmatism and Criticism* (*Philosophische Briefe über Dogmatismus und Kriticismus*), Schelling takes up the question of freedom in post-Kantian philosophy. Published anonymously when Schelling was twenty, the *Philosophical Letters* depict an early effort in Schelling's project, which extends at least through the following decade, of reconciling an understanding of human freedom with a scientific knowledge of natural causality. Schelling's philosophical approach is famously protean and underwent substantial changes every few years at this stage, but at least through 1805, it affords a central place to works of art, and to tragedy most of all. In tragedy, Schelling finds an insight into the common ground of freedom and nature, a way to unify the opposed realms of Kantian philosophy. Schelling at this stage does not so much philosophize about tragedy as through it: Greek tragedy provides a model for representing conflict and division under the sign of reconciliation.

Kantian philosophy appears to the Schelling of 1795 as a primarily negative effort, sweeping away the untenable assumptions of previous philosophy, but not setting any positive course for the future. Kant's division between pure reason (the realm of nature) and practical reason (the realm of freedom) allows for two equally justified but irreconcilable courses. The elaboration of a philosophy based on the freedom of the subject leads to "Criticism," embodied by the work of Fichte. Fichte's philosophy postulates the subject's unconditioned freedom and constructs an external world in relation to the I, and so leads to an "absolute subject." The alternative, "Dogmatism," is represented by Spinoza's monistic thought,[17] which had become notorious in the 1780s in the Pantheism Controversy between F. H. Jacobi and Moses Mendelssohn.[18] The Spinozist position, as Schelling understands it, is a philosophy of the "absolute object," which affords the natural world the only reality and suggests that human subjectivity and freedom

---

[16]See Claus-Artur Scheier, "Kants dritte antinomie und die Genese des tragischen Gedankens: Schelling 1795–1809," *Philosophisches Jahrbuch* 103 (1996).

[17]There is also, particularly in the first four letters, a polemic against what Schelling terms *Dogmatizismus*, the attempt of Tübingen theologians to harmonize Kantian critique with a theoretical certainty of God—an apologetic perversion that is to be distinguished from the consequent forms of both Criticism and Dogmatism.

[18]See Bowie, *Schelling and modern European philosophy*: 17–25.

are merely epiphenomena. Philosophy finds itself with a choice between two, both problematic, ways forward: "One of the two must occur: either no subject, and an absolute object, or no object and an absolute subject" (*LDC* 167; *AA* 1.3, 65).

Schelling's Idealism consists in the conviction that the opposed philosophical systems result from a division in the originary unity of "the absolute," conceived as the ground of all human existence and cognition. The absolute is a state of pure identity in which there is no consciousness or differentiation, and therefore no division between *phenomenon* and *noumenon*. In order for division to be experienced, Schelling reasons, there must once have been union. He outlines a quasi-historical narrative, which sees humanity as having emerged from a state of unconscious identity with nature: "Only insofar as we step out of the absolute does the conflict against it begin, and only through this *originary* conflict in the human spirit itself does the conflict of philosophers begin" (*LDC* 163; *AA* 1.3, 59). In becoming self-conscious (which entails distinguishing an I from a Not-I), the mind opposes what originally was one, and so becomes opaque to itself. Modern philosophy is characterized, for Schelling, by a hopeless effort to recapture the original state of union. Schelling's therapeutic effort attempts to understand the opposition of Criticism and Dogmatism as the empirical—and therefore necessarily divided—manifestation of a single absolute truth.

The conflict of the two systems is undecidable because both offer means of approaching the same absolute unity, but from different sides. Neither Criticism nor Dogmatism can prove the validity of its first principle, and so both systems are essentially proleptic, awaiting a validation that philosophy cannot provide. Nor can one, according to Schelling, deduce the unity of the two systems rationally; the only means of demonstrating the identity of theoretical and practical reason is through an action in which necessity and freedom are simultaneously realized:

> For both systems there thus remains nothing more than to make the absolute, since it cannot be an object of *knowledge*, into an object of *action*, or to *demand* the *action* through which the absolute is realized. In this necessary action *both* systems *are united.* (*LDC* 190–91; *AA* 1.3, 103)

The question for Schelling is how freedom, which cannot be an object of theoretical reason, can nevertheless be experienced. As Schiller had argued, this is only possible through negative representation, an action in which the freedom of the subject becomes apparent in struggling against necessity. Schelling's demonstration is aimed at showing how freedom (indeed, practical action in general) can be reconciled with natural causality. He argues for the necessity of a pre-theoretical union of freedom and nature, which would explain their opposition in modern philosophy.

The final letter illustrates the possible identity of the two systems by recalling Greek tragedy's depiction of the struggle of the individual against fate. Schelling sees such struggle as proving, paradoxically, the mutual inclusion of freedom and necessity: the subjection of the individual to fate proves the power of objective causality, while the ability to struggle against such determination proves the freedom of the subject: "A mortal—determined by destiny [Verhängniß] to become a criminal, himself fighting *against* this destiny, and still awfully punished for the crime, which was the work of fate! [Schicksal]" (*LDC* 192; *AA* 1.3, 106). The tragic hero—and Schelling is clearly thinking of Oedipus—becomes a criminal not through a free action, but through the work of fate. Though objectively, he is undeniably guilty, he remains subjectively innocent of the crime, and defends his innocence against the necessity that would condemn him. The futility of such struggle acknowledges Dogmatism's deterministic principle, while its very possibility proves Criticism's assertion of individual freedom. Oedipus cannot overcome necessity, but he can oppose it, and thereby demonstrate the simultaneous validity of the two principles.

By vindicating both natural causality and human freedom, tragedy for Schelling gives an insight into the undivided state of the absolute. Freedom, properly understood, encompasses necessity within itself.[19] In order for the one to exist, the other must as well—even though the two are only unified in the absolute (while in the phenomenal world they can only be opposed). Tragedy does not provide a conceptual proof of this unity, but a pre-rational, aesthetic perception, a possibility that "even though it has long vanished in the light of reason, must still be retained for art—for the highest in art." (*LDC* 192; *AA* 1.3, 106). Art, for Schelling, does not end the theoretical conflict of critical and dogmatic worldviews, but points backwards to the moment of identity before their difference. Greek tragedy appears to represent the pre-theoretical moment in which freedom and necessity could be reconciled.

Oedipus has a dual character for Schelling, as an object of necessity and a subject of freedom. Though the terms of this understanding are defined by eighteenth-century discussions of the *OT* as a tragedy of fate, Schelling's argument gives it a Schillerian twist by finding in the submission to fate a simultaneous recognition of human freedom:[20] "That the criminal, who was *laid low* only by the strength of fate, still more was *punished*, was an acknowledgement of human freedom, *honor* which was due to freedom" (*LDC* 193; *AA* 1.3, 107). The mechanism of negative representation (free-

---

[19] Reinhard Loock, *Schwebende Einbildungskraft: Konzeptionen theoretischer Freiheit in der Philosophie Kants, Fichtes, und Schellings* (Würzburg: Königshausen & Neumann, 2007), 322.

[20] See Lurje, *Die Suche nach der Schuld*: 229–31. Lurje points to the roots of Schelling's understanding of the *OT* in Terrasson and Marmontel, but underestimates the changes wrought on this model by Schiller's notion of the sublime.

dom proven through its struggle against fate) is at the heart of the sublimity of tragedy for Schelling just as it was for Schiller. The final step, though, is wholly original, and makes of Oedipus a kind of philosophical martyr, whose free assumption of guilt and self-destruction becomes a sublime beacon of human freedom: "It was a *great* thought [ein *großer* Gedanke], willingly to bear the punishment for an *unavoidable* crime, and so through the loss of freedom itself to prove that very freedom, and with a declaration of free will to go down" (*LDC* 193; *AA* 1.3, 107). The sublimity of tragedy appears when the hero chooses what fate had ordained, making freedom and necessity appear indistinguishable, simultaneously mortified and vindicated.[21]

The theological roots of this conception have often been overlooked: Schelling makes Oedipus into a kind of Christ figure, his guilt a *felix culpa* that brings a demonstration of human freedom. The tragic hero recalls Christ in accepting and affirming his own suffering.[22] This *interpretatio Christiana* will be even more apparent in the thought of Hegel and Hölderlin, who, with Schelling, were educated in theology at the Tübingen Stift (the three were even briefly roommates). Christian-tinged concepts of martyrdom and self-sacrifice provide the frame for Schelling's image of Oedipus' blinding as a redemptive act of submission.

But Oedipus' sacrifice for Schelling remains a limited one, confined to the aesthetic realm. "Such a struggle is only imaginable for the purpose of tragic art: it could not become a system of action for this reason alone, that such a system would presuppose a race of titans" (*LDC* 194; *AA* 1.3, 108). Tragic heroes appear as superhuman beings, endowed with the strength to demonstrate their freedom even in the moment of destruction. Whether such an action is possible in the present is unclear, and the conflict of the philosophical systems is not resolved. Tragedy is therefore of limited use to Schelling, since its realization of the absolute is only possible aesthetically. Schelling's turn to tragedy in the *Philosophical Letters* has a paradoxical aim: to advance philosophy by regress to a no-longer-valid origin.[23] The possibility of Oedipus' action "has long vanished in the light of reason," and so seems unrealizable in modernity. Schelling's account of freedom finds itself confronted with the problem of historical process, as Greek tragedy suggests a means of reconciliation, but one that is importantly distanced from the present. The discussion ends in a state of aporia, with Greek tragedy

---

[21] Courtine, "Tragedy and sublimity," 161.

[22] This concept echoes importantly in Hegel's *Spirit of Christianity*, discussed in chapter 5, as well as later in Kierkegaard and Nietzsche.

[23] Lore Hühn, "Die Philosophie des Tragischen: Schellings *Philosophische Briefe über Dogmatismus und Kriticismus*" in *Die Realität des Wissens und das wirkliche Dasein: Erkenntnisbegründung und Philosophie des Tragischen beim frühen Schelling*, ed. Jörg Jantzen (Stuttgart: frommann-holzboog, 1988), 115–17.

simultaneously offering a way back to wholeness, and a reminder of the ir-reconcilable division of modern subjectivity.

The account of tragedy is a microcosm of the *Philosophical Letters* as a whole, a representation of philosophical opposition as necessary and essential, grounded in a division that is uniquely modern. Schelling interprets this in a positive light in the closing paragraph: "We do not wish to mourn, but rather to be happy that we stand finally at the crossroads, where division is unavoidable" (*LDC* 196; *AA* 1.3, 111). There is an echo here of Oedipus at the place where three roads meet that reinforces the affinity of ancient tragedy and modern philosophy, both depictions of a fundamental ambiguity of human freedom. But the difference is even more important: the action of tragedy cannot offer a conceptual solution, and ultimately emphasizes only the irreconcilability of the philosophical problem. Greek tragedy's representation of an action uniting freedom and necessity is no longer credible in modernity. The "fate" of Schelling's philosophy is that it must either accord the subject or the object primacy, choosing one path while neglecting the other. In the *Philosophical Letters*, Schelling seeks, like Oedipus, to determine the cause of this double bind. The ultimate causality that Oedipus ascribes to Apollo, Schelling finds in the tragic division of the absolute.

SCHILLER'S SYSTEM OF TRAGIC FREEDOM

Tragedy is curiously absent from Schiller's most important contribution to philosophy, *On the Aesthetic Education of Man in a Series of Letters* (*Über die ästhetische Erziehung des Menschen in einer Reihe von Briefen*, 1795). The absence is significant, both in the context of Schiller's own thought, and for the development of other idealist theories. In the *Aesthetic Letters*, Schiller offers his most sustained argument for the power of aesthetic experience to unify the realms of human nature and cognition that Kant had sought to keep apart. Schiller's theory of aesthetic education is the most important link between Kantian aesthetics and the idealist philosophy of art, and an important influence on Schelling, A. W. Schlegel, Hegel, and Hölderlin. Hegel, in his *Lectures on Aesthetics*, would point to Schiller's concepts of "unity" (*Einheit*) and "reconciliation" (*Versöhnung*) as a major advance over Kantian thought, and the first major step towards a philosophy of art (*Aesthetics* 61; *WZB* 13, 89). Self-serving as the narrative is, there is truth in it, for Hegel as much as for other idealist thinkers. Schiller's *Aesthetic Letters* elaborate and extend the third *Critique*'s circumspect notion of beauty's mediation between sense and reason into an account of the unifying role of art in existence. In particular, Schiller's connection between aesthetic and social experience, and his elegy for the role of art in Greek culture were decisive for the Tübingen Stiftler. Yet the *Aesthetic Letters* also became a spur in their very incompleteness: for Schiller as for his contemporaries, Greek tragedy seemed to represent the highest form of art, yet its characteristic mode, the sublime, was not discussed in the text (at least explicitly).[24] This lacuna would be addressed later by Schiller himself, leading him to a bifurcated aesthetics, which viewed beauty and sublimity as opposing modes of experience. Schiller was unusual in emphasizing the challenge posed by the tragic sublime, differing in this respect from the Schlegels and Schelling, who assimilated tragedy to reconciliatory models. Schiller's emphasis on the disjunctive elements of tragedy constitutes a great part of the modernity and continuing appeal of his thought.

The *Aesthetic Letters* represent Schiller's response to the twin revolutions of French politics and Kantian critique, elaborating a concept of freedom that explicitly binds political liberalism and aesthetic autonomy. To many, the affinity of Kantian philosophy and revolutionary politics was self-evident: their apparently destructive qualities, their effort to construct a rational system *ex nihilo*, their emphasis on human freedom.[25] Though Schiller, like many German intellectuals, initially supported the Revolution, he seems to have turned against it by the time of the execution of Louis XVI in January 1793.[26] While following the course of events in France with increasing despair, Schiller was engaged in formulating his concepts of the beautiful and the sublime. Both revolutionary politics and aesthetics seemed to lead to aporia, as the exaltation of human freedom revealed a darker side. The Reign of Terror showed the horrific effects of political liberation, while Kant's insistence on the subjective character of aesthetic judgment threatened to undermine the power of works of art. Schiller's way out of this dual impasse is based on the conviction that the two issues are linked, that true autonomy is impossible without the sense of beauty, and that aesthetic experience is a means of grounding a mature political freedom.

In 1793, Schiller began a series of letters to his patron, Herzog Friedrich Christian von Augustenburg, which document his changing thoughts on the relation of aesthetics and politics and contain the germ of the *Aesthetic Letters*. The *Augustenburg Letters* make explicit the dual crisis that provides the impetus for Schiller's thought, merging political and philosophical language: "The revolution in the philosophical world has shaken the basis on

---

[24]This is controversial. A good discussion is Carsten Zelle, *Die doppelte Ästhetik der Moderne: Revisionen des Schönen von Boileau bis Nietzsche* (Stuttgart: Metzler, 1995), 170–84. Zelle notes correspondences between Schiller's vague concept of "energetic beauty" and the sublime, but resists the tendency to map one onto the other. Rather than expecting systematic connections between Schiller's terminology in different texts, he suggests that we should recognize opposing clusters of related though not identical concepts, tending either to a "utopian" or a "tragic anthropology" (162).

[25]Well discussed by Pinkard, *German philosophy*: 82–85.

[26]See Peter-André Alt, *Schiller: Leben—Werk—Zeit*, 2 vols. (Munich: Beck, 2000), 2, 121–25.

which aesthetics was conducted. [. . .] Kant has already, if not given, then at least prepared the foundations of a new theory of art" (*FA* 8, 492). Because of its denial of an objective concept of beauty, Kant's aesthetics appeared frustratingly incomplete to Schiller.[27] Though Kant had laid out the conceptual apparatus for discussing the interactions of different cognitive faculties, he had not, Schiller believed, offered the last word on how these interactions proceed. This philosophical problem was matched by a political one, demonstrated in the catastrophic events in France. If the philosophical revolution had failed to attain its end, the political one seemed to have achieved its goal too early:

> The effort of the French people to establish for itself its holy human rights and achieve a political freedom has only brought its inability and unworthiness to light, and hurled back not only this unhappy people, but with it a considerable part of Europe and a whole century, into barbarity and servitude. (*FA* 8, 501)

The failure of the ideals of the Revolution appears to Schiller not only as a catastrophe for those caught up in it, but as a setback for the entire project of Enlightenment. The political freedom his generation had so fervently desired seems to have come too early, liberating a people not yet prepared to exercise their freedom for good ends. "That man is not yet ready for *civic* [*bürgerlich*] freedom," Schiller writes, "to whom still so much is lacking in *human* [*menschlich*, sc. freedom]" (*FA* 8, 501).

Before humans are able to act as independent political agents, Schiller argues, they must first develop themselves intellectually and morally. Schiller points to two paths for the improvement of character: philosophy, which seeks "*justification of concepts* [*Berechtigung der Begriffe*]," and aesthetic culture, which leads to "*purification of feelings* [*Reinigung der Gefühle*]" (*FA* 8, 505). Coming at the end of a century of Enlightenment, Schiller finds that the first task has been sufficiently accomplished, but the second remains unfinished—indeed, has been largely forgotten in the concentration on the first. The human mind has rationally deduced the rights of man, but man's feelings are still prey to confusion, selfishness, and brutality. The *Augustenburg Letters* seek to correct the cognitive bias of Kantian critique through the "purification of feelings." The concept recalls Aristotelian *catharsis*, but Schiller is quite vague on the means of it (and at this point, his knowledge of Aristotle seems to have been largely at second hand). Schiller uses the notion of "purification" to describe the ennobling effect of aesthetic culture on the individual.[28] Political liberation and rational critique, for Schiller, must

---

[27] Schiller discusses the shortcomings of Kant in the "Kallias-Briefe": *FA* 8, 276–329. See Beiser, *Schiller as philosopher*: 47–53.

[28] The *Augustenburg Letters*, unlike the *Aesthetic Letters*, do make clear gestures towards an opposition between the beautiful and the sublime (*FA* 8, 520–21), but without discussing tragedy. Since these passages seem quite closely related to those in the essay "Concerning the sub-

be combined with an enlightenment of feelings and morality. "It is here [...] where art and taste lay their developing hand on man and prove their ennobling influence" (*FA* 8, 505).

The *Aesthetic Letters*, like the *Augustenburg Letters*, set out a biting critique of modern culture: "Here wildness, there lethargy: the two extremes of human decline, and both united in one time!" (Letter 5: *Essays* 96; *FA* 8, 568). As often in Schiller's thought, modern alienation is contrasted with the idealized wholeness of ancient Greece. The Greeks, for Schiller as for many of his contemporaries, represent both a historical reality and, because of their cultural achievements, a universal ideal. They provide the paradigm of a culture in which the individual develops as a totality, without prioritizing reason or sense: "At once full of form and full of plenitude, philosophizing and developing, tender and energetic, we see them unite the youth of fantasy with the virility of reason in a glorious humanity" (*Essays* 98; *FA* 8, 570). Where the Greeks followed "all-uniting nature," moderns are defined by "all-dividing understanding [Verstand]" (Letter 6: *Essays* 99; *FA* 8, 571). Schiller describes a Rousseauist fall narrative that sees modernity as a period of division and conflict. Schiller's disaffection with reason and the spirit of critique, though, is not total. It is the "onesidedness" (*Einseitigkeit*) of modern culture that is so troubling, not its rational spirit *per se*. What is needed, Schiller argues (against Rousseau), is not a return to nature, but the development of a new interplay of reason and sense through a renewed aesthetic culture.

Schiller places Kant's suggestion that aesthetic judgment bridges theoretical and practical reason in a social and historical context. The experience of beauty for Schiller unifies the opposing realms of human activity, and so recreates the natural wholeness of antiquity by artificial means. Artistic beauty is able to provide the totalizing and intra-subjective experience lacking in modern society. In Schiller's description, works of art take on an epiphanic quality, with the power to shock their society out of its unhappy complacency. The artist must commit an act of purifying violence, countering the historical world with an ahistorical ideal. Schiller employs the language of tragedy to describe the power of aesthetic experience to resist historical circumstances:

> The artist is indeed the son of his time, but alas for him if he is also its pupil or even its favorite [Günstling]. Let a benevolent godhead tear him as an infant early from his mother's breast, nurse him with the milk of a better age, and let him ripen to maturity under a distant Greek sky. When he has become a man, then let him return, an alien figure, to his age; but not to please it with his

lime" (discussed below), one can speculate that Schiller originally sought to integrate the two into a single program, before coming to see them as serving fundamentally different roles in the project of aesthetic education.

appearance, rather, terribly, like Agamemnon's son, to purify it [furchtbar wie Agamemnons Sohn, um es zu reinigen]. (Letter 9: *Essays* 108; *FA* 8, 583–84)

Here we see a trace of Schiller's disjunctive notion of tragedy. Like Orestes, the modern artist finds himself an alien in his own homeland, and must act against the current of his time to restore a lost order. The experience of "a better age" in Greece provides a challenge to the present.[29] Modernity appears as degenerate and corrupt, to be saved by the cathartic appearance of a tragic avenger (*Reinigung* again recalls *catharsis*). This, the closest Schiller comes to considering tragedy in the *Aesthetic Letters*, points forward to a central element of Schiller's later thought: tragedy is a means of redeeming modernity by its violent untimeliness.

The *Aesthetic Letters*, in broadly Kantian fashion, return repeatedly to the opposition of intellect and sense. Schiller, though, conceives of the two as dynamic forces realized in "drives" (*Triebe*), which are understood anthropologically, as characteristics of all human activity. The "form-drive" (*Formtrieb*) is the expression of man's rational side, which seeks to impose order on existence. The "matter-drive" (*Sachtrieb* or *Stofftrieb*, sometimes translated "sense-drive"), on the contrary, constitutes man's sensuous nature, demanding satisfaction of immediate needs and appetites. The two drives tend in opposite directions, one pressing to impose reason, the other seeking to satisfy sense. The ideal is a state of "reciprocity" (*Wechselwirkung*) of the two drives, in which they oppose and temper one another.[30] In this state, a third drive becomes active, the "play-drive" (*Spieltrieb*), in which the will of the individual rises above the contingent demands of sense and the constraining demands of reason: "The play-drive, then, as that in which the two [drives] act together, will constrain the disposition morally and physically at once. It will, because it annuls [aufhebt] all contingency [Zufälligkeit], also annul all constraint [Nötigung], and set man, physically and morally, in freedom" (Letter 14: *Essays* 127; *FA* 8, 608). Paradoxically, Schiller argues that true freedom emerges from reciprocal constraint, as each drive is neutralized by the other. The version of dialectic here is characteristic of Schiller's thought, which posits oppositions with the aim of an ideal tension, a third state in which the onesidedness of each is negated.[31] In the state of play, neither drive predominates, but both, through their reciprocal negation, contribute to the fullest autonomy of the subject.

[29] See further Nicholas Martin, *Nietzsche and Schiller: untimely aesthetics* (Oxford: Clarendon, 1996), 123–29.

[30] See Sieglinde Grimm, "Von der 'sentimentalischen Dichtung' zur 'Universalpoesie': Schiller, Friedrich Schlegel und die 'Wechselwirkung' Fichtes," *Jahrbuch der deutschen Schillergesellschaft* 43 (1999).

[31] Schiller's dialectic is a substantial influence on Hegel, but Hegel will transform Schiller's oppositions founded in the nature of man into oppositions created by the immaturity of reason. Schiller envisions an anthropological (and so constant) dialectic, Hegel a historical and progressive one.

Schiller's anthropology of human freedom leads through the aesthetic to the political. Schiller has described, in individual terms, the way freedom emerges from the reciprocity of the two drives, as a mediation between reason and sense. This can only be an aesthetic condition. Beauty, like the play-drive, is defined by the "most perfect possible union and *equality* of reality and form" (Letter 15: *Essays* 132; *FA* 8, 614). The freedom attained in the aesthetic condition is adumbrated in the concept of play, which Schiller appropriates from Kantian terminology to describe an act that is without ulterior aim, but which is nevertheless governed by internal rules. The play of the aesthetic condition therefore resists the onesidedness that is characteristic of modernity for Schiller, releasing man from constraints of reason and sense alike.[32]

Schiller's concept of aesthetic freedom brings him full circle to the question of political freedom. Having described how an individual subject attains genuine autonomy, he can now imagine a political freedom that is more than the absence of hierarchy. It would be based on a community of individuals who "appear [to one another] only as a figure [Gestalt], confront [one another] as object of free play. The basic principle of this realm is *to give freedom through freedom [Freiheit durch Freiheit zu geben]*" (Letter 17: *Essays* 176; *FA* 8, 673–74). The collective freedom of the aesthetic state is guaranteed by the individual freedom and interconnection of its members, and so is based on a firmer foundation than the political freedom of the French Revolution. By imagining a state of aesthetic harmony within and between individuals, Schiller's utopian vision seeks to reconcile the oppositions it inherits from Kantian thought: individual and collective, theory and practice, necessity and freedom.

Though the *Aesthetic Letters* are concerned with art's relation to human freedom, they do not explicitly discuss the sublime. Indeed, their theory of reconciliation through beauty leaves little room for the mixed pleasure of the sublime.[33] Schiller seems to have been aware of this silence, as is clear in his selection of essays for the third volume of his *Shorter Prose Writings* (*Kleinere prosaische Schriften*), published in 1801. The volume bookends the *Aesthetic Letters* with two essays, "Concerning the Sublime" ("Über das Erhabene") and "Concerning the Pathetic" ("Über das Pathetische").[34] The latter we have already encountered, as it forms the second half of the essay

---

[32] Beiser, *Schiller as philosopher*: 131.

[33] A similar depotentiation of the sublime takes place in Schelling's *System of Transcendental Idealism*, where beauty is understood as the overarching concept, of which the sublime is a simple instance. See Loock, *Schwebende Einbildungskraft*: 461.

[34] *Essays* confuses things by entitling "Über das Pathetische" "On the pathetic," thus corresponding to the translation of "Vom Erhabenen" as "On the sublime." But the correspondence should be between the titles "Über das Erhabene" and "Über das Pathetische." Schiller's organization is quite clear, even if the exigencies of editorial practice have made it seem obscure.

"On the Sublime," where it completed the general account of the sublime with a detailed discussion of tragedy's "pathetic sublime." "Concerning the Sublime" was first published in the 1801 collection, though probably written some years before.[35] Whatever the history of the essay, and whatever Schiller's plans for the sublime in the *Aesthetic Letters*, the 1801 volume suggests that the sublimity of tragedy and the aesthetic education of beauty are complementary.[36] Together, the essays on the sublime and its instantiation in tragedy form the counterpart to the analysis of beauty in the *Aesthetic Letters*, and outline a concept of freedom that undermines or at least complicates the utopian vision of the *Aesthetic Letters*.[37]

"Concerning the Sublime" describes a mode of aesthetic education, but of a very different kind from that of the *Aesthetic Letters*. The essay begins by asserting man's freedom from compulsion in the words of Lessing's *Nathan the Wise*: "no man is obliged to be obliged [Kein Mensch muß müssen]," defining man's particularity as "the being that wills [das Wesen, welches will]" (*Essays* 70; *FA* 8, 822). Yet this primacy of the will is importantly limited by circumstances—most of all, the possibility of violence and death, which threaten to rob man of the freedom that is essential to humanity, in Schiller's definition. Physical strength can protect one to a limited extent, but ultimately there is no means of exerting human will over external forces. All that is left is a purely intellectual assertion of man's superiority over nature,

> *wholly and completely to negate* [*ganz und gar aufzuheben*] *a relation* that is so disadvantageous to [man], and *to annihilate according to its concept* [*dem Begriff nach zu vernichten*] a violence that he must suffer in fact. To annihilate a violence according to its concept, however, means nothing other than to subject oneself to it voluntarily. (*Essays* 71–72; *FA* 8, 823)

A new element has entered Schiller's understanding of freedom, which may reflect the influence, direct or indirect, of Schelling's "Tenth Letter": by accepting voluntarily what nature has dictated, man transforms the work of necessity into the work of freedom. Previously, Schiller had sought to demonstrate the superiority of human freedom in the struggle against necessity; now, he seeks to negate necessity by proving it identical to freedom. Schiller's theory has taken a stoic turn, emphasizing "resignation to necessity" (*Essays* 72; *FA*

---

[35] Barone, *Schiller und die Tradition des Erhabenen*: 112–14. Barone argues for a late dating of the essay (1796 or after), which seems plausible, though parts of it may well date to earlier in Schiller's career. All that can really be deduced is that in 1801, the essay reflected Schiller's thoughts on the sublime.

[36] See Pugh, *Dialectic of love*: 319–23. Pugh describes the contrast between the two analyses in terms of the Plotinian concepts of *methexis* (unification, associated with the beautiful) and *chorismos* (division, associated with the sublime).

[37] Zelle, *Doppelte Ästhetik*: 179.

8, 824).[38] It is the role of the sublime in art to prepare the individual for this practice of resignation. This is a substantially darker view of the possibilities of human freedom than Schiller had put forward in "On the Sublime" and reflects a pessimism that seems at odds also with the reconciliatory vision of the *Aesthetic Letters*.

Schiller addresses the relation of the beautiful and the sublime explicitly in "Concerning the Sublime." Where the beautiful leads to a feeling of harmony as the sensory world seems to conform to rational purposes, the sublime begins in a feeling of disharmony and of conflict with reality. By confronting us with the difference between our moral and sensible natures, the sublime teaches "that we have an autonomous principle in us, which is independent of all sensory stirrings" (*Essays* 74; *FA* 8, 827). The harmony felt in the apprehension of beauty appears insufficient in a world in which reason and sense cannot conform. The freedom perceived in beauty remains within nature, while the freedom of the sublime raises the subject above nature. The sublime is thus the more important for our moral constitution, since it "creates for us an exit from the sensory world in which the beautiful would gladly hold us forever" (*Essays* 77; *FA* 8, 830).

Schiller introduces a hierarchy into the Kantian description, preferring the bracing effect of the sublime to the calming effect of the beautiful. The sublime, for Schiller, is a shock that recalls man's moral nature, just as Mentor reminded Odysseus of his duty (*Essays* 77; *FA* 8, 830).[39] Sensitivity to the sublime, Schiller writes, comes later than the ability to perceive beauty, and occurs only when the subject becomes fully conscious of its intellectual powers. Through repeated observation of the chaotic and contradictory, the individual learns to impose a rational order on what appears incomprehensible to the senses. This freedom, the ability to discern oneself "as a citizen and co-ruler of a higher system" (*Essays* 80; *FA* 8, 834) is the essence of Schiller's later theory of the sublime, which is directed to the subjective perception of freedom rather than the objective proof of it. The sublime is now a power (*Kraft*) of the subject, not a property of action.[40] This brings Schiller closer to Kant than he had been in the earlier essays and makes his later theory a significant expansion of the Kantian sublime into the realm of the mimetic arts.[41]

Schiller's later theory of the sublime is less affirmative than his earlier understanding, but it is far more historically engaged. The sublime for Schiller becomes a way of viewing history, which finds a subjective perception

[38] Barone, *Schiller und die Tradition des Erhabenen*: 124–27. Barone notes this stoic sense, but it is more likely to come from Schelling's "Tenth Letter" than from Schiller's scanty reading of ancient philosophy.

[39] Schiller is thinking of Fénélon's *Telemaque*, rather than the *Odyssey*, in which Hermes visits Calypso and urges her to send Odysseus home (Book 5).

[40] Barone, *Schiller und die Tradition des Erhabenen*: 117.

[41] I am grateful to Lucas Zwirner for pointing this out.

of order in a chaotic succession of events and actions. At the heart of this concept is a sense of man not being at home in nature. This is not, as in the *Aesthetic Letters*, a reversible social alienation, but a constant and insurmountable alienation caused by historical existence itself:

> The world, as a historical object, is basically nothing else than the conflict of the powers of nature with one another and with the freedom of man, and history tells the result of this struggle. [...] If one approaches history with great hopes of light and knowledge—how much one finds oneself disappointed! All well-intentioned efforts of philosophy to bring what the moral world *demands* into agreement with what the real world *permits* are refuted by the testimonies of experiences. (*Essays* 81; *FA* 8, 835)

Intellect and experience appear irreconcilable, the conflict of reason and sense unending. The pessimism of these words contrasts sharply with Schiller's earlier thoughts on *Universalgeschichte*, which had been dominated by a faith in progress and a belief that historical reality could be understood by philosophical abstraction.[42] Irrationality, destruction, and chaos appear to be unalterable facts of existence, which no philosophy can improve. This pervasive disharmony between self and world makes the sublime ability to impose a subjectively rational order a pressing need for all humans. "Observed from this point of view, and *only* from this, is world history [Weltgeschichte] a sublime object for me" (*Essays* 81; *FA* 8, 835).

The individual's ability to withstand real chaos, Schiller argues, is increased by exposure to mimetic scenes of pathos. The sublime takes on a stoic characteristic, as an awareness of the inevitable failure of human freedom. Viewing history as sublime is a form of enlightened spectatorship, through which one attains a distance and perspective on suffering. The experience of the pathetic becomes a rehearsal for the catastrophes of life. "The pathetic, one can say, is an inoculation from inescapable fate [eine Inokulation des unvermeidlichen Schicksals], through which it robs fate of its evil and deflects its attack to the strong side of man" (*Essays* 83; *FA* 8, 837). It is only near the end of the essay, in an extraordinary rhetorical display, that Schiller makes explicit the connection to tragedy:

> Towards this acquaintance ["with the dangers surrounding us"] we are assisted by the terrible majestic spectacle [das furchtbar herrliche Schauspiel] of all-destroying alternation, which recreates and again destroys—of the ruinations that sometimes creep up slowly and sometimes attack quickly; we are assisted by the pathetic pictures of man struggling with fate, of the unstoppable flight of

---

[42] Wolfgang Riedel, "'Weltgeschichte ein erhabenes Objekt': zur Modernität von Schillers Geschichtsdenken," in *Prägnanter Moment: Studien zur deutschen Literatur der Aufklärung und Klassik*, ed. Peter-André Alt et al. (Würzburg: Königshausen & Neumann, 2002).

happiness, of deceptive security, of triumphant injustice and defeated innocence which history arrays in rich measure, and tragic art brings before our eyes in imitation [die tragische Kunst nachahmend vor unsre Augen bringt]. (*Essays* 83; *FA* 8, 837–38)

Tragedy and history alike are representations of events that cannot be grasped as belonging to any sort of order. And this very inscrutability is what recommends them as forms of education. By making us aware of the catastrophes that have befallen others, they prepare us to face the "eternal faithlessness of all the sensible [ewige . . . Untreue alles Sinnlichen]" (*Essays* 83; *FA* 8, 838). Schiller sees history as governed by a tragic law, which renders all attempts at rationalization impotent. In the tragic and historical sublime, though, we learn to perceive chaos as order, preparing ourselves to turn the work of necessity into the work of freedom. This makes the tragic sublime—and not the beautiful—the conclusion to Schiller's project of aesthetics: "thus the sublime must be added to the beautiful, in order to make *aesthetic education* [*ästhetische Erziehung*] into a complete whole" (*Essays* 84; *FA* 8, 838).

CRITICISM AND SCHOLARSHIP: A. W. SCHLEGEL AND GOTTFRIED HERMANN

The understanding of Greek tragedy as proof of human freedom spread quickly. Very often, Schiller's and Schelling's ideas were abstracted from their contexts and merged, apparently unconsciously, into a single theory. The considerable impact on Hegel and Hölderlin will be considered in later chapters, while here it remains to consider two more systematic (though somewhat less original) reflections on the sublimity of tragedy, both of which emerge from readings of Schiller and Schelling. August Wilhelm Schlegel's Jena lectures of 1798 and Berlin lectures of 1801–1803 seem to have been the first transformation of Schelling's remarks in the *Philosophical Letters* into a full-blown theory of tragedy—a step that is hardly suggested by Schelling's text. As the earliest use of an idealist approach to tragedy as a critical tool, the lectures are path-breaking. Gottfried Hermann's 1802 commentary on Aristotle's *Poetics* similarly applies idealist premises within the realm of classical philology. He employs concepts gained from idealist theories as a means for understanding *catharsis*, and as the foundation of a post-Kantian theory of genre. Though neither Schlegel nor Hermann acknowledges these debts, the influence of earlier theories is clear in their descriptions of tragedy as defined by the sublime conflict between freedom and necessity. In just a few years, then, the approach suggested by Schiller and Schelling seems to have entered the intellectual bloodstream in Germany.

Unusually for their time, both August Wilhelm Schlegel and his younger brother Friedrich had the benefit of a university training in classical philology.

As law students in Göttingen in the early 1790s, both attended the famous seminar of Christian Gottlob Heyne, and were impressed by his integrative approach to antiquity. Both took from the seminars a sense of antiquity's educative value and an understanding of philology as a field of critical synthesis, in which the history and literature of the ancient world were understood to form an essential unity.[43] Together and individually, their writings of the 1790s returned repeatedly to ancient texts, and theorized, more self-consciously than any of their contemporaries, the relation of Greek to modern, "Romantic" (a term they popularized) literature. August Wilhelm's most important contribution to thought on Greek tragedy was three courses of lectures delivered beginning in 1798 and culminating in the famous 1808 Vienna lectures, in which he described the fundaments of a Romantic philosophy of art, and discussed a broad range of dramatic traditions. Though Greek drama remained at the heart of his project, defining the terms in which the entire dramatic tradition was discussed, August Wilhelm was particularly influential in directing attention to the drama of other nations and times—especially the English and the Spanish. For both Schlegels, theory, history, and criticism (in the sense of evaluation) of art were indivisible, and the task of a philosophical approach to art was to show the necessary interrelations between these spheres of knowledge.

When A. W. Schlegel delivered his first series of *Lectures on Philosophical Aesthetics* (*Vorlesungen über philosophische Kunstlehre*) in 1798–99, he was an extraordinary professor in Jena, dividing his time between university teaching, coediting the journal *Athenäum* with Friedrich, and translating foreign literature (including versions of Shakespeare that remain classics). For recent critics, August Wilhelm has often remained under the shadow of the younger and undeniably more brilliant Friedrich, and it is often assumed that August Wilhelm's lectures were largely derived from his brother's thoughts. This is not entirely fair: August Wilhelm's particular talent lay in applying concepts of philosophical aesthetics to concrete critical instances—something that, it must be said, neither Friedrich nor their friend Schelling did with the same success. The lectures are indeed largely derivative in their theoretical framework, but their critical insights are often quite novel. This is clear in the theory of the tragic sublime: Schlegel adds little that is new, but brings together the scattered, unsystematic reflections of Schelling and Schiller into a coherent critical approach. Indeed, Schlegel may have been the first person to transform Schiller's and Schelling's descriptions of a conflict between freedom and necessity into an understanding of tragedy as an inherently dialectical form.

The Jena lectures define tragedy as doubly dialectical, in generic form and plot. Building on his brother's argument that tragedy "determines, puri-

[43]Martin Bäuerle, *Kommunikation mit Texten: Studien zu Friedrich Schlegels Philologie.* (Würzburg: Königshausen & Neumann, 2008), 34.

fies, raises, unifies, and orders all the individual perfections of earlier forms, ages, and schools into a new form" (*Study* 60; *KFSA* 1, 296), A. W. Schlegel describes drama as "an absolute synthesis of both other opposed major forms, the epic and lyric" (*KAV* 1, 83). Here, we see August Wilhelm schematizing the intuition of his brother, placing tragedy into a clear generic structure that is only vaguely suggested by Friedrich's writings. This notion of tragedy as a historical and formal synthesis of epic and lyric will be important to both Schelling and Hegel (as well as to Nietzsche much later), who will similarly take drama to be the fullest manifestation of the possibilities of literature.[44] August Wilhelm treats artistic and literary genres as ideal forms, each having a unique essence that can be placed into dialectical relation with the other forms.[45] He discusses "pure tragedy" and "pure comedy" as general principles that transcend any particular example (though both are instantiated in Greek works most of all), hinting at the hypostasization of "the tragic" that will become widespread in the years following. Throughout Schlegel's lectures, it is the Greek forms of the genre that define the norm against which later examples are judged.

August Wilhelm's understanding of the plot of tragedy elaborates Schelling's description of the identity of freedom and necessity into a generic principle. In doing so, he elides the aporetic tinge of the *Philosophical Letters*, and sees tragedy (like his brother Friedrich) as essentially reconciliatory: "Tragedy is the immediate representation of an action, in which the conflict between humanity and fate is resolved in harmony" (*KAV* 1, 83). Describing the end of tragedy as a harmonious coexistence of fate and free will, Schlegel interprets the moral aim of *catharsis* as "to produce for us that sublime mood [jene erhabene Stimmung]" (*KAV* 1, 84). Where both Schiller and Schelling had preserved disjunctive elements of the Kantian mixed pleasure in their descriptions of the tragic sublime, Schlegel emphasizes the harmonious end of sublime experience. Though citing Schelling, Schlegel describes a complementarity of necessity and freedom that differs from the absolute identity of the *Philosophical Letters*: "Everything occurs with necessity, except for where the free being acts" (*KAV* 1, 84). Schlegel's conclusion is far less philosophically ambitious than Schelling's, but it represents a first effort to read a spectrum of Greek tragedies in idealist terms. His discussion of the construction of tragic plots, principles of representation, and his innovative perspective on the chorus are guided by a concern for the autonomy of art, which he understands as the power of "elevation over nature [Erhebung über die Nature]" (*KAV* 1, 84).

Tragedy for Schlegel is bifurcated, divided (in the 1801–1804 Berlin lectures) between "inner freedom and outer necessity ... the poles of the tragic

---

[44]Most, "Schlegel, Schlegel und die Geburt eines Tragödienparadigmas," 164–66.
[45]Susanne Holmes, *Synthesis der Vielheit: die Begründung der Gattungstheorie bei August Wilhelm Schlegel* (Paderborn: Schöningh, 2006), 160–63.

world. Each idea is brought to appearance first through the opposition with the other" (*KAV* 1, 721–22). The sublimity of tragedy teaches the inconsequence of the sensible world and the need for struggle against necessity. Schlegel cites the third *Critique*'s discussion of the sublime, though his understanding of the "moral teaching" (*KAV* 1, 725) of tragedy is far closer to Schiller's "On the Sublime" than it is to Kant's theory. The concept of fate provides a usefully elastic measure for critical evaluation as well: the works of Sophocles and Aeschylus are both praised for representing "the thought of indignation against fate [Empörung gegen das Schicksal]" (*KAV* 1, 738; cf. 743), which steels the audience to withstand fate in their own lives. The works of Euripides, on the other hand, are deficient because they fail to treat freedom and necessity as genuinely opposed. They do not address themselves to the moral freedom, but rather to the passions of the audience (*KAV* 1, 747).[46] Schlegel is interested in the critical insights that can be gleaned from the philosophical discussions, and his free use of terminology from Schiller and Schelling demonstrates, far more than their more original discussions, the power of an idealist dialectic to organize the events of Greek tragedy into a philosophical content. His definition of tragedy's essence as the sublime struggle against fate elevated the genre above all other art forms for its depiction of human freedom.

Gottfried Hermann's education was parallel to that of the Schlegel brothers: born the same year as Friedrich (1772), he studied law in Leipzig, but was increasingly drawn to the study of Greek literature during his time at university. While engaged in classical studies, Hermann read heavily in Kantian philosophy and attended the important Kantian Karl Leonhard Reinhold's Jena lectures in 1793–94. Hermann's first term teaching in Leipzig found him lecturing on Kant's third *Critique* and on Sophocles' *Antigone* (!). The interest in philosophy is visible as early as his 1794 *On the Types of Poetry* (*De Poeseos Generibus*), which applies concepts from the third *Critique* to a taxonomy of poetic forms and theory of poetic beauty.[47] The work decries the use of empirical categorizations, seeking to determine the *a priori* necessity of all poetic forms.[48] A similar approach informs his 1799 *Handbook of Metre*, which begins with a substantial "general theory of rhythm" before moving on to classifying the extant verses in the second part. Here, too, Hermann protests against an empirical method, demanding that his readers be grounded in philosophy in order to understand the principles of his

[46] On Schlegel's polemic against Euripides, see Behler, "*Damnatio*."

[47] See Michael Schramm, "Hermann und Kant: Philologie als (Kantische) Wissenschaft," in *Gottfried Hermann (1772–1848): internationales Symposium in Leipzig, 11.-13. Oktober 2007*, ed. Kurt Sier and Eva Wöckener-Gade (Tübingen: Narr, 2010), 85–91; Clémence Couturier-Heinrich, "Gottfried Hermann, un philologue kantien," *Revue germanique internationale* 14 (2011).

[48] Gottfried Hermann, "De poeseos generibus," in *Opuscula* 1 (Leipzig: Fleischer, 1827), 43.

work.[49] Later in life, philosophical interests would be less obvious in his scholarship, which made its greatest impact in the field of textual criticism, with tragedy a particular focus. Hermann's editions of individual plays and, especially, his lifelong project of editing Aeschylus, were milestones in editorial practice, and remain fundamental for modern editors.[50]

The impact of idealist theories of tragedy is clear in Hermann's 1802 edition of Aristotle's *Poetics*, which prints the Greek text with Latin translation, extensive notes, and a "Commentary on Tragic and Epic Poetry" of Hermann's own (all in Latin, still the major scholarly language). The work contains a diatribe against Aristotle's empirical procedure, and the unsystematic conclusions drawn in the text. Most of this polemic is confined to Hermann's own disquisition, but the explanatory notes often draw attention to unclear distinctions and seek to bring systematic coherence to the recondite text.[51] Throughout the notes, Hermann interprets the *Poetics* in light of modern aesthetics' investigation of the sensations produced by beauty, downplaying and denying outright Aristotle's understanding of tragic emotions.[52] This is evident in Hermann's most obviously idealist intervention, which consists in a complete revision of the Aristotelian theory of *catharsis* along Schillerian lines:

> For it is not by pity and terror of that kind that the purification of the soul takes place, but by sublimity [non enim per miserationem et terrorem istiusmodi purgatio animi perficitur, sed per sublimitatem], which, although Aristotle should have noted most of all in his definition of tragedy, he grasped least of all. For this [sublimity] causes that even in pity and fear we feel ourselves to be greater, nor are our spirits overwhelmed by these emotions. This is truly to possess emotions of the spirit that have been purged: to be touched by them, but not conquered [tangi iis, nec vinci].[53]

For Hermann, tragedy's sublime effect explains Aristotelian *catharsis*. This was certainly suggested by Schiller's and Schelling's theories, but it was not explicit, as neither engaged directly with the *Poetics*. For Schiller and Schelling, the concept of the sublime may have rendered *catharsis* unnecessary to explain how tragedy's negative emotions could be transmuted into positive ones. Hermann tries to integrate the sublime into an Aristotelian

---

[49] Gottfried Hermann, *Handbuch der Metrik* (Leipzig: Fleischer, 1799), viii.

[50] See Roger D. Dawe, "Hermann and tragedy," in *Gottfried Hermann (1772–1848): internationales Symposium in Leipzig, 11.-13. Oktober 2007*, ed. Kurt Sier and Eva Wöckener-Gade (Tübingen: Narr, 2010).

[51] Gottfried Hermann, *Aristotelis de arte poetica liber cum commentariis* (Leipzig: Fleischer, 1802). See for example, the long opening note on *mimesis* (83–89), and that on the parts of tragedy (127–30), which postulates a lacuna in order to make Aristotle's divisions correspond from one part of the text to another.

[52] See the discussion of plots in which bad people are rendered unhappy: ibid., 145–47.

[53] Ibid., 115.

theory—somewhat awkwardly—and indeed, when he returns to the sublime in his essay, *catharsis* is absent. Yet the argument proved influential in the years following, and provoked a substantial backlash against such a curious hybrid of Aristotle and idealist philosophy.[54]

Most striking in the edition, though, is Hermann's "Commentary on Tragic and Epic Poetry," which follows the *Poetics* notes. In it, Hermann develops a relatively thorough idealist theory of tragedy from systematic premises. The essay begins with a surprising declaration for a commentator on Aristotle: "There is a double task for those who interpret ancient philosophers: not only what they thought, but whether they thought rightly must be explained."[55] The words are an index not only of Aristotle's diminished authority, but also of the newly ambitious goals of philology, which increasingly saw itself as capable of taking on literary and philosophical questions (rather than relating narrowly to textual and historical ones). Hermann's first major disagreement with Aristotle concerns the nature of the pleasure gained from poetry. For Hermann, the concept of *mimesis*, and the associated pleasures of recognition and learning, fail to grasp the purely sensory nature of poetry, which pleases by its beauty (*pulcritudo*), and cannot be referred to any concepts.[56] Hermann divides *pulcritudo*, in good Kantian fashion, into *venustas* or *formositas* (both essentially meaning "beauty") and *sublimitas*, illustrating the sublime at length with examples from Homer and Aeschylus. Hermann seeks to specify the means of creating beautiful and sublime effects in poetry—essentially writing a counter-*Poetics* on Kantian principles.

For Hermann, the distinguishing characteristic of both tragedy and epic is their sublime action. To show their sublimity, Hermann moves beyond the Kantian influence of his preceding discussion, employing an idealist framework. Sublime action is described as "consisting in the contention of freedom and necessity."[57] Hermann describes a logic of equality that seems closest to Schelling: necessity cannot be conquered, or it would not be necessity; freedom cannot be conquered or the subject would not be free.[58] An action that would depict both principles, then, would have to be one "in which each equally has power, but that power is so divided that what

---

[54] See James I. Porter, "Tragedy and the catharsis of modernity," in *Tragedy and the idea of modernity*, ed. Joshua Billings and Miriam Leonard (Oxford: Oxford University Press, forthcoming).

[55] Hermann, *De arte poetica*: 197.

[56] Ibid., 198.

[57] Ibid., 248.

[58] Hermann, though, is more systematic than Schelling in defining generic characteristics, differentiating between the sublimity of drama and epic: where drama shows human freedom assaulted by necessity, epic shows necessity transgressed by human freedom (the model presumably being Achilles in the *Iliad*): ibid., 251–53.

the one is able to do, the other cannot. This is truly human nature, which is both ruled by freedom and obeys necessity [quae et libertate regitur, et necessitati paret]."[59] Drama depicts this paradoxical coexistence in the struggle of the individual against fate: "Necessity threatens ruin; freedom invites it freely; necessity brings evils; freedom endures; necessity causes sorrows; freedom restrains them; necessity destroys man; freedom scorns death, immune from ruin."[60] The language recalls much more the breathless style of Schelling's "Tenth Letter" than Kant's sober discussion, and shows the immediate influence of idealist accounts of tragedy throughout learned circles.

It is hard to gauge the influence of Hermann's *Poetics* because it would soon be joined by far more accessible discussions in German—most of all, Schlegel's Vienna lectures—which overshadowed Hermann's work in the popular imagination. In fact, Hermann does not seem to have been particularly proud of the edition, which was never reprinted, or the "Commentary," which was not taken up into his eight-volume *Opuscula* later in life. One can speculate that Hermann came to be embarrassed by his youthful enthusiasm for Kantian and post-Kantian philosophy—just as many scholars seem to have been, in ignoring this major work of one of the most important philologists of all time. Hermann never again addressed tragedy in such theoretical terms, perhaps seeing philosophical aesthetics as a diversion from the serious business of textual and historical scholarship. Still, the edition represents a fascinating document of Hermann's early thoughts on tragedy and the philosophy of art. Hermann's systematic discussion not only transfers a philosophical approach to the heart of academic philology, but also is a significant philosophical achievement itself, one of the first systematic philosophies of poetry on idealist premises.

When viewed retrospectively, all of the theories examined in this chapter can look quite similar: all view human nature as divided between sense and reason, all engage with Greek tragedy as a representation of the limits of human reason, and all understand tragedy through the Kantian concept of the sublime as a relation of freedom and necessity. These strands are uniquely post-Revolutionary and post-Kantian, and emerge from the effort to negotiate a place for human freedom within historical causality. The cumulative impact of the theories is hard to overestimate, and they represent, as Szondi rightly suggests, the first major theoretical approach to tragedy to move out of the shadow of Aristotle's concept of *mimesis*—even as they circle back to crucial issues of the *Poetics* such as *catharsis*, the ideal plot, and the tragic protagonist.

Nevertheless, one should not overlook the differences between the theories: not only do they lead to divergent interpretations of Greek tragedy,

[59] Ibid., 250.
[60] Ibid.

but, more importantly, they advance idealist readings of tragedy to quite different ends. Schiller seeks to answer the question of how tragedy can be pleasurable or useful even as it represents events that are painful to watch; Schelling is not interested in interpreting tragedy, but finds it a useful model for understanding how freedom and necessity can be reconciled in the absolute; August Wilhelm Schlegel is the first to engage with broader generic questions, setting tragedy into a systematic philosophy of the arts; and Hermann seeks to elaborate a new, rational approach to generic distinctions within ancient Greece. Though they read tragedy in similar ways, they do not have anything like a common theory of tragedy—much less a single "philosophy of the tragic." Their deepest commonality does not lie in their interpretations or philosophies, but in an approach that finds Greek tragedy uniquely meaningful for understanding the existence of the subject within history, divided between freedom and compulsion. Idealism's focus on freedom in tragedy allows it to argue that tragedy of all art forms represents the possibilities of human action at their fullest.[61] Despite its temporal remoteness, Greek tragedy appears to offer a unique insight into the possibilities for free action in the revolutionary present. The modernity of Greek tragedy, from Idealism onward, lies in this paradoxical sense of contemporaneity.

[61] See Allen Speight, "Tragedy and the human image: German Idealism's legacy for theory and practice," in *The impact of Idealism: the legacy of post-Kantian German thought*, ed. Nicholas Boyle et al. (Cambridge: Cambridge University Press, 2013).

CHAPTER 4

Greek and Modern Tragedy

"THE PROBLEM OF OUR POETRY appears to me to be the unification of the essentially modern with the essentially ancient," writes Friedrich Schlegel to his brother in 1794 (27.2.1794: *KFSA* 23, 185). This could describe the program for much of Schlegel's writing and thought of the 1790s; it could equally apply to Schiller's "classical dramaturgy" and, in philosophical context, to Schelling's thought on art. For all three, the challenge for modern artworks and thought on art is to incorporate elements of ancient practice, and to conceive of a possible union of what appear to be opposed principles. The names for these principles and the vision of their union varies—not only between thinkers, but in the thought of each one over time—but it is tragedy most of all that provides the ground for their historical imaginations.

By this point, Sophocles and Shakespeare had been firmly established as the essential ancient and modern dramatist, and they came to define an opposition of antiquity and modernity more broadly. With the publication of Goethe's *Faust: A Fragment* in 1790, a third, contemporary term began to suggest itself, which promised to incorporate lessons from ancient and modern drama alike into a new synthesis. As German thinkers were reeling from the revolutions discussed in the previous chapter, they looked to the past for direction. Tragedy, which had offered a means of representing the upheavals of the early 1790s, towards the end of the decade came to seem a way beyond the intellectual and artistic dilemmas of the time. Thinking Sophocles and Shakespeare in dialectic, idealist thinkers outlined a positive program for the tragic in modernity.

This chapter will consider idealist thought on the difference of antiquity and modernity, returning to the constellation of problems defined by the *Querelle des Anciens et des Modernes*. Yet the *Querelle* in the 1790s took

---

*General bibliography on the major figures is given in the previous chapter. For background on the ancient/modern distinction in the period, see Peter Szondi, "Antike und Moderne in der Ästhetik der Goethezeit," in *Poetik und Geschichtsphilosophie I*, ed. Senta Metz and Hans-Hagen Hildebrandt (Frankfurt: Suhrkamp, 1974). David S. Ferris, *Silent urns: Romanticism, Hellenism, modernity* (Stanford: Stanford University Press, 2000). Particularly important for the argument of this chapter is Hans Robert Jauß, "Schlegels und Schillers Replik auf die 'Querelle des anciens et des modernes,'" in *Literaturgeschichte als Provokation* (Frankfurt: Suhrkamp, 1970). Jauß is largely followed by two recent and more in-depth discussions: Oergel, *Culture and identity*; Urs Müller, *Feldkontakte, Kulturtransfer, kulturelle Teilhabe: Winckelmanns Beitrag zur Etablierung des deutschen intellektuellen Felds durch den Transfer der "Querelle des anciens et des modernes"* (Leipzig: Leipziger Universitätsverlag, 2005).

on quite different contours than it had in the 1690s, 1730s, or 1770s. The question was no longer one of comparative evaluation or normative poetics; both lines of inquiry had been effectively demolished by Herder and Goethe's encomia to Shakespeare. Schlegel, Schiller, and Schelling all took the greatness of Sophocles and Shakespeare for granted; the new challenge was to mediate between the two, to determine a relation of antiquity and modernity that would create the conditions for a flowering of contemporary art. The disastrous course of the French Revolution completed the reorientation in taste that had been in process since Winckelmann, in which German artists turned their attention to ancient as much as modern artists for inspiration, and to English rather than French modernity. In this climate, Herder's rigorous differentiation between antiquity and modernity increasingly seemed to burden rather than liberate the present, as it threatened to deprive artists of the constructive examples of the Greeks. The 1790s saw a new wave of philhellenism, almost as powerful as that introduced by Winckelmann, oriented not to visual art but to literature and especially tragedy. One of Schiller's satirical distiches describes the turn to the Greeks as one of "two fevers" afflicting Germans in the 1790s: "Kaum hat das kalte Fieber der Gallomanie uns verlassen / Bricht in der Gräkomanie gar noch ein hitziges aus" (*Xenion* 320: *FA* 1, 618: "Barely has the cold fever of Gallomania left us, when a hot one of Graecomania breaks out.").

The starkest statement of the opposition of antiquity and modernity comes in Friedrich Schlegel's *On the Study of Greek Poetry* (*Über das Studium der griechischen Poesie*). The essay, published in 1797, though complete by the end of 1795, has often been overshadowed by Schiller's concurrent and independently conceived *On Naive and Sentimental Poetry* (*Über naive und sentimentalische Dichtung*, 1795–96). While there are surprising similarities between the two essays (especially given the largely opposed poetics of the authors), their juxtaposition very often obscures a fundamental difference in intent: where Schlegel's essay is concerned with ancient poetry (and tragedy most of all) as a concrete historical phenomenon, Schiller's understands much ancient poetry as an example of the "naive," a category that transcends history.[1] Schlegel aims to outline a program for a creative relation to antiquity, while Schiller seeks to grasp the philosophical significance of differing relations to nature.[2] However, Schlegel and Schiller are closer in some re-

[1] There is a tension, never fully resolved by Schiller, between his understanding of "naive" and "sentimental" as historical categories (differentiating ancient and modern poetry) and modes of writing (differentiating two relations to nature, which can obtain in any time and place): see Szondi, "Antike und moderne," 149–83.

[2] See Karl Heinz Bohrer, *Das absolute Präsens: die Semantik ästhetischer Zeit* (Frankfurt: Suhrkamp, 1994), 128, which deplores Schiller's *Geschichtsphilosophie*. The opposing case is stated by Alt, *Schiller*: 2, 224–27.

spects than has been noticed—except that it is the Schiller of 1797 and after whose thought forms the more illuminating comparison, especially around tragedy. Though Schiller ridiculed the historical thought of Schlegel's *Study* essay on its publication, he nevertheless incorporated some of its lessons when he turned intensively to the study of Aristotle and Sophocles.

Schlegel and Schiller, for all their disagreements, agree on the fundamental difference between ancient and modern tragedy, and their different powers over the audience. Schelling, to the contrary, insists on a possible similarity, an aesthetic principle that would allow modern tragedy to have the same effect as ancient works. Indeed, it is crucial to his philosophical viewpoint that he be able to show the continuity in the possibilities of art from antiquity to the present. This leads him first to aporia and then to contortions, as he searches for a modern work that would have the same reconciliatory power that Sophoclean drama did. Historicization undermines the search for philosophical universals that drives Schelling's version of Idealism, and complicates the relation between systematic considerations and empirical data. All systematic philosophy of art must grapple with the tension between history and theory, between the drive to recognize particularity and the drive to subsume individuality under broader categories. Idealism never resolves this problem (if it ever could be resolved), but it establishes the modern terms of the question.

FRIEDRICH SCHLEGEL: NATURE, ART, REVOLUTION

The *Study* essay was intended as the first of a series of works through which the young Friedrich Schlegel (twenty-three at the time of writing) hoped to establish his name. Inspired by his university teacher Heyne, Schlegel conceived of his early writings as an effort, "to revive the study of the ancients, at least in Germany" (to A. W. Schlegel, 20.1.1795: *KFSA* 23, 226). His attention, though, quickly turned to editing the famous journals of the Romantic movement, the *Athenäum* and *Lyceum*, and he expressly disavowed the *Study* essay for its "revolutionary objectivity-fury [Objektivitätswut]" (*Lyceum*-Fragment 66: *KFSA* 2, 155). Yet Schlegel's project is more continuous than he wished to admit. One of the *Athenäum*-Fragments formulates the need for a universalism that would complement the historicization introduced by Winckelmann:

> The systematic Winckelmann, who read all the ancients at once as a single author, saw everything as a whole and concentrated his entire power on the Greeks, laid the ground for a material understanding of antiquity through his perception of the absolute difference between the ancient and the modern. Only when the standpoint and conditions of the absolute identity of the ancient and modern,

which was, is, or will be, is discovered, can one say that at least the contour of this science is complete, and then the methodological execution can be considered. (*Athenäum*-Fragment 149: *KFSA* 2, 188)

This is, in effect, an effort to formulate a speculative universalism after the historicizations of Winckelmann and Herder. The perception of the "absolute difference" of antiquity and modernity is incomplete until one recognizes the possibility of their "absolute identity." What exactly such a standpoint might entail remains, like so much in Schlegel's writing, fascinatingly obscure. But one can understand the *Study* essay as a first attempt to elaborate such a position, to describe the conditions for a synthetic knowledge of antiquity and modernity.

Schlegel's parallel of ancient and modern literatures takes a new route, historicizing artistic process rather than artistic products (as Herder had, by referring all process to nature). Schlegel preserves a single atemporal standard of excellence, but suggests that the paths to it must be different in antiquity and modernity, based on the age's respective principles of development, *Bildung*. He describes two models of *Bildung*: ancient, natural *Bildung* and modern, artificial (*künstliche*) *Bildung*. In the ancient world, culture followed a spontaneous, organic process of growth and decline. Works of art were created through an innate talent, and reflected the purity and wholeness of the natural world. Modern culture, on the other hand, takes its direction from individual reason rather than natural process, and so follows no single course. Though individual artists may create extraordinary works, the culture as a whole is so chaotic that no direction can be discerned for the present or future—and therefore, no artistic progress is possible. Schlegel points to a moment of catastrophe in antiquity, an undefined turning point, in which the natural *Bildung* of society degenerated, opening the way for artificial *Bildung*. In the phase of artificial *Bildung* that stretches into the present, it is no longer the principle of beauty that guides art, but rather that of "the interesting:" "*Interesting* is any original individuality, which contains a greater quantity of intellectual content or aesthetic energy" (*Study* 35; *KFSA* 1, 252). Schlegel ascribes to modern art the opposite of Kant's description of "disinterested pleasure" as the basis of the judgment of beauty.[3] "Interesting" art, unlike beautiful art, appeals directly to cognition and the individuality of the person who perceives it. Where the "objective" art of antiquity proceeded naturally from culture as a whole and was free of the marks of its creator, the "characteristic" art of modernity is always a product of the will, and reflects the personality of the artist. Though Schlegel draws sharp and even polemical distinctions between ancients and moderns, he grounds these contrasts in a historical narrative that diagnoses the problem and, if only dimly, outlines a form of therapy.

---

[3] Bäuerle, *Kommunikation*: 66.

Schlegel's discussion of Greek tragedy bears the marks of his continuing engagement with Winckelmann's *History*, especially in the *Study* essay's historical narrative and tone of rhapsodic praise.[4] In Winckelmannian fashion, Schlegel outlines a biological model of growth, fulfillment, and decline, which he maps onto the three Greek tragedians—an assessment he saw as an important critical advance.[5] After the primitive beginnings of Aeschylus and the perfection of Sophocles, the ancient ideal enters into a phase of decadence in Euripides, which corresponds to the beginning of modern *künstliche Bildung*. Sophocles represents "the *ideal of beauty*" (*Study* 62; *KFSA* 1, 300) to Schlegel, his works leading to a feeling of "*fullest satisfaction*" (*Study* 63; *KFSA* 1, 301). Though the sublime is occasionally mentioned in the text, it is the category of the beautiful that seems most applicable to Greek tragedy. Schlegel interprets Aristotelian *catharsis* as an equilibrium of positive and negative emotions, which leads to a feeling of harmony. Sophocles "knows how to mix terror and emotion beneficently in most perfect equality" (*Study* 62; *KFSA* 1, 298) and so ensures the emotional balance of the spectator. This conception will be ridiculed by Schiller and Goethe for suggesting that there is a kind of emotional reconciliation in works like the *OT*, but it will be important for August Wilhelm's lectures, and for Schelling and Hegel. Schlegel's idealization of the effect of ancient tragedy is, for better and for worse, one of his most important legacies, and is taken up powerfully by other idealist thinkers.

Though Shakespeare represents the apogee of modern art for Schlegel, his works have none of the beauty or harmony of Sophoclean tragedy. Schlegel argues, like Herder, that Shakespeare must be evaluated on different criteria from ancient tragedians, but Schlegel denies even a correspondence in their process. Post-classical art no longer reflects the wholeness of the natural world, but instead the divided subjectivity of its creator. Shakespeare's works appear as the height of artifice and individuality, creating an effect diametrically opposed to that of Greek works. Shakespeare is the exemplary modern author and *Hamlet* the exemplary modern work, because "there is perhaps no more perfect representation of the insoluble disharmony that is the actual object of philosophical tragedy" (*Study* 33; *KFSA* 1, 248). Where Sophocles' "aesthetic tragedy" moderates negative impressions with positive ones, Shakespeare's "philosophical tragedy" creates a "*maximum of despair*," making manifest "the eternal *colossal dissonance* that infinitely separates humanity and fate" (*Study* 33; *KFSA* 1, 248).

[4] See Stefan Matuschek, "Winckelmänner der Poesie: Herders und Friedrich Schlegels Anknüpfung an die *Geschichte der Kunst des Altertums*," *Deutsche Vierteljahrsschrift für Literaturwissenschaft und Geistesgeschichte* 77 (2003).

[5] *KFSA* 23, 212 (to A. W. Schlegel, 18.11.1794) mentions an essay concerning "Beurtheilung des Aeschylus, Sophokles, Euripides," and plans for a history of tragedy crop up repeatedly in the letters.

Despite presenting a forceful contrast of antiquity and modernity, Schlegel is far from arguing (as Herder did) that the products of the two must be viewed as utterly and irreconcilably opposed. The difference between natural and artificial development, he argues, has a history, and the two structures a necessary relation. Natural development proceeds cyclically, as a spontaneous process of growth to a "relative maximum, an unsurpassable *fixes proximum*" (*Study* 55; *KFSA* 1, 288) beyond which it can only decline, as all natural products wither and die. Artificial development, on the contrary, is governed by the restless demands of reason, which admit of no complete fulfillment. This development is progressive, striving towards an absolute that can never be reached because "there is no *highest interesting*" (*Study* 35; *KFSA* 1, 253). Yet as modern art achieves ever-greater heights of individuality, it finds itself in need of the natural principles by which it could be regulated:

> The excess of the individual therefore leads naturally to the objective; the interesting is the preparation of the beautiful, and the last aim of modern poetry can be none other than the *highest beautiful*, a maximum of objective aesthetic perfection. (*Study* 35; *KFSA* 1, 253)

Just as natural development spontaneously degenerated, so now, artificial development seems to be approaching a moment of transition, in which modern individuality and ancient objectivity will be combined. This age will, Schlegel suggests, surpass even the achievements of the ancients by combining the principles of the interesting and the beautiful.

The Greeks will lead the way to this artistic utopia. Modern artists can find in ancient Greek art "the *general natural history of art* [*allgemeine Naturgeschichte der Kunst*]" (*Study* 47; *KFSA* 1, 273) a distillation of artistic possibilities that will correct the excessive individuality and artificiality of modern art. Schlegel finds a way to value modernity's rational spirit by directing it to the "study of Greek poetry." Grasping the development of Greek art intellectually, modern artists can gain the intuition (*Anschauung*) necessary to restore the natural principle in their own works. Schlegel combines the two historical narratives at the heart of the *Querelle*, describing a change from the cyclical history of antiquity to the progressive history of modernity. He directs attention beyond the question of superiority to the problem of a reunion of antiquity and modernity.

Schlegel's understanding of how this union of the ancient and modern could be accomplished in practice is vague, but seems to be based equally on philosophical and artistic developments. Modern culture appears to be at a moment of transition, in which "here and there *the unmistakable beginnings of objective art and objective taste* are already stirring" (*Study* 89; *KFSA* 1, 356). The interrelation of the two spheres, creative and critical, is essential to Schlegel's vision for the future of poetry. He detects signs of a revival of taste in Kantian aesthetics, and finds new directions in creative practice being explored by Goethe, especially in *Faust*. "*The time* is *ripe*," Schlegel writes, "for an important revolution of aesthetic development [eine wichtige Revolution der ästhetischen Bildung]" (*Study* 89; *KFSA* 1, 356). Though the essay contains only one brief and rather detached nod to the French Revolution (*Study* 92; *KFSA* 1, 361–62), it is suffused by a revolutionary consciousness, which sees the present as a turning point in world history—though not, in the first instance, a political one.[6] More important for Schlegel is the "great moral revolution" that will prepare the way for a cultural revival in Germany:

> Aesthetic development has *reached the decisive point*, where left to itself it can no longer sink, but only be arrested in its progress through external violence, or (as in a physical revolution) be completely destroyed. I mean the great moral revolution, through which freedom in its battle with fate (within development) finally gains a decisive advantage over nature [die Freiheit in ihrem Kampfe mit dem Schicksal (in der Bildung) endlich ein entschiedenes Übergewicht über die Natur bekommt]. (*Study* 40; *KFSA* 1, 262)

The "battle with fate" recalls Schiller's description of the tragic protagonist, figuring modern development as a sublime struggle to assert humanity's control over nature. Schlegel forecasts a "moral revolution" as autonomy comes to be the guiding principle within culture, a step made possible by Idealist philosophy's (presumably Fichte's) delineation of the conditions of human freedom. From this understanding of human freedom, Schlegel suggests, will come liberation from the "*aesthetic prejudices*" that have damaged modern art—most of all, the remnants of a neoclassical theory of imitation (*Study* 41; *KFSA* 1, 263).[7] Schlegel's concept of an "aesthetic revolution" (*Study* 45; *KFSA* 1, 269) imagines a reciprocal influence of philosophical and artistic developments, in which modern reason will artificially recreate the natural qualities of Greek poetry.

When Schlegel came to revise the *Study* essay for an 1823 edition of his collected works, he redacted most uses of the word "revolution." Schlegel's later discomfort with the transformational fervor of the essay is evidence of the pregnancy of these words in their original form. This has often been viewed in a concrete political light, as an expression of Schlegel's support for the French Revolution, but the valences of Schlegel's usage are much

[6]See Ernst Behler, "Einleitung: Friedrich Schlegels Studium-Aufsatz und der Ursprung der romantischen Literaturtheorie," in *Friedrich Schlegel, Über das Studium der griechischen Poesie: 1795–1797* (Paderborn: Schöningh, 1981), 35–51. Schlegel's repeated use of the word "revolution" cannot, though, be divorced from the political completely.

[7]Towards the end of the essay, Schlegel reinterprets the doctrine of *Nachahmung* as imitation of "the *spirit of the whole—the pure Greekness*" rather than any particular "local form" (*Study* 83–84; *KFSA* 1, 346–47).

broader: moral, aesthetic, political, and anthropological at once. A famous *Athenäum*-Fragment describes the French Revolution, Fichte's *Wissenschaft-slehre*, and Goethe's *Wilhelm Meister* as "the greatest tendencies of the age" (*AF* 216: *KFSA* 2, 198), and the sentiment seems equally to characterize the Schlegel of the *Study* essay. Philosophical, artistic, and political forms were in transition, but these revolutionary movements remained only "tendencies" (*Tendenzen*), "without thorough execution [ohne gründliche Ausführung]" according to a draft of the fragment (*KFSA* 18, 85). By directing his contemporaries to the study of the Greeks, Schlegel hoped to give a more coherent form to the revolutionary impulses of his time. His vision of an "aesthetic revolution" is an implicit counterpart—a correction even—to the French Revolution. The study of Greek poetry is a means of orienting the revolutionary energies of the time to an aesthetic end.

Like Schiller in the *Aesthetic Letters*, Schlegel believes that modernity's revolutionary tendencies needed to be based on a firmer foundation in order to realize their potential, and (again like Schiller), he seeks this foundation in Greek art. The two differ profoundly, though, in their vision of how modernity should relate to ancient Greece: for Schiller, the value of ancient Greece lies in its ideal quality, which provides a counter-image to alienated modernity. For Schlegel, in contrast, it is not the ideal quality of Greek art that is primarily important (though his image of ancient Greece is profoundly idealizing), but its real historical existence. It is thus misleading to label Schlegel the "ancient" and Schiller the "modern," as is often done.[8] Schlegel is at once more immersed in the ancient and more emphatically modern than Schiller (which explains how it was possible for Schlegel to become the central figure of the Romantic movement). Their more profound difference concerns the status of history: for Schiller, history is a neutral container of events, a stage for individuals, cultures, and epochs to appear and be judged against an ideal that is essentially ahistorical (though is usually imagined through ancient Greece). For Schlegel, in contrast, history is a mode of existence, a dynamic force that creates its own unique possibilities at each moment. Schlegel's historical thought does not envision a teleology for modernity (as Schiller's does in the "aesthetic state" or "the ideal"), but an ongoing, progressive mode of self-creation. From his study of philology, perhaps, Schlegel gained a sense of both the reality and ideality of Greek culture. The relationship to the Greeks is characterized by a dynamic of desire and necessity that creates poetry out of the mutual implication of antiquity and modern: "From what the moderns desire, one must learn what poetry should become. From what the ancients do, what it must be. [Aus dem, was die Modernen wollen, muß man lernen, was die Poesie

---

[8] See Jauß, "Schlegels und Schillers Replik." Another way of putting this point is that the *Querelle* is simply not a useful lens through which to view Schlegel, though it may be for Schiller.

werden soll: aus dem, was die Alten tun, was sie sein muß]" (*LF* 84: *KFSA* 2, 157). The *Querelle*'s question, "antiquity or modernity?" is transformed into an imperative: antiquity *and* modernity.

SCHILLER: "THE LIMITS OF ANCIENT AND MODERN TRAGEDY"

When Schiller diagnosed the fever of "Graecomania," he was responding to the publication of excerpts from Schlegel's *Study* essay in 1796, especially the rhapsodic praise for Sophocles. Schiller's distich comes from a series of elegiac couplets entitled *Xenien* (guest-gifts), which appeared under the joint names of Schiller and Goethe in 1797. A number of them parody Schlegel's arguments, especially his description of Greek tragedy as a harmonious, satisfying art form:

> "Griechische und moderne Tragödie"
> Unsre Tragödie spricht zum Verstand, drum zerreißt sie das Herz so,
>   Jene setzt in Affekt, darum beruhigt sie so!
> "Entgegengesetzte Wirkung"
> Wir Modernen, wir gehn erschüttert, gerührt aus dem Schauspiel,
>   Mit erleichterter Brust hüpfte der Grieche heraus!

> [Greek and modern tragedy: Our tragedy speaks to the understanding, therefore it tears the heart so. The other creates affect, therefore it calms so!
> Opposed effect: We moderns, we go shocked, moved from the play; with lightened breast the Greek skipped out!] (*Xenien* 325–26: *FA* 1, 619)[9]

There is some irony to Schiller's attack; not only is it unfair to the consciously paradoxical nature of Schlegel's discussion of Greek tragedy, but it parodies a historical opposition of ancient and modern not so different from Schiller's own. Schiller seems to have been primarily incensed at Schlegel's denial of qualities of beauty and harmony to modern works (though the essay's praise of Goethe at his implicit expense could not have helped). Schlegel's conviction that modern tragedy had not achieved the heights of Sophocles would have been particularly galling to Germany's leading tragedian. Despite Schiller's idealization of the ancient world, he was not a great admirer of Greek tragedy in 1796. His tastes ran much more to modern works, and his knowledge of ancient tragedy and poetics was still rather sketchy. Between 1797 and 1803, however, an important change in Schiller's attitude to Greek tragedy is visible, which has never been adequately charted. Schiller's conversion to the Greeks in the late 1790s is a turning point in his creative practice, forming the dramaturgical basis for

---

[9]Cf. also the following two *Xenien*.

his "classical" tragedies, and especially for his appropriation of Greek forms in the 1803 *Bride of Messina* (*Die Braut von Messina*). Ultimately, Schiller will come to a view of Greek tragedy that sees antiquity as providing a ground for reflection on historical difference and the particular character of modernity.

Schiller's engagement with Greek tragedians began in 1788, by which point the twenty-nine-year-old had a concept of tragedy extensively formed by Shakespeare, French classical tragedy, Lessing, and Goethe, among others. The previous year had seen the publication of Goethe's *Iphigenia* and Stolberg's Sophocles translation, so Schiller's interest in the Greeks was timely and perhaps even opportunistic. Until the late 1790s, Schiller's comparisons of ancient and modern tragedies nearly always come out in favor of modernity, usually on the grounds of its more developed morality.[10] Characteristic of this judgment is the essay "On Tragic Art" ("Über die tragische Kunst"), the second of three essays on tragedy to be published in 1792–93. Schiller understands Greek tragedy to be based on a capricious divine necessity, which forecloses any perception that the events of tragedy are guided by "a teleological connection between things, a sublime order, a benevolent will" (*Essays* 9; *FA* 8, 261). He dislikes the struggle against fate portrayed in ancient works because "blind subjection to fate is always humiliating and insulting for a free, self-determining being. This is what leaves something to be desired even in the most splendid pieces of the Greek stage" (*Essays* 9; *FA* 8, 261). In 1792, the goal of tragedy is to prove the order of the world by demonstrating the power of human freedom. Greek works are unsuited to the task because they are animated by an inscrutable theology. Schiller accordingly decides the parallel of tragedies in favor of modernity: "If we moderns really must abandon the effort ever to restore Greek art, let alone to surpass it, tragedy alone might constitute an exception. To tragedy alone, perhaps, our scientific culture restores the loss it has brought about for art generally" (*Essays* 10; *FA* 8, 262).

This faith in progress, however, did not last. The turning point in Schiller's thought on Greek tragedy came in 1797, when, at the suggestion of Goethe, he studied Sophoclean tragedy and Aristotle's *Poetics*. The impact of this encounter has largely not been recognized by critics who overlook the scattered, though highly significant theoretical discussions of Schiller's letters.[11] Importantly, this was also the period when Schiller was turning his attention back to playwriting after a hiatus of almost ten years, and traces of

[10] Joachim Latacz, "Schiller und die griechische Tragödie," in *Tragödie: Idee und Transformation*, ed. Hellmut Flashar (Stuttgart: Teubner, 1997), 243.

[11] Major recent articles concerning Schiller and Greek tragedy miss the significance of the exchanges with Goethe: Latacz, "Schiller und die griechische Tragödie"; Ernst-Richard Schwinge, "Schiller und die griechische Tragödie," in *Schiller und die Antike*, ed. Paolo Chiarini and Walter Hinderer (Würzburg: Königshausen & Neumann, 2008).

the engagement with Greek tragedy and poetics are visible throughout his later plays. Responding especially to the *OT*, Schiller reconsiders dramatic representation of human freedom and comes to value tragedy's presentation of autonomy as radically limited. In Schiller's later theory and practice, free will and forms of necessity become inextricably entwined, as they seem to be for Oedipus. One can speculate that Goethe, who held a much darker view of tragedy, was an important influence.[12] Between 1797 and his death in 1805, Schiller wrote four tragedies (*Wallenstein, Mary Stuart, The Maid of Orleans*, and *The Bride of Messina*) pervaded by the lessons of Sophocles and Aristotle, while at the same time sketching, in letters and a preface, a historical poetics of tragedy. This period is known as Schiller's "classical" phase for good reason: throughout these works, Schiller strives for a tension of ancient and modern elements, employing forms and motifs gained from Greek practice. Ancient and modern principles do not merge for the later Schiller (as Schlegel hoped they would), but remain productively opposed in the creation of a form of high tragedy that recognizes both its descent and its distance from the Greeks.

The lessons Schiller draws from Aristotle and Sophocles mainly concern the creation of tragic plots: "That [Aristotle] lays the greatest weight on the connection of events [Verknüpfung der Begebenheiten] in tragedy, is to hit the nail straight on the head" (5.5.1797: *FA* 12, 246). The focus on construction and causality is notable in comparison with Schiller's earlier writings, which concentrate more on the representation of suffering and the viewer's response to pathos. After a reading of Sophocles' works, he writes to Goethe: "I find, the more I consider my own work and the treatment of tragedy among the Greeks, that the whole *cardo rei* lies in the art of creating a poetic fable" (4.4.1797: *FA* 12, 261). Poetic depiction, Schiller continues, can be more truthful than reality, a means of showing "the eternal basis [ewigen Grund] of human nature" (4.4.1797: *FA* 12, 261). The symbolic character of poetic truth now licenses the non-naturalistic characters of Greek tragedy, who are "ideal masks and not real individuals, as I find in Shakespeare's and your [Goethe's] pieces. [. . .] One obviously gets on much better with such characters in tragedy, they present themselves more quickly and their characteristics are more permanent and strong" (4.4.1797: *FA* 12, 262). The lack of internality that had seemed to mark ancient tragedy as inferior to modern works now appears to have a dramatic justification, as a means of presenting the action of the piece more directly. Psychology is now subordinated to a dramatic plan—a change in focus mirrored by the shift in Schiller's theory of the sublime from the earlier model of heroic struggle

[12] On Goethe's theory of tragedy, see Marie-Christin Wilm, "Die 'Construction der Tragödie': zum Bedingungsverhältnis von Tragischem und Ästhetischem in Goethes Tragödientheorie," *Goethe-Jahrbuch* 123 (2006); Boyle, "Goethe's theory of tragedy."

to the later model of historical observation. The freedom of the tragic hero is henceforth never pure, but manifests itself only within a chain of events conditioned by external forces.

The *OT* most of all inspires Schiller to develop his notion of freedom in tragedy. He reports to Goethe that he has been searching for a similar subject for his own work. In Sophocles' play

> the action [Handlung] has already happened, and therefore falls completely outside of the tragedy. Moreover, that which has happened, since it is irrevocable, is by its nature far more frightening, and the fear that something might *have happened*, grasps the mind quite differently from the fear that something may happen. (2.10.1797: *FA* 12, 330–31)

By setting the decisive actions outside of the stage time, Sophocles heightens the sense of inevitability, directing the audience's attention to the causal linkages that make up the action. Schiller famously describes the *OT* as a "tragic analysis. Everything is there already and it is simply unfolded" (2.10.1797: *FA* 12, 331). The analytic structure of the piece sets freedom wholly out of the picture; in Oedipus' investigation, we discover only the terrifying power of necessity. The pleasure of such a work lies, as Schiller suggests in "Concerning the Sublime," only in the subjective perception of causality, as the poet makes necessity—which in reality is blind and chaotic—into an object of rational analysis. The rational necessity of tragedy's poetic fable serves as an inoculation against the blind contingency of reality.

It is partly through the example of Shakespeare that Schiller articulates his changing views on poetics. In November 1797 he reads *Richard III* and writes to Goethe that it is "one of the most sublime [erhabenste] tragedies that I know. No Shakespearean piece reminded me so much of Greek tragedy" (28.11.1797: *FA* 12, 344). The judgment bespeaks the later concept of the sublime, which is now created by rational spectatorship of horror, rather than vicarious triumph of freedom. "It is so to speak the pure form of the tragic frightful that one enjoys," Schiller writes, "a high nemesis moves through the piece in all appearances, and one does not escape the feeling from the beginning to the end" (28.11.1797: *FA* 12, 344). The frightful, the sublime, and the Greek qualities of the work are linked in Schiller's description—an index of the changes in his thought from five years previous. Sublimity is created by the frightening perception of *nemesis*, an ineluctable force of retribution called up by the actions of the protagonist. The power of necessity no longer undermines sublimity, but comes to define it for Schiller. From this point forward, he will measure his work by the standards of "pure" or "real" tragedy gained from his reading of the Greeks.

In his massive *Wallenstein* trilogy (performed in 1798–99 and published in 1800), Schiller sought to put his theory into practice, applying the lessons of the *Poetics* to a historical theme taken from the Thirty Years' War. With reference to Aristotle, he writes that "discounting the insurmountable difference of modern from ancient tragedy, I believe I have afforded and will afford him satisfaction in all the essential demands" (to Körner, 3.6.1797: *FA* 12, 283).[13] The consciousness of difference—though it will never recede—now allows for commonality to emerge, based on tragedy's staging of freedom and determination. The trilogy explicitly thematizes the role of fate by portraying the main character's reliance on astrology for guidance. A powerful general fighting for the Holy Roman Empire, Wallenstein is tempted to betray the Emperor and conclude a separate peace with the Swedish enemy. Waiting for a signal from the stars, though, he delays taking decisive action until his plot has been discovered. Though his crime has not yet been committed, Wallenstein finds himself trapped in the very possibility of betrayal: "Bahnlos liegt's hinter mir und eine Mauer / Aus meinen eignen Werken baut sich auf, / Die mir die Umkehr türmend hemmt" (*Tod* 156–8: *FA* 4, 160: "Behind me there is no way, and a wall of my own works builds itself, which towering, stops me from turning back"). While waiting for the sign of a transcendent fate, Wallenstein has delivered himself to historical necessity.[14]

The final irony comes later, once the counterplot is already in motion. Wallenstein ignores the warnings of his astrologer and, in doing so, makes himself subject to the disaster foretold by the stars, as he is murdered at the hands of his lieutenant.[15] The moment Wallenstein rejects superstition, asserting his freedom from external determination, he brings on his own downfall. Like the *OT*, *Wallenstein* is concerned with the limits of human autonomy, but Schiller's work is profoundly ambivalent about the true power of fate. Individual freedom in *Wallenstein* appears caught between astrological determination and historical causality. This aporetic conception links the *Wallenstein* trilogy with the essay "Concerning the Sublime," and reflects an uncertainty towards the very possibility of freedom that is irreconcilable with Schiller's early theory of tragedy.[16] Schiller's reading of Sophocles and Aristotle seems to have been the catalyst for his reconception of tragic freedom as inextricable from the contingencies of historical existence.

Schiller is adamant that *Wallenstein* should not be regarded as an attempt to revive Greek tragedy.[17] Nevertheless, the importance of the ancient model was recognized immediately after its creation, in Johann Wilhelm Süvern's 1800 *Concerning Schiller's Wallenstein with Regard to Greek Tragedy*

---

[13] On the influence of Aristotle on *Wallenstein*, see Hartmut Reinhardt, "Schillers *Wallenstein* und Aristoteles," *Jahrbuch der deutschen Schillergesellschaft* 20 (1976).

[14] See Hans Feger, *Poetische Vernunft: Moral und Ästhetik im Deutschen Idealismus* (Stuttgart: Metzler, 2007), 105–34.

[15] Mario Zanucchi, "Die 'Inokulation des unvermeidlichen Schicksals': Schicksal und Tragik in Schillers *Wallenstein*," *Jahrbuch der deutschen Schillergesellschaft* 50 (2006): 159.

[16] See Michael Hofmann, "Die unaufhebbare Ambivalenz historischer Praxis und die Poetik des Erhabenen in Friedrich Schillers *Wallenstein*-Trilogie," *Jahrbuch der deutschen Schillergesellschaft* 43 (1999).

[17] See the letter to Körner, 8.1.1798: *NA* 29, 184.

(*Über Schillers Wallenstein in Hinsicht auf griechische Tragödie*). The short book recounts Schiller's trilogy in detail, arguing that it conforms to the essence of Greek tragedy by presenting an action ruled by fate. Yet Süvern finds that Wallenstein does not sufficiently demonstrate his freedom in the struggle with fate, that the "conclusion is more suffering than action."[18] This is, ironically, the reproach Schiller had directed at Greek tragedy almost ten years earlier. Schiller responds in a letter that sketches his understanding of the difference between ancient and modern works:

> I share with you the unconditioned admiration for Sophoclean tragedy, but it was a phenomenon of its time that cannot return, and to subject the living product of a certain individual present to a completely different time as a measure and model, is to kill rather than enliven art, which must always arise and act dynamically and vividly. Our tragedy, if we have anything of the kind, must struggle with the weakness, the inertness, the characterlessness of the spirit of the time, and with a base way of thinking. It must show power and character, it must seek to shake the mind, to raise it up, but not to relax it. Beauty is for a happy race, but one must seek to move an unhappy one in a sublime way [ein unglückliches muß man erhaben zu rühren suchen]. (to Süvern, 26.7.1800: *FA* 12, 522)

Schiller finds himself surprisingly close to Schlegel's notion that ancient tragedies create a sense of harmony while modern works leave us "shocked, moved" (in Schiller's parody). Schiller integrates a historical differentiation of the effect of tragedy with his earlier reflections on the quality of the sublime, seeing sublimity as an essentially modern form of experience.[19] Modern culture's alienation calls for a different form of art than ancient culture's wholeness. Modern artworks should afford audiences a mixed pleasure, shocking them out of complacency and steeling them against the disappointments of living in a degenerate age. Tragedy, which in ancient Greece had reflected the harmony of existence, in modernity has the task of reconciling viewers to disharmony.

The year 1802 brought Greek tragedy to the Weimar stage. August Wilhelm Schlegel's adaptation of Euripides' *Ion* was premiered on January 2, and cre-

---

[18] W. Süvern, *Über Schillers Wallenstein in Hinsicht auf griechische Tragödie* (Berlin: Königliche Realschule, 1800), 209.

[19] This had been suggested also in "Concerning the sublime," where sublimity was the later principle temporally, proceeding from a moral capacity that beauty's sensible play did not touch. See the parable of the two genii: *Essays* 73; *FA* 8, 826. Cf. also from the *Augustenburg Letters*: "For the man in the hand of nature, the need is therefore not so much for the sublime as for the beautiful, since he has long been moved by size and power before he begins to be receptive to the charms of beauty. For the man in the hand of art, the need is on the contrary for the sublime, since in the state of refinement he all too gladly fritters away the power that he brought with him from the state of wildness" (*FA* 8, 520).

ated a minor scandal for its unexpected mixture of tragedy and comedy. It was followed in May by Schiller's adaptation of Goethe's *Iphigenia* (unfortunately lost) and Friedrich Schlegel's classicizing tragedy *Alarcos*, widely judged a failure.[20] The string of performances revived Schiller's long-postponed notion of a tragedy "according to the most strict Greek form" (to Körner, 13.5.1801: *FA* 12, 570).[21] This resolution bore fruit in *The Bride of Messina, or the Enemy Brothers: A Tragedy with Choruses* (*Die Braut von Messina, oder die feindlichen Brüder: ein Trauerspiel mit Chören*), begun in summer 1802 and finished in February 1803. *Bride* implicitly responds to the earlier works, which Schiller saw as failed efforts to recreate Greek tragedy. Though Schiller had praised Goethe's *Iphigenia* as a thorough revival of Greek tragedy on its publication, he is now shocked by its modernity[22]:

> It [the *Iphigenia*] is so astonishingly modern and un-Greek that one cannot understand how it was possible ever to compare it to a Greek piece. It is wholly and only ethical [sittlich], but the sensible power, the life, the movement and everything that makes a work truly dramatic, is quite missing. (to Körner, 21.1.1802: *FA* 12, 593)

Schiller reproaches the piece for its failure to recognize the "limits of ancient and modern tragedy [Grenzen des alten und neuen Trauerspiels]" (22.1.1802: *FA* 12, 595), a critique that could have applied to all the classicizing dramas of 1802. Goethe's work appears to lack the gripping power that Schiller had found in Aristotle's notion of plot. Schiller's conception of modern drama requires a vigorous representation of conflict, which would challenge the audience's rational powers, rather than calming them. Modern tragedy, he suggests, must be more violent and frightful than Greek works, directed to the sublime rather than the beautiful. The works of Goethe and the Schlegel brothers seem to lack the basis in a philosophy of history that would allow them to achieve the sublime effect of tragedy.

Schiller's model in *Bride* has taken on an Aeschylean tinge, coinciding with his study of the 1802 translation by Friedrich Leopold Graf zu Stolberg. This is obvious in the central importance of the chorus and the motifs of family guilt and brotherly hatred. Though Schiller may also have been inspired by the *OT* and *Phoenician Women*, the plot of *Bride* recommended itself because "the piece allows itself to be an Aeschylean tragedy" (to Körner,

[20] See Hellmut Flashar, *Inszenierung der Antike: das griechische Drama auf der Bühne*, 2nd ed. (Munich: Beck, 2009), 47–57; Georg Reichard, *August Wilhelm Schlegels 'Ion': das Schauspiel und die Aufführungen unter der Leitung von Goethe und Iffland* (Bonn: Bouvier, 1987).

[21] The idea dates back to Schiller's first reading of the Greeks in 1788. See the letter to Körner, 20.8.1788: *FA* 11, 317.

[22] See Lesley Sharpe, "Schiller and Goethe's *Iphigenie*," *Proceedings of the English Goethe Society* 54 (1985); Benedikt Jessing, "Schillers Rezeption von Goethes *Iphigenie*," *Goethe-Jahrbuch* 122 (2005).

9.9.1802: *FA* 12, 626).[23] The work includes many of the typical forms of Greek tragedy: a prologue followed by a choral entrance song, stichomythia, choral odes, monodies, etc.[24] Moreover, Schiller preserves the unities of time, space (roughly), and action, and strews the piece with *sententiae* and other linguistic reminiscences of Greek tragedy. Yet any comparison—with Aeschylus, Sophocles, or Euripides—is limited: most obviously, the work takes place in medieval Sicily, centers around an amorous intrigue, and divides the chorus into two inimical groups (which may have been suggested loosely by the *Eumenides*). But this is all to be expected if one recalls Schiller's historical philosophy and reflections surrounding *Wallenstein*: *Bride* is not, and cannot be a Greek tragedy.[25] Though it employs Greek forms and themes, its dramatic core is, according to Schiller's historical theory, resolutely modern: the interweaving of individual freedom and historical causality. Where Schiller found in Greek tragedy a depiction of human freedom struggling to assert itself against divine necessity, in modern works he sought to depict freedom as essentially tragic, subject to contingent and inscrutable forces.

Bride seems to combine the analytical principle Schiller found in the *OT* with the frightful nemesis of Shakespearean works. The story concerns the ruling family of Messina, centered around its matriarch, Isabella. Her two sons, Cesar and Manuel, have hated one another from a young age, but have decided, following the death of their father, to reconcile. Unbeknownst to one another, though, both have fallen in love with Beatrice, who has been mysteriously confined in a cloister since birth. In the inevitable confrontation, Cesar kills his brother, and abducts Beatrice—only to learn, on bringing his beloved to Isabella, that Beatrice is his own sister. Tormented by guilt over the murder of his brother and his incestuous love, Cesar kills himself, dying at the feet of his wretched sister and mother. The plot includes reminiscences of a number of Greek tragedies: the motif of brotherly hatred recalls the *Seven* and *Phoenician Women*, the oracular utterances and incest motif the *OT*, the parent-child reunion the *Ion*. Yet these plot elements are so thickly interwoven that the work seems closer to the complex intrigues of baroque drama than any Greek tragedy. As Walter Benjamin pointed out, the work's "reflexive mirroring" of freedom and determination in historical

---

[23] See also the letter to Körner, 15.11.1802: *NA* 31, 171.

[24] See Wolfgang Schadewaldt, "Antikes und modernes in Schillers 'Braut von Messina,'" *Jahrbuch der deutschen Schillergesellschaft* 13 (1969). Bernhard Zimmermann, "Teoria e utilizzo del coro in Friedrich Schiller," in ". . . un enorme individuo, dotato di polmoni soprannaturali": *Funzioni, interpretazioni, e rinascite del coro drammatico greco*, ed. Andrea Rodighiero and Paolo Scattolin (Verona: Edizioni Fiorini, 2011).

[25] Some commentators overlook Schiller's historical philosophy, which describes how Greek forms are to be revived under modern conditions: e.g., Martin Mueller, *Children of Oedipus, and other essays on the imitation of Greek tragedy, 1550–1800* (Toronto: University of Toronto Press, 1980), 141–42.

events approaches the baroque's melancholy view of a world pervaded by the guilt of original sin.[26]

The final words, spoken by the chorus, express a response to the potential of human pursuits to miscarry catastrophically: "Das Leben ist der Güter höchstes *nicht*, / Der Übel größtes aber ist die *Schuld*" (2839: *FA* 5, 384: "Life is not the highest of goods, but the greatest of evils is guilt"). Schiller's conception of guilt (*Schuld*) internalizes the ancient concept of fate, making the individuals of the play morally responsible for the disastrous outcome.[27] The chorus at one point invokes the Furies of the *Eumenides* pursuing Orestes (2011–27: *FA* 5, 358), but the difference is more striking than the similarity: Schiller's mechanism of punishment is entirely psychological (closer to that of Euripides' *Orestes*, though there is no evidence of Schiller's ever reading the play). It is not based on a retributive concept of justice, but on a roughly theological concept of sin. On recognizing his incestuous desire, Cesar sees no possibility of purification: "So bin ich schuldig einer Greueltat / Die keine Reu und Büßung kann versöhnen" (2482–83: *FA* 5, 373: "Then I am guilty of an awful deed, which no regret or atonement can reconcile"). No *catharsis* is possible for the characters of *Bride*, who find themselves caught within an inscrutable logic of transgression and guilt. The only response possible—here as in the essay "Concerning the Sublime"—seems to be the chorus's stoical acceptance of the power of contingency: "Nicht an die Güter hänge dein Herz, / Die das Leben vergänglich zieren, / Wer besitzt, der lerne verlieren, / Wer im Glück ist, der lerne den Schmerz" (2305–8: *FA* 5, 367: "Do not hang your heart on goods that adorn life temporarily. Whoever possesses, let him learn to lose, whoever is in happiness, let him learn pain").

Schiller does not discuss the sublime explicitly in his preface to the work, entitled "On the Use of the Chorus in Tragedy" ("Über den Gebrauch des Chors in der Tragödie"), yet traces of the concept are present in his theory of the role of the chorus.[28] Schiller describes the chorus as a means of regulating the affective participation of the audience. By thematizing the observation of suffering, the chorus refracts the audience's response, helping the viewers to retain their autonomous power of judgment in the midst

---

[26] Benjamin, *Ursprung des deutschen Trauerspiels*, 301. The point is followed in more detail by Rolf-Peter Janz, "Antike und Moderne in Schillers 'Braut von Messina,'" in *Unser commercium: Goethes und Schillers Literaturpolitik*, ed. Wilfried Barner, Eberhard Lämmert, and Norbert Oellers (Stuttgart: Cotta, 1984).

[27] On the transformation of the ancient concept of fate, see Monika Ritzer, "Not und Schuld: zur Funktion 'antiken' Schicksalsbegriffs in Schillers 'Braut von Messina,'" in *Schiller heute*, ed. Hans-Jörg Knobloch and Helmut Koopmann (Tübingen: Stauffenburg, 1996).

[28] Schiller's practice is somewhat different from his theory; see Joachim Müller, "Choreographische Strategie: zur Funktion der Chöre in Schillers Tragödie *Die Braut von Messina,*" in *Friedrich Schiller, Angebot und Diskurs: Zugänge—Dichtung—Zeitgenossenschaft*, ed. Helmut Brandt (Berlin: Aufbau, 1987).

of sympathetic identification with the protagonists.[29] Within tragedy, the choral lyrics preserve the principle of freedom and form a counterpart to the suffering of the protagonists:

> If the blows with which tragedy touches our heart followed on one another without interruption, then suffering would triumph over action [so würde das Leiden über die Tätigkeit siegen]. We would become wrapped up in the matter [Stoff] and no longer float above it. In that the chorus holds the scenes apart, and steps between the passions with its calming observations, it gives us back our freedom, which would be lost in the storm of feelings. (FA 5, 289)

The reflections of the chorus fashion a space for the audience to abstract themselves from the powerful effect of tragedy; in this oscillation between affective participation and rational cognition, one recognizes the outlines of Schiller's theory of the sublime. Tragedy's "economy," its alternation of pathetic scenes and reflective odes realizes the division between sense and reason that informs Schiller's understanding of human faculties. The chorus appears as the rational instance within tragedy, an assertion of spiritual freedom against the suffering portrayed on stage.

Schiller's understanding of the "limits of ancient and modern tragedy" entails differentiating the ancient from the modern chorus. The historical dialectic of antiquity and modernity that has run through Schiller's thought receives one of its fullest expressions in *Bride*'s preface:

> Ancient tragedy, which originally concerned itself with gods, heroes, and kings, used the chorus as a necessary accompaniment. Tragedy found the chorus in nature, and used it because it found it. The actions and fates of heroes and kings are in themselves public, and were even more so in the simple primitive time. The chorus was consequently more a natural organ in ancient tragedy, it followed from the poetic form of real life. In modern tragedy it becomes an artificial organ, it helps *to bring forth* poetry. The modern poet no longer finds the chorus in nature, he must create it poetically and introduce it—that is, he must perform a transformation of the story he treats, whereby it is set back into that childlike time and into that simple form of life. (FA 5, 286)

Ancient and modern choruses have different origins and serve different functions. The modern chorus is useful because it is so utterly out of place, and therefore sets the poetic world of tragedy outside of contemporary experience. The chorus responds to alienation from nature with alienation from culture. It should be "a living wall [lebendige Mauer] that tragedy erects around itself in order to cut itself off purely from the real world and

---

[29]Michael Böhler, "Die Zuschauerrolle in Schillers Dramaturgie: Zwischen Aussendruck und Innenlenkung," in *Friedrich Schiller: Kunst, Humanität und Politik in der späten Aufklärung*, ed. Wolfgang Wittkowski (Tübingen: Niemeyer, 1982).

preserve its ideal basis, its poetic freedom" (*FA* 5, 285). The "poetic freedom" of tragedy is created by its existence in an autonomous sphere of representation, not bound to the everyday world of the senses. The chorus, as an anti-naturalistic element, ensures that the world of the drama is set off from the world of sense, just as it divides the action of drama into reflection and engagement. This, though, is quite different from its function in antiquity, when the chorus was simply the necessary accompaniment to the plots of tragedy. Where ancient tragedy conformed to natural surroundings, modern tragedy struggles against its artificial culture.

Schiller's differentiation of the effects of ancient and modern tragedy conforms to his historical opposition of the beautiful and sublime. The chorus appears as the answer to the modern need for sublimity—both for its resistance to naturalistic expectations and for its abstraction from the suffering of the protagonists. In both ways, it opposes the sensible world and asserts the rights of reason. In Schiller's historical thought, this is a uniquely modern need: "the chorus thus performs a far more necessary service to the modern tragedian than to the ancient poet" (*FA* 5, 286). In antiquity, before culture diverged from nature, the chorus was a harmonious element, part of the beautiful effect of ancient tragedy; now, the chorus is an aesthetic shock, which creates the educative disharmony of the sublime. Only in modernity does the full power of tragedy emerge, its ability to liberate its viewers from the world of sense. Schiller's thought on antiquity is based on a constant opposition of the role of art in ancient and modern cultures. This distinguishes him from Schlegel, who aimed ultimately at understanding their "absolute identity." For Schiller, modern tragedy cannot and should not seek to emulate the beauty of Greek works, but should seek to "move an unhappy race in a sublime way."

SCHELLING: IDENTITY AND HISTORY IN THE *PHILOSOPHY OF ART*

For Schlegel and Schiller, antiquity and modernity are divided by a chasm that appears difficult or impossible to bridge. Schelling's theory of the tragic in history seeks, almost desperately, to transcend this gulf. In lectures on the *Philosophy of Art* (*Philosophie der Kunst*) delivered between 1802 and 1805, Schelling sets himself a paradoxical task: on the one hand, to distinguish between the principles of ancient (Greek) and modern (Christian) art, and on the other, to show that these differences are philosophically insignificant. Schelling's method at this stage in his career is known as "identity philosophy" because it sought to understand the diversity of existing things as emanating from the unity of the absolute. Just as the body of a single organism has many parts with various functions, so too, Schelling argued, reality should be thought of as an infinitely differentiable whole (*Philosophy*

27; *SW* 1.5, 23–24). The absolute cannot be experienced as such, but only in one or the other of its "potences" (*Potenzen*): reality, ideality, or a balance of the two, "indifference" (*Indifferenz*). The potences, in differing degrees, circumscribe the possibilities of reality, and so give an *a priori* necessity to all of existence. Consequently, the work of philosophy is essentially "construction," the process of showing how experience proceeds from the absolute in its various potences. Though Schelling understands the absolute as unchanging and unaffected by history, his task of construction is a historical one in that it seeks to determine the ontological necessity pervading all past, present, and future existence.[30] All historical objects should be comprehensible as particular emanations of the ahistorical absolute. As in the *Philosophical Letters*, Schelling's approach aims to account for the apparent bifurcation of the worlds of sense and intellect (the real and ideal potence), and does so with a historical narrative pervaded by tragedy.

The function of art for Schelling is to represent the absolute—a task shared with philosophy, though the two are differentiated by potence: art represents the absolute in real, philosophy in ideal form. Understanding the significance of art means constructing its relation to the absolute, the way a particular work or form distills an infinity. The only idea that human imagination can form of the infinite, Schelling argues, is as divinity, so religion is the necessary basis for all artwork. In the mythologies of a religion (and Schelling is thinking mainly of Greek polytheism), individual gods represent different spheres of the absolute, but together they manifest its wholeness. Mythology allows the absolute to appear in real form, while remaining itself absolute, and thus provides "the necessary condition and first content of art" (*Philosophy* 45; *SW* 1.5, 405).[31] Schelling's interest in myth was a constant throughout his career, and binds his thought on art to that of his Stift comrades Hegel and Hölderlin. For all three, art is a means of negotiating a relationship to the divine—a theological approach that will be discussed in more detail in the next chapter. Mythology's representation of divinity in corporeal form achieves an interpenetration of universal and particular, and so forms the bridge between the absolute and the world of sense.

Schelling sees two fundamental forms of mythology, reflecting divinity either in the real or ideal potence: Greek mythology is oriented to the here and now and is characterized by a natural, realistic potence, while Christianity's eschatology makes it fundamentally historical, looking forward to the ideal and the infinite. Though these terms of opposition are unsurpris-

---

[30] The systematic difficulty of integrating history into Schelling's identity philosophy is discussed further in Devin Zane Shaw, *Freedom and nature in Schelling's philosophy of art* (London: Continuum, 2010), 104–12.

[31] See Bernhard Barth, *Schellings Philosophie der Kunst: Göttliche Imagination und ästhetische Einbildungskraft* (Freiburg: Alber, 1991), 150–54.

ing, Schelling is unusual in seeking to account historically for the transition from Greek to Christian worldviews:

> The material of Greek mythology was nature, the general intuition of the universe as nature; the material of Christian mythology was the general intuition of the universe as history, as a world of providence [Vorsehung]. This is the actual turning point of ancient and modern religion and poetry. The modern world begins when man tears himself loose from nature, but since he does not yet have any other home, he feels abandoned. When such a feeling comes over an entire race, it turns either voluntarily or compelled by an inner urge to the ideal world to make itself at home there. (*Philosophy* 59; *SW* 1.5, 427)

Schelling sees Christian modernity as defined by loss, by the absence of ancient gods and beliefs. Christianity became popular, Schelling suggests, at the moment when the decadence of the Roman Empire caused its citizens to turn away from the world surrounding them and seek solace in an ideal future. Such a future was offered by Christianity, which saw all of existence as governed by a moral order established by providence. Where Greek mythology produced "a representation of the infinite as such in the finite," Christianity sought "to take up the finite into the infinite" (*Philosophy* 61; *SW* 1.5, 430). From these opposed relations to the sensible world, opposed forms of art developed.

Schelling reverses the typical opposition of ancient beauty and modern sublimity. Greek art does not recognize the existence of an ideal world beyond it and seeks to make the finite itself infinite; this "rebellion [Aufstand]" of the real against the ideal is the principle of sublimity, and fundamental to ancient art.[32] Modern art, however, seeks to shed its finitude and reach the infinite through "surrender [Hingabe]" of the human to the divine; this leads it to the principle of beauty (*Philosophy* 62; *SW* 1.5, 430). Christianity's idealistic quality deprives its artwork of the real points of reference that the Greeks could rely on, making modern art more individualistic, as both Schlegels had argued.[33] Modernity's individualistic, original art appears to Schelling as a deficiency, since it deprives works of the universality that ancient art could attain. Christian art, since it is based on the principle of particularity, exists "only as a transition or as being non-absolute in opposition to the first [Greek]" (*Philosophy* 82; *SW* 1.5, 456). In order for Christianity to attain a developed artistic basis, a "new mythology" is needed, which would afford Christianity's idealism a deeper grounding in the real world (and therefore be more communicable than individual imagination). Schelling

---

[32] The notion seems related to A. W. Schlegel's description of tragedy's "Empörung gegen das Schicksal" (*KAV* 1, 738).

[33] The *Study* essay is almost certainly an influence, and Schelling also borrowed A. W. Schlegel's manuscript Berlin lectures while preparing his own.

suggests that developments in the sciences may help to bring this about by striving towards a universalizing knowledge of the natural world, which would "plant its [Christianity's] ideal divinities into nature itself" (*Philosophy* 76; *SW* 1.5, 449). This sense of modernity as a period of transition, along with the hope for a new mythology, was common to the Tübingen Stiftler (and shared by Friedrich Schlegel) around 1800.[34] All looked forward to a future in which elements of Greek religion would be restored to Christianity, and modern spirituality would appropriate ancient aesthetic culture. Schelling's historical thought is distinguished by its insistence that the antithesis of ancient and modern is "merely formal"—that is, inessential to the character of the art each age produces, which always presents the "absolute identity of the general and the particular" (*Philosophy* 78; *SW* 1.5, 452). For Schelling, artistic process is the same in antiquity and modernity, and the discrepancy between their two products is attributable only to the differing mythological materials available to the artist.[35] Schelling describes these differences as starkly as Schlegel or Schiller, but he accounts for them by contingent and reversible factors, which are seen as inessential to art's philosophical significance. This has led many commentators to brand Schelling's identity philosophy as ahistorical, a reproach that gains much of its piquancy from the retrospective contrast with Hegel's thought.[36] Yet Schelling's method is more audacious in its relation to history than is generally recognized: his view of historical difference does not ignore the importance of history, but explicitly denies it. He recognizes fully the historicity of artistic phenomena, but denies that this has any ontological validity. In comparison to the constant oppositions of antiquity and modernity of the time, this must be understood as a principled position, and not as a failure to attain Hegel's historicization of ontology. Schelling's system is not so much ahistorical as anti-historical.[37] The consequences for his approach to tragedy are particularly striking: the proverbial antithesis of Sophocles and Shakespeare becomes problematic and must be transformed in order to establish a continuity between ancient and modern tragedy.

Drama is the capstone of Schelling's discussion of the forms of art, closing the investigation of poetry and the entire course of lectures. Tragedy's

[34] See Manfred Frank, *Der kommende Gott: Vorlesungen über die neue Mythologie* (Frankfurt: Suhrkamp, 1982); George S. Williamson, *The longing for myth in Germany: religion and aesthetic culture from Romanticism to Nietzsche* (Chicago: University of Chicago Press, 2004), 56–59.

[35] Berbeli Wanning, *Konstruktion und Geschichte: das Identitätssytem als Grundlage der Kunstphilosophie bei F.W.J. Schelling* (Frankfurt: Haag + Herchen, 1988), 59.

[36] Explicitly in Peter Szondi, "Schellings Gattungspoetik," in *Poetik und Geschichtsphilosophie II*, ed. Wolfgang Fietkau (Frankfurt: Suhrkamp, 1974), 307. Essential for Szondi's critique is Jürgen Habermas, *Das Absolute und die Geschichte: von der Zwiespältigkeit in Schellings Denken* (Bonn: Bouvier, 1954), 196–98.

[37] See Gerhard Plumpe, *Ästhetische Kommunikation der Moderne I: Von Kant bis Hegel* (Opladen: Westdeutscher Verlag, 1993), 193.

interpenetration of fate and free will exemplifies the general function of art, as the appearance of absolute identity in sensible form.[38] Despite its idealist premises, though, Schelling's approach to tragedy is surprisingly Aristotelian. Much of it appears as an effort to deduce the *Poetics a priori*, following from the premise that "the essence of tragedy is a real and objective struggle between freedom in the subject and necessity" (*Philosophy* 251; *SW* 1.5, 693). The tragic conflict described is familiar from the "Tenth Letter," parts of which Schelling repeats verbatim. One major point of difference is worth noting and corresponds to the identity philosophy's general approach to art. Schelling poses the question of reconciliation far more urgently than he had earlier: "Are [. . .] these contradictions not purely shattering," he asks, "and where lies the basis of the beauty which the Greeks nevertheless achieved in their tragedies?" (*Philosophy* 253; *SW* 1.5, 696).

Though Schelling's discussion of tragedy is oriented primarily to philosophical content, it cannot avoid the question of tragic effect, and the meaning of *catharsis*. Tragedy, for Schelling, must resolve the conflict it establishes in order to afford a purifying glimpse into the unity of the absolute. This is possible, as we know from the *Letters*, through a sublime action in which the innocent hero accepts guilt and punishment, sacrificing and proving his own freedom in the same instant. Sublimity for Schelling (as for Hermann) is the ontological basis of Aristotelian *catharsis*: "This is the basis of the reconciliation and harmony which lies in them, that they do not leave us feeling shattered, but healed, and, as Aristotle says, purified" (*Philosophy* 254; *SW* 1.5, 697). Reconciliation (*Versöhnung*) and *catharsis* describe the same process, a reconstitution of affective harmony from the discord of tragic events.[39] Even though Schelling sees this process, in speculative terms, as the attainment of an ontological insight, his approach to tragedy remains defined by an Aristotelian crux.[40]

The theory of tragedy in the *Philosophy of Art* is pervaded by an imperative of reconciliation, conceived simultaneously as an affective state and a philosophical insight. Tragedy's proof of the absolute union of freedom and necessity now brings with it an affirmation far more comprehensive than it did in the *Philosophical Letters*, in which Oedipus' sublime acceptance of necessity had appeared impossible in the modern age. Some of this change

[38] Dieter Jähnig, *Schelling: die Kunst in der Philosophie*, 2 vols. (Pfullingen: Neske, 1966/99), 2, 244.

[39] See Marie-Christin Wilm, "Ultima Katharsis: zur Transformation des aristotelischen Tragödiensatzes nach 1800," in *Die Tragödie der Moderne: Gattungsgeschichte—Kulturtheorie—Epochendiagnose*, ed. Daniel Fulda and Thorsten Valk (Berlin: de Gruyter, 2010).

[40] In more superficial ways, as well, Schelling shows his debt to Aristotle. See the discussions of tragedy's morality (Aristotle's ἦθος), the miraculous (τὸ θαυμαστόν), and the *deus ex machina* (*Philosophy* 256–58; *SW* 1.5, 701–703). The one profoundly non-Aristotelian element is Schelling's discussion of the chorus, which is largely derivative from A. W. Schlegel's lectures.

can be attributed to the influence of the Schlegels, who similarly emphasized ancient tragedy's reconciliatory power. Schelling discusses a number
of ancient works, which, he argues, are united by their reconciliatory character. The *Eumenides* and *OC* take on great importance for their representation of characters attaining reconciliation with their own situations.[41] Re-
gardless of whether the end is a happy one, Schelling argues, tragedy must
portray its characters accepting the outcome of the drama: "Only from this
inner reconciliation proceeds the harmony that we demand for completion" (*Philosophy* 258; *SW* I.5, 703). Orestes' acquittal and Oedipus' peaceful
death appear as alternative ways of demonstrating human freedom in the
struggle with fate, but with more affirmative conclusions. When Schelling
describes "the one true *tragic* in tragedy [das einzig wahrhaft *Tragische* in der
Tragödie]" (*Philosophy* 254; *SW* 1.5, 697), he is speaking most of all of the
process of reconciliation.

As the depiction of a universal conflict in humanity's constitution, tragedy
has a constant character in antiquity and modernity. Yet Christian religion
transforms the ancient concepts of freedom and necessity, with important
implications for tragedy. At the heart of Schelling's description of Greek
works was a notion of fate as a natural force powerful enough to undermine
individual freedom radically. Schelling's reading of the *OT* assumes that necessity is strong enough to make Oedipus guilty of a crime against his own
will. Guilt in antiquity could be conditioned purely by circumstance, and
so carried no moral implications. Christianity, by contrast, sees the universe
as "a moral world," and freedom as its essential quality (*Philosophy* 61; *SW*
1.5, 430). For such a worldview, guilt is always immoral, since it must ema-
nate from a free action. An unavoidable crime—which Schelling sees as the
ideal plot of tragedy—is impossible under Christianity. Christian religion
appears unable to recognize the essential tragic conflict of freedom and
necessity, and so to be incapable of tragedy. Variations of this point will be
articulated by Hegel, Nietzsche, and Benjamin, and a related thesis (though
blaming the Enlightenment rather than Christianity) is central to George
Steiner's argument for the "death of tragedy."[42] Though rarely acknowledged
as such, Schelling is an important precursor of these discussions, one of the
first thinkers explicitly to question whether tragedy is possible in modernity.

Schelling first demonstrates the possibilities for modern, Christian tragedy in the plays of Shakespeare. Just as certain Greek plays substantially
formed notions of ancient tragedy, there was a similarly restricted Shake-

[41]Cf. A. W. Schlegel, *KAV* 1, 735–37 and 742–44.
[42]George Steiner, *The death of tragedy* (London: Faber and Faber, 1961), 193. Important
recent responses are Eagleton, *Sweet violence*. Christoph Menke, *Tragic play: irony and theater
from Sophocles to Beckett*, trans. James Phillips (New York: Columbia University Press, 2009).

spearean canon at this moment, which emphasized *Macbeth* and *Hamlet* especially.[43] Consciously or not, part of the appeal of these works must have lain in their concentration on a single central figure, whose errors and downfall could be made to conform to Aristotelian notions of tragic plot and protagonist. Lacking a concept of fate, Shakespeare's plays represent necessity subjectively, as a facet of character: "Character appears in the place of ancient fate in his [Shakespeare's] works, but he lays such a powerful *fatum* into that character that it can no longer be counted as freedom, but appears as insurmountable necessity" (*Philosophy* 269; *SW* 1.5, 720). Macbeth would be the paradigm of such a figure, becoming guilty through an action in which "there is no objective necessity," so "it is character that is decisive" (*Philosophy* 269; *SW* 1.5, 721). Macbeth's drive for power is strong enough, Schelling argues, to function like the necessity imposed by fate in ancient works, but this form of necessity is not insurmountable, nor is it blameless. Shakespearean tragedies represent *nemesis* in the downfall of their guilty figures, but this is not the fate of the Greeks. Rather, it is a force operative within history, governed by a causal logic of action and reaction. Shakespeare does not represent either guilt or retribution as absolute necessity, but depicts "*freedom* struggling *with freedom*" (*Philosophy* 270; *SW* 1.5, 722). For Schelling, this makes his works too mired in the contingent to afford the properly tragic insight into the absolute.

Though Shakespeare fails to create the sense of reconciliation that is essential to tragedy, his works nevertheless have a different type of beauty. Like Herder, Schelling describes Shakespeare as portraying human existence in all its individuality, where Greek tragedy created a closed totality. Tragedy in modernity appears an entirely different instrument than it did in antiquity:

> That ancient lyre enticed the whole world with *four* strings; the new instrument has a thousand strings, it splits the harmony of the universe in order to create it, and therefore is always less calming for the soul. The severe, all-soothing beauty can exist only with simplicity. (*Philosophy* 271; *SW* 1.5, 723)

Though Shakespeare's works achieve a kind of harmony, it is chaotic and unsettling, commensurate with the complex reality of modernity. Indeed, characteristic of modern drama is a "*mixing of opposites*" in which tragedy and comedy interpenetrate (*Philosophy* 267; *SW* 1.5, 718). The hybrid quality of modern drama destroys insight into the tragic, which is based on seeing through opposition to identity.[44] Whereas Greek tragedy achieved

---

[43] The range of reference may have been wider for Shakespeare than for Greek tragedy, though; Germany had a complete translation of Shakespeare in 1782: see Paulin, *Shakespeare in Germany*: 127–32.

[44] Wanning, *Konstruktion und Geschichte*: 243.

a reconciliatory clarity detached from the passion of events on stage, Shakespeare leaves our thoughts and emotions impure. His works plunge us deeper into the sensible, rather than raising us to a vision of absolute identity.

The perceived difference between Sophocles and Shakespeare strikes at the heart of Schelling's concept of historical construction, which must be able to prove that true, reconciliatory tragedy is possible in modernity. Otherwise, modern art would be unable to represent the absolute in its purest form—an argument Hegel's historical philosophy countenances, but Schelling's identity philosophy cannot. In order to prove the possibility of an identity of ancient and modern art, he must show that Christian tragedy is possible.[45] Though Schelling has based his account of modern drama entirely on Shakespeare, he is forced to look elsewhere for the true tragic in modernity: "we must be able to hope for a Sophocles of the differentiated world, for a reconciliation within what we call *sinful* art" (*Philosophy* 273; *SW* 1.5, 725–26). The answer to this hope, Schelling finds, "is suggested from a previously little-known side," the Spanish dramatist Calderón de la Barca, whose *Devotion of the Cross* (*La Devoción de la Cruz*) had recently been translated into German by A. W. Schlegel (*Philosophy* 273; *SW* 1.5, 726). Though Schelling has only read this one play, he finds realized in it the reconciliatory possibilities of modern tragedy that had been so lacking in Shakespeare. As a Catholic, Calderón appears to have a different relationship to guilt and sin. Schelling distinguishes between the purely spiritual religion of (Protestant) Christianity and Catholicism, which is "according to its nature a mixture of the sacred and profane, which assumes sin in order to prove the power of grace in their reconciliation" (*Philosophy* 269; *SW* 1.5, 720). Where Protestantism sees sin as a choice of the individual, Catholicism considers it (as original sin) unavoidable, but reconcilable. It thus allows for a true conflict of freedom and necessity, which will be resolved not by human action, but by divine forgiveness.

Calderón's surprising and barely-anticipated entrance as *deus ex machina* is crucial to Schelling's historical construction of tragedy, which must demonstrate the continuity of the genre from antiquity to modernity. Schelling's relief at finding a genuine modern tragedy is palpable in a letter he wrote to A. W. Schlegel just after reading the piece: "I see that what in theory one thought to be a problem whose solution lay in the distance, here really is solved" (21.10.1802: *AA* 3.2.1, 502). Schelling had evidently been seeking just such a work, which would prove that art in the modern world could serve the same reconciliatory end it did in antiquity. The tragic element in Calderón's work lies in the way it portrays a modern, Christian counterpart to ancient fate:

---

[45] Ibid., 245.

The first principle and, so to speak, the basis of the entire edifice of his art is admittedly what the Catholic religion has given him, to whose view of the universe and of the divine order of things it essentially belongs that there be *sin* and sinners so that through the mediation of the church God may prove his grace on them. Thus is introduced a general necessity of sin, and in Calderón's piece under discussion the entire fate [Schicksal] develops out of a kind of divine predestination [Schickung]. (*Philosophy* 273; *SW* 1.5, 726)

Where the tragic in antiquity depicted guilt as a result of unavoidable error, Calderón recognizes a "general necessity of sin" that makes humans guilty through divine necessity. Schelling's description of the play emphasizes that the characters, like Oedipus, become guilty through circumstances beyond their control. Yet whereas ancient tragedy depicted necessity in order to show the triumph of human freedom, Calderón aims to demonstrate the benevolence of the divine. The tragic in paganism leads to a vindication of the immanent (as human freedom), in Catholicism to a proof of the transcendent (the grace of God). Both reach the reconciliation that is fundamental to the tragic, but Calderón's is appropriate to the differentiated Christian world, in which meaning resides solely in God.

The tragic in Calderón affords a vision of order beyond the divisions of earthly existence. Like the Greek tragedians, Calderón offers a quasi-philosophical insight in his works. He is characterized by reason (*Vernunft*, in contrast to Shakespeare's *Verstand*, "understanding"), and depicts "the absolute world itself" (*Philosophy* 275; *SW* 1.5, 729). The parallel of Calderón and Sophocles replaces the conventional Shakespearean one to prove that the tragic is possible in modernity. Where the consideration of Shakespeare led the parallel into aporia, Calderón allows it to proceed on the basis of identity. Calderón's drama, like Sophocles', represents the relation between man and god, demonstrating the order of the absolute in real actions. The miraculous occurrences portrayed in Calderón's works prove the benevolence of God, even to the guilty and unfortunate. Schelling recounts the story of the *Devotion of the Cross*, which concludes with the sinner Julia promising atonement while clasping a cross, which levitates and draws her up into heaven. Such a miraculous ending leads to a Christian form of reconciliation, which "calms, like the end of Oedipus or the final lot of Antigone" (*Philosophy* 276; *SW* 1.5, 731).

The weakness, if not the scandal, of Schelling's argument is hard to deny. Two systematic imperatives lead Schelling to introduce Calderón in so transparently willful a manner: on one hand, the need to establish a continuity of ancient and modern artworks; and on the other, the need to demonstrate the reconciliatory end of tragedy. Looking back to Schlegel and Schiller, one can discern continuities in both efforts. The writings of all three are pervaded by a consciousness of the divide between ancient and modern tragedies. What is most missing in modern works, they agree, is a sense of reconciliation; for Schlegel and Schelling, this is to be lamented; for Schiller, it is to be affirmed. The recognition of difference leads each to search for a means of restoring some form of continuity: Schlegel's hopes for an aesthetic revolution, Schiller's composite tragedy *Bride*, Schelling's advocacy of Calderón. None of these was very convincing in its time, and the flaws are only more apparent today. Yet they are indicative of a growing interest in the antiquity of the ancient—what distinguishes the Greeks from us—and, reciprocally, what makes modernity modern. Thinking about tragedy spurs them all to stretch their notions of modernity to encompass the unexpected, and to conceive of themselves as part of a larger historical process. In many ways, Hegel and Hölderlin will offer more compelling visions of the place of tragedy in history, but this first stage of idealist thought is unique in the tenacity with which it considers modernity as a problem. Art, and tragedy in particular, appears to offer some kind of solution, a way of finding meaning in the apparent chaos of history. From this period, Greek tragedy becomes profoundly, and often paradoxically, implicated in questions of historical existence. For idealist thinkers, thinking about tragedy was an essentially historical endeavor, and the challenge for historical thought, reciprocally, was to confront tragedy.

CHAPTER 5

Tragic Theologies

SCHELLING, HEGEL, AND HÖLDERLIN were all trained to be pastors—not philosophers, poets, or philologists.[1] This is often forgotten in discussions of Idealism, but crucial to understanding the reasons why all three turn to tragedy in the 1790s. On leaving the Tübingen Stift—Hegel and Hölderlin in 1793, and Schelling in 1795—they were expected to enter the clergy of Württemberg, the duchy in the southwest of Germany in which they grew up. In Tübingen, they had received five years of education free of charge, of which the latter three were devoted to theology. Their course of study included extensive training in ancient languages and philosophy, which were seen as necessary auxiliary competencies for church service. The Stift was both a religious and a political institution, ensuring clerical orthodoxy while binding educated citizens to the rulers—an especially important role in an age of changing ideas of authority.[2] The close connection between church and state hierarchies made the Stift atmosphere particularly fraught in the late 1780s, when the Pantheism Controversy and the French Revolution seemed to threaten received ideas of religion and civic organization alike. Meeting with the critical impulses of Kantian philosophy, these challenges to prevailing orthodoxy grew still more explosive, drawing teachers and students into heated disputes.[3]

The details of these controversies are often quite esoteric, but a central question for Idealism is the role of reason in religious metaphysics. Kant's position in the first two *Critiques* was equivocal: reason denied the theoretical certainty of religion (since any statements about God would pertain

*English biographies of Hegel are Terry Pinkard, *Hegel: a biography* (Cambridge: Cambridge University Press, 2000), and (in much greater depth, on the early years), H. S. Harris, *Hegel's development: toward the sunlight, 1770–1801* (Oxford: Clarendon, 1972); H. S. Harris, *Hegel's development: night thoughts (Jena 1801–1806)* (Oxford: Clarendon, 1983). The major English biography of Hölderlin is David Constantine, *Hölderlin* (Oxford: Clarendon, 1988). On tragedy in the works of both, the best English reference is Schmidt, *On Germans and other Greeks*. There are good essays on both in Miguel de Beistegui and Simon Sparks, eds., *Philosophy and tragedy* (London: Routledge, 2000).

[1] Schelling and Hegel, of course, went on to complete their dissertation and habilitation in philosophy, but somewhat later.

[2] The context is sketched by Wilhelm G. Jacobs, *Zwischen Revolution und Orthodoxie? Schelling und seine Freunde im Stift und an der Universität Tübingen* (Stuttgart: frommann-holzboog, 1989).

[3] See Dieter Henrich, "Philosophisch-theologische Problemlagen im Tübinger Stift zur Studienzeit Hegels, Hölderlins und Schellings," *Hölderlin-Jahrbuch* 25 (1987).

to the *noumenon*), but, practically, reason demanded that one act as if the postulates of Christian religion were absolutely valid. Kant's middle road sought to show that critical philosophy was compatible with Christianity, but at the same time, its argument that God could not be experienced immediately armed detractors with a new and powerful tool to assault religious certainty. These tensions deepened with the Pantheism Controversy, in which F. H. Jacobi imputed Spinozist positions to Lessing, arguably the major figure of the German Enlightenment before Kant.[4] Jacobi argued that Spinozism—understood as the concept of a single, divine substance as the ground of all reality—was the necessary conclusion of religion based on reason alone. Spinozism was dangerous to Christianity because it denied any division between divine and human will, and so seemed to sweep away freedom and grace at once. The Controversy (launched in 1785) and Kantian critique combined to make the question of the relation of religion and reason urgent throughout the German-speaking world. The young Idealists, especially Schelling and Hölderlin, were impressed by the Spinozist position, but at the same time seem to have recoiled from the rationalistic extremes of Enlightenment thinkers.[5] The challenge, as they saw it, was to fashion a place for reason within religion and for faith within philosophy.

This chapter will trace the nexus of religion, philosophy, politics, and tragedy, concentrating on Hegel and Hölderlin in their years after the Stift.[6] Both Hegel and Hölderlin understand Greek tragedy—especially the *OT* and *Antigone*—through the lens of theology, and see Sophocles' works as the representation of a moment of transition within Greek religion. In broad terms, their theories differ from Schelling's and Schiller's in seeing Greek tragedy as a historical and progressive art form: tragedy does not just exist within temporality, but is itself a historical force, which reflects and contributes to changes in ancient Greek theology. Both conceive religion as a (and even *the*) central element of social existence, and not as a sphere separated from political life.[7] Hegel's and Hölderlin's approaches to tragedy are not

---

[4] On the Pantheism Controversy, see Frederick C. Beiser, *The fate of reason: German philosophy from Kant to Fichte* (Cambridge, MA: Harvard University Press, 1987), 75–83.

[5] As in Hegel, *WZB* 1, 21–33 (from the *Fragmente über Volksreligion und Christentum*); Hölderlin, *SWB* 3, 78–79 (to Johanna Gock, 14.2.1791); Schelling's (somewhat more positive) attitude in the *Letters* has been sketched in Chapter 3. Sources are helpfully collected in Christoph Jamme and Frank Völkel, eds., *Hölderlin und der deutsche Idealismus: Dokumente und Kommentare zu Hölderlins philosophischer Entwicklung und den philosophisch-kulturellen Kontexten seiner Zeit*, 4 vols. (Stuttgart: frommann-holzboog 2003), 1, 320–73.

[6] The Christological roots of Schelling's notion of sacrifice in tragedy have been discussed in the previous chapter, as have his views on religion. Though there would be more to say about religion in Schelling, Christian theology pervades his early writings on tragedy to a lesser extent than it does those of Hegel and Hölderlin.

[7] See Thomas A. Lewis, *Religion, modernity, and politics in Hegel* (Oxford: Oxford University Press, 2011), 17–24.

only more historically contextualized than those discussed previously, but more immediately engaged politically.[8] Indeed, to distinguish religion from other concerns in their early thought is artificial, but nevertheless useful for showing the ways that theological interests ground understandings of tragedy that, in their developed forms, are not obviously Christianizing. Hegel would distance himself from the religio-political conceptions of his early writings, in favor of a more rigid distinction between spheres of meaning and historical epochs (as Hölderlin, though more ambiguously, does as well).

Understanding the religious background to Hegel's and Hölderlin's theories of tragedy draws out a crucial (and controversial) aspect of their thought: a focus on reconciliation as the end of tragedy. For both, the fundamental problem of tragedy is how it can present reconciliation as the end of conflict and division.[9] The urgency of this question stems from an inquiry into the relation of human and divine spheres that Hegel and Hölderlin undertook together and separately in the late 1790s, which left its marks on their understandings of tragedy well beyond. For both, tragedy represents processes that appear incomprehensible in such a way that they can be apprehended as rationally necessary. This makes tragedy a uniquely privileged mode of historical thought, for it offers the possibility of finding meaning in events that seem irreducibly chaotic. Tragedy is particularly compelling at this time of religious, philosophical, and political controversy, because it orders conflict and upheaval into a meaningful and even reconciliatory form.

A Poetic Religion

Tracing the roots of Hegel's and Hölderlin's understanding of tragedy requires looking back to a period of close interchange in the years 1797–1800, when both were living in the Frankfurt area. Hölderlin had been employed as a private tutor in the house of a wealthy banker from 1796, and he secured a similar post for Hegel, who arrived in early 1797. Their friendship seems to have continued through Hölderlin's flight to nearby Homburg in 1798, following the discovery of his affair with the mistress of the house. The close interactions between them only came to a close towards the end of 1800, when Hegel left for Jena, where he would begin life as a professional philosopher. It was in these years that the distinctive features of both of their understandings of tragedy began to emerge, though the intellectual

[8] This is not to deny the political context of Schiller's and Schelling's appeals to freedom (which was emphasized in the previous chapters). Hegel and Hölderlin, though, emphasize the *particular* historical content and context of tragedy far more—where for Schiller and Schelling, the political valences of tragedy are broadly conceived as universal.

[9] On Hegel's notion of reconciliation, see Michael O. Hardimon, *Hegel's social philosophy: the project of reconciliation* (Cambridge: Cambridge University Press, 1994), 95–119.

questions that tragedy would answer had been evolving since Tübingen. In their first years after leaving the Stift, Hölderlin's philosophical thought developed far more quickly than Hegel's, and produced a significant challenge to Fichte's subjective idealism.[10] Hölderlin's philosophical approach at this stage was directed towards reconstituting a moment of preconscious union, which, he argued, must have preceded the division between subject and object that forms the basis of conceptual knowledge. Beauty seemed to offer a glimpse of such a nonrational, but nevertheless perfectly ordered state, preserving the memory of such a union. Hölderlin's "philosophy of union" (*Vereinigungsphilosophie*) is expressed in the penultimate version of his novel *Hyperion*, as the hope, "to end that eternal conflict between our self and the world, to bring back the peace of all peace, which is higher than any reason, to unite ourselves with nature in one infinite whole" (*SWB* 2, 256).

Hölderlin's goal of reunion with nature through aesthetic experience was social as well as individual, and imagined a broader cultural reorientation that would remodel society according to aesthetic principles. From their time in Tübingen, Hegel and Hölderlin both had high hopes for political transformation, which they conceived as inextricable from philosophical, aesthetic, and religious critique and reform. The cultural organization of the Greek *polis* provided a model for conceiving of a modern *Volksreligion*, which would bind together the disparate spheres of political, religious, and artistic life.[11] The best-known document of this interest is a short text of Hegel's, probably written in 1797, and showing strong indications of his exchanges with Hölderlin.[12] The text is known (somewhat misleadingly) as the "Oldest System Program of German Idealism" ("Älteste Systemprogramm des deutschen Idealismus") and has been attributed, since its discovery in 1917 to Schelling, Hölderlin and others—despite being unmistakably in Hegel's handwriting (the presumption being that he copied the text).[13] Around the same time, and probably in some connection to Hegel's text, Hölderlin considered similar themes in a "Fragment of Philosophical Letters" (assumed to

---

[10] See Dieter Henrich, *Hegel im Kontext*, rev. ed. (Frankfurt: Suhrkamp, 2010), 9–40.

[11] Christoph Jamme, "*Ein ungelehrtes Buch*": die philosophische Gemeinschaft zwischen Hölderlin und Hegel in Frankfurt, 1797–1800 (Bouvier: Bonn, 1983), 53–54.

[12] On the dating, see (with a grain of salt) Frank-Peter Hansen, "*Das älteste Systemprogramm des deutschen Idealismus*": Rezeptionsgeschichte und Interpretation (Berlin: de Gruyter, 1989), 374–76. Jamme and Schneider argue for a slightly later dating, at the beginning of Hegel's Frankfurt period: Christoph Jamme and Helmut Schneider, eds., *Mythologie der Vernunft: Hegels "ältestes Systemprogramm des deutschen Idealismus"* (Frankfurt: Suhrkamp, 1984), 36–43. Both essentially agree, though, that the text shows a moment of transition from the Bern to the Frankfurt writings on religion.

[13] The grounds for doubting Hegel's authorship were always tenuous, and in the absence of any concrete evidence to the contrary, one can assume that Hegel is indeed the author and not merely a copyist. Of course, this does not rule out Schelling's or Hölderlin's influence on Hegel's thinking in the text—and indeed, both seem quite likely.

come from a series of "New Letters on Aesthetic Education" that Hölderlin mentions; the text is also known as "On Religion"). Though little concrete evidence of their closeness survives, the similarities between the two texts suggest a lively interchange between the two school friends, while their differences also suggest deeper divisions between their approaches.[14]

Hegel and Hölderlin seek a way beyond the controversies between rational and revealed religion, or Spinozistic pantheism and orthodox monotheism. They hope for a future religion that would encompass both an infinite aesthetic diversity and a unified philosophical and religious conception. For Hegel, this takes the form of "monotheism of reason and heart, polytheism of imagination and art" (SP 511; WZB 1, 235–36) while Hölderlin imagines a world in which "everyone honors his own god and all honor one common god in poetic representations" (E&L 239; SWB 2, 568).[15] Aesthetic imagination appears as a form of mediation between faith and reason, and so offers a response to the problems of theology and philosophy alike. Both texts challenge the authority of the modern church for imposing forms of cultural life without developing their spiritual basis. In place of such a hierarchical notion of spirituality, both seek to establish a horizontal one, which would emerge organically from the life of the culture and reach to all spheres of activity.

Hegel and Hölderlin are strongly influenced by Schiller's *Aesthetic Letters*, which similarly imagines the way from an alienated present to a future of individual wholeness through aesthetic imagination. The critique of the "System Program," though, cuts even deeper, to the very idea of an organizing state: "the state is something mechanical . . . every state must treat free men as mechanical cogs, and it should not. Therefore the state must end" (SP 510; WZB 1, 234–35). The organization of contemporary society appears to lack the living principle that would allow it to recognize the autonomy of its citizens (an argument that will recur in Hegel's essay *Natural Law*, though without the revolutionary conclusion).[16] As for Schiller, beauty appears as a form of mediation between individual and collective, and between reason and emotion—a conception that the "System Program" extends to embrace all of cultural life.[17] Hegel imagines a reciprocity of mythical imagination and philosophical reason, which will make "the

[14] See Jamme and Schneider, *Mythologie der Vernunft*, 49–53. The chronology of the two texts and the direction of the influence, though, remain uncertain.

[15] Eckart Förster, "'To lend wings to physics once again': Hölderlin and the 'Oldest System-Programme of German Idealism,'" *European Journal of Philosophy* 3 (1995): 192. Förster points out that the first phrase recalls Goethe's maxim (which might have been picked up in conversation): "We are pantheists when investigating nature, polytheists when writing poetry, monotheists morally."

[16] Hansen, *"Das älteste Systemprogramm"*: 357.

[17] On the influence of Schiller's *Aesthetic Letters*, see Annemarie Gethmann-Siefert, *Die Funktion der Kunst in der Geschichte: Untersuchungen zu Hegels Ästhetik* (Bonn: Bouvier, 1984).

people rational" and "the philosophers sensible" as the basis of a "new religion, [which] will be the last greatest work of humanity" (*SP* 511–12; *WZB* 1, 236).

Hölderlin is less interested in the details of religion, but nevertheless views it as the foundation of any human society. Religion is not a structure of faith or belief but a "relation" (*Verhältnis*) or "connection" (*Zusammenhang*), a means by which an individual experiences the world as full of meaning. Such experience was the basis of ancient Greek religion for Hölderlin, but it has been debased by the strictures of Christianity, which turn the feeling of connection into an "an arrogant moral, partly a vain etiquette or an empty rule of taste" (*E&L* 237; *SWB* 2, 564). This stems from an excessive emphasis on the rational and the moral, which forecloses a closer, "living" relationship to nature. Hölderlin conceives of true religious experience as the unification of what he calls the intellectual and the historical, which are mediated in myth. As a concrete representation of action, myth has a firm physical basis, yet always remains concerned ultimately with the spiritual realm. Myth is a representation of divinity entering history, and so mediates between the world of sense and the world of reason. This form of connection to the divine is for Hölderlin the essence of poetry, so that "all religion would be in its essence poetic" (*E&L* 239; *SWB* 2, 568). For Hölderlin, the divine can only be experienced as beauty, and so religious and aesthetic experiences are one.

Both the "System Program" and Hölderlin's "Fragment" consider aesthetic experience as fundamental to religion, but they differ at least partly in their vision of spirituality. For Hegel, religion, art, and philosophy are all grounded in a unitary concept of reason, and the challenge is to make the rational sensible (through art, religion, or philosophy). For Hölderlin, an artistic religion is itself the highest aim, and would constitute an alternative to conceptual knowledge. Both notions of the relation of art, religion, and philosophy are deeply influenced by Plato's dialogues, especially the *Timaeus*, *Phaedrus*, and *Symposium*, which were studied in the Stift.[18] Hegel and Hölderlin's project at this stage is a kind of "aesthetic Platonism" in that it sees sensible beauty as a means of philosophical enlightenment.[19] This could be suggested by the writings of Kant and especially Schiller, but the Idealists are far more emphatic in their sense of the significance of beauty. "I am now convinced," Hegel writes in the "System Program," "that the highest act of reason, the act in which it encompasses all the ideas, is an aesthetic act, and that *truth and goodness* are united *only in beauty*" (*SP* 511; *WZB* 1, 235).

---

[18] On Plato in the Stift, see Jamme and Völkel, *Hölderlin und der deutsche Idealismus*, 1, 134–68.
[19] Klaus Düsing, "Ästhetischer Platonismus bei Hölderlin und Hegel," in *Homburg von der Höhe in der deutschen Geistesgeschichte: Studien zum Freundeskreis um Hegel und Hölderlin*, ed. Christoph Jamme and Otto Pöggeler (Stuttgart: Klett-Cotta, 1981).

For Hegel, beauty's synthetic power makes it the ideal of reason, and the point of union between theoretical and practical philosophy.[20]

Hölderlin's position is less orthodox, and at this point imagines the ideal of spiritual experience as a state of originary union with nature, from which humanity has been cut off by culture. Beauty is a means of reconstituting this union, and is therefore a state of philosophical and religious enlightenment. If for Hegel, beauty and philosophy are ultimately one, for Hölderlin, beauty is the basis of philosophy, since it alone gives access to the ground of thought, and therefore guides philosophical inquiry (which is necessarily imperfect because mediated by concepts). The first part of Hölderlin's *Hyperion*, published in 1797, contains a eulogy of the beautiful that shows a profound debt to Plato's *Symposium* in its notion of beauty as the guide of reason: "If the divine εν διαφερον εαυτῳ [sic: "one differentiated in itself," a reference to Heraclitus quoted at *Symposium* 187a] shines forth, the ideal of beauty to striving reason, then reason does not seek blindly, and knows why and to what end it seeks" (*Hyperion* I, XXX: *SWB* 2, 94).[21] Hyperion's vision of the future at the end of the first volume seems to restate Hölderlin's understanding of the path through beauty to the divine: "There will be only one beauty, and man and nature will unite themselves in one all-encompassing divinity" (*Hyperion* I, XXX: *SWB* 2, 101).

"Problems of Fate": "The Spirit of Christianity" and *Empedocles*

The optimism of Hegel's "System Program" and Hölderlin's *Hyperion* I leaves little room for the divisions and contradictions of tragedy, and indeed, the genre plays a relatively minor role in the writings of both before the late 1790s. Though they read and admired Sophocles and Euripides at the Stift, their interest seems to have focused on tragedy's poetic achievements and its characters (most importantly, Antigone crops up in the writings of both in an ethical context).[22] Neither engages particularly with generic questions, or with the problems of division and reconciliation that will pervade their theories of tragedy—indeed, these issues are dealt with primarily in religious and philosophical contexts, with aesthetics considered, quite abstractly, as a realm of synthesis and wholeness. But especially from 1798, tragedy begins to take a major place in the thought of both, and is seen in relation to fundamental questions of philosophy and theology. Hegel's notes known as "The

---

[20] Frank, *Der kommende Gott*: 183–85.

[21] On *Hyperion* and the *Symposium*, see Joshua Billings, "Hyperion's symposium: an erotics of reception," *Classical Receptions Journal* 2 (2010).

[22] For the poetic achievement, see Hölderlin's *Magister-Specimen* (*SWB* 2, 489); for Antigone, Hegel's Bern-period "Die Positivität der christlichen Religion" (*ETW* 155; *WZB* 1, 205) and Hölderlin's "Fragment of Philosophical Letters" (*E&L* 236; *SWB* 2, 563).

Spirit of Christianity and Its Fate" ("Der Geist des Christentums und sein Schicksal") and Hölderlin's sketches for a tragedy based on the life of the pre-Socratic philosopher Empedocles both show an understanding of tragedy as a genre of sacrifice. This coincides with the development of a darker version of the philosophy of union, in which division from nature is seen as a necessary and irrevocable stage in development, rather than a lamentable obstacle to be overcome.[23] The question for both, then, becomes, how to understand destruction as part of a greater logic, how to see conflict as a stage in a reconciliatory process. The problem is religious, philosophical, and historical at once, and leads both Hegel and Hölderlin to tragedy.

Running through Hegel's and Hölderlin's engagements with tragedy from 1798 is an unusual concept of fate (Schicksal, from the verb schicken, to send), which seems to combine Greek and Christian elements. This corresponds to a development away from the hopefulness of their earlier thought, and shows them focusing on processes of reconciliation rather than reconstitution.[24] Both understand fate in theological terms, as a form of connection to divinity that underlies human actions in history. Schicksal is not an externally imposed force of determination (as for Schelling), but a possibility of meaning in human existence, which can be more or less present at different moments in time. The paradigmatic figure of Schicksal is Jesus, a human figure whose sacrifice established a relation between man and god. The pattern of human sacrifice establishing or altering the relation to divinity crops up repeatedly in Hegel's and Hölderlin's writings, and is applied to Orestes, Oedipus, Antigone, and Hölderlin's own tragic protagonist, Empedocles. The religious background of the concept is never wholly absent, though overtly it recedes after Frankfurt. Hegel's relatively optimistic religious conception leads him to a view of Schicksal as a progressive force of destruction and reconstitution.[25] Hölderlin, on the other hand, holds a darker, hermetic view of religion and history, and sees modernity as essentially fateless (schicksallos), waiting for the return of absent gods. For all the differences between the two notions of fate and theories of tragedy, though, they have a common root in a philosophical and theological approach to the question of reconciliation.

"The Spirit of Christianity and Its Fate" is the name given to a series of fragmentary texts dated to the years 1798–1800. The texts are problematic in a number of ways: beyond substantial difficulties of language, edition, and

[23] Jamme, "Ein ungelehrtes Buch": 326.

[24] Ibid., 390–95.

[25] Miguel de Beistegui similarly draws attention to the role of Schicksal (which he translates "destiny") in Hegel's early thought: Miguel de Beistegui, "Hegel: or the tragedy of thinking," in Philosophy and tragedy, ed. Miguel de Beistegui and Simon Sparks (London: Routledge, 2000), 12–16. See also Pierre Bertrand, "Le sens du tragique et du destin dans la dialectique hégélienne," Revue de Métaphysique et de Morale 47 (1940).

chronology, they present a condemnation of Judaism that has justifiably disturbed readers. Hegel considers Judaic religious practice essentially flawed, and sees a deficient theology as the root of the Jewish people's wanderings and sufferings. Though the anti-Judaism of the text cannot be apologized or explained away, it is worth remembering that Hegel's negative opinion of Judaism is theological rather than racial—and so should be understood in a different context from the nationalistic anti-Semitism that began to take root in the period. Indeed, the inadequacy of Jewish theology for Hegel, its "positivity," is typical of forms of Christianity as well, and pervasive in contemporary German society. "Positive" for Hegel describes a subjective principle that is taken to be objective—typically, an internal sense of morality or duty that is given external form as a law or dictate. Judaism abounds in such laws, understanding religious practice as obedience to an impersonal God rather than an individual, reflective relation to divinity: "The root of Judaism," Hegel writes, "is the objective, that is, service, servitude of a foreign one [Knechtschaft eines Fremden]" (*ETW* 206; *WZB* 1, 298). Hegel describes this tendency as a response to the early history of the religion, when Noah found himself so overwhelmed by the power of nature that he could only subsist by imagining an all-powerful divinity, who ruled man and nature alike, and set down certain laws for human conduct. Thus, "Noah secured himself against the hostile power [of nature] in that he subjected it and himself to one more powerful" (*ETW* 184; *WZB* 1, 276). From this first abdication of human autonomy to divine inscrutability, Hegel writes, Judaism has understood itself always in opposition to the outside world, and has been unable to recognize the intimate connections to god or other people that constitute "living" relationships.

Hegel exemplifies the positivity of Judaism through the contrast with the Greeks.[26] Instead of the true autonomy that existed between subjects in ancient Greece, Hegel argues, the Jewish people understand the world around them as a pure object, either subordinated or subordinating, with which they can never be in harmony. Hegel contrasts the invisible, unrepresentable God of the Jews with the Eleusinian Mysteries: whereas the secret of the Jewish God was "thoroughly alien," inaccessible even to the priests, from the Eleusinian Mysteries "no one was excluded, but they could not be spoken of, since they would be desecrated by words" (*ETW* 193; *WZB* 1, 285). By setting its God wholly out of the world, Judaism removes all holiness from everyday existence and religious observance. Greek religion, on the contrary, understands earthly life as saturated with the divine and sacred. Hegel's dream of a "living" Christianity takes much of its inspiration from

[26] On the Greek/Jew dichotomy, see Miriam Leonard, *Socrates and the Jews: Hellenism and Hebraism from Moses Mendelssohn to Sigmund Freud* (Chicago: University of Chicago Press, 2012), 65–104.

Greek polytheism, but is elaborated throughout his early writings in primarily negative terms. His utopian vision stands in contrast not only to Judaism but to the current state of philosophical metaphysics and ethics, defined by Kant's theoretical agnosticism and practical ethic of duty. Hegel's idealizing view of ancient Greece and vision for future Christianity are articulated through opposition to a state of division and submission that characterizes both Judaism and German Enlightenment modernity. In contrast to these forms of positivity, Hegel imagines a religion based on intimate relations between independent subjects, and an ethics based on mutual recognition.

Hegel's fragment closes with a pregnant paradox, which considers the fate of the Jewish people:

> The great tragedy [Trauerspiel] of the Jewish people is no Greek tragedy [Trauerspiel], it can awaken neither fear nor pity, since both are created only by the fate [Schicksal] of a necessary error of a beautiful being; it can awaken only disgust. The fate of the Jewish people is the fate of Macbeth, who stepped out of nature itself, relied on alien beings, and then in their service had to trample and kill all that is holy in human nature, had to be finally deserted by his gods (since they were objects, he was the servant) and destroyed by his faith itself. (*ETW* 204–5; *WZB* 1, 297)

Behind these words lies a normative conception of tragedy, which sees only certain works as genuinely tragic. In finding that Judaism's fate can "awaken only disgust [Abscheu]," Hegel recalls Aristotle's comment on a tragic plot in which a good man falls from happiness: "This is not frightful or pitiable but repulsive [μιαρός]" (*Poetics* 1452b). Like Aristotle, Hegel distinguishes between tragic and untragic suffering, with the contrast—a chilling one to modern readers—centering on Greek and Jewish relations to divinity. The fate of the Jews is created by their dependence on an unseen, unknowable God, which leads them to despise the world around them. Recognizing no source of meaning within human action, Judaism, like Macbeth, treats nature as a means to an end, and finds itself abandoned by the divinity in which it had trusted. Though the description of Greek tragedy as based on a "necessary error" recalls Schelling's *Philosophical Letters*, the phrase "beautiful being" points to a different model of the tragic hero—more Antigone than Oedipus, and in this context, Jesus most of all. Hegel's notion of tragedy, like Schelling's, entails a consciousness and acceptance of guilt, by which the tragic hero becomes a martyr. As becomes clear in Hegel's discussion of the concept of fate, this notion of sacrifice is deeply informed by theology.

In another fragment, Hegel develops a conception of morality based on subjectivity rather than objectivity, opposing the Jewish-Kantian concept of duty (*Pflicht*) with a Christian concept of inclination (*Neigung*).[27] To il-

---

[27]The following discussion refers to the fragment beginning "Die Positivität der Juden . . ." (*ETW* 224–53; *WZB* 336–69).

lustrate the opposition, Hegel describes two ways of understanding the individual relation to morality, as "law" (*Gesetz*) or as "fate" (*Schicksal*).[28] The first is based on a positive (in Hegel's terminology) worldview, in which existence is governed by abstractions that impose a punishment on any transgressions.[29] *Gesetz* mechanically enacts a penalty equal to the crime: "the punishment lies immediately in the offended law; the criminal loses the same right that through the crime was damaged in another" (*ETW* 225; *WZB* 1, 338). Between crime and punishment there is no possibility of mediation, and no forgiveness or leniency can change the fact of guilt: "the punishment follows the deed; their connection is unbreakable" (*ETW* 227; *WZB* 1, 340). The inflexibility of *Gesetz* means that, once transgressed, it can never be made good again, condemning criminals to a permanent self-damnation: "the criminal sees himself always as a criminal, he has no power over his action in reality, and this his reality is in contradiction with his consciousness of the law" (*ETW* 227; *WZB* 1, 340). *Gesetz* creates an indelible consciousness of sin, which makes the present state of punishment appear as a permanent alienation from morality, without possibility of redemption.[30]

Schicksal is based on an understanding of morality as a connection between individuals, rather than a rigid, impersonal law. In one respect, this makes transgression more damaging, since it now injures another subject (rather than the law):

> It [life] is immortal, and when murdered it appears as a terrifying ghost that unleashes all its branches, lets loose its Eumenides. The illusion of the crime—that it had destroyed an alien life and thus expanded itself—dissolves when the departed spirit of the injured life returns to oppose it, just as Banquo, who came to Macbeth as a friend, was not destroyed by his own murder, but took his seat at the table right after he had been killed, not as a companion for the meal, but as an evil spirit. (*ETW* 229; *WZB* 1, 342)

Schicksal makes crime an issue between agents (rather than between an agent and an abstraction) and so creates a need for revenge of the injured on the injurer. Yet *Schicksal* also allows for a process of reconciliation that is hinted at by calling the Furies by their later appellation, "kindly ones." As in the fragment on Judaism, *Macbeth* occurs in the context of crime and punishment.[31] The work seems to have appealed to Hegel for the way it depicts a hero destroyed by reliance on esoteric knowledge, which ultimately

---

[28] Since Hegel's usage of the terms is highly idiosyncratic, I leave them untranslated to preserve their strangeness.

[29] See Bernard Bourgeois, *Hegel à Francfort, ou Judaïsme—Christianisme—Hegelianisme* (Paris: Vrin, 1970), 66–68.

[30] There are interesting parallels to Hölderlin's fragmentary essay "Über den Begriff der Strafe" (*E&L* 229–30; *SWB* 2, 499–501).

[31] The reference was quite current, as A. W. Schlegel's translation had only appeared in 1797.

rebounds against the agent.[32] Macbeth's transgressions appear as injuries to himself, and his punishment as a self-imposed alienation from the continuity of life.

In seeing crime and punishment as two stages of the same process, an understanding of *Schicksal* prepares the way for their reconciliation: punishment is not the action of an immutable, external law, but the negative side of a immanent dynamic. "Because the enemy is felt as life," Hegel writes, "therein lies the possibility of a reconciliation of *Schicksal*" (*ETW* 232; *WZB* 1, 345). Such reconciliation is a reunion with the self, a reconstitution of the living, moral totality that the crime had riven apart.[33] Punishment is experienced as a necessary reconstruction of normal human relations, rather than an arbitrary, external imposition. The recognition of the commonality of life leads to genuine repentance, and to a sense of all individuals as connected by love: "The feeling of life, which finds itself again, is love, and in it, *Schicksal* reconciles itself" (*ETW* 232; *WZB* 1, 346). Love, understood as a binding force between equals, appears as the completion of fate, the mechanism through which the wound in life created by crime is healed, and a sense of harmony restored.[34]

Hegel describes the path to reconciliation in terms that unmistakably recall Schelling's description of tragedy in the "Tenth Letter." *Schicksal*, unlike *Gesetz*, has no connection to justice—it punishes injuries done intentionally or not, and therefore "often appears to cross into the most crying injustice, when it appears so much more terribly faced with the most sublime guilt, the guilt of innocence [der erhabensten Schuld, der Schuld der Unschuld gegenüber]" (*ETW* 232–33; *WZB* 1, 347). The description of sublime, guiltless guilt surely comes from Schelling, as does the response to punishment for a crime of which one is subjectively innocent: "in order to save himself, man kills himself; in order not to see his own in an alien power, he no longer calls it his own, and thus destroys himself" (*ETW* 235; *WZB* 1, 350). Through willful renunciation and self-destruction, the individual proves his independence, even in the loss of freedom: "he has at the same time raised [erhoben] himself above all fate; life has become unfaithful [untreu] to him, but he not to life" (*ETW* 236; *WZB* 1, 350).[35] With the concept of sacrifice, the connection to Jesus becomes explicit. Renunciation of all that is impure, for Hegel, represents the essence of Christ's teaching, "to leave everything in order not to come into a compact with the degraded world"

---

[32] *Macbeth* returns in the *Phenomenology* (discussed in Chapter 6), where his reliance on the witches is at issue. Further, see Igor Primoratz, *Banquos Geist: Hegels Theorie der Strafe* (Bonn: Bouvier, 1986), 15–26.

[33] Otto Pöggeler, *Hegels Idee einer Phänomenologie des Geistes* (Freiburg: Alber, 1973), 85.

[34] See Harris, *Toward the sunlight*: 295–98.

[35] The concept of unfaithfulness (*Untreue*) will be important again in Hölderlin's Sophocles "Notes," where it also describes the tragic hero's response to catastrophe.

(*ETW* 236; *WZB* 1, 350). Hegel has transformed elements of Schelling's description of Oedipus into a description of Christ. Oedipus' punishment for a crime he did not intend provides the pattern for Christ's sublime acceptance of guilt on behalf of humanity. Hegel's thought mixes the tragic figures of Greece and Christianity, seeing both as the embodiment of true ethical consciousness.

Though Hegel does not explicitly refer to tragedy in the fragment, it should be clear that concepts of the tragic pervade "The Spirit of Christianity."[36] Like Schelling, Hegel understands Greek tragedy through the Christian concept of sacrifice, and, reciprocally, conceives of the Passion in terms of a Greek concept of fate. Acceptance of an unavoidable guilt—whether Christ's or Oedipus'—paradoxically demonstrates the subjection to fate and the possibility of sublimity: "Thus can the highest guilt be united with the highest guiltlessness, the highest, most unlucky *Schicksal* with elevation [Erhabenheit] over all *Schicksal*" (*ETW* 236; *WZB* 1, 351). The tragic hero's sacrifice of self both recognizes and transcends the contradictions of earthly existence.[37] Though it is too often forgotten in studies that abstract ethical content from religious context, Hegel's concepts of tragic division, conflict, and reconciliation are rooted in Christian theology.[38] Tragedy's ethical implications will always be framed by a religious context, either implicitly (in the notion of sacrifice of the *Natural Law* essay) or explicitly (in the *Phenomenology*'s "Religion" chapter). For Hegel—and, it will be argued, for Hölderlin as well—the concept of *Schicksal* understands tragic fate on the model of Christ's death and resurrection, envisioning reconciliation with divinity as the necessary end of tragedy.

"*All tragic persons* [. . .] are in their characters and expressions more or less attempts to solve the problems of *Schicksal*," Hölderlin writes in the "Basis for Empedocles" ("Grund zum Empedokles," *DoE* 148; *SWB* 2, 433). This short, hermetic text was sketched at a moment of transition in Hölderlin's poetological thought, following two aborted efforts to write a tragedy on the story of the pre-Socratic philosopher Empedocles. Hölderlin views Empedocles, expanding a story reported in Diogenes Laertius, as an advocate of civic

---

[36] This is recognized by Georg Lukács, *Der junge Hegel: ueber die Beziehungen von Dialektik und Oekonomie* (Zürich: Europa, 1948), 267–70.

[37] See further Werner Hamacher, *Pleroma—reading in Hegel: the genesis and structure of a dialectical hermeneutics in Hegel*, trans. Nicholas Walker and Simon Jarvis (London: Athlone, 1998), 143–55.

[38] The tendency to focus on the ethical at the expense of the religious is particularly marked in Annemarie Gethmann-Siefert, *Einführung in Hegels Ästhetik* (Munich: Fink, 2005); Michael Schulte, *Die "Tragödie im Sittlichen": zur Dramentheorie Hegels* (Munich: Fink, 1992); and the chapter in Schmidt, *On Germans and other Greeks*. Christoph Menke also pursues an ethical reading, but acknowledges that his is an appropriative one: Christoph Menke, *Tragödie im Sittlichen: Gerechtigkeit und Freiheit nach Hegel* (Frankfurt: Suhrkamp, 1996).

freedom, a revolutionary figure who seeks to lead his society out of its dependence and immaturity.[39] Unable to bring about this transformation in life (for reasons that change in each draft), Empedocles chooses a spectacular death, leaping into Etna, an act that he predicts will bring about a new closeness to divinity. In the first draft, Empedocles explains his suicide to the people of Agrigento through a logic of sacrifice:

> Menschen ist die große Lust
> Gegeben, daß sie selber sich verjüngen.
> Und aus dem reinigenden Tode, den
> Sie selber sich zu rechter Zeit gewählt,
> Erstehn, wie aus dem Styx Achill, die Völker. (1497–1501: *SWB* 2, 340)

> [To men is given the great desire that they make themselves young. And from
>   the purifying death that they choose for themselves at the right time, the
>   people rise up, as Achilles out of the Styx.] (*DoE* 90)

Empedocles describes himself as the "purifying death" through which his people will gain a new coherence and autonomy—a vision related to that of the "Fragment" and the close of *Hyperion* I. In Empedocles, individual and collective *Schicksal* coincide. Hölderlin understands Empedocles' fate as *geschickt* (sent) in a double sense: it is the destiny that has been assigned to him, and he is a figure sent to his people for their renaissance. Echoes of the Christian Passion are obvious, as well as of Sophocles' *OC*, which similarly depicts the willing death of an individual leading to the collective good.[40] These two sources mutually reinforce the theme of sacrifice, and the eschatological hope for divine presence. Empedocles' sacrifice, like Christ's, reconfigures the relation to the gods, pointing his errant people to their collective fate.

The most striking difference between Hölderlin's and Hegel's understanding of fate in tragedy concerns forms of eschatology. Hölderlin grew up in a milieu that was strongly influenced by pietism, a movement within Protestantism that emphasized individual faith and religious study, and the practical application of Biblical principles. The teachings Hölderlin would have experienced in Württemberg also had strong hermetic and chiliastic tendencies, seeing human history as defined by varying degrees of divine presence.[41] This relatively fluid view of revelation allowed Hölderlin to view

---

[39]Diogenes reports that Empedocles declined the kingship of Agrigento when it was offered to him (*Lives* 8, 63).

[40]Hölderlin could also draw on the *Ajax* for the theme of tragic suicide. The play was important to him from the first drafts of *Hyperion*, and exerts a particularly strong influence on the first drafts of *Empedocles*. See R. B. Harrison, *Hölderlin and Greek literature* (Oxford: Clarendon, 1975), 192–219.

[41]Gerhard Schäfer, "Der spekulative württembergische Pietismus des 18. Jahrhunderts—Systeme und Ausstrahlung," in *Hölderlin und Nürtingen*, ed. Peter Härtling and Gerhard Kurz (Stuttgart: Metzler, 1994).

Greek and Christian religion syncretically, as varying manifestations of a single divinity—most famously, in the poem "Bread and Wine" ("Brod und Wein"), which blends the figures of Dionysus and Christ in its imagination of the return of "the heavenly ones" from their self-imposed exile.[42] Though Hegel seems to have been influenced by both the eschatological and syncretic tendencies in his friend (as in a poem addressed to Hölderlin in 1796, "Eleusis": WZB 1, 230–33), his religious views placed a far greater emphasis on reason and progress.[43] After the Frankfurt period (where the influence of Hölderlin is the strongest), parallels of tragic figures and Christ do not have the same importance in Hegel's writings, and he consistently describes the transition from Greek to Christian religion as a progressive development of reason. Hegel's view of history was teleological, seeing tragedy as a constant and progressive quality of existence governed by fate; Hölderlin's view, on the other hand, was eschatological, conceiving of tragedy as a moment of revolutionary rupture, which restores human fate through a new relation to divinity.

Both Hegel and Hölderlin bind political and religious notions of revolution. Hegel is less explicit on the connection, but it is operative in his contrast of Judaism's hierarchical tendency with the egalitarian ethos of ancient Greece, as well as in more conventionally political writings from his Bern and Frankfurt years.[44] Hölderlin's Empedocles concentrates religious and republican ideals of revolution, and his changing depictions of the philosopher are often seen to reflect an increasing pessimism towards the course of the French Revolution.[45] The effects of the Revolutionary Wars would have been inescapable during the time in Frankfurt: the city was occupied three times in the 1790s, and Hölderlin was evidently following events closely when Napoleon dissolved the Directory in 1799 and "became a kind of dictator" (to Johanna Gock [Hölderlin's mother], 11.16.1799: E&L 168; SWB 3, 404). The eclipse of Hölderlin's hopes for republicanism within contemporary politics seems to have led him to transfer his revolutionary ideals to a more distant future, and to complicate the form he imagined such a revolution taking. If the French Revolution had initially made the return of a republican polytheism on the model of ancient Greece seem within reach (as witnessed in the "Fragment"), the deepening crisis of the Wars made the engagement with Greek tragedy appear a way of preserving republican ideals in a world hostile to them.

[42] See Frank, Der kommende Gott: 285–307.

[43] Laurence Dickey, Hegel: religion, economics, and the politics of spirit, 1770–1807 (Cambridge: Cambridge University Press, 1987), 143–50.

[44] Jamme, "Ein ungelehrtes Buch": 197–205.

[45] See Christoph Prignitz, Hölderlins Empedokles: die Vision einer erneuerten Gesellschaft und ihre zeitgeschichtlichen Hintergründe (Hamburg: Buske, 1985). The identification of Empedocles and Napoleon is obvious in a manuscript page containing the poem "Empedokles" on one side, and "Buonaparte" on the other (SWB 1, 241 and 374; cf. 667).

Hölderlin's changing views on religious and political revolution are unmistakable in the final draft of *Empedocles*, which complicates the vision of rebirth of the first versions. Two scenes are particularly important: first, a wrenching confrontation between Empedocles and his student Pausanias, which juxtaposes an apparently naive regret at death with the philosopher's resolve; and second, a new confrontation between Empedocles and the blind seer Manes, which questions the very possibility of revolution that Empedocles had promised. In the third version, Empedocles' decision seems to arise mainly from a consciousness of fate, a belief that his own individuality must be subsumed into a larger plan. As he explains to Pausanias, "Und was ich mein', es ist von heute nicht, / Da ich geboren wurde, wars beschlossen. / Sieh auf und wags! was Eines ist, zerbricht" ("And what I intend, it is not of today; when I was born it was decided. Look up and dare! What is one—shatters") (165–67: *DoE* 177; *SWB* 2, 404). Along with this understanding of the inevitability of individual destruction goes a prophetic consciousness of rebirth, with which Empedocles comforts his despairing pupil: "Geh! fürchte nichts! es kehret alles wieder, / Und was |geschehen soll, ist schon vollendet" ("Go! fear nothing! all returns again, and what should happen is already completed") (319–20: *DoE* 182; *SWB* 2, 409). This cyclical notion of existence follows reports of Empedocles' own philosophy, which finds a constant process of union and separation at the heart of history: ἄλλοτε μὲν Φιλότητι συνερχόμεν᾽εἰς ἕν ἅπαντα, / ἄλλοτε δ᾽αὖ δίχ᾽ἔκαστα φορεύμενα Νείκεος ἔχθει (*Lives* 8, 76: "At one time by love all things coming together in one, at another time each thing borne apart by the hatred of strife"). The process must have appealed to Hölderlin as a revision of the philosophy of union, which envisions becoming and passing away as necessarily linked, but without end.[46] Yet Hölderlin retains an eschatological belief in the redemption of time, as moments of divine presence punctuate the constant alternation of love and strife.[47] Empedocles' justification of his suicide to Pausanias performs Hölderlin's chiliastic pietism in the setting and dramatic form of ancient Greece.

The following scene, the last that Hölderlin sketched in any detail, continues and complicates this questioning of the meaning of the death of the tragic hero. It introduces the character of Manes, a blind prophet recalling Sophocles' Tiresias, who comes to warn Empedocles against suicide.[48]

---

[46]On Hölderlin's philosophical affinities with Empedocles, see Véronique M. Fóti, *Epochal discordance: Hölderlin's philosophy of tragedy* (Albany: State University of New York Press, 2006), 55–64.

[47]Uvo Hölscher, *Empedokles und Hölderlin* (Frankfurt: Insel, 1965), 57.

[48]The name could suggest a number of origins: the Greek μάντις, "seer," the German *mahnen* and Latin *moneo*, both meaning "to warn," and the *Manes*, Roman chthonic divinities, believed to be spirits of the dead.

Manes has recognized that the transitional nature of the time requires an individual to mediate between man and divinity:

Der Eine doch, der neue Retter faßt
Des Himmels Strahlen ruhig auf, und liebend
Nimmt er, was sterblich ist, an seinen Busen,
Und milde wird in ihm der Streit der Welt.
Die Menschen und die Götter söhnt er aus
   Und nahe wieder leben sie, wie vormals. (372–77: *SWB* 2, 412)

[The one, though, the new savior grasps the rays of heaven calmly, and lovingly takes what is mortal to his breast, and in him the conflict of the world becomes calm. Man and god he reconciles, and again they live close, as before.] (*DoE* 184)

Manes, though, questions whether Empedocles is this figure, suggesting a new uncertainty in Hölderlin's understanding of tragic fate. "Dir hat der Schmerz den Geist entzündet, Armer" ("Pain has kindled your spirit, poor man") (481: *DoE* 187; *SWB* 2, 415), Manes reproaches, and asserts that Empedocles' dream of transformation is a mere illusion.[49] The question of a reconciliation between man and god is a recurring element in Hölderlin's thought on tragedy, and here takes on a conflictual tone—bringing it closer to the *Antigone*, and to Hegel's developing conception of tragic conflict.[50] Reconciliation for Hölderlin must now be won out of strife, and the figures of tragedy appear as "attempts to solve the problems of fate" in that they combat the fatelessness of a world without divinity. Tragedy is the genre of rupture and renewal for Hölderlin, and the tragic hero a catalyst for a transformation that is political and religious at once. Hölderlin's notes for the continuation ultimately suggest that Empedocles will be recognized, like Christ and the Colonean Oedipus, as the one able to bring the blessings of the gods on men through his death. Manes will acknowledge "that he [Empedocles] is the one called, who kills and gives life, in whom and through whom a world at once dissolves and renews itself" (*DoE* 194; *SWB* 2, 445).

Hölderlin describes his fundamentally theological understanding of Greek art in a letter of 1800, writing that the sole aim of ancient poetry was

to bring the gods and humans closer together. Tragedy shows this *per contrarium*. God and man appear one, upon which a fate [ein Schicksal, sc. comes], which arouses all the humility and pride of man, and at the end leaves behind, on one hand, respect for the heavenly ones and, on the other, a purified mind as the property of man. (*E&L* 184; *SWB* 3, 412)

---

[49] The concept of an illusion (*Trugbild*) occurs also in the "Basis" (*DoE* 145; *SWB* 2, 430).
[50] It has often been suggested that Manes is inspired by Hegel. See Pöggeler, *Hegel's Idee*: 108.

Tragic action is a change in human relation to divinity, as an immediate but unstable coexistence is transformed into a mediate but more stable one. This could be a description of the action of *Empedocles*, in which the main character's insight into the depths of existence brings him so close to divinity that his sacrifice becomes necessary. Empedocles' suicide is the purifying death that restores a stable relation of god and man. Though the most obvious models for this action are Christ and the Oedipus of the *OC*, it will become clear in Hölderlin's "Notes" on Sophocles that he sees this process of reckoning with the divine at the heart of Greek tragedy quite broadly. While writing *Empedocles*, however, Hölderlin seems to have come to acknowledge that the theological purpose of tragedy must be transformed in Christian modernity. This leads him, following his final abandonment of the drama, in two directions: to the creation of a new, "hymnic" genre of poetry on the one hand, and to translations of Sophocles and Pindar on the other. The purpose of "bring[ing] gods and humans closer together" remains, though the means of doing so change, according to Hölderlin's developing logic of the opposition and reciprocal necessity of antiquity and modernity (discussed in Chapter 7). Developing a more differentiated conception of *vaterländisch* poetry, Hölderlin will grapple with a newly historicized conception of poetry and poetics.

The Power of the Sacrifice: The *Natural Law* Essay

From their discussions in Frankfurt, Hegel and Hölderlin both came away with ideas of tragedy deeply imbricated with theological conceptions. Hölderlin's centers quite concretely on the tragic hero as a transformative figure in the relation of man and god, while Hegel's remains at a level of greater abstraction and sees tragedy as a model for understanding historical process as rational. A response to a reading of Schiller's *Wallenstein*, dated around 1800, exhibits the state of Hegel's thought on tragedy just before leaving Frankfurt. The short text sketches an implicit contrast of ancient and modern tragedy that recalls Schiller's satirical *Xenien*, but in complete earnest: "Life against life, but only death rises up against life, and unbelievable! Horrible! Death triumphs over life! This is not tragic, but awful! This tears (see *Xenien*) [the heart], one cannot leap out with a lightened breast!" (*WZB* 1, 619–20). Repeating Schiller's words, Hegel suggests an opposition of ancient, reconciliatory tragedy, and modern, heartrending tragedy. The end of *Wallenstein* seems to prove the point Schiller had made in jest: ancient works afford the audience a kind of satisfaction, whereas modern works plunge the viewers deeper into despair. This was also the contrast suggested by Hegel's fragment on the tragedy of Judaism, and the normative conception of the tragic recurs in the *Wallenstein* piece, with a formulation even closer to the *Poetics*: the work "is not tragic but awful [entsetzlich; cf. μιαρός]!" The ending of *Wallenstein* is so shocking to Hegel because it seems unguided by any kind of justice, poetic or divine. Wallenstein has been murdered suddenly and ignominiously, while the friend who betrayed him finds himself elevated, to his own horror, to Wallenstein's position. The final image, one of Schiller's great *coups de théâtre*, is not a retrospective gesture, as in nearly all ancient and Shakespearean tragedies, but the stage direction "Octavio goes pale and looks, full of pain, to heaven" (*FA* 4, 293). Hegel seems just as shattered by the conclusion of the work, seeking a heavenly justification that will not come: "When the piece ends, everything is over, the realm of nothing, of death has gained triumph; it does not end as a theodicy" (*WZB* 1, 618).

The mention of "theodicy" is important: tragedy for Hegel cannot be divided from its religious background, or from a particular enlightenment conception of progress.[51] Hegel may not intend a strong reference to Leibniz's 1710 *Theodicy* (which coined the term), but, like Leibniz, Hegel will seek to validate the rational nature of existence—though replacing "God" with "substance" as the motive force in history. In the *Wallenstein* fragment and *Natural Law* essay, we see this form of reason taking shape, before it is expressed in monumental form in the 1807 *Phenomenology of Spirit*. Throughout Hegel's writings, Greek tragedy provides a model for the power of reason to think beyond opposition to reconciliation. Tragedy's depiction of conflict is always a means to the attainment of a higher, affirmative viewpoint, from which suffering appears necessary for the progress of spirit. Though this does not conform to modern concepts of tragedy, which tend to emphasize negative and disjunctive elements, it is not necessarily "untragic."[52] It could be argued that the overwhelming negativity of most modern notions of the tragic is no less alien to Greek works (some of which end happily) and Aristotelian poetics (which includes the concept of *catharsis*) than Hegel's apologetic tragic philosophy. Though a Hegelian reconciliatory reading can seem inadequate to a work like the *OT* or *Antigone*, it may capture the emotional dynamics of the *Oresteia* and the *OC* better than a more disjunctive interpretation.[53]

Hegel's first formulation of tragedy as a historical dialectic comes in the essay on *Natural Law* (*Naturrecht*), published in 1802–1803.[54] Moving from

---

[51] See especially Roland Galle, "The disjunction of the tragic," in *Tragedy and philosophy*, ed. N. Georgopoulos (Basingstoke: Macmillan, 1993).

[52] The charge is made in the otherwise superb discussions of both Pöggeler and de Beistegui, as well as in many less sensitive ones.

[53] On the *OC* and German Idealism, see Joshua Billings, "The ends of tragedy: *Oedipus at Colonus* and German Idealism," *Arion* 21 (2013).

[54] The full title is *Über die wissenschaftlichen Behandlungsarten des Naturrechts, seine Stelle in der praktischen Philosophie und sein Verhältnis zu den positiven Rechtswissenschaften (On the sci-*

Frankfurt to Jena in 1801, Hegel reconnected with Schelling and turned his attention fully to philosophy. Together, the two wrote and published a journal (with all essays appearing anonymously) in the years 1802–1803, before Schelling left for a post in Würzburg. Over the course of Hegel's time in Jena, differences from Schelling emerge, which center around the interaction of philosophical theory and empirical reality. For Schelling, historical facts are more or less incidental to the single, timeless truth of absolute identity. For Hegel, on the other hand, the absolute only exists historically, and philosophical knowledge is necessarily historical knowledge. Where for Schelling the concept of the absolute subsumes historical individuality, in Hegel's understanding, the absolute is always emergent from individuality in history. This process of emergence is for Hegel a dialectic, in which (to put it most broadly) opposed positions are reconciled in the moment of "sublation" (*Aufhebung*, from the verb *aufheben*, which can mean "to negate," "to preserve," and "to raise up"—all senses that are encompassed in Hegel's usage).[55] From this higher viewpoint, elements that appeared contradictory or incompatible reveal themselves as parts of the same unified whole. Philosophy's aim for Hegel is the attainment of a viewpoint in which difference and division appear as constructive. The philosopher, like the tragic spectator, cannot reunite what the play of history opposes, but can rationally reconcile himself to the consequences. For Hegel, history is tragedy, and philosophy *catharsis*.

Approaching Hegel's published writings from his earlier notes on religion makes clear how profoundly his understanding of historical process is indebted to a confluence of tragic and theological models. The *Natural Law* essay shows both Greek and Christian inheritances in its description of the decline of Greek culture as a process of self-sacrifice. Sacrifice (*Opfer*) had been central to the fragments on Christianity, but the concept is most thoroughly formulated in a fragment known as the "System Fragment of 1800." In it, Hegel describes a process of renunciation that individuals must undertake in order to gain abstraction from the "objective" relations of everyday existence and enter into the infinite life of religion. The sacrifice of something real simultaneously degrades the finite and acknowledges the power of the infinite, thereby preparing the individual for religious experience. "And therefore he [man] gives up from his property [Eigentum], the necessity of which is his fate [Schicksal], something as a sacrifice [Opfer]—only a certain thing, for his fate [Schicksal] is necessary and cannot be negated [aufgehoben]" (*ETW* 316; *WZB* 1, 424–25). Religion aims at the elevation of

---

entific ways of treating natural law, its place in practical philosophy, and its relation to the positive sciences of law).

[55]The next chapter discusses Hegelian dialectic in greater depth; in 1802 the process is still developing in Hegel's mind.

the individual over the finitude of *Schicksal* (which here means something like the connection to other living things, as in "The Spirit of Christianity"); in order to realize this elevation within life, though, the individual must sacrifice something to death, an act that establishes a form of mediation between the finite and the infinite. It is essential to Hegel's view of sacrifice that what is destroyed be understood as part of a larger organism, which attains to a higher stage through the sacrifice. When Hegel returns to the concept of sacrifice in the *Natural Law* essay, it will be in a social context, describing the fall of a part of the collective in order to ensure the stability of the whole.[56]

The *Natural Law* essay approaches the question of the rights of the individual within society through a historical narrative.[57] Hegel argues that modern individuality can only be understood as emerging from a contradiction in ancient political existence. His account of natural law does not begin with the individual (as most theorists of the time did), but with the *Volk*. True ethical life for Hegel can be conceived only in terms of a collective, in which individuals make no distinction between their own freedom and that of the people. Hegel's model is the ancient Greek polis, which he views as a complex and internally differentiated social organism. The need to defend against external dangers on the one hand and to satisfy the physical demands of the city on the other leads to a division of the people into two classes: the free citizenry, who are willing to fight and die for the collective; and a subordinate class of workers, who ensure the self-sufficiency of the city.[58] Unlike the first class, which enjoys the full benefits of democracy, the second class has no stake in civic life, but enjoys the protection of the state. The ethical consciousness of the first class, Hegel argues, is "absolute" because it places its own freedom wholly at the hands of the collective. The consciousness of the second class, on the other hand, is only relative, since their day-to-day life does not make ethical demands on them or place them in existential danger. Where the first class offers life to the state and receives freedom in return, the second class offers freedom to the state and receives life in return. Still, the lower class is essential to the functioning of the state, since its labor supports the system by which the first is able to perpetuate itself. Only through the relative lack of freedom of the second class can the absolute freedom of the first be maintained. Hegel sees this internal duality

---

[56] See especially Peter Furth, "Antigone—oder zur tragischen Vorgeschichte der bürgerlichen Gesellschaft," *Hegel-Jahrbuch* 1984/5 (1988).

[57] A good overview of the complicated discussion is H. B. Acton, "Introduction," in *G.W.F. Hegel, Natural law: the scientific ways of treating natural law, its place in moral philosophy, and its relation to the positive sciences of law* (Philadelphia: Univerity of Pennsylvania Press, 1975).

[58] There is also a third mentioned (*NL* 100; *WZB* 1, 490), which seems to be made up of farmers and others who live outside of the political life of the state but can be expected to support the first class in war. Their development is never treated directly.

as an unsustainable contradiction, which will be resolved in a dialectical movement, whereby the opposed classes become one.

Hegel points to a moment of transition in the Roman Empire, in which both slavery and aristocratic privileges were abolished, and the two classes made equal under a system of laws. Hegel summarizes this in a paradox, "with the end of freedom, slavery necessarily ended as well" (*NL* 101; *WZB* 2, 491). Now that the collectively minded first class has been abolished, the entire polity lives according to private (and occasionally antisocial) desires, and the need for a system of laws arises. Hegel describes this process as the sacrifice of the freedom of the first class to the rule of law. The danger that the first class had previously taken solely on itself (the relation to the "chthonic powers") is now felt universally, as the need for protection of property. Where previously the ethical dialectic of the state had been concentrated in the first class, it is now spread out across the community: each citizen is subjected to a milder necessity and receives a less extensive freedom in return. The value and necessity of a bourgeois, law-governed state is that it shares sacrifice equally across the community.

Hegel understands the creation of the modern state as the sacrifice of absolute ethical life to empirical reality. The sacrifice takes place in "the ethical" (*das Sittliche*) itself, as the absolute ethical life of the state-as-collective is replaced by an "inorganic" regime of laws for the state-as-individuals. This sacrifice of absolutely ethical collectivity to relatively ethical individuality stabilizes the community's relation to death by erecting mechanisms for protection and punishment. Hegel writes,

> The power of the sacrifice consists in the vision [Anschauen] and objectification of the entanglement with the inorganic, through which vision [Anschauung] the entanglement is undone, the inorganic divided, recognized as it is, and itself taken up into indifference; the living, however, in that it places what it knows to be a part of itself in the inorganic, sacrificing it to death, has at once acknowledged [anerkannt] death's right and purified [gereinigt] itself from it. (*NL* 104; *WZB* 2, 494–95)

The collective, by setting up a system of laws and punishments, makes death a permanent but confined element of existence. Absolute freedom is sacrificed for the good of the individual citizens, effecting the renunciation that Hegel had called for in the "System Fragment." The dialectic of freedom and compulsion that determines ethical life has changed its form: where it used to involve a collective relation to death, it now takes the form of an individual subjection to the law. "Acknowledgment" (*Anerkennung*) and "purification" (*Reinigung*) in this context cannot but recall Aristotelian *anagnorisis* and *catharsis*, figuring the downfall of absolute ethicality as a tragic moment. Hegel understands social life as a constant process of sacrifice, in which the ethical takes on a tragic character.

From the subjective process of acknowledgment and purification (the experience of the collective in relation to death), Hegel turns to the life of the ethical itself:

> It is nothing other than the performance of the tragedy in the ethical [die Auffüh-rung der Tragödie im Sittlichen], which the absolute always plays with itself, in that it always brings itself forth in objectivity, in this form gives itself over to suf-fering and death, and raises itself out of its ashes into glory. (*NL* 104; *WZB* 2, 495)

The description mixes reminiscences of the Christian Passion and the phoe-nix of Egyptian religion to characterize the existence of the absolute in his-tory. It is characteristic of Hegel's thought that he views the absolute as a whole that is only realized partially at any one moment in time. The partial realization here takes the form of a sacrifice: in becoming real, the absolute subjects a part of itself to the fate of all life—suffering and death—only to rise again, in a new form. This describes of course the story of Christ, and is quite similar to Hölderlin's understanding of Empedocles as the "purifying death" out of which, "the people, rise up, as Achilles out of the Styx." The life of the ethical is experienced as an *Aufführung* in that it is the particular realization of a constant process, predetermined by the dialectical struc-ture.[59] Tragedy is an appropriate "script" for the absolute not only because it depicts the death of the individual, but because it shows this death to be necessary and effects a reconciliatory *catharsis* of tragic emotions. In trag-edy, as in Hegel's history of social life, the viewer understands individual destruction as necessary, acknowledging and transcending the relation to death.

Hegel understands the tragedy of the ethical ahistorically, as a constant necessity of sacrifice that persists in all societies. Yet ancient Greece seems to have a unique relation to this process, which is manifest in the content of Attic tragedy. Hegel describes the *Eumenides* (which, not coincidentally, had been translated for the first time in 1802) as a representation of the dia-lectical process whereby destructive, chthonic powers are simultaneously acknowledged and reconciled. He sees the conclusion of the *Eumenides* not as a historical occurrence, but as an example of the process by which a col-lective acknowledges and reconciles itself to the chthonic powers. The ap-propriation of the figures of Eumenides here develops earlier reflections on crime and punishment, but places the revenging powers of fate in a social context. It is now the integration of the Furies into culture as the Eumen-ides that is of interest to Hegel, as an illustration of the transformation of the Greek polis from a state ruled by (collective, reflective) fate to one ruled by (individual, impersonal) laws:

[59] Bernhard Lypp, *Ästhetischer Absolutismus und politische Vernunft: zum Widerstreit von Re-flexion und Sittlichkeit im deutschen Idealismus* (Frankfurt: Suhrkamp, 1972), 186.

> The image of this tragedy, defined more for the ethical, is the outcome of the trial between the Eumenides (as powers of the law, which is in difference) and Apollo (the god of indifferentiated light) concerning Orestes before the ethical organization, the people [Volk] of Athens. In human fashion [menschlicherweise], as the Areopagus of Athens, the people lay equal votes in the urns of both powers, acknowledge the coexistence of both, and thus do not calm the conflict, and define no connection and relation between the powers. In divine fashion [göttlicherweise], Athena of Athens returns Orestes wholly to the people, entangled as he is in difference by the god himself, and with the division of the powers, both of which had a claim to the criminal, also undertakes reconciliation, so that the Eumenides would be honoured by the people as divine powers and have their seat in the city, and from the altar erected to them in the city below, their wild nature would enjoy the view of Athena throned high on the mountain across, and thereby would be calmed. (NL 105; WZB 2, 495–96)

The basic figure of this extremely complicated passage is the self-sacrifice of the absolute: in entering reality, ethical nature necessarily becomes divided into two spheres, human and divine (or relative and absolute). This establishes a tension at the heart of ethical consciousness, as both spheres make a claim in the trial, which cannot be decided "in human fashion." Only through Athena's intervention, convincing the Furies to give up their right of revenge in exchange for a place of honor, can the conflict be resolved.[60] The absolute right of revenge is sacrificed for the relative right of honor, just as the absolute freedom of the first class of citizens gave way to the relative freedom of the new individuality. The *Eumenides* would depict the process of absolute ethicality giving way to a law-governed society. For Hegel, this process is not bound to Athens (and indeed, does not seem possible to locate historically), but is a constant necessity of collective existence. The "tragedy of the ethical" for Hegel performs the process of social constitution from the contradictions of collective existence.

The description of tragedy brings Hegel to the concept of *Schicksal*, returning to his own earlier reflections in "The Spirit of Christianity." Hegel sees tragedy and comedy as inverses of one another, with tragedy animated by recognition of necessity, and comedy by insubstantial drives:

> If *tragedy* lies in the fact that the ethical nature, in order that it not entangle itself with the inorganic, divides the inorganic from itself and opposes it to itself as a fate [Schicksal], and through the acknowledgment [Anerkennung] of the same

---

[60] Hegel does not address the interpretive crux of whether Athena's vote for acquittal creates a majority for Orestes or (as seems more likely) an equality, which then leads to a judgment of *non liquet*. He is interested in the social transformation of the conclusion rather than in the concrete circumstances of Orestes' acquittal: Bernard Bourgeois, *Le droit naturel de Hegel (1802–1803): Commentaire* (Paris: Vrin, 1986), 457.

fate in struggle against it, is reconciled to the divine essence as the unity of both, then *comedy* in contrast, in order to complete the picture, would fall on the side of fatelessness [Schicksallosigkeit]. (*NL* 105; *WZB* 2, 496)

Schicksal here is a development of the reflections on punishment in "The Spirit of Christianity," and suggests a creation of ethical nature—rather than a destiny externally imposed. Hegel's conception of *Schicksal* seems to refer to a relation to necessity more than to the necessity itself. By transforming the powers that divide the city into *Schicksal* (i.e., establishing the Eumenides as a permanent force in the city), ethical life reconciles itself to the fall of absolute *Sittlichkeit*. *Schicksal* has the role of mediating between empirical and absolute understandings of ethical life; it is the way in which objective necessity can be grasped by subjective consciousness. In contrast, comedy's *Schicksallosigkeit* appears in its playful relation to all forms of absolute—an argument that recurs in the *Phenomenology*, where comedy appears as a destructive religious force, opposed to the theological seriousness of tragedy. Though the vocabulary and context will change, Hegel's conception of drama as fundamentally concerned with the role of divinity in human existence, and depicting a change in this role, will remain constant through the *Phenomenology* and *Aesthetics*. The existence of the absolute in history for Hegel is tragic, but tragedy is understood, on the model of the Christian Passion, as the sacrifice of a part of the divine that allows for the whole to "raise itself out of its ashes into glory."

Before moving on to a full discussion of the place of tragedy in the *Phenomenology* in the next chapter, it is important to note how disparate the contexts of tragic thought have been in Hegel's writings before 1807. At no point has he offered anything that could be considered a theory of tragedy, in the sense of an account of the form and meaning of the literary genre (as, for example, Hölderlin does in a number of places). Yet Hegel's early writings outline an idea of the tragic, which, though changing over time, has relatively constant features that will continue to be central to his thought. Greek tragedy for Hegel illustrates the dialectical process whereby contradiction and conflict are reconcilied through a higher insight. As a representation of *Schicksal*, tragedy is a means of attaining a standpoint from which historical process appears rational. Tragedy and philosophy alike seek to make *Schicksal* comprehensible as a force for progress. This teleological understanding of history as tragedy remains central to Hegel's method of philosophy well after his idealization of ancient Greek religion and society has given way to a more affirmative conception of the progress of spirit. Hegel's understanding of tragedy is inextricable from his broader notion of the task of thinking, which takes shape in discussions with Hölderlin that must have ranged widely across philosophy, art, and religion. The marks of their religious training in Tübingen remain profound through their early writings, in which they first formulate distinctive approaches to tragedy and philosophy. Though this chapter has argued that the origins of Hegel's and Hölderlin's thought on tragedy are importantly theological, in the next two chapters it will become clear that the developed theories of both serve ends that are more thoroughly historical, and are substantially engaged in questioning the modernity of Greek tragedy. What in the early writings is often figured as a problem of understanding divine necessity manifests itself later as a need for rational reconciliation in the human sphere. Placing Greek tragedy more firmly in history, Hegel and Hölderlin come to see the limits of tragic reconciliation as a solution to modern division, while at the same time maintaining the formative importance of tragedy for modern thought. They thus crystallize the distinctive quality of the modern concept of the tragic: its engagement with the antiquity of the ancient and the modernity of the modern.

TRAGIC TEXTS

CHAPTER 6

Hegel's *Phenomenology*: The Fate of Tragedy

TRAGEDY FOR HEGEL is the emergence of union from contradiction. It begins in opposition, as the latent instability of one form of consciousness becomes apparent, and progresses through the destruction of the terms of opposition to a new state of (provisional) stability. In the *Natural Law* essay, Hegel described this process at work in the ethical life of societies; in "The Spirit of Christianity," he demanded it in religious life. *The Phenomenology of Spirit (Die Phänomenologie des Geistes)* treats tragedy both as a model for historical processes in ancient Greek society, and, for the first time, as a literary genre in its own right, with a particular historical place and cultural role within the Athenian *polis*. In both contexts, tragedy is the process through which loss becomes constructive, furthering the development of consciousness in and beyond antiquity—a progressive notion that must have emerged from discussions with Hölderlin in Frankfurt. Yet Greek tragedy is also importantly limited for Hegel: both its content and its form have been rendered irrevocably past by the very historical transformations it represents. Hegel's theory of tragedy encompasses moments of both loss and gain, and the power of his appropriation in the *Phenomenology* results from the tension between the insight into historical necessity that tragedy offers on one hand and the emotion of sorrow that it brings with it on the other. As a representation of, and reflection on historical process, tragedy is a central figure of thought in Hegel's system.

*There is no satisfactory translation of the *Phenomenology* in book form; Miller's Oxford text is the standard reference, but it is problematically interpretive as well as frustratingly inconsistent in use of terminology. Far better is Terry Pinkard's draft translation, with facing German text, available online at http://terrypinkard.weebly.com/phenomenology-of-spirit-page. html [accessed July 2, 2013]. I have consulted Pinkard's translation extensively, and encourage readers to do the same. Paragraph numbers refer to Pinkard's edition, which in the chapter "Spirit" (though not in "Religion") are lower by one than Miller's numbering.

Literature on Hegel and the *Phenomenology* is vast. Important recent English books include Robert B. Pippin, *Hegel's idealism: the satisfactions of self-consciousness* (Cambridge: Cambridge University Press, 1988); Terry Pinkard, *Hegel's Phenomenology: the sociality of reason* (Cambridge: Cambridge University Press, 1994); Michael N. Forster, *Hegel's idea of a phenomenology of spirit* (Chicago: University of Chicago Press, 1998). On tragedy in the *Phenomenology*, see Schulte, *Die "Tragödie im Sittlichen"*; Menke, *Tragödie im Sittlichen*; Allen Speight, *Hegel, literature, and the problem of agency* (Cambridge: Cambridge University Press, 2001); Theodore G. George, *Tragedies of spirit: tracing finitude in Hegel's Phenomenology* (Albany: State University of New York Press, 2006). I am particularly thankful to Allen Speight for discussions of Hegel.

With Hegel's *Phenomenology*, we reach the first of two chapters devoted to single texts, and the method turns from thematic discussion to close reading. The reason for this shift in focus lies in the object itself: both Hegel's and Hölderlin's texts are forbidding in their conceptual complexity and linguistic difficulty, and are only accessible to a reading that pays scrupulous attention to details of structure and expression. It is assumed that these texts, no matter how recondite at times, have a recognizable argument, and are written in language that is comprehensible within its own terms. A focus on structure distinguishes the discussion presented here from most other treatments of these texts, which rarely attempt to read at both the microscopic, linguistic level, and the macroscopic, architectural level—a synoptic method demanded by both works. It is important to remember that, unlike most of the texts examined in the last chapter, both the *Phenomenology* and the Sophocles "Notes" were published by their authors at the time of composition. Though their language is extremely idiosyncratic, they are somewhat more accessible than the notes intended for personal use and further development (like Hegel's "Spirit of Christianity" and Hölderlin's "Basis for Empedocles"). An adequate reading, then, should take seriously this exoteric quality and seek to present a reading of the text as a whole.

A close reading of both texts is particularly important because Hegel and Hölderlin are the thinkers of the idealist era most influential for current discussions of tragedy, even though it is only in the last half-century that Hölderlin's "Notes" have been widely known, and Hegel's theory was fairly obscure in English-speaking circles until A. C. Bradley's *Oxford Lectures on Poetry* (1909). Today, both are objects of frequent discussion, appropriation, and criticism, but the difficulty of the texts often makes the basis of such discussions rather shaky. The historical and contextual approach adopted here is intended to correct a number of widespread tendencies in understanding these writings. In particular, there is a tendency to read both theories in isolation from their roots in particular Greek works—to apply Hegel's approach to tragedy in ancient Greece far beyond its historical reference frame, and to isolate Hölderlin's notion of the tragic from its roots in a reading and translation of two particular plays. Hegel and Hölderlin, it is argued here, offer appropriations of tragedies in the first instance (which, to be sure, are thoroughly conditioned by their broader philosophical approach), and theories of the tragic in the second. This distinguishes both from Schelling or Schlegel, in whose thought the systematic basis often overwhelms the recognition of particularity. Hegel's and Hölderlin's theories of the tragic emerge directly from their readings of Greek tragedies (mainly the *Antigone* and *OT*), and their range is far more circumscribed than is often thought. The close connection of their theories to the details of particular tragic texts and their refigurations of concepts of *mimesis* and *catharsis* make them, paradoxically, the last great Aristotelians in their thinking about tragic poetics, and the first to show the power of a genuinely non-Aristotelian philosophy of the tragic.[1] Seeing them in both contexts is essential to understanding their importance for modern thought.

The readings of the *Phenomenology* and the Sophocles "Notes" will build on the discussion of religion in the last chapter, but will also reflect back on the formative idealist understandings of subjectivity and modernity discussed in Chapters 3 and 4, as well as on the major continuities emphasized in the earlier chapters: the engagement with the *Poetics*, especially its concept of *catharsis*, and a sense of tragedy's political implications. Hegel and Hölderlin, though, differ radically from their contemporaries in their understanding of history. All the idealist-era thinkers discussed have engaged profoundly with historical questions in their theories of tragedy, but Hegel and Hölderlin pursue substantially more complex approaches to the interaction of history and genre. Indeed, for both the inquiry into tragedy is fundamentally an inquiry into temporality itself. Tragedy is a figure for understanding historicity: How it is that moderns could experience the world so differently from the Greeks, and what losses and gains has historical change brought? The ambition and strangeness of Hegel's and Hölderlin's approaches only emerge fully when contrasted to the historical thinking of their time. Though their questions are best understood as emerging from the ferment of tragic thought around 1800, their answers remain uniquely challenging. Today, thinking about the relation of antiquity and modernity, the genre of tragedy, and the possibility of philosophical literary criticism still has a great deal to learn from a close engagement with these writings.

THE ETHICAL WORLD OF TRAGEDY

The problem of the *Phenomenology* is the central question of Kantian epistemology: the correspondence of subjective consciousness with objective reality. As in the *Natural Law* essay, Hegel argues that an adequate answer is only possible within a dialectical account of the problem's emergence—that is,

---

[1] This is not to deny, as Halliwell has shown, that concepts of *mimesis* have a formative role in modern aesthetics: Stephen Halliwell, *The aesthetics of mimesis: ancient texts and modern problems* (Princeton: Princeton University Press, 2002), 344–81. Since the late eighteenth century, it is no longer possible to take Aristotle as *the* authority on tragic poetics, though many philosophers have found thinking with Aristotle extremely productive for understanding tragedy and the tragic: for example, Hans-Georg Gadamer, *Wahrheit und Methode: Grundzüge einer philosophischen Hermeneutik. Gesammelte Werke* 1 (Tübingen: Mohr Siebeck, 2010), 133–39; Martha C. Nussbaum, *The fragility of goodness: luck and ethics in Greek tragedy and philosophy*, rev. ed. (Cambridge: Cambridge University Press, 2001); Jonathan Lear, *Open minded: working out the logic of the soul* (Cambridge, MA: Harvard University Press, 1999), 167–90.

a "science of the experience of consciousness" (*Wissenschaft der Erfarhrung des Bewusstseins*, Hegel's original title for the work).[2] Such a history would describe how the present state of doubt and contradiction came about, and provide the insight necessary to dissolve opposition. Hegel largely accomplishes this in the first part of the work, which traces the development of consciousness from the most basic sensory perceptions through self-consciousness to reason. But, as the change in Hegel's title recognizes, the work became much more than an account of the development of consciousness; it became the narrative of consciousness within history. It emerges in the course of the work that reason always exists within historical structures of meaning. For Hegel, changing forms of consciousness must be investigated within the social context that defines them. The relation of consciousness to its world constitutes *Geist* (spirit).[3] Understanding *Geist* in history turns investigation of the "experience of consciousness" into a "phenomenology of spirit," which takes in first individual, and then social development, and leads progressively to the moment at which the principle of development is recognized as "absolute knowledge"—in the final chapter of Hegel's text.

Hegel's account is "phenomenological" because it treats all the different ways of grounding consciousness as so many necessary appearances of spirit—and not as contingent or contradictory moments. The succession of states observed phenomenologically is guided by an abstract "concept" (*Begriff*, related to *begreifen*, "grasp" or "comprehend"), which manifests itself concretely in ever-changing ways, undergoing constant mutation in its progress towards full realization. At every stage of Hegel's work, spirit finds that its present mode of grounding its own certainty leads necessarily into contradiction, which can only be resolved through a new realization of the concept, which sees the previously opposed principles as elements of a higher unity. "Spirit," Hegel writes, "is this movement, to become an *other* to *itself*, that is an *object of itself*, and to sublate this being-other [Geist ... ist diese Bewegung, *sich* ein *Anderes*, d. h. *Gegenstand seines Selbsts* zu werden und dieses Anderssein aufzuheben]" (§36; *WZB* 3, 38). Since spiritual progress can only come about through an insight into the insufficiency of the current state of understanding and a reformulation of that understanding, the moment of negation and preservation (both meanings of the German word *Aufhebung*, typically translated "sublation") is of central importance

---

[2] On the change in conception, see: Pöggeler, *Hegels Idee*: 170–230.

[3] The seminal account of spirit as a relational quality is Pinkard, *Hegel's Phenomenology*. I have learned a great deal from Pinkard's sensitive reading of the text, though my overall approach to the work leans towards a more analytic reading than Pinkard's unitarian one. (That is, I tend to see more loose ends and unresolved questions, which I take to result from changes in the work's design and ambivalences in Hegel's own thought).

in Hegel's text.[4] It describes an act whereby the internal contradiction of a state of consciousness is recognized, and superseded by a new, *aufgehoben* (with echoes of a third meaning, "to raise") state from which the previously opposed elements are seen to be partial truths. It is unmistakably a tragic (in Hegel's sense) moment.[5]

The *Phenomenology* develops and extends elements of Hegel's earlier historical thought into a dialectical method. Self-alienation and recognition had been at the heart of Hegel's philosophical concerns since his earliest writings, and—as the previous chapter has shown—are often understood through tragic and theological models. The concept of *Schicksal* in "The Spirit of Christianity" and the "tragedy in the ethical" in the *Natural Law* essay both entail processes of contradiction, negation, and reconciliation that are clear forebears of Hegel's mature method. In these works, and again in the *Phenomenology*, tragedy appears as a form of spiritual reconciliation. By the time of the *Phenomenology*, though, Hegel's syncretic tendencies had largely been abandoned in favor of seeing Greek and Christian religion as historically separate entities, and ancient paganism as the contradictory form that Christianity supersedes. As throughout Hegel's later thought, the progressive, positive element of this experience comes to outweigh the sorrow experienced at the sacrifice of a previous state of consciousness. Where the *Natural Law* essay saw tragedy as an unending process of division and reconstitution (and therefore not a progress), the dialectic, performed over and over in the *Phenomenology*, is now each time a means of resolving contradictions in existence and moving to a higher state of spirit.[6] The irony of Hegel's tragic dialectic, however, is that Greek tragedy is relegated to a stage of consciousness that Hegel's philosophy seeks to overcome.[7] For Hegel,

[4]"Sublation," though the most common translation of *Aufhebung*, is unsatisfactory. *Aufhebung* literally means "raise up" (from the Germanic verb *heben*, "to hold" and the preposition *auf*, "up" or "away") and by extension, "take away," "destroy." "Sublate" comes from the past participle of the Latin verb *tollere* (which, like the German, can mean both "lift up" and "abolish"), but in its rare English usage means primarily "negate" or "deny." The translation, though, is useful precisely for its artificiality: it serves as a reminder of the untranslatable German word.

[5]See Eliot L. Jurist, *Beyond Hegel and Nietzsche: philosophy, culture, and agency* (Cambridge, MA: MIT Press, 2000), 87–94. Jurist sketches an interpretation of the *Phenomenology* on the model of Greek tragedy. It is, though, reasonable to wonder whether Hegel's dialectical thought emerges from his reading of tragedy or *vice versa*. As the previous chapter has shown, the religious model of sacrifice is crucial to both Hegel's tragic notion of dialectic and his dialectical notion of tragedy. Further, see Schmidt, *On Germans and other Greeks*: 94–96.

[6]For Hegel's self-critique in the *Phenomenology*, see Schulte, *Die "Tragödie im Sittlichen"*: esp. 97–101.

[7]See Jean Hyppolite, "Le tragique et le rationnel dans la philosophie de Hegel," *Hegel-Jahrbuch* (1964). Hyppolite describes Hegel's development as a victory of panlogism over pantragism.

tragedy in ancient Greece is the manifestation of a primitive form of ethical and religious thought and its inevitable crisis. Tragedy necessarily leads beyond itself, as the social organization of ancient Greek culture is *aufgehoben* in modernity.[8]

Though Hegel's use of tragedy and tragic models often takes place on a level of forbidding abstraction, it reveals nevertheless a strong interest in the concrete political life of ancient Greece. This distinguishes the *Phenomenology* from the volumes published as *Lectures on Aesthetics* (*Vorlesungen über die Ästhetik*), a posthumous collation of lecture notes that has become part of the standard edition of Hegel's works.[9] The *Aesthetics* is often reproached for its normative classicism and tendency to dissolve empiry in abstraction. Yet much of what appears implausibly generalizing in the *Aesthetics* lectures makes more sense in the context of the *Phenomenology*. Here, the discussion of tragedy is exemplary rather than interpretive, and thoroughly historicizing (if not concretely historical): the dilemmas of tragedy are seen as meaningful only for a particular moment in time, demonstrating a transient stage of individual and social development. Greek tragedy is seen as a representation of the moment at which ancient social organization and religion begin to unravel, preparing the transition to Christian modernity. As previously, Hegel conceives of tragedy in terms of a contrast between tragic antiquity and untragic modernity, but the *Phenomenology* offers a way of understanding and affirming this opposition. Hegel accounts for the absence of the tragic in modernity by a theory of progress, in which antiquity itself is subject to a tragic fate.

The *Phenomenology* employs tragedy in two places, both times seeing it as central to understanding the role of ancient Greece in the development of spirit: first, in the chapter "Spirit [Geist]," the ethical aspect of tragic conflict is primarily at issue; then, in the chapter "Religion," theological and aesthetic aspects of the genre are treated. Between the two passages, the basic understanding and models of tragedy remain fairly constant, with Sophocles' Theban plays and Aeschylus' *Oresteia* dominating (though Hegel

---

[8] The self-negation of tragedy in Hegel's thought has often led to his being described more as a "comic" than a "tragic" thinker: see Gary Shapiro, "An ancient quarrel in Hegel's *Phenomenology*," *The Owl of Minerva* 17 (1986). Mark William Roche, *Tragedy and comedy: a systematic study and a critique of Hegel* (Albany: State University of New York Press, 1998). Though this is an important aspect of Hegel's theory, I would maintain that comedy is an inadequate model for understanding Hegelian dialectic as a whole because it does not represent historical process (it falls on the side of *Schicksallosigkeit*, in the *Natural Law* essay). It is further a misunderstanding to see an affinity with comedy in the concept of reconciliation, since tragedy for Hegel is itself reconciliatory.

[9] The 1832–45 *Werke* forms the basis of *WZB*, which remains the only complete edition of Hegel's works (a historical-critical edition, *Gesammelte Werke*, still lacks the crucial volume in which "Der Geist des Christentums" appears). For the case against relying on the *Aesthetics* lectures, see Gethmann-Siefert, *Einführung*.

also makes important reference to *Macbeth* and *Hamlet*).[10] In both chapters, tragedy is a genre of transition: ethically, from an externally given notion of right conduct to a reflective one; religiously, from a polytheistic to a monotheistic understanding of divinity; and aesthetically, from art's role as the manifestation of the most important interests of a collective to a secondary place in society. Though both chapters are fundamentally accounts of societal development, they are not strictly descriptions of Greek history. Hegel's discussion of ancient Greece uses tragedy to present a stage in spirit's development, but this stage is a logical rather than a historical one. Tragedy appears to distill tensions in Greek culture in such a way that the state of spirit in this period is legible. In the first moment, "Spirit," Hegel employs tragic models to illustrate the ethical life of ancient Greece, finding in tragedy a reflection of conflicts in society at large; in the second moment, "Religion," Hegel considers the artistic form of tragedy as a representation of ancient theology, which ultimately makes visible the instability of Greek religion. The two chapters build on one another: Hegel shows, first, a contradiction inherent to ancient ethics, which is only understood fully in the second chapter, with an account of the religious foundation of ancient culture. Where the first chapter focuses on ethical conflict, the second strives towards religious reconciliation. The responsion of the two chapters is rarely given sufficient critical weight, likely because of the tendency to see Hegel's thought on tragedy mainly in terms of a theory of conflict.[11] Both elements, conflict and reconciliation, are essential to understanding Hegel's engagement with tragedy.

The chapter "Spirit" begins at a crucial juncture in the *Phenomenology*: having passed through the stages of individual development, consciousness has finally attained adequate form as *Geist*, as it recognizes its essential reliance on community. This comes about in the previous chapter, "Reason," as the rational subject of Kantian thought finds its own self-determination inadequate to ethical action, since it is without grounding in any particular society. Reason, the Kantian agent finds, must henceforth be understood as a social practice.[12] With this transition to a genuinely ethical outlook comes also a shift in Hegel's descriptive focus from the individual to the society

[10] It is misleading to see a change in tragic models from Hegel's earlier writings to the *Phenomenology*, as Pöggeler does: Pöggeler, *Hegels Idee*: 91. The *Antigone* and the *Oresteia* are exemplary for different elements of the tragic process (as are Sophocles' two *Oedipus* plays as well).

[11] The tendency, which is especially strong in English secondary literature, goes back to Bradley's *Oxford Lectures*, but was given particular weight in Michelle Gellrich, *Tragedy and theory: the problem of conflict since Aristotle* (Princeton: Princeton University Press, 1988). Though Hegel is certainly interested in tragic conflict, it is misleading to see this as the essence of his understanding of tragedy. As in every aspect of his thought, Hegel is interested in the dialectical progress through contradiction to unity; conflict is necessary for tragedy, but it is not sufficient.

[12] Pinkard, *Hegel's Phenomenology*: 135.

in which the subject exists. Hegel's narrative in "Spirit" will offer an exemplary account of social regimes of ethics from the ancient world to his own present. He will then begin again (for the third time!) with religion, and describe the progress of the consciousness of the absolute through ancient religions and Christianity to the absolute knowledge of his own philosophy. The shift in focus from ontogeny to phylogeny is appropriate to the social understanding that consciousness has gained in becoming *Geist*. With the broadening of consciousness to embrace collective existence, the *Phenomenology* shows "instead of forms merely of consciousness, forms of a world [statt Gestalten nur des Bewußtseins, Gestalten einer Welt]" (§440; WZB 3, 326).

Ancient Greece for Hegel exemplifies the most basic way of understanding ethical life in relation to communal notions of reason. Greek *Sittlichkeit* —related to *Sitte*, "customs" or "*mores*," indicating the ethical norms of a culture—was given by generally accepted and unquestioned laws. Hegel describes this relation to ethics as "immediate" (*unmittelbar*), since it does not reflect on the duties it is assigned. Such immediacy is first presented at the close of the chapter "Reason" in a quotation from *Antigone*, which describes the subject's adherence to timeless norms of ethical action: "The *relation* of self-consciousness to them [heavenly forms] is just as clear and simple. They *are*, and nothing more,—makes up the consciousness of its relation. Thus they count for the Antigone of Sophocles as the *unwritten* and *infallible* law of the gods [Das Selbstbewußtsein ist ebenso einfaches, klares *Verhältnis* zu ihnen (himmlische Gestalten—au). Sie *sind*, und weiter nichts,—macht das Bewußtsein seines Verhältnisses aus. So gelten sie der Antigone des Sophokles als der Götter *ungeschriebenes* und *untrügliches* Recht]" (§436; WZB 3, 321–22). To demonstrate this immediate consciousness, Hegel quotes Antigone's words in his own translation: "Nicht etwa jetzt und gestern, sondern immerdar / lebt es, und keiner weiß, von wannen es erschien" ("Not at all now and yesterday, but always / it lives, and no one knows from whence it appeared"), translating οὐ γάρ τι νῦν γε κἀχθές, ἀλλ᾽ ἀεί ποτε / ζῇ ταῦτα, κοὐδεὶς οἶδεν ἐξ ὅτου φάνη (456–57: "For it is in no way of today and yesterday, but always it lives, and no one knows from where it appeared"). Hegel is scrupulous in the citation and translation: a footnote refers to the line number of the original, and the translation follows Greek word order closely, introducing archaisms that correspond better to Greek structure (*immerdar* for ἀεί ποτε, *von wannen* for ἐξ ὅτου, where *immer* and *wovon* would have been more idiomatic). This is important to note because Hegel will take significant liberties with two other passages from *Antigone* later. The character of Antigone for Hegel embodies the immediate ethical consciousness of ancient Greece, which represents an alternative to the self-legislating Kantian subject.[13] The cita-

---

[13] Ibid., 137.

tion of her account of duty is pivotal as a bridge from the individual consciousness that Hegel has been describing in the previous chapters to the social consciousness that will be the object of the chapters following.[14] For Hegel, tragedy is from the first embedded in the account of collective existence.

The words "tragedy" and "Greece" are absent from the chapter "The true spirit. Ethicality" ("Der wahre Geist. Die Sittlichkeit."), yet the chapter's narrative of the development of spirit is unmistakably a narrative of the ancient polis and its dissolution, described on the model of Sophocles' Theban plays (especially, though not exclusively, *Antigone*). As in the *Natural Law* essay, this is understood as the playing-out of a "tragedy in the ethical," in which the internal tensions within a collective become so strong that they force a change in the form of social organization. Hegel describes the "ethical world" of the Greeks as divided into the two fundamental realms that give the sub-chapter its heading, "Human and divine law, the man and the woman [Das menschliche und göttliche Gesetz, der Mann und das Weib]" (*WZB* 3, 328). This division is a result of the way in which the underlying order of a community, which Hegel calls "substance," realizes itself in consciousness. At this relatively primitive stage of spirit, an individual can only know one element of substance, and cannot comprehend the full totality of *Sittlichkeit*. Concretely, this entails a rigid division between the various spheres of society, which reach a functional but inherently unstable equilibrium.[15] Hegel's account of the interaction of spheres in ancient Greek society is highly complex, and has formed the crux of most interpretations of his thought on tragedy, especially those that seek to criticize or deconstruct it.[16] Gender has often been the matrix on which Hegel's understanding of *Antigone* has been read, but this is only one aspect of his thought.[17] For the present purposes, it is important to see how deeply the structure of Greek tragedy pervades Hegel's entire account of the ethical life of the polis. Ethical life in Greece is characterized by an antithetical structure that will have to be sublated if spirit is to progress. Tragedy represents this process of opposition, negation, and reconstitution.

[14]See Speight, *Hegel, literature, and the problem of agency*: 51–53.

[15]The details of this division are different from the equilibrium between the different classes of the *Natural Law* essay, but the way of understanding society as an internally-differentiated whole remains.

[16]On some of the major critiques (Lacan, Irigaray, Derrida), see Leonard, *Athens in Paris*: 95–156.

[17]Important in recent years are Judith Butler, *Antigone's claim: kinship between life and death* (New York: Columbia University Press, 2000); Honig, *Antigone, interrupted*. For a discussion of gender in Hegel and his readers, see Peter Burian, "Gender and the city: *Antigone* from Hegel to Butler and back," in *When worlds elide: classics, politics, culture*, ed. Karen Bassi and J. Peter Euben (Lexington: Lanham, 2010).

Hegel understands the ancient polis as divided between the realms of human and divine law, which have corollaries in oppositions between man and woman, and between state and family. Where civic life entails duty to an abstract collective, family life binds its members to one another as individuals. The family seeks to preserve its members, yet each member also has duties to the state, in which individuality is subsumed into the collective. The exceptions to the rule of the state are women, who do not contribute to the protection of the collective, and the dead, who no longer have a role in it. Only when dead does a (male) individual belong exclusively to the family; alive, he is bound to offer himself to the state. The care of the dead is thus the prerogative of the family, the only element of familial life that is not subject to state imposition. Through burial of its dead, the family asserts the role of divine law in human society (while all other actions are governed by the human law of the state): "This final duty makes up the complete *divine* law or the positive *ethical* action towards the individual [Diese letzte Pflicht macht also das vollkommene *göttliche* Gesetz oder die positive *sittliche* Handlung gegen den Einzelnen aus]" (§452; WZB 3, 334). Where the state negates individuality, the family preserves it, yet the two sides of culture are generally complementary, since the family's power begins where the state's ends. When the rights of one are transgressed by the other, however, the immanent contradiction of these two sides of life will become clear.

Having set out the opposition of family and state, Hegel discusses the varieties of relations within the family at great length. The digression is an odd one and much commented on, but there is a close link between *Antigone* and Hegel's theory. He sees only the relation of brother to sister as "pure [rein]," that is, free from desire (which characterizes marital relations) or asymmetry (which characterizes parental relations). The equality between a brother and sister is given once and for all by birth; their relation is without all contingency, and allows for the fullest realization of the self and other: "The moment of the *individual self*, recognizing and being-recognized, can here observe its right, since it is linked with the equality of blood and desire-free relation [Das Moment des anerkennenden und anerkannten *einzelnen Selbsts* darf hier sein Recht behaupten, weil es mit dem Gleichgewichte des Blutes und begierdeloser Beziehung verknüpft ist]" (§456; WZB 3, 337–38). This exposition, and Hegel's surprising paean to fraternal bonds, has to be understood as a response to the *Antigone*. Hegel calls attention to a particular crux of the work, Antigone's speech at lines 905–12, in which she prioritizes duty to her brother over that to a husband or children—words that famously scandalized Goethe:[18]

---

[18] And not only Goethe: they have often been suspected by textual critics for their odd construction and parallels with Herodotus 3.119, but now are largely accepted.

πόσις μὲν ἄν μοι κατθανόντος ἄλλος ἦν,
καὶ παῖς ἀπ' ἄλλου φωτός, εἰ τοῦδ' ἤμπλακον,
μητρὸς δ' ἐν Ἅιδου καὶ πατρὸς κεκευθότοιν
οὐκ ἔστ' ἀδελφὸς ὅστις ἂν βλάστοι ποτέ. (909–12)

[If my husband were dead, there could be another, and a child from a different man, if I lost one, but when my mother and father are covered in Hades, there could never grow another brother.]

Interest in the passage goes back to Aristotle, who uses it as an example of the need to give reasons for an otherwise unbelievable ethical assertion (*Rhetoric* 1417a). Hegel seems to find the notion similarly incredible, but he responds by historicizing the sentiment, describing Antigone's duty to her brother as the expression of the specific way in which public and private spheres relate in Greek society. A brother offers the only "pure" connection that a woman has to the public sphere of men, and so represents for a sister the irreplaceable link between family and state. A brother is thus definitive for the sister's role in the collective in a way no other family member can be. Greek ethical understanding, for Hegel, dictates Antigone's absolute adherence to family bonds, which takes the double form of duty to her brother and duty to the dead.

ERROR AND RECOGNITION

Hegel has set the stage for conflict by describing a collective in which ethical consciousness is divided between two realms. From this static portrait of society, Hegel turns in the next sub-chapter to the action of an agent. The agent can only act in such a way as to realize one or another power of ethical substance, which it understands as a single law to be followed absolutely. There is within the subject "no willfulness, no struggle, no indecisiveness [keine Willkür und ebenso kein Kampf, keine Unentschiedenheit]" (§464; WZB 3, 342). Such consciousness cannot comprehend other ethical imperatives and so understands resistance to its actions "as an *unhappy* collision of duty with lawless *reality* merely [als eine *unglückliche* Kollision der Pflicht nur mit der rechtlosen *Wirklichkeit*]" (§465; WZB 3, 343). Hegel demonstrates the conflict with recalcitrant reality with the example of Antigone. The human laws of the state seem violent and unjust in opposing her chthonic duty. With a consciousness that knows only one half of the ethical imperative, she neglects another, equally valid claim. In acting on the basis of one duty, the subject creates "the opposition of the *known* and *unknown* in consciousness [am Bewußtsein der Gegensatz des *Gewußten* und des *Nichtgewußten*]" (§466; WZB 3, 344) It is crucial that Hegel places both claims, human and divine law, within a single consciousness, even though at this stage of spirit the subject can only be aware of one or the other.

It might seem strange that ethical obligation coincides in Hegel's mind with an agent's knowledge, but this is characteristic of the regime of *Sittlichkeit*: both *Sittlichkeit* and knowledge are given immediately, and are not subject to processes of reflection. The evidence of the senses and the dictates of custom are equally taken to be absolute guides. In acting on such dictates, ethical consciousness necessarily transgresses its own, unknown half, and "through the deed becomes *guilt* [wird also durch die Tat zur *Schuld*]" (§467; *WZB* 3, 346). Guilt is not a result of evil or avoidable error, but of the limits of ethical understanding at this state of spirit.[19] Hegel's understanding of tragic guilt reconceives Aristotelian *hamartia*, with Schelling, as a necessary fault. This fault, though, is not the work of fate, but a blindness inherent to the ethical world of ancient Greece.

In acting on the basis of a onesided commitment, the ethical subject necessarily transgresses another right, and calls up an opposed, vengeful power. Confronted with the inevitable reaction, the agent comes to recognize —in a version of Aristotelian *anagnorisis*—that its action has injured the substance that underlies both its own and the opposing law. The agent's recognition recalls the concept of *Schicksal* from "The Spirit of Christianity," which arose from the acknowledgment of a continuity between the criminal and victim. The coming-to-light of a contradiction immanent to the agent binds together the tragedies of Oedipus, Antigone, and Creon, as Hegel describes a series of recognitions in the events of the house of Labdacus, beginning with Oedipus:

> Reality holds the other side, which is alien to knowledge, hidden in itself and does not show itself to consciousness as it is in and for itself—does not show the son the father in the man who insults him, nor the mother in the queen that he takes as his wife. In this way the ethical self-consciousness is pursued by a power that avoids the light, and breaks forth only once the deed is already done.

> [Die Wirklichkeit hält daher die andere, dem Wissen fremde Seite in sich verborgen und zeigt sich dem Bewußtsein nicht, wie sie an und für sich ist,—dem Sohne nicht den Vater in seinem Beleidiger, den er erschlägt,—nicht die Mutter in der Königin, die er zum Weibe nimmt. Dem sittlichen Selbstbewußtsein stellt auf diese Weise eine lichtscheue Macht nach, welche erst, wenn die Tat geschehen, hervorbricht.] (§468; *WZB* 3, 347)

Oedipus' story exemplifies the partiality of knowledge for agents in the Greek world of immediate consciousness. Since they do not reflect on the basis of their knowledge, their actions are subject to a "power that avoids the light," which undermines intentionality. Oedipus, the most knowledge-

---

[19] See the sensitive discussion of errancy and *hamartia* in George, *Tragedies of spirit*: 87–92.

able and most ignorant of men, is paradigmatic of the partiality of knowledge. Ethical consciousness at this stage of spirit can only recognize the full truth of its actions retrospectively (a version of Aristotelian *anagnorisis*).

From the unknown side of Oedipus' actions, Hegel moves to the unacknowledged right injured by Antigone's deed. Hegel effectively revises the Aristotelian preference for the *OT* through his focus on consciousness within tragedy. Antigone is a more interesting case for Hegel because she knowingly transgresses the complementary law: "ethical consciousness is more complete, its guilt purer, when it *knows* the law and the power that it opposes *beforehand*, considers them violent and unjust, an ethical contingency, and knowingly, like Antigone, commits the crime [das sittliche Bewußtsein ist vollständiger, seine Schuld reiner, wenn es das Gesetz und die Macht *vorher kennt*, der es gegenübertritt, sie für Gewalt und Unrecht, für eine sittliche Zufälligkeit nimmt und wissentlich, wie Antigone, das Verbrechen begeht]" (§469; *WZB* 3, 348). Because she is aware of the opposing power from the beginning, there is the possibility that Antigone can acknowledge her transgression as Oedipus could not, making her a more reflective ethical agent.[20] In the consequences of her deed, Antigone comes to recognize that the opposed principle is based in the same substance that makes up her own consciousness:

> The ethical consciousness must, for the sake of this reality and for the sake of its deed, acknowledge what is opposed as its own, must acknowledge its guilt:
>
> *Because we suffer, we acknowledge that we have erred.*
>
> This acknowledgment expresses the sublated conflict of the ethical *purpose* and *reality*, it expresses the return to an ethical *attitude*, which knows that nothing is valid but the law. With it, however, the actor gives up his *character* and the *reality* of himself, and has perished.

> [Das sittliche Bewußtsein muß sein Entgegengesetztes um dieser Wirklichkeit willen und um seines Tuns willen als die seinige, es muß seine Schuld anerkennen:
>
> *weil wir leiden, anerkennen wir, daß wir gefehlt.*
>
> Dies Anerkennen drückt den aufgehobenen Zwiespalt des sittlichen *Zweckes* und der *Wirklichkeit*, es drückt die Rückkehr zur sittlichen *Gesinnung* aus, die weiß, daß nichts gilt als das Rechte. Damit aber gibt das Handelnde seinen *Charakter* und die *Wirklichkeit* seines Selbsts auf und ist zugrunde gegangen.]
> (§469–70; *WZB* 3, 348)

Hegel again cites the reference, to *Antigone* line 926, where the full sentence reads: ἀλλ᾽ εἰ μὲν οὖν τάδ᾽ ἐστὶν ἐν θεοῖς καλά, / παθόντες ἄν ξυγγνοῖμεν ἡμαρτηκότες (925–26: "But if these things are [deemed] good among the

[20]On this quality of retrospectivity, see Speight, *Hegel, literature, and the problem of agency*: 53–56.

gods, then in suffering we would know that we have erred"). Hegel's translation ignores the fact that the citation is the second part of a conditional sentence, with the optative verb expressing irreality. Where Sophocles' Antigone expresses only a slight uncertainty about the justice of her action, Hegel's ethical subject acknowledges that suffering is proof of error. This would be an obvious misreading of Sophocles if Hegel were making an interpretive argument. Yet it is not the specific instance of Sophocles' play that is at issue, but rather ethical consciousness at this stage of spirit. Antigone's words here represent for Hegel the possibility of acknowledging the opposed principle, which has emerged out of the reaction to her act. Whether Sophocles' Antigone actually does so is for Hegel immaterial; what she shows is that catastrophe has opened ethical consciousness to recognizing its own error. This is a step beyond its previous certainty, and shows a glimmer of the reflective ethical understanding that is emerging. Yet, as Hegel well knows, Antigone does not take this step—indeed, it is only incipient within Greek ethicality, and will first become possible at a higher stage of spirit.

To complete the vindication of the unity of ethical substance, Creon must also be punished for his onesidedness. Hegel introduces this symmetry with the next lines of Antigone's speech (this time uncited): "It [ethical individuality] has the certainty that the individuality whose pathos is the opposed power, *does not suffer more evil than it inflicts* [Sie (die sittliche Individualität—au) hat aber dabei die Gewißheit, daß diejenige Individualität, deren Pathos diese entgegensetzte Macht ist, *nicht mehr Übel erleidet, als sie zugefügt*]" (§471; *WZB* 3, 349). Again, Hegel translates only the result of the conditional sentence, which follows directly on the previous citations, and reads: εἰ δ᾽ οἵδ᾽ ἁμαρτάνουσι, μὴ πλείω κακὰ / πάθοιεν ἢ καὶ δρῶσιν ἐκδίκως ἐμέ (927–28: "But if these men err, let them not suffer greater evils than they do unjustly to me"). Antigone's expression of equality to the injury on both sides (rather than her desire for retribution) is the crux of Hegel's citation. It may not be an accident that both passages cited in the chapter include the verb ἁμαρτάνω, used by Aristotle for the error committed by the hero of tragedy. Antigone's advancing ethical consciousness recognizes that both powers have been injured, and that both guilty parties will suffer. It is only then that the end of the ethical action is attained, and the destruction within the play reveals the hand of fate: "Only in the equal subjugation of both sides is the absolute law first completed and the ethical substance emerges as the negative power that engulfs both sides, or the all-powerful and just *fate* [Erst in der gleichen Unterwerfung beider Seiten ist das absolute Recht vollbracht und die sittliche Substanz als die negative Macht, welche beide Seiten verschlingt, oder das allmächtige und gerechte *Schicksal* aufgetreten]" (§471; *WZB* 3, 349). The true subject of tragedy—which can only emerge at the end of the work—is the ethical substance, not any character or action. In the recognition of the justice of fate, the ethical agent comes to acknowledge the equal validity and invalidity of the two partial claims to justice. Though Hegel has shown this on the model of *Antigone*, his exposition is not exactly an interpretation of the work itself, but an illustration of the process of recognition that spirit undergoes in its transformation.[21] He sees tragedy as the depiction of a necessary stage in the development of spirit; the inadequacy of the Greek ethical world forces spirit to take on a negative quality.[22]

The opposition of family and collective on which the ancient state rests has shown itself to be irreconcilable. With the stories of tragedy in mind, Hegel summarizes the contradiction of Greek society:

> Since the commonwealth gives itself existence only through the disturbance of family happiness and the dissolution of self-consciousness into the general, it makes an internal enemy out of what it oppresses, which is at the same time essential to it—femaleness itself. By intrigue, femaleness—the eternal irony of the commonwealth—changes the general purpose of the government into a private purpose, transforms its general activity into a work of this particular individual, and converts the general property of the state into a possession and ornament of the family.

> [Indem das Gemeinwesen sich nur durch die Störung der Familienglückseligkeit und die Auflösung des Selbstbewußtseins in das allgemeine sein Bestehen gibt, erzeugt es sich an dem, was es unterdrückt und was ihm zugleich wesentlich ist, an der Weiblichkeit seinen inneren Feind. Diese—die ewige Ironie des Gemeinwesens—verändert durch die Intrige den allgemeinen Zweck der Regierung in einen Privatzweck, verwandelt ihre allgemeine Tätigkeit in ein Werk dieses bestimmten Individuums und verkehrt das allgemeine Eigentum des Staats zu einem Besitz und Putz der Familie.] (§474; *WZB* 3, 352)

The "eternal irony of the commonwealth" is that the collective, in order to function as a collective, must make the individual inimical to it. The female is this internal enemy in polis society, a figure that preserves the contradiction of social constitution, and ultimately, asserts the right of the individual and the importance of private life. The privatization of life that Hegel had seen in the emerging bourgeoisie now has its roots in female self-assertion and subversion of collective aims in service of the family. This splintering of the state appears to Hegel as the necessary end of collective existence, which

---

[21] See Menke, *Tragödie im Sittlichen*: 94–96. Menke offers a particularly interesting reading of this citation and process of recognition, arguing that it forms a hinge between the ethical concerns of "Spirit" and the aesthetic concerns of "Religion," via Antigone's attainment of distance on her own actions.

[22] The next stage of his argument (§472; *WZB* 3, 350–51) also uses the model of tragedy, suggesting that the conflict between Eteocles and Polyneices is similarly a conflict between the human law of primogeniture and the divine law which makes them equal as brothers.

cannot resolve the tension between individual, familial aims, and collective, political goals. The immediate ethical consciousness of *Sittlichkeit* leads ultimately to contradiction, and makes visible the need for a more reflective, and therefore more individual, social existence.

Geist necessarily develops beyond the immediate consciousness of the ethical world, as Greek society is transformed into the Roman state of laws (*Rechtzustand*). In this condition, there is no longer any identification of the individual with the state, and individuals are bound simply by an externally imposed rule of law. The state is now "geistlos," lacking the organic legitimacy of a basis in communal *Sittlichkeit*, but its citizens are now recognized individually as holders of legal rights. *Antigone* appears as a depiction of the growing individualism in Greek society, and a first stage in this process of transition. By making plain the onesidedness of ethical consciousness in the ethical world, Sophocles offers an insight into the unacknowledged unity of substance. In this insight, however, the possibility of Greek *Sittlichkeit*, based on immediate consciousness of duty, is past. Tragedy appears as a representation of the necessary transition within ancient society—indeed, as the form of necessity itself.

Before turning to the second major appropriation of tragedy in the *Phenomenology*, it is worth pausing to consider the precise status of tragedy in the "Spirit" chapter. The *Antigone* seems to function as more than a mere epiphenomenon or example of Greek culture as a whole, yet Hegel at no point addresses its character as a work of art, nor offers an account of why it should have a particularly important role for understanding *Geist* in ancient Greece. In a genealogical perspective, this is hardly surprising: in the decade preceding the *Phenomenology*, Hegel has often—and without explicit theorization of their status—used literary models to understand and figure social transformations. He will continue to do so throughout the *Phenomenology*, using the works of Diderot and Jacobi especially to explore different stages of spirit.[23] Though this may seem curious for a text that proclaims itself to be *Wissenschaft*, it is wholly of a piece with Hegel's tendency to think historical process through works of art. At this point in the *Phenomenology*, it is hard to say more. A more satisfying answer, however, will come in the "Religion" chapter, which argues for the place of artworks, on the model of tragedy, as a form of *Er-Innerung*, "internalization" or (its common meaning) "recollection." Only at the close of both appropriations of tragedy will their philosophical status become clear, as Hegel describes the significance of past art forms for the self-consciousness of the present. To anticipate this discussion, it is as "conceptualized history," a rendering of past transformations into comprehensible form, that tragedy is valuable to the *Phenomenology*. This, it will be shown, is what distinguishes Greek tragedy from the artistic

---

[23] Explored in depth by Speight, *Hegel, literature, and the problem of agency*.

and social forms that follow: it is both a form within history and the form of the *Phenomenology*'s history.

Tragic Knowing and Forgetting

Hegel's appropriation of tragedy in the "Spirit" chapter of the *Phenomenology* is not a theory of the genre nor even an interpretation of Sophocles' plays. Rather, Hegel uses tragedies (primarily, but not exclusively the *Antigone*) as phenomena through which to understand the ethical world of ancient Greece and its transformation. He does not generalize about the genre, nor does he seek to account for its artistic form in any way. Yet many commentators on tragedy in the *Phenomenology* have taken the passages in "Spirit," and sometimes only those concerning *Antigone*, to be definitive for Hegel's understanding of tragedy.[24] This is usually based on a retrospective imposition of the model of the *Aesthetics* lectures, in which the *Antigone*'s ethical conflict does seem to be definitive for Hegel's very concept of tragedy. Yet such a reading is methodologically unsound, as Hegel did not oversee the publication of the later text, and moreover, the introductory nature of the lectures may have precluded a more complex inquiry into the genre (there is also the more obvious question of whether Hegel's understanding of tragedy remained the same over twenty-odd years). The only explicit theory of tragedy that Hegel ever *wrote* (and published) comes in the *Phenomenology* chapter "Religion," in which Hegel gives an account of the genre and its role in Greek culture. Throughout Hegel's early thought, tragedy has been associated with theological understanding in various ways; in the *Phenomenology* (and henceforth in Hegel's thought), it is seen in a religious teleology that leads from pagan religion to Christianity. For Hegel, tragedy has a specific cognitive role in a specific historical moment: it is the medium through which ancient Greece becomes aware of the inadequacy of its form of religion.

Both the chapters "Religion" and "Spirit" describe forms of reflection that bind communities together; they differ mainly in that religious reflection, for Hegel, is conscious of its need for an authority outside of itself (where the unifying force in "Spirit" is purely immanent to the community), which is found in representations of divinity.[25] The teleology of "Religion" as a whole leads from representations of the absolute as objects of nature in eastern religions, through Greek figurations of the absolute as

---

[24]Especially so in: Steiner, *Antigones*; Schulte, *Die "Tragödie im Sittlichen."* Many others, even if they recognize "Religion" as important, will see it as an expansion of the earlier chapter—rather than the central exposition of Hegel's thought on tragedy.

[25]See Pinkard, *Hegel's Phenomenology*: 221–28.

anthropomorphic gods, to the incorporeal God of Christianity. Religion, for Hegel, grows more individual and reflective as religious subjects recognize the contradictions of positing the absolute in any concrete form. Greek culture now appears at a different stage of development, representing the second major form of religious life, where it had been the first manifestation of spirit. Hegel describes the "natural religion" of Egypt (among others) as "immediate," in the same sense that Greek *Geist* was: supernatural power is understood to lie in a mysterious, inaccessible realm, which can only be grasped through symbols. In the course of fashioning symbols, though, the figures increasingly are attributed consciousness and come to resemble their creators, until they become anthropomorphic. At this point, Greek "art-religion" (*Kunstreligion*) begins, as divinity is understood to be comprehensible in the terms of human consciousness and representable in human form. Divinity in Greek religion is no longer something outside of society but an integral part of community, existing in a relationship of reciprocity with humans.

Because Greek gods lend themselves to anthropomorphic representation (rather than symbolic indication), Greek religion finds its adequate expression in works of art. Ultimately, this artistic religion, too, will find itself unable to represent developing concepts of divinity, as philosophical abstraction begins to undermine the concreteness of the Greek pantheon and religion comes to be understood as an individual relation to divinity. Greek religion, though, produces "absolute art" (§702; WZB 3, 514) in that it is through artistic representation that the community's values and understanding of the absolute are captured. It is only in Greek art-religion that religious consciousness finds its adequate manifestation in artistic works. [26] Before, substance is too material; later, it is too spiritual (§702; WZB 3, 514). Hegel's treatment of Greek art-religion, despite its teleological framework, is notable for its nostalgic quality. Like every other form of spirit examined previously, it is seen as a stage in the larger narrative of progress; yet as "absolute," it is also an end in itself. Hegel, unusually, will pause to reflect on the end of art's highest possibility, and the fate of Greek culture. The *Phenomenology*'s account of ancient Greece is conditioned by a tension between the absolute validity of its art, and the relative validity of its religion, and stands out in the work for its ambivalence.

Drama is created at the point when Greek art reaches the height of its religious consciousness. Hegel describes three stages of art-religion, characterized by increasingly anthropomorphic representations of the divine: "the abstract artwork" of sculpture, oracles, and cult-worship, in which divinity is hierarchically separated from humanity, gives way to "the living artwork"

[26]This thesis recurs famously in the *Aesthetics* lectures, where it grounds Hegel's argument for the "past-character of art": after the end of Greek religion, no other age has represented its highest concerns in artistic form, and thus, art's moment of greatest importance has passed.

of mysteries and religious festivals, in which divinity is understood as mysteriously present in collective existence. In the final stage, "the spiritual artwork," the gods take on subjectivity as they themselves are represented as the agents of necessity ruling human existence in epic and drama. This is the moment at which the Pantheon of gods acquires form, as each divinity is given individual traits and powers. With this new individualization, a representation of divinity as a concrete, active force first becomes possible. The epic bard has the task of describing the concrete relation of gods and heroes, focusing on the way divine necessity and human will interact. The necessity depicted in epic, though, is removed from human consciousness so much that it inevitably appears capricious and inscrutable. Tragedy will close the gulf between human and divine consciousness by depicting humans animated with substantial aims, "*self-conscious* people, who *know* their right and their purpose, the power and the will of their determination, and know how to *speak* them [*selbstbewußte* Menschen, die ihr Recht und ihren Zweck, die Macht und den Willen ihrer Bestimmtheit *wissen* und zu *sagen* wissen]" (§733; *WZB* 3, 534). Tragedy is born for Hegel when divine substance becomes the content of human speech, as characters express their religious consciousness and obligations in words.

The relation of human and divine in tragedy is broadly familiar from the chapter "Spirit," but Hegel now accounts for the theatrical medium in a way he did not earlier. Hegel understands tragedy's form as characterized by an internal temporality, created by the opposition of the chorus and protagonists. The chorus's consciousness for Hegel is primitive and discontinuous, "*the general ground*, on which the movement of these figures [the protagonists] created by the concept takes place, it is the consciousness of the first representing speech and its selfless, disparate content [*der allgemeine Boden* worauf die Bewegung dieser aus dem Begriffe erzeugten Gestalten vorgeht, ist das Bewußtsein der ersten vorstellenden Sprache und ihres selbstlosen, auseinandergelassenen Inhalts.]" (§734; *WZB* 3, 535). This consciousness is analogous to that of epic ("the first representing speech") in that it sees divinity as something wholly external, and fails to make distinctions between duties to one god and another. Seeking to satisfy a myriad of incompatible divine imperatives, the chorus's religious consciousness is empty of the particularity that could render it a basis for action. The chorus does not take a clear position on the ethical aims of the protagonists, but only offers irrelevant and promiscuous praise of the gods. Its religious consciousness has not moved beyond the archaic Pantheon of capricious divinities, and sees the divine world as irreducibly chaotic, ruled by a threatening, alien fate.[27]

---

[27] Further on the chorus for Hegel, see Joshua Billings, "Choral dialectics: Hölderlin and Hegel," in *Choral mediations in Greek tragedy*, ed. Renaud Gagné and Marianne Hopman (Cambridge: Cambridge University Press, 2013).

The protagonists, on the contrary, are too immediately bound up in divine substance, and recognize only a single ethical duty. In them, spirit appears "in the simple division of the concept. [. . .] Its substance shows itself therefore split into its two extreme powers [in der einfachen Entzweiung des Begriffs. [. . .] Seine (Geists—au) Substanz zeigt sich daher nur in ihre zwei extremen Mächte auseinandergerissen]" (§735; *WZB* 3, 536). Hegel now interprets the onesidedness of the characters in religious terms: their ethical consciousness shrinks the chorus's undifferentiated Pantheon to the two opposed realms that Hegel locates at the center of Greek culture. Hegel's description of the content of tragic action harks back to the "Spirit" chapter, briefly recalling the conflict of human and divine law, man and woman, family and state as "the nature and realization of the ethical substance [Natur und Realisierung der sittlichen Substanz]" (§736; *WZB* 3, 536). The religious consciousness of tragic protagonists can only recognize a single god, just as their ethical consciousness could only adhere to a single obligation. Tragic protagonists are poised between particular and general for Hegel, as individuals who represent a single element of universal substance. This dual quality makes them the most complete manifestation of religious consciousness, just as the anthropomorphic gods of the Pantheon were the most complete realization of divinity in art. Yet the interpenetration of human, finite form and divine, infinite consciousness will reveal itself to be unstable as the art-religion of the Greeks becomes conscious of its inherent contradiction.

Though Hegel has referred back to his discussion in the "Spirit" chapter, he now expands on it substantially, moving away from the model of *Antigone* and towards the *Eumenides*. This may be explained by a change in the focus of Hegel's discussion: where previously, tragedy had been seen as a representation of social conflict, now it appears as a form of religious reconciliation. The narrative Hegel presents centers on the opposition of tragic knowledge and ignorance. Tragic characters take their knowledge wholly from the divine, but, since their "immediate" access to divinity can reveal only one side of the totality of substance, knowledge is always bound up with ignorance in a single consciousness: "The actor thus finds himself in the opposition of knowing and not-knowing [der Handelnde befindet sich dadurch im Gegensatz des Wissens und Nichtwissens]" (§737; *WZB* 3, 537). This appears paradigmatically in the case of oracles, whose words represent a divine truth that remains obscure to the protagonists until it is too late. Hegel demonstrates the relation of divine language to tragic knowledge successively on the figures of Oedipus, Orestes, Macbeth and Hamlet. All of them seem to be destroyed by a religious knowledge that they are unable fully to comprehend.

Hegel describes tragedy as the emergence of full truth from partial knowledge. The partiality of knowledge gained from divinity links a series of tragic characters, all of whom commit crimes because their theological understanding is incomplete. The religious knowledge of tragedy appears as a manifestation of a truth that nevertheless remains half hidden:

> He, who himself was able to unlock the riddling Sphinx, like the childish trusting one, is sent to ruin by that which the god revealed to him. This priestess through whom the beautiful god speaks is none other than the double-meaning fate-sisters, who, with their promises, drive the person who relied on the apparent meaning of what they said to crime, and deceive through the double-tongued character of what they presented as certainty.

> [Der, welcher die rätselhafte Sphinx selbst aufzuschließen vermochte, wie der kindlich Vertrauende werden darum durch das, was der Gott ihnen offenbart, ins Verderben geschickt. Diese Priesterin, aus der der schöne Gott spricht, ist nichts anderes als die doppelsinnigen Schicksalsschwestern, die durch ihre Verheißungen zum Verbrechen treiben und in der Zweizüngigkeit dessen, was sie als Sicherheit angaben, den, der sich auf den offenbaren Sinn verließ, betrügen.]
> (§737; WZB 3, 537)

Hegel points to ambiguous language as a cause of destruction in tragedy. Taking words at face value, all these figures are destroyed by ambiguities of divine revelation: in seeking to avoid the fate prophesied for him, Oedipus makes himself subject to it, while Orestes carries out the order of Apollo only to find that he has transgressed the right of the Erinyes. Similarly, Macbeth's crimes, motivated by the words of the witches, lead him to destruction. In tragedy, the words of the gods are always riddles, and the protagonists' knowledge is never free from ignorance.[28] Hamlet appears as a more circumspect figure, who "after the revelation which the ghost of his father himself made of the crime that killed him, hesitates with revenge and sets up still other proofs [auf die Offenbarung, die der Geist des Vaters selbst über das Verbrechen, das ihn mordete, machte, mit der Rache zaudert, und andere Beweise noch veranstaltet]" (§737; WZB 3, 538). Hamlet seems to take account of the uncertainty of revelation, in a way that Oedipus, Orestes, and Macbeth fail to—but not, obviously, to the point that he is able to transcend the partiality of knowledge.[29] Even as tragedy brings religious consciousness on stage, it demonstrates the inscrutability of divinity in the downfall of the protagonists.

Hegel's focus on the theme of knowledge in tragedy is continuous with the *Antigone* quotations in the "Spirit" chapter. These related to the possibility of a

---

[28]On riddling in tragedy (in the context of Aristotle's *Poetics*), see George, *Tragedies of spirit*: 110–15.

[29]Hegel may be suggesting a historical differentiation of Greek and Shakespearean tragedy, like he would make in the *Aesthetics* lectures and like Schelling had made recently in his lectures on the *Philosophy of Art*, but it is not explicit.

secure knowledge of the will of the gods, which seems only to emerge through punishment for an action that is retrospectively judged to be wrong. Tragedy for Hegel is the process of knowledge turning against the knower, revealing a catastrophic truth that had been hidden from consciousness:

> Action itself is this inversion of the *known* into its *opposite, being*. It is the transformation of the right of character and knowledge into the right of the opposed, with which it is connected in the essence of substance,—into the Erinys of the other inimical and agitated power and character.

> [Die Handlung selbst ist diese Verkehrung des *Gewussten* in sein *Gegenteil*, das *Sein*, ist das Umschlagen des Rechts des Charakters und des Wissens in das Recht des Entgegengesetzten, mit dem jenes im Wesen der Substanz verknüpft ist,—in die Erinnye der anderen feindlich erregten Macht und Charakters.]
> (§738; WZB 3, 538)

Hegel describes tragedy as a complex of action and reaction, returning to reflections on crime and punishment from "The Spirit of Christianity." As in the earlier text, the Erinyes of the *Eumenides* appear as avengers of an injury to life (or here, substance) itself. Hegel's focus on justice in tragedy is unique within idealist thought, and connects him to the moralizing tradition of thought on tragedy represented by Dacier, among others. But for Hegel, the crime is never known until it is punished; only in suffering can one acknowledge error.

Consciously or unconsciously, Hegel's understanding of tragic knowledge and ignorance follows Aristotle's tripartite discussion of the elements (μέρη) of tragic plot: *peripeteia, anagnorisis,* and *pathos* (1452a-b). For Hegel, though, it is only after reversal that recognition becomes possible, as the punishment reveals the truth of the crime (in contrast to *Poetics* 1452a, where Aristotle lauds the coincidence of *peripeteia* and *anagnorisis* in the *OT*). Out of reversal and suffering, recognition emerges teleologically.[30] This outline of tragic actions binds together the appropriations of tragedy in the two chapters of the *Phenomenology,* and the stories of Antigone, Oedipus, and Orestes. In all these cases, a truth emerges out of tragic onesidedness and punishment:

> However, the truth of the opposed powers of content and consciousness is the result that both are equally right, and therefore, in the opposition that the action creates, equally wrong. The movement of the deed shows their unity in the reciprocal downfall of both powers and the self-conscious characters.

> [Die Wahrheit aber der gegeneinander auftretenden Mächte des Inhalts und Bewußtseins ist das Resultat, daß beide gleiches Recht und darum in ihrem Gegen-

---

[30] See Terence Cave, *Recognitions: a study in poetics* (Oxford: Clarendon, 1988), 150–62. Cave points out that this is a substantial widening (or corruption) of the Aristotelian concept. This is of course characteristic of idealist appropriations of Aristotelian terminology.

satz, den das Handeln hervorbringt, gleiches Unrecht haben. Die Bewegung des Tuns erweist ihre Einheit in dem gegenseitigen Untergange beider Mächte und der selbstbewußten Charaktere.] (§740; WZB 3, 539)

This insight seems to relate as much to the audience as to the protagonists of tragedy, though Hegel does not distinguish clearly, and may see both as possible. In viewing (or experiencing) collision and suffering, one comes to recognize the insufficiency of the forms of knowledge represented on stage. From this standpoint, the opposing sides of the protagonists' consciousnesses—known and unknown, the laws of state and family—are shown to be manifestations of a single unity (a structure not so different from Schelling's notion of tragedy as the proof of the absolute identity of freedom and necessity). As the unity behind opposition is recognized, reconciliation becomes possible.

Since the *Poetics*, tragic knowledge and recognition have been associated with the figure of Oedipus. He appears in three guises in the *Phenomenology*: as the solver of the riddle of the Sphinx (not portrayed in any extant Greek tragedy, but referred to by Sophocles), as the parrincest of the *OT*, and, somewhat more sketchily, as the redeemed sufferer of the *OC*. These three moments in Oedipus' story outline the tragic process for Hegel: (partial) knowledge, reversal and suffering, and reconciliation. Hegel goes on to describe a reconciliation (*Versöhnung*) through forgetting (*Vergessenheit*). As the characters give up their previous certainties, they attain something like an Aristotelian *catharsis*:

> The reconciliation of the opposition with itself is the *Lethe* of the *underworld* in death, or the *Lethe* of the *upper world* as acquittal not from guilt (since consciousness cannot deny this because it acted), but from the crime, and its expiatory calm. Both are *forgetfulness*, the disappearance of reality and the deed of the powers of substance, their individualities, and the powers of abstract thought of good and evil.

> [Die Versöhnung des Gegensatzes mit sich ist die *Lethe* der *Unterwelt* im Tode,— oder die *Lethe* der *Oberwelt*, als Freisprechung nicht von der Schuld, denn diese kann das Bewußtsein, weil es handelte, nicht verleugnen, sondern vom Verbrechen, und seine sühnende Beruhigung. Beide sind die *Vergessenheit*, das Verschwundensein der Wirklichkeit und des Tuns der Mächte der Substanz, ihrer Individualitäten, und der Mächte des abstrakten Gedankens des Guten und des Bösen.] (§740; WZB 3, 539–40)

The two possibilities for reconciliation, death and absolution, are not explicitly connected to particular characters; they apply most obviously to Antigone's death and Orestes' acquittal in the *Eumenides*. But the Oedipus of the *OC* may lie behind both, as a character whose death, unlike Antigone's, has a clearly reconciliatory quality, and who, to a Christian readership, seems to attain something like redemption for his earlier crimes by his reception in Athens. Both

Oedipus' and Orestes' death could bring a recognition of "the equal honor and therefore the equal unreality of Apollo and the Erinyes, and the return of their spirituality and action into the single Zeus [die gleiche Ehre und damit die gleichgültige Unwirklichkeit Apollos und der Erinnye, und die Rückkehr ihrer Begeistung und Tätigkeit in den einfachen Zeus]" (§740; WZB 3, 540). Hegel exploits a symmetry between the stories of Orestes and Oedipus: the partial knowledge of both comes from Apollo (Orestes' command of revenge, Oedipus' oracle), and redemption comes from a reconciliation with the Erinyes/Eumenides. Such reconciliation is essential to Hegel's concept of tragedy. It completes a progress beyond the opposed realms of Athenian divinity he had pointed to in the *Natural Law* essay, and beyond the onesidedness of ethical and religious consciousnesses he has described previously in the *Phenomenology*. The religious truth that emerges from tragedy sublates the conflict and destruction portrayed. For Hegel, it is the redemptive endings of the *Oresteia* and *OC* that depict the essential process of tragedy, the progress from division to reconciliation.

THE END OF TRAGEDY

The end of tragedy brings the end of the art-religion of the Greeks. Tragedy's reconciliatory insight into the unity of substance renders the individualized gods of the Pantheon obsolete: "This fate completes the depopulation of heaven, the thoughtless mixing of individuality and essence [Dieses Schicksal vollendet die Entvölkerung des Himmels, der gedankenlosen Vermischung der Individualität und des Wesens]" (§741; WZB 3, 540). Greek tragedy reveals that divine substance (or essence) cannot be individualized as *pathos* or knowledge; the onesidedness of tragic characters demonstrates the incoherence of Greek religious consciousness, which can only grasp the divine as single beings. Divinity, Greek culture is beginning to realize, cannot be atomized as discrete individuals—but no alternative has presented itself (it will only come in Christianity's incorporeal god). The demonstration of the inadequacy of Greek knowledge of the divine is a shared end of tragedy and philosophy.

Hegel sees Socrates' questioning as analogous to tragedy's "expulsion of such essence-less representations [Vertreibung solcher wesenlosen Vorstellungen]" (§741; WZB 3, 540). Tragedy, in representing the too-immediate unity of human and divine, is both the peak of art-religion and the moment at which its inadequacy first appears. After the insight of tragedy, the apparent unity of individuality and divine substance is broken, introducing a division between actor and role: "The hero who appears before the audience decomposes into his mask and the actor, into the person and the real self [Der Held, der vor dem Zuschauer auftritt, zerfällt in seine Maske und in den Schauspieler, in die Person und das wirkliche Selbst]" (§742; WZB 3, 541). The mask (*persona* in Latin) that had identified the actor with a mythical hero now appears as "hypocrisy" (playing on the Greek ὑποκριτής, actor).[31] The substantial interests of the community can no longer be represented by a single-minded mythical character, but are now recognized as subject to the contradiction, debate, and ambiguity of real existence.

The art form of the real self in everyday existence is comedy, which now becomes the definitive expression of Greek consciousness. In the parabasis (the moment when the chorus speaks in the person of the author), comedy depicts an interplay of the masked self and the real one, now separated and at odds. The self-consciousness of comedy can put on and take off the mask at will, and the fluidity of its identity represents the dissolution of tragic certainty. With the transition from tragedy to comedy, the art-religion reaches the height of anthropomorphism; yet in doing so, it has revealed the insufficiency of artistic representation to the substantial interests of consciousness. Comedy's irony has a tinge of bitterness to it, as the vacuum of certainty left by the disappearance of the tragic Pantheon is experienced as a loss. Private goals, rather than religious or social obligation, become the reigning principle, a change that reveals—as in both the "Spirit" chapter and the *Natural Law* essay—fissures in the unity of the polis, "the complete emancipation of the purposes of immediate individuality from the general order and the individual's ridicule of this order [die gänzliche Befreiung der Zwecke der unmittelbaren Einzelnheit von der allgemeinen Ordnung und der Spott jener über diese]" (§745; WZB 3, 543). Comedy's anarchic relation to accepted values and beliefs elevates the individual above the collective, and brings about the end of Greek religion and communal life alike: "The *individual self* is the negative power, through and in which the gods as well as their moments, existing nature, and thoughts of their determinations, disappear [Das *einzelne Selbst* ist die negative Kraft, durch und in welcher die Götter sowie deren Momente, die daseiende Natur und die Gedanken ihrer Bestimmungen, verschwinden]" (§747; WZB 3, 544). Drama dissolves the communal life of the polis, guaranteed by immediate knowledge of the divine, into the private life of the Roman state of laws. The art-religion, as both a stage in development and a representation of the transition (in drama), is a *mise-en-abîme* of Hegel's historical thought.[32] Greek culture as a whole is subject to a tragic recognition of the partiality of its own knowledge, which forces the spirit onward into what appears an abyss of uncertainty.

Having lost the divine grounding for human activity, consciousness experiences "[the loss] of substance as well as of self; it is the pain, which

[31]On the mask, see Werner Hamacher, "(The end of art with the mask)," in *Hegel after Derrida*, ed. Stuart Barnett (London: Routledge, 1998).

[32]Rüdiger Bubner, "The 'religion of art,'" in *Hegel and the arts*, ed. Stephen Houlgate (Evanston: Northwestern University Press, 2007).

reveals the harsh word that *God has died*. [(der Verlust—au) der Substanz wie des Selbsts; es ist der Schmerz, der sich als das harte Wort ausspricht, daß *Gott gestorben ist*]" (§752; *WZB* 3, 547). No other rupture in the *Phenomenology*'s constant process of transformation leaves such a void behind it. Hegel pauses to remember the religion of ancient Greece and his language takes on a rare elegiac tone:

> The sculpted columns are now corpses, from which the enlivening soul has flown, like belief from the words of hymns; the tables of the gods are without spiritual food and drink, and the happy unity of self and essence does not return to consciousness from its games and festivals.

> [Die Bildsäulen sind nun Leichname, denen die belebende Seele, so wie die Hymne Worte, deren Glauben entflohen ist, die Tische der Götter ohne geistige Speise und Trank, und aus seinen Spielen and Festen kommt dem Bewußtsein nicht die freudige Einheit seiner mit dem Wesen zurück.] (§753; *WZB* 547)

Ancient religion has lost the sense of divinity animating human consciousness, becoming alienated from its own source of meaning. Rather than seeing religious life hierarchically, in terms of (divine) substance and (human) consciousness, it must recognize that divinity and humanity are inextricably interwoven in reflection. This realization will eventually change the form of spirit from that of "substance" into that of a "subject" in the "revealed religion" of Christianity (§748; *WZB* 3, 545). Hegel describes this transition as the *Schicksal* of Greek religion, deploying the concept of fate in an idiosyncratic sense familiar from his previous writings on tragedy. *Schicksal* for Hegel describes the process of consciousness recognizing dialectical necessity (not the more usual sense, found in Schelling, of an externally imposed necessity). The structure of the *Phenomenology* has been the coming-to-consciousness of *Schicksal*, a process both represented and completed in drama. Though Hegel recognizes the necessity and rationality of the *Schicksal* that has rendered art inadequate to the expression of the divine, he does so with a sadness that very much recalls Schiller's or Hölderlin's more nostalgic moments.

Hegel's elegiac look back at the arts in ancient Greece, though, attains a form of reconciliation in the concept of memory or recollection, *Erinnerung*. The passage is worth quoting at length for its beauty and for its melancholic, reflective tone, which is rare if not unique in the *Phenomenology*:

> The works of the muses lack the power of spirit, which gained its certainty of self from the crushing of gods and men. They are now what they are for us—beautiful fruits broken from a tree. A friendly fate offered them to us, like a girl presenting us with those fruits. There is no real life to their existence, not the tree that bore them, not the earth and the elements that made their substance, not the climate that made their particularity, not the change of seasons that governed

the process of their becoming. Thus fate gives us, with the works of that art, not their world, not the spring and summer of ethical life in which they bloomed and ripened, but alone the veiled memory of that reality.

[Den Werken der Muse fehlt die Kraft des Geistes, dem aus der Zermalmung der Götter und Menschen die Gewißheit seiner selbst hervorging. Sie sind nun das, was sie für uns sind,—vom Baume gebrochene schöne Früchte: ein freundliches Schicksal reichte sie uns dar, wie ein Mädchen jene Früchte präsentiert; es gibt nicht das wirkliche Leben ihres Daseins, nicht den Baum, der sie trug, nicht die Erde und die Elemente, die ihre Substanz, noch das Klima, das ihre Bestimmtheit ausmachte, oder den Wechsel der Jahreszeiten, die den Prozeß ihres Werdens beherrschten.—So gibt das Schicksal uns mit den Werken jener Kunst nicht ihre Welt, nicht den Frühling und Sommer des sittlichen Lebens, worin sie blühten und reiften, sondern allein die eingehüllte Erinnerung dieser Wirklichkeit.] (§753; WZB 3, 547–48)

All that remains from the *Schicksal* of ancient Greece is the memory of the form of life it incorporated. The final metaphor is important in the history of historical thought: Herder's "Shakespeare" essay uses the image of the seed and the shell (*eingehüllt* is literally "en-shelled") in order to demonstrate that the essence of Greek tragedy was still somehow accessible, and could be compared to Shakespearean works. For Hegel, penetrating the shell of ancient art is impossible; its power remains only a memory, and a veiled one at that. The loss of the Greek world makes the process of recollection the fate of modern consciousness, a constitutive moment for self-understanding. Though the forward motion of Hegel's dialectic is relentless, he pauses here to look back at what has been lost. More than at any other moment in the *Phenomenology*, the sorrows of tragedy seem to weigh on Hegel's logic of progress.

Yet Hegel does find a way to reconcile himself to the loss of ancient immediacy. Through a play on the word *Erinnerung*, he suggests that the memory of antiquity is simultaneously its dialectical preservation, as something internal (*er-innern*; to make internal). The dialectic allows Hegel to describe how the artistic products of ancient Greece remain essential beyond their time, as a memory through which spirit comes to understand itself. Tragedy is an essential moment in spirit's path, and its meaning is integrated into more advanced forms of consciousness. The *Phenomenology* as a whole can be understood as a work of *Er-Innerung*, a recollection of the stages of spirit that internalizes the entire history of consciousness.[33] The play on words

---

[33] See Donald Phillip Verene, *Hegel's recollection: a study of images in the Phenomenology of Spirit* (Albany: State University of New York Press, 1985). Verene, though, does not discuss the way that the two uses of *Er-Innerung* relate. Hegel uses the form only these two times in the whole work, and the responsion of the two is surely not incidental.

here looks forward to the final paragraph of the work, where Hegel writes that "*Er-Innerung* has preserved [the earlier forms of spirit], and is the inner and in fact higher form of substance [die *Er-Innerung* hat sie aufbewahrt und ist das Innere und die in der Tat höhere Form der Substanz]" (§808; *WZB* 3, 591). *Er-Innerung* denotes the process by which spirit incorporates previous losses as meaningful, creating "conceptualized history" as the "recollection and Golgotha of absolute spirit [begriffene Geschichte ... die Er-innerung und die Schädelstätte des absoluten Geistes]" (§808; *WZB* 3, 591). Tragedy is both a form of this process of recollection and an object of it; it exists in time as a means of conceptualizing historical necessity, but is itself subject to the same historical necessity. For this reason, tragedy is not simply a reflection or model of dialectical process, but dialectic's formative moment. In tragedy, spirit conceptualizes itself as a recollecting subject and for the first time grasps the truth of its own path. Though the forms of the past have lost their meaning, they have been internalized and even redeemed in recollection. This process is first theorized through Greek tragedy but is essential to Hegel's project in the *Phenomenology*. *Er-Innerung* preserves Greek art-religion as the tragic fate of spirit:

> But just as the girl who offers the plucked fruits is more than the nature that presents them immediately, broken up into all their conditions and elements—the tree, light, air, etc.—since she brings all this together in a higher way in the gleam of her self-conscious eye and the offering gesture, thus is the spirit of the fate which these artworks present more than the ethical life and reality of that people, for it is the *Er-Innerung* of the spirit that was still *expressed* in them. It is the spirit of tragic fate, which collects all the individual gods and attributes of substance into one pantheon, into spirit become conscious of itself as spirit.

> [Aber wie das Mädchen, das die gepflückten Früchte darreicht, mehr ist als die in ihre Bedingungen und Elemente, den Baum, Luft, Licht usf. ausgebreitete Natur derselben, welche sie unmittelbar darbot, indem es auf eine höhere Weise dies alles in den Strahl des selbstbewußten Auges und der darreichenden Gebärde zusammenfaßt, so ist der Geist des Schicksals, der uns jene Kunstwerke darbietet, mehr als das sittliche Leben und Wirklichkeit jenes Volkes, denn er ist die *Er-Innerung* des in ihnen noch *veräußerten* Geistes,—er ist der Geist des tragischen Schicksals, das alle jene individuellen Götter und Attribute der Substanz in das eine Pantheon versammelt, in den seiner als Geist selbst bewußten Geist.]
> (§753; *WZB* 3, 548)

CHAPTER 7

Hölderlin's Sophocles: Tragedy and Paradox

"THE MEANING OF TRAGEDIES," HÖLDERLIN WRITES in an undated note, "is most easily grasped through paradox" (*E&L* 316; *SWB* 2, 561). Paradox, the co-presentation of opposites, is the guiding principle of Hölderlin's thought on tragedy. Unity, Hölderlin believes, can only be grasped through difference, presence through absence, continuity through change: "for everything original [alles Ursprungliche], since all potential is justly and equally divided, does not in fact appear in original strength, but actually in its weakness" (*E&L* 316; *SWB* 2, 561). The tragic is based on a tension between an infinite signified and its finite signifier, in which "the sign in itself is meaningless, ineffective, but the original comes straight out [das Ursprüngliche ist gerade heraus]" (*E&L* 316; *SWB* 2, 561). "The sign" is the human world, which reveals its transience and fragility in tragedy, but in doing so, gives a glimpse into "the original." The dissolution of the represented world is the negative manifestation of an ontological fullness—a structure Hölderlin takes over from Schiller's and Schelling's theory of the sublime. The pattern of negative representation is characteristic of all existence for Hölderlin: nature's power only becomes visible in its negation, "when [nature] presents itself in its strongest talent, the sign = 0 [das Zeichen wenn sie (die Natur) sich in ihrer stärksten Gabe darstellt = 0]" (*E&L* 316; *SWB* 2, 561). Tragedy, as the form in which existence appears at its most fragile, is simultaneously the form in which existence appears at its fullest.

Two relatively concrete oppositions structure even Hölderlin's most abstract thought on tragedy: god and man, antiquity and modernity. The action of tragedy for Hölderlin is always the catastrophic meeting of god and man; tragedy's co-presence of human and divine is an ecstatic state, a time outside of time in which the paradoxical becomes real and changes the course of history. Much of this process is familiar from Hölderlin's earliest thought on tragedy and his drafts and notes for *Empedocles* (discussed in Chapter 5). Around 1801, though, Hölderlin abandons his effort to write a

---

*English secondary literature on Hölderlin's Sophocles translations and "Notes" is growing. A good place to start is the chapter in Schmidt, *On Germans and other Greeks*. A more detailed and philological treatment is in Harrison, *Hölderlin and Greek literature*. Véronique Fóti is the most extensive discussion of the topic currently, though I disagree with many of her conclusions: Fóti, *Epochal discordance*. Useful also are the essays by Courtine, Dastur, Krell, and Lacoue-Labarthe collected in de Beistegui and Sparks, *Philosophy and tragedy*.

modern tragedy on an ancient theme, and devotes himself to the challenge of writing an ancient tragedy in modern language, culminating in his 1804 translations of Sophocles. In Hölderlin's later thought, tragedy offers a way of thinking the relation of antiquity and modernity, defining "the proper" (or "one's own," *das Eigene*) through "the foreign" (*das Fremde*). The paradoxical play of ancient and modern, for Hölderlin, places the forms of Greek tragedy definitely in the past, even as it gives "the tragic" a transhistorical meaning. Tragedy is the condition of historical existence, defined by absolute stasis and absolute change. The Greeks, then, are indispensable, and the Greeks are unnecessary. Tragedy is impossible and tragedy is unavoidable. Or, as Hölderlin wrote during his madness (in lines referring to Oedipus), "Life is death and death is also a life" (*SWB* 1, 481).

Tragedy in Hölderlin's thought is consistently linked to historical process, as a representation of the creation of the new from the destruction of the old. His theory of the tragic can be understood as an effort to redeem history, by referring what passes in time to what remains outside of time. Hölderlin's tragic thought, like that of his friend and interlocutor Hegel, has a progressive element to it, which sees the genre as a representation of the meeting of contraries and the emergence of a new order. Unlike Hegel, however, Hölderlin sees no teleology in history, but only a constant, cyclical process of destruction and creation. In Hölderlin's own writing, moreover, Greek tragedy has a forward-looking quality: it is the form through which he trains himself as a lyric poet. Modernity for Hölderlin only comes to full consciousness of itself through engagement with the alterity of antiquity. The notion of self-definition through otherness is central to Hegelian dialectic as well, but Hölderlin's historical thought is distinguished by its refusal to afford one age a priority. Though Hölderlin has no doubt that he must define himself wholly as a modern, he sees the continuous engagement with antiquity as the only way to make that modernity authentic. For Hölderlin, antiquity is a living presence whose urgency comes from its untimeliness.

The reading of Hölderlin's Sophocles "Notes" ("Anmerkungen") presented in this chapter (like the reading of the *Phenomenology* in the previous) will emphasize the coherence of the whole and its engagement with specific works of tragedy. The structure of the "Notes" has often been obscured by selective readings that appropriate and develop isolated elements of Hölderlin's thought.[1] At the same time, the close connection between particular passages of Sophocles' text and Hölderlin's commentaries are overlooked in readings that view Hölderlin primarily as a theorist of the tragic as a

---

[1] Particularly interesting appropriations are Krell, *The tragic absolute*; William S. Allen, *Ellipsis: of poetry and the experience of language after Heidegger, Hölderlin, and Blanchot* (Albany: State University of New York Press, 2007); Menke, *Tragic play*.

transhistorical concept, in the mode of Schelling's or Hegel's lectures.[2] In contrast, this chapter argues that the "Notes" should be understood as a coherent, though paradoxical, reading of Sophocles' texts, which presents a poetics of the tragic *in and of* history. Though this reading attempts to distinguish between the interests and approaches of Hölderlin and Hegel, it opposes readings that place Hölderlin beyond Idealism, and make of him a theorist of absolute disjunction.[3] Just as Hegel's thought on tragedy is often found wanting for its tendency towards reconciliation, Hölderlin's is valorized for its integration of horror and irresolution. This does injustice to the paradoxical quality of Hölderlin's understanding: tragedy is as much about mourning as it is about joy, and as much about destruction as about creation. Paradox, in the end, is not a negation of meaning, but a figure for the fullness and even the excess of meaning that tragedy presents.[4] Tragedy for Hölderlin is the genre of absolute contraries, and represents paradox as the condition of human existence.

Tragedy and *Vaterland*

The shift in Hölderlin's thought around 1801 is often articulated around the concept of the *Vaterland* (literally, "father-land," it could be translated "nation" or "country;" the adjectival form *vaterländisch* can mean both "national" and "patriotic"). In this period, Germany was a confederation of states of varying sizes, religions, and forms of government, loosely united as the Holy Roman Empire. Hölderlin had been absent from his birthplace of Swabia since he left for Frankfurt in 1796, and he returned in 1800 during a period of despondency, having given up *Empedocles*, his affair with the mistress of the house in which he was employed, and his hopes for a political revival led by Napoleon. The concept of the *Vaterland* crystallizes his hope for a sense of belonging within culture and history, for a kind of collective *Schicksal*. The *Vaterland* for Hölderlin is only loosely linked to a particular place or people (it is not "nationalistic" in any political sense), and can take on an extraordinary variety of meanings, denoting by turns Swabia, German modernity in general, the Occident, and even a purely

[2] Especially in Szondi's wake: Szondi, *Essay*; Lambropoulos, *The tragic idea*; Judet de la Combe, *Les tragédies grecques sont-elles tragiques?*

[3] For example Françoise Dastur, *Hölderlin: le retournement natal* (La Versanne: Encre Marine, 1997); Fóti, *Epochal discordance*. This reading is particularly indebted to the work of Philippe Lacoue-Labarthe, especially Lacoue-Labarthe, "The caesura of the speculative." Lacoue-Labarthe, though, is self-consciously paradoxical in posing the question of "a demarcation of the speculative" (211) in Hölderlin's thought.

[4] I take this excess to be a part of what Lacoue-Labarthe identifies as Hölderlin's "hyperbologic": Lacoue-Labarthe, "The caesura of the speculative," 231.

spiritual state of totality.[5] Common to all these meanings is a sense, which may be more or less geographically and temporally localized, of a sphere of existence characterized by wholeness and essential relations between all parts.[6] The *Vaterland* is a state in which nature and culture reach a stable and productive relation, such as existed in ancient Greece and will, Hölderlin hopes, be established again in modernity. It does not denote a particular national collective, but a spiritual community centered on political and aesthetic ideals.[7] Though Hölderlin's interest in the *Vaterland* coincides with his giving up *Empedocles* and an increasing pessimism about the French Revolution, it does not represent a turn to modern Germany or away from ancient Greece—rather, it is an orientation to a future, imagined state of union of the essential qualities of the two.[8]

Hölderlin first indicates the importance of the concept of the *Vaterland* in a poetological essay written while struggling with the final version of *Empedocles*. The essay, "The declining fatherland . . ." ("Das untergehende Vaterland . . .")[9] marks his breaking-off from the drama, and seems to be a final attempt to collect his thoughts before abandoning the project for good. It begins by indicating a conception of the *Vaterland* as a realm poised between real particularity and ideal representation: "The declining fatherland, nature and humans in so far as they stand in a particular reciprocity, constitute a *particular* world become ideal and connection between things . . . [Das untergehende Vaterland, Natur und Menschen insofern sie in einer besondern Wechselwirkung stehen, eine *besondere* ideal gewordene Welt, und Verbindung der Dinge ausmachen]" (*E&L* 271; *SWB* 2, 446). Hölderlin's concern in the essay is to understand how the fall of one "particular reciprocity" can be represented in such a way that it appears simultaneously as the creation of another—how decline (*Untergang*) can be

---

[5] Johann Kreuzer, *Erinnerung: zum Zusammenhang von Hölderlins theoretischen Fragmenten "Das untergehende Vaterland . . ." und "Wenn der Dichter einmal des Geistes mächtig ist . . ."* (Königstein: Hain, 1981), 19.

[6] Ulrich Gaier, "Hölderlins vaterländische Sangart," *Hölderlin-Jahrbuch* 25 (1987).

[7] Anke Bennholdt-Thomsen and Alfredo Guzzoni, *Analecta Hölderliniana* 2: *Die Aufgabe des Vaterlands* (Würzburg: Königshausen & Neumann, 2004), 203. They argue that Hölderlin increasingly finds this ideal unrealisable after 1803—a thesis that I believe is untenable in relation to the Sophocles "Anmerkungen."

[8] Hölderlin scholarhip has often noted this turn. It was interpreted first in nationalistic terms, as a "turn to the Occident" (Michel) and then, following Szondi, as an "overcoming of classicism:" Wilhelm Michel, *Hölderlins abendländische Wendung* (Weimar: Feuerverlag, 1922); Peter Szondi, "Überwindung des Klassizismus: der Brief an Böhlendorff vom 4. Dezember 1801," in *Schriften I* (Frankfurt: Suhrkamp, 1978). Both narratives impose distorting teleologies on Hölderlin's thought; the central change, I agree, relates to the understanding of the relation of antiquity and modernity. However, this is not a reversal in the hierarchy of ancient and modern, but a new focus on a third state that would integrate elements of antiquity and modernity alike: the *Vaterland*.

[9] Also known as "Das Werden im Vergehen" ("Becoming in Passing-Away").

experienced as transition (*Übergang*). This was one of the central poetological problems of *Empedocles*, which sought to depict the death of the individual as the catalyst for social transformation. The essay can be read as an outline for a poetics of tragedy that would look forwards and backwards while representing the gap between the old and the new.[10] Tragic language for Hölderlin has a retentive and progressive character: by preserving the past ideally, it enables a transition to the future. Tragedy is the representation of moments of catastrophic change, and its objectifying form allows for change to be understood as productive and necessary.

Hölderlin's understanding of the *Vaterland* runs through his writings after 1800, and elaborates a poetic ideal that can be understood as a dynamic balance of ancient and modern elements. This is most visible in a famous letter to his friend Casimir Ulrich Böhlendorff, dated late 1801. When Hölderlin wrote it, he was preparing to leave his family home to take up a post as a tutor in Bordeaux, undertaking much of the weeks-long journey by foot. He would return a year later, having given up the job soon after arrival, ragged and almost raving. The period in between seems an abyss in Hölderlin's life, and his friends would remark on the changes in him upon his return.[11] The immediate impetus for Hölderlin's letter is a response to Böhlendorff's drama, *Fernando*, a work in the tradition of bourgeois tragedy, centering on forbidden love, and notable mainly for its strong artist-mythology.[12] Though the work is subtitled "A Dramatic Idyll" Hölderlin judges it "on the whole, a *true* modern tragedy"—a label Hölderlin does not use lightly, shortly after abandoning his own effort at *Empedocles* (12.4.1801: *E&L* 208; *SWB* 3, 460). It is difficult to see what in the work Hölderlin was responding to, given its mediocre quality and its extraordinary distance from Hölderlin's own poetry. Yet it is an index of Hölderlin's changing thought on the relation of antiquity and modernity that he describes *Fernando* in this way, using the occasion to formulate his developing notion of historical creation.

Nowhere before in Hölderlin's thought do we find so sharp a distinction between ancient and modern tragedy—or between ancient and modern poetry in general. The reflections surrounding *Empedocles* had all assumed that "the tragic" was a constant quality, and the work, though not adhering strictly to Greek forms, employed ancient dramaturgical elements and themes freely. This no longer seems possible in 1801. The possibilities of literature are now firmly based on a historical dynamic between *das Eigene*

---

[10] For an in-depth reading of "Das untergehende Vaterland..." see the commentary in David Farrell Krell, ed. *Friedrich Hölderlin: The death of Empedocles, a mourning-play* (Albany: State University of New York Press, 2008); Helmut Hühn, *Mnemosyne: Zeit und Erinnerung in Hölderlins Denken* (Stuttgart: Metzler, 1997), 117–64.

[11] Hegel, *Briefe* 1, 71–73 depicts the reactions of Hegel and Schelling.

[12] An excerpt is in Jamme and Völkel, *Hölderlin und der deutsche Idealismus*, 4, 35–44.

and *das Fremde*: *das Eigene* for Hölderlin denotes characteristics that are in-
digenous to modern poetry—"clarity of presentation," "presence of spirit
and talent of presentation"; *das Fremde* describes qualities associated with
the Greeks, "fire from heaven," "beautiful passion" (*E&L* 207; *SWB* 3, 460).
Hölderlin sees the natural constitution of moderns as fundamentally different from that of ancients, and therefore requiring a different tendency in
art. The fiery Greeks needed "occidental" sobriety to balance their tempera-
ment, while Böhlendorff has attained the warmth that will complete his
naturally sober tendency. There is an echo of Schiller's *Form-* and *Stofftriebe*,
understood as a historical dialectic: antiquity is characterized by its raw, passionate materials, which require the coolness of modern forms as a counter-
weight (and vice versa). Hölderlin understands all art, ancient and modern,
as requiring a balance between nature and artifice, and thereby recognizes
a historicity and processual quality to Greek culture that is unusual for its
time.[13] He draws attention to the fundamental difference between ancient
and modern works, but sees them as representing complementary processes.

The logic of this historical philosophy is only dimly apparent in the letter,
and will become clearer in the Sophocles "Notes." Hölderlin understands all
poetry as responding to needs created by the particular historical place of a
culture—as in some way *vaterländisch*. His conception, though, is unusual
in placing the engagement with alterity at the heart of culture. Poetry does
not reflect its culture (as Herder or, in a way, Hegel would argue), but is produced by a dynamic of identity and difference. Hölderlin continues:

> For us it is the reverse. Therefore it is also so dangerous to abstract rules of art
> only and alone from Greek excellence. I have long labored at it and know now
> that besides that which must be the highest for the Greeks and us—that is, living
> relation and skill—we cannot well have anything *common* with them.
>
> But the proper must be learned as well as the foreign. Therefore the Greeks
> are indispensable to us. Still, we will not match them precisely in that which is
> our proper and native to us, because, as I said, the *free* use of *the proper* is the most
> difficult. (*E&L* 207–8)

> [Bei uns ists umgekehrt. Deswegen ists auch so gefährlich, sich die Kunstregeln
> einzig und allein von griechischer Vortrefflichkeit zu abstrahieren. Ich habe
> lange daran laboriert und weiß nun daß außer dem, was bei den Griechen und
> uns das höchste sein muß, nämlich dem lebendigen Verhältnis und Geschick,
> wir nicht wohl etwas *gleich* mit ihnen haben dürfen.
>
> Aber das eigene muß so gut gelernt sein, wie das Fremde. Deswegen sind uns
> die Griechen unentbehrlich. Nur werden wir ihnen gerade in unserm Eigenen,
> Nationellen nicht nachkommen, weil, wie gesagt, der *freie* Gebrauch des *Eigenen*
> das schwerste ist.] (*SWB* 3, 460)

---

[13] Szondi, "Antike und moderne," 190. See also Szondi, "Überwindung des Klassizismus."

Hölderlin rejects one form of engagement with antiquity, the abstraction of rules for creation, in favor of another, following the example of the Greeks in order to learn "the *free* use of the *proper*." This seems a specifically modern problematic for Hölderlin, resulting from the power of the example of the Greeks, which threatens to overwhelm the modern poet and lead to naive imitation.[14] Similarly, in a letter to Schiller a few months earlier, Hölderlin describes his study of antiquity as having proceeded, "until it had given me back the freedom which it had taken so easily at the beginning" (*E&L* 202; *SWB* 3, 454). The end of an engagement with the Greeks is a new poetic freedom, which incorporates ancient and modern without subordinating the demands of one age. Like Schiller in *On Naive and Sentimental Poetry*, Hölderlin describes the challenge of the contemporary artist as coming to terms with the difference between ancient and modern art. Having done so, the poet will be able to reconstitute the "living relation and skill" of Greek poetry, but this will necessarily take on a different form.

Hölderlin's notion of the opposed poetics of ancients and moderns informs a new understanding of the tragic, which represents an implicit rejection of the *Empedocles* project. Tragedy appears to take on a different form in modernity:

> For this is the tragic with us, that packed in some sort of container, we quietly depart from the realm of the living—not that, consumed by flames, we atone for the flames we were not able to tame.
>
> And truly! the first moves the inmost soul as well as the last. It is not so imposing a fate, but a deeper one, and a noble soul accompanies such a dying one with fear and pity, and holds the spirit up amid the fury. (*E&L* 208)

> [Denn das ist das tragische bei uns, daß wir ganz stille in irgend einem Behälter eingepackt vom Reiche der Lebendigen hinweggehn, nicht daß wir in Flammen verzehrt die Flamme büßen, die wir nicht zu bändigen vermochten.
>
> Und wahrlich! das erste bewegt so gut die innerste Seele, wie das letzte. Es ist kein so imposantes, aber ein tieferes Schicksal und eine edle Seele geleitet auch einen solchen Sterbenden unter Furcht und Mitleiden, und hält den Geist im Grimm empor.] (*SWB* 3, 460–61)

Hölderlin's contrast between "the tragic" in antiquity and modernity suggests that between Böhlendorff's *Fernando* and Hölderlin's *Empedocles*. The

---

[14]This is why Hölderlin congratulates Böhlendorff at the beginning of the letter on his increase in "precision and supple efficiency," both "national" qualities, while he describes Homer appropriating "foreign" ones (*E&L* 207; *SWB* 3, 459). Hölderlin says nothing about Homer needing to learn "the free use of the national," and so suggests that, even though both ancient and modern poetry are created dynamically, this dynamic is different in modernity, as a function of the errancy or lack of *Geschick* that Hölderlin so often diagnoses. The point is nearly always missed in readings of the letter, which assume that the processes are strictly symmetrical.

title character in Böhlendorff's drama is imprisoned, "packed in some sort of container," at the time that his lover dies, while Hölderlin's title character is "consumed by flames." Hölderlin now recognizes the latter as a distinctly antique fate, not possible in modern drama, and commends Böhlendorff for portraying a tragic fate suited to the modern world. The tragic in modernity must have a more spiritual content than it did in antiquity. The effect of tragedy, the Aristotelian dyad of fear and pity, has become "deeper," though less imposing. Hölderlin sees a universal validity to the quality of the tragic, yet at the same time he recognizes the pastness of the fate depicted in Greek tragedies. It is this dual consciousness that motivates Hölderlin's translation of Sophocles. In the works of antiquity, "the tragic" is visible in an alien form, and translation is a way of appropriating this foreignness. Translation embodies the dynamic of proper and foreign that is at the heart of poetic creation for Hölderlin.[15] Hölderlin's translations will be the means of attaining the freedom necessary for this dynamic, discovering the *vaterländisch* through the alien. Hölderlin's later thought continually anticipates the emergence of *vaterländisch* song. A year later, on returning from France, he writes a second letter to Böhlendorff, which records his hopes for modern poetry "because we, since the Greeks, again begin to sing patriotically and naturally, actually originally [eigentlich originell]" (*E&L* 214; *SWB* 3, 467).

SOPHOCLES, ANCIENT AND MODERN

Hölderlin pursued his *vaterländisch* song mainly in lyric poetry, and in the short time left before he descended finally into madness, produced some of the most beautiful and mysterious poems in the German language. Translation was a means to the end of original creation, and not the end itself. Hölderlin's dedication of his Sophocles volume is clear on this point:

> I have now chosen this endeavor, since a poet among us must also do something for the necessary or the pleasurable, because it is bound in laws that although alien, are fixed and historical. Otherwise I wish, if there is time, to sing the parents of our dukes and their seats and the angels of the holy fatherland.

> [Jetzt hab'ich, da ein Dichter bei uns auch sonst etwas zum Nötigen oder zum Angenehmen tun muß, dies Geschäft gewählt, weil es zwar in fremden, aber festen und historischen Gesetzen gebunden ist. Sonst will ich, wenn es die Zeit gibt, die Eltern unsrer Fürsten und ihre Sitze und die Engel des heiligen Vaterlands singen.] (*SWB* 2, 785)

[15]Throughout the chapter, my use of "dynamic" as a key concept for Hölderlin's translation and theory is heavily indebted to Charlie Louth, *Hölderlin and the dynamics of translation* (Oxford: Legenda, 1998).

Hölderlin is drawn, as in the Böhlendorff letter, to the foreignness of the Greeks as a starting-point for the modern, *vaterländisch* poet. "Fixed and historical" suggests laws that are clear and firm, but belonging to another moment. This is characteristic of Hölderlin's approach to Sophocles: Greek tragedy reveals something essential about poetry, but it does not offer a guide for modernity. Its value to the present lies in its historical quality, its alternative perspective on common concerns. Translation is a means of preparing for creation because it affords an intuitive insight into the poetic process. Hölderlin's translations and notes have the dual purpose of illuminating ancient tragic poetry and modern tragic poetics.

Though it is not often remarked, Hölderlin's 1804 *Die Trauerspiele des Sophokles* substantially represented the arrival of idealist thought on the tragic within public discourse. Neither the brief discussions in Schelling's *Letters on Dogmatism and Criticism* nor in Hegel's *Natural Law* essay offered anything like a theory of tragedy, and neither mentions "the tragic" (although Schelling's lectures on the *Philosophy of Art* were contemporaneous to Hölderlin's translations, they were not published at the time). This novelty may account in part for the universal bafflement that greeted the publication of Hölderlin's "Notes," which persisted long after Hölderlin's rehabilitation as a poet. The "Notes" remains an extremely difficult text, but not impossibly so; its major concern, opening and closing the volumes, is to juxtapose ancient poetic achievement with modern poetic possibility. Sophocles represents an alien culture in its fullest achievement, and so distills the laws of Greek poetry for the modern poet. Beyond this historical and poetological intention, there is also a more specific reason that Hölderlin is drawn to tragedy and to Sophocles in particular (when the technical aim could probably be just as well fulfilled by translation of Pindar, which Hölderlin did as well). From the time of *Empedocles*, Hölderlin understood tragedy as a representation of societal change, as the depiction of a transformation that has an analogy with the process of translation. Not only does he find in Sophocles' plays indications of revolutionary upheaval within ancient Greece, but he seems to view this as a formative stage in the creation of modern society. The act of translation, for Hölderlin, is incipient to ancient tragedy, which is in its essence a genre of transition and transformation.[16] Beyond the technical proficiency to be gained by translating ancient poetry generally, then, there is a particular historical consciousness that tragedy provides, and that translation brings out. History is not only the stage of tragedy, but its action and language as well.

The most striking characteristic of Hölderlin's translation practice is its transparency, its replication of Greek literal meaning and structure in German word choice and syntax. Hölderlin rarely seeks to create idiomatic

---

[16]On the analogy of tragedy and translation, see ibid., 224–30.

German out of Sophocles' Greek (even when the original is relatively idiomatic). Notoriously, Hölderlin translates the practically incomprehensible Greek opening of the *Antigone* into practically incomprehensible German: "Gemeinsamschwesterliches! o Ismenes Haupt!" (1: "Common-sisterly! O Ismene's head!") translates Ὦ κοινὸν αὐτάδελφον Ἰσμήνης κάρα (Juntina/ OCT 1: "O common sisterly head of Ismene"),[17] where a more idiomatic rendering might replicate the sense of the address.[18] Likewise, in *Oedipus*, the chorus' words of the fourth stasimon are exact to the point of near nonsense: "Wie zähl ich gleich und wie nichts / Euch Lebende" (1204–5: "How I count equal and like nothing you living ones") replicates the curious construction of ὡς ὑμᾶς ἴσα καὶ τὸ μηδὲν / ζώσας ἐναριθμῶ (Juntina 1195– 96; OCT 1187–88: "How I count you equal and nothing while living"). In the chorus' next words, Hölderlin pushes a complex construction to the edge of sense: "Denn welcher, welcher Mann / Trägt mehr von Glück, / Als so weit, denn ihm scheint, / Und der im Schein lebt, abfällt" (1206–69: "For whichever, whichever man bears more of happiness than so far, as it appears to him, and who lives in appearance, falls away"). The Greek reads τίς γὰρ τις ἀνὴρ πλέον / τᾶς εὐδαιμονίας φέρει, / ἢ τοσοῦτον, ὅσον δοκεῖν, / καὶ δόξαντ', ἀποκλῖναι (Juntina 1197–1200; OCT 1189–92: "For whichever, whichever man bears more of happiness than as much as seems to exist, and seeming, falls away").[19] Hölderlin barely alters the syntax (except for the introduction of an indirect object of δοκεῖν: "as it appears *to him*"), but his fidelity to the literal meaning renders the text almost incomprehensible. These passages, to be sure, are difficult ones, their translation subject to debate even now, but Hölderlin's translation makes no effort to solve the difficulties; rather, he replicates the strangeness of Sophocles' Greek in German.[20]

There is also a more interpretive form of translation, which willfully adapts the text to emphasize Hölderlin's sense of the modernity of Sopho-

---

[17] Hölderlin's exact sources are still somewhat unclear, but the only Greek text he is known to have possessed (and some of whose readings he reproduces) is *Sophoclis tragoediae septem, cum interpretationibus uetustis et ualde utilibus* (Frankfurt: 1555), known as the Juntina. Hölderlin certainly used another text in addition, but it has not been definitively identified. The Juntina is reproduced in volume 16 of the *Frankfurter Hölderlin Ausgabe*, and cited here by line number. I have added accents to the capital letters in this text, but have otherwise reproduced it exactly; major divergences from the OCT are mentioned in footnotes.

[18] Stolberg translates "Ismäna, mein geliebtes Schwesterherz" and Solger (who was unusually concerned with accuracy for the time) would settle on "O theures, mitgebornes Haupt, Ismene, sprich": Stolberg, *Sofokles*: 2, 7; Karl Wilhelm Ferdinand Solger, *Des Sophokles Tragödien*, 2 vols. (Berlin: Realschulbuchhandlung, 1808), 1, 169.

[19] The OCT punctuates as a question; the Juntina continues the sentence into the next line (though Hölderlin prints a period).

[20] There are also, as Schadewaldt documents, many strangenesses introduced by false readings in the Juntina and by Hölderlin's misunderstandings: Wolfgang Schadewaldt, "Hölderlins Übersetzung des Sophokles," in *Hellas und Hesperien* (Zürich: Artemis, 1970), 278–87.

cles' plays.[21] This is especially stark in *Antigone*, the later in sequence of events, which represents for Hölderlin a hinge between antiquity and modernity.[22] Hölderlin draws attention to some of his interventions in the "Notes," where he describes his aim as "to make it closer to our mode of representation [um es unserer Vorstellungsart mehr zu nähern]" (*E&L* 328; *SWB* 2, 916). The effect is visible in the continuation of Antigone's first speech: "Weißt du etwas, das nicht der Erde Vater / Erfuhr, mit uns, die wir bis hieher leben, / Ein Nennbares, seit Oedipus gehascht ward?" (2–4: "Do you know anything that the father of earth did not experience with us, we who live to this point, something nameable, since Oedipus was seized?"). The resemblance to the Greek is so vague that it cannot be an issue of misunderstanding: ἆρ᾽ οἶσθ᾽ ὅ, τι Ζεὺς τῶν ἀπ᾽ οἰδίπου κακῶν / ὁποῖον οὐχὶ νῷν ἔτι ζώσαιν τελεῖ (Juntina/OCT 2–3: "Do you know anything of the evils of Oedipus that Zeus does not bring to pass for us still living?").[23] Hölderlin makes the god—"father of earth" rather than Zeus—suffer along with the girls, after Oedipus "was seized" (probably a reference to his fall in the *OT*).[24] Changes in the names of the gods occur throughout the translations (and are partly explained in the "Notes"), and have the effect of making the divine power more comprehensible in modern terms. The "father of earth" seems to take part in human affairs in a way that Zeus does not, experiencing the trials of living on with Antigone and Ismene. Antigone's locution, "Do you know … something nameable," establishes a concern with the possibilities of human knowledge that will be important for Hölderlin's understanding of the action of the play. Antigone's question suggests that the forces at work in human existence are not yet clear to historical agents; the "Notes" will explain that this is because divinity is in transition, as the ancient forms of meaning are converted into modern, *vaterländisch* ones. Hölderlin's translation is an effort to bring out the modern tendencies in the Greek text, even as it brings out the latent Greekness of the modern language.[25]

[21] Beissner reasonably (though without concrete evidence) assigns this to a latter stage of composition, alluded to in a letter to his publisher (12.8.1803: *E&L* 216; *SWB* 3, 469): Friedrich Beissner, *Hölderlins Übersetzungen aus dem Griechischen* (Stuttgart: Metzler, 1961), 105.

[22] Here I disagree with Lacoue-Labarthe, who argues that *Antigone* requires more modernization because it is more "ancient" than *Oedipus*: Lacoue-Labarthe, "The caesura of the speculative," 220–22. Not only is this contention unfounded in anything Hölderlin says about the "modernity" of either text, but it does not fit at all with the descriptions of Antigone's character or *vaterländische Umkehr*, all of which place the *Antigone* closer to the modern, "republican" age.

[23] The OCT breaks up the syntax even more, printing a dash marking aposiopesis at the end of line 2 and beginning line 3 ἅ, ποῖον …

[24] See Harrison, *Hölderlin and Greek literature*: 181–82. The verb *haschen* seems to describe man's being seized by a kind of madness, which results from coming too close to the divine—a process Hölderlin sees as the essence of both Oedipus' and Antigone's downfall. There is a parallel use at *Antigone* 993, where *haschen* translates ζεύχθη ("was yoked": Juntina 953; OCT 955).

[25] This is nicely summed up in the three senses of translation noted by Wolfgang Binder, "Hölderlin und Sophokles," *Hölderlin-Jahrbuch* 16 (1972): 25. The article is a good, concise

These two tendencies—making German language transparent and showing Greek theology in transition—exert disparate, though importantly interrelated, influences on the text. Both are part of a strategy of bringing out the dynamics inherent to Greek art. A glimpse of Hölderlin's reasoning is given in a letter to his publisher, which justifies his translation practice:

> I hope to present Greek art, which is foreign to us because of the national convenience and error on which it has always relied, to the public with more liveliness than usual by bringing out more the oriental that Greek art has denied, and by improving its artistic error wherever it occurs. (To Wilmans, 9.28.1803: *E&L* 215; *SWB* 3, 468)

These words can be understood with help from the Böhlendorff letter: Hölderlin sees the process of Greek art as a move away from "the oriental" (or the "fire from heaven") to the "occidental Junonian sobriety." In the translations, he seeks to counteract this movement by bringing out the original qualities in Greek art. Hölderlin's defamiliarization and intensification of the German language seems to fulfill this aim, bringing out the strangeness that Greek culture has repressed.[26] This is not strictly opposed to the other tendency noted, bringing the Greek text "closer to our mode of representation," which similarly relates to a process that Hölderlin finds inherent in Sophocles, and which his translation emphasizes. Hölderlin envisions translation not as the reproduction of a text in a different language, but as the uncovering of possibility within a text in its dynamic transposition. Hölderlin can see this process as an improvement on the original, since it brings out tendencies that Sophocles could not grasp in his time. For Hölderlin, translation completes Greek tragedy.

"THE LAWFUL CALCULUS"

Hölderlin's "Notes" to *Oedipus* and *Antigone* pursue two primary aims: on the one hand, they delineate the differences between ancient and modern poetry; on the other, they seek to define "the tragic" as it is manifested in Sophocles' works. The first task, in essence, goes back to the *Querelle* and its "revival" in the 1790s (on which see Chapter 4), while the second is uniquely idealist, though powerfully mediated by Aristotle's *Poetics*. Religious and historical conceptions form the link between the two aims. The differ-

---

description of Hölderlin's translation practice, of which I only scratch the surface. For greater detail, Beissner's book is still essential: Beissner, *Hölderlins Übersetzungen aus dem Griechischen*.

[26] Similarly, a few months later he writes that he believes himself "to have written in the direction of the eccentric enthusiasm [gegen die exzentrische Begeisterung], and so to have reached Greek simplicity" (to Wilmans, 4.2.1804: *E&L* 220; *SWB* 3, 473). This is well discussed by Louth, *Hölderlin and the dynamics of translation*: 60–68.

ence between ancient and modern poetry results, according to Hölderlin, from their respective theologies, and tragedy's generic essence lies in its confrontation of god and man and the historical change that ensues. Both aims invoke the dynamic interchange of ancient and modern suggested in Hölderlin's letters and his concept of translation. The addition of notes to the Sophocles translation (which Hölderlin intended to supplement with an introductory volume) allows Hölderlin to make these dynamics explicit, and to advocate for a new approach to ancient poetry among his contemporaries. It is this exhortatory aim that opens and closes the "Notes." Hölderlin envisions his work as the spur towards a more philosophical conception of poetry, which would be based on the products of antiquity. As an essentially historical concept, the tragic is a privileged ground for the historical poetics Hölderlin will elaborate.

Both sets of notes, to *Oedipus the Tyrant* (*Oedipus der Tyrann*, the title an example of Hölderlin's alienation through transparency) and *Antigone*, are divided into three sections, which can roughly be labelled "technical," "interpretive," and "historical." Hölderlin begins both notes with a discussion of the form of tragedy generally, in which he describes the poetic laws to be gained from Greek works, and suggests what their application to modernity might be. This is followed, in the second section, by a discussion of passages, in which Hölderlin unfolds his interpretations of the plays and justifies his translation practice. The second sections of both "Notes" focus on two temporalities, which Hölderlin suggests are analogous: that internal to the tragedies, the individual and social changes undergone within the time of the play, and that of translation, the process whereby ancient Greek becomes modern German. The third sections then turn to the question of presentation (*Darstellung*), and develop a theory of the interplay between tragedy's form (the concern of the first section) and the temporalities of the works themselves (the concern of the second section).[27] Combining the technical concerns of the first sections and the interpretive concerns of the second, the third sections describe the tragic within and as historical process. Between the two sets of notes, moreover, there is a developmental structure: those to *Oedipus* establish the fundaments for the *Antigone* discussion, which often refers backwards. Because of the parallelism between the two sets of notes, it will be easier to treat each of the sections separately, in order to show the continuities and developments between the discussions of the two plays.

Hölderlin begins with a statement of historical difference and desired similarity: "It would be good, in order to secure for poets, among us as well,

---

[27] See Jeremy Adler, "On tragedy: 'Notes on the Oedipus' and 'Notes on the Antigone,'" *Comparative Criticism* 5 (1983): 214. Adler labels the three sections "form," "content," and "conclusion"—which is accurate, though vague.

a civic existence, if one raised poetry, among us as well, discounting the difference of times and constitutions, to the μηχανή of the ancients [Es wird gut sein, um den Dichtern, auch bei uns, eine bürgerliche Existenz zu sichern, wenn man die Poësie, auch bei uns, den Unterschied der Zeiten und Verfassungen abgerechnet, zur μηχανη der Alten erhebt]" (E&L 317; SWB 2, 849). Placed at the beginning of Hölderlin's "Notes," these words have a programmatic function. μηχανή (machine, device) is the word used for the crane on which gods appeared in later fifth-century tragedy, and suggests here that Greek poetry was a means of making divinity appear (as at *Poetics* 1454b).[28] Raising poetry to the level of the ancients entails making it once more the site of an encounter with the divine. Hölderlin's hope to secure a civic role for poets suggests that his goal is nothing less than the (re)introduction of poetry into larger cultural life, political as well as religious. The same ambition is present in the dedication's promise to "sing the parents of our dukes and their seats and the angels of the holy *Vaterland.*" Here, as ever, the Greeks are the model: Sophocles was the *vaterländischste Mann* to Stolberg, and from the time of *Empedocles*, Greek tragedy appealed to Hölderlin as a civic form of art. Though Hölderlin has no doubt that the forms of poetry must change, he hopes that the role of poets may be restored.

Yet, before this is possible, a reform of modern artistic process is necessary. Hölderlin judges modern poetry to be chaotic, lamenting its unreliability in comparison to Greek works. Modernity's lack of artistic skill is related to a philosophical deficit in understanding, a failure to comprehend the means of poetry: "One must, among humans, in everything, look primarily to see that it is something—that is, that it is cognizable in the mode (*moyen*) of its appearance, that the way that it is created can be determined and taught [Man hat, unter Menschen, bei jedem Dinge, vor allem darauf zu sehen, daß es Etwas ist, d.h. daß es in dem Mittel (*moyen*) seiner Erscheinung erkennbar ist, daß die Art, wie es bedingt ist, bestimmt und gelehret werden kann]"(E&L 317 SWB 2, 849). Hölderlin describes a philosophical mode of cognition at the heart of poetic process, a marked difference from the genius mythologies of his time. By analyzing ancient works, Hölderlin will come to understand "the mode of [their] appearance," and "how [they are] determined." In order to transfer this knowledge to modern works, he suggests, what is needed are "more secure and characteristic principles and limits. First among these is that same lawful calculus [sicherer und charakteristischer Prinzipien und Schranken. Dahin gehört einmal eben jener gesetzliche Kalkul]" (E&L 317; SWB 2, 849). The "lawful calculus" would direct modern poetry by delineating its own "characteristic" possibilities.

---

[28] Sophocles may well have used the device for the epiphany of Hercules in the *Philoctetes*, but Hölderlin seems to be taking the term metaphorically.

Sophocles will teach the general, lawful process that will show moderns how to discover their own particular, characteristic forms.

The law governing a work of poetry cannot be dictated in advance, but must be related to its individual content. It is here that Hölderlin begins to describe the particularity of the tragic:

> The law, the calculus, the way that a system of feeling, the whole human, develops itself as if under the influence of the element, and representation and feeling and reasoning follow one another in different successions, but always according to a secure rule, in the tragic is more balance than pure sequence. (*E&L* 317–18)

> [Das Gesetz, der Kalkul, die Art, wie, ein Empfindungssystem, der ganze Mensch, als unter dem Einflusse des Elements sich entwickelt, und Vorstellung und Empfindung und Räsonnement, in verschiedenen Sukzessionen, aber immer nach einer sichern Regel nacheinander hervorgehn, ist im Tragischen mehr Gleichgewicht als reine Aufeinanderfolge.] (*SWB* 2, 849–50)

Hölderlin describes two dynamics possible for the poetic law: a dynamic of succession, in which the whole is to be grasped from the various parts emerging and passing away, and a dynamic of simultaneity, in which the whole is to be grasped as a balance of conflicting elements.[29] The dynamic of succession is proper to language as such, but the specificity of tragic language is that it establishes an element of simultaneity, through which the whole can be grasped. The element of simultaneity is particularly important in tragedy because the changes brought about by succession are particularly catastrophic. The diachronic instability of tragedy must be counteracted by its specific rhythm, which is governed by balance, since "the tragic *transport* is in fact actually empty, and the most unbound [der tragische *Transport* ist nämlich eigentlich leer, und der ungebundenste]" (*E&L* 318; *SWB* 2, 850). "Transport" for Hölderlin seems to refer to the way tragedy shows the hero in transition from one state to another through *peripeteia*. Tragic *transport* is "actually empty" because it is only a superficial expression of the law of the genre, and "the most unbound" because it has an eccentric tendency, pulling the individual out of security into chaos. As in the notes to *Empedocles*, Hölderlin describes temporality as the essence of tragedy's content, but the temporality represented in tragedy (*transport*, succession) now exists in a tension with a temporality in tragedy's form (balance).

The balance of tragic form is ensured by the "rhythm" particular to tragedy. In order to counteract the threatening *transport* of tragic content, there must be an equality between the two halves of the drama. Hölderlin describes a "caesura" (the technical term for a pause in sense in the middle of a line of poetry) as the guarantee of the spectator's affective and cognitive balance:

[29] Monika Kasper, *"Das Gesetz von allen der König": Hölderlins Anmerkungen zum Oedipus und zur Antigonä* (Würzburg: Königshausen & Neumann, 2000), 19.

"The counter-rhythmical interruption [is] necessary in order to meet the tearing alternation of representations at its *summum*, so that from then on it is not the alternation of representation that appears, but the representation itself [die gegenrhythmische Unterbrechung notwendig, um nämlich dem reißenden Wechsel der Vorstellungen, auf seinem Summum, so zu begegnen, daß alsdann nicht mehr der Wechsel der Vorstellung, sondern die Vorstellung selber erscheint]" (*E&L* 318; *SWB* 2, 850). The caesura is the moment at which the audience gains the distance necessary to understand the wholeness of "the tragic *transport*," apprehending the transience of succession as a secure simultaneity. The caesura offers a vision of what lies behind the "tearing alternation" depicted in tragedy, and so has a therapeutic aim, allowing for reflection amid chaos.[30] Since tragedy represents a catastrophic change in the world depicted, it must afford a standpoint outside of that world in order for the necessity of change to become clear. In both *Antigone* and *Oedipus*, this takes the form of a prophetic moment in which the tragic course of nature is revealed:

> In both pieces the caesura is constituted by the speeches of Tiresias.
>
> He enters the course of fate, as the overseer of natural power, which tragically bears man from his sphere of life, from the midpoint of his inner life, into another world, and tears him into the eccentric sphere of the dead. (*E&L* 318)

> [In beiden Stücken machen die Zäsur die Reden des Tiresias aus.
>
> Er tritt ein in den Gang des Schicksals, als Aufseher über die Naturmacht, die tragisch, den Menschen seiner Lebenssphäre, dem Mittelpunkte seines innern Lebens in eine andere Welt entrückt und in die exzentrische Sphäre der Todten reißt.] (*SWB* 2, 851)

The prophetic speeches of Tiresias offer a perspective on the whole action, grasping the succession of stages that the tragic figures undergo in simultaneity. The caesura offers a secure insight into historical change, making chaotic events comprehensible through artistic representation.

The placement of the caesura, Hölderlin continues (in a passage repeated almost verbatim in the corresponding section of the *Antigone* notes), should be determined by the "rhythm of representations [Rhythmus der Vorstellungen]" so that the two halves of the drama have an equal weight or power over the viewer. The caesura moderates the intensity of impressions by providing a distanced perspective, which allows for greater reflection on the part of the audience. If, as in *Oedipus*, "the *first* [representations] are torn along more by the *following* [die *ersten* mehr durch die *folgenden* hingerissen sind]," then

---

[30] In reading the concept of caesura as therapeutic for the viewer, I am thinking especially of "The declining fatherland . . . ," where such an aim is explicit. It is only implicit in the Sophocles "Notes," but the reception-focused perspective is suggested by the notion that in the caesura, "the representation itself appears."

the caesura should come early in the work, "so that the first half so to speak is protected against the second [so daß die erste Hälfte gleischsam gegen die zweite geschützt ist]" (*E&L* 318; *SWB* 2, 850). Hölderlin suggests that placing Tiresias' speech early in the *Oedipus* prevents the quickening tempo of the second half from overwhelming the effect of the more expositional first scenes. The insight Tiresias' words provide into the course of nature gives the audience a form of distance that prepares them for the "tearing" pace of the second half. The reverse is the case in *Antigone*: "the *following* [representations] are more pressed by the *beginning* [die *folgenden* mehr gedrungen sind von den *anfänglichen*]" so the additional weight of the caesura comes later in the work (*E&L* 325; *SWB* 2, 913). The rising action of the *Antigone* begins from the very first words and leads to a confrontation that reaches its climax with Antigone's final exit to her death. Tiresias' speech comes immediately after and puts the previous scenes and their catastrophic outcome in a perspective that lends the final scenes additional pathos. Hölderlin sees the caesura as a break that establishes a balance between the violent *transport* of tragedy and the more distanced contemplation of the viewer. Hölderlin's theory of the caesura seeks to reconcile historical transience with the security of poetic form.

"The Boldest Moment"

In his readings of *Oedipus* and *Antigone*, Hölderlin focuses on decisive moments—not the caesurae themselves, but the scenes just before, which would constitute the *summa* of the action. The second sections of the "Notes" take the form of commentaries, juxtaposing passages of Hölderlin's translation with exegetical remarks. Both of Hölderlin's commentaries point to moments of theological excess, in which characters transgress the bounds of human consciousness and come too close to divinity. In *Oedipus*, this is a speech act, a *nefas* (literally, "unspeakable," but a common Latin word for crime), which leads to divine retribution; in *Antigone*, the transgression is Antigone's political opposition to Creon, coupled with a blasphemous appropriation of divinity. In both works, the protagonists place themselves in a new relation to the gods, which is at once profane and sacred. For Hölderlin, the action of tragedy remains fundamentally theological, beginning in a state (as in the letter of 1800 quoted in Chapter 5) in which "god and man appear one," and developing from this illusory oneness through catastrophe to "leave behind on one hand, respect for the heavenly ones and, on the other, a purified mind as the property of man" (*E&L* 184; *SWB* 3, 412). Hölderlin interprets the actions of *Oedipus* and *Antigone* as resulting from an unstable closeness to divinity, which calls for a purification of human consciousness through a demonstration of the power of the gods.

The end of this cathartic process of union and separation is a new relation to the divine, which Hölderlin (like Hegel) will suggest is the beginning of monotheistic religion.

The *Oedipus* notes describe an act of theological excess as the key to the work as a whole: "The *comprehensibility* of the whole depends primarily on envisioning the scene where Oedipus *interprets* the oracular utterance *too infinitely,* is tempted *to nefas* [Die Verständlichkeit des Ganzen beruht vorzüglich darauf, daß man die Szene ins Auge faßt, wo Oedipus den Orakelspruch *zu unendlich deutet, zum nefas* versucht wird]" (*E&L* 319; *SWB* 2, 851). Oedipus, in Hölderlin's reading, misinterprets the oracle brought by Creon, which should have been construed as commanding him in general terms to maintain just order in the city during the plague. Rather than understanding the oracular command in civic terms, "Oedipus however immediately responds as a priest [Oedipus aber spricht gleich darauf priesterlich]" (*E&L* 319; *SWB* 2, 851). He understands his duty as ritual purification through the expulsion of an individual, going far beyond the broad command of the oracle. When Creon explains the story of Laius' death, Oedipus—falsely, in Hölderlin's interpretation—conflates the broad, social degeneracy pointed out by the oracle with the unsolved crime, establishing causality where none necessarily existed.[31] Oedipus' *nefas* consists in his cursing of the as-yet-unknown murderer, by which he "takes the sin as infinite [die Sünde als unendlich nimmt]" (*E&L* 319; *SWB* 2, 852).[32] In assuming the priestly role, Oedipus has in effect created a sin where none existed, and this seems to initiate a progressive disintegration in Oedipus' psychology. Behind all this is surely the Aristotelian concept of *hamartia,* which Hölderlin understands (very much contrary to Aristotle) as an act of intellectual excess, precipitating a longer mental descent.[33] Hölderlin's Oedipus is a man at the verge of sanity, struggling to retain control of consciousness as it slips away. Antigone, too, will appear as a tragic figure struggling to maintain her soundness of mind—which it is hard not to see as a projection of Hölderlin's own deteriorating mental state at the time.

Throughout his interpretation, Hölderlin calls attention to the violence of language. The turning point of the story is Oedipus' *nefas,* rather than (as for Hegel) the revelation of truth or (as for Schelling) Oedipus' acceptance of guilt. Oedipus is doomed by words spoken in the play, not by actions

---

[31] For an attempt to make such a reading plausible, see Menke, *Tragic play:* 14–36.

[32] Hölderlin had used the word also in the first draft of *Empedocles* to denote a crime of *hubris.* It may have a Senecan provenance, as it occurs many times in the corpus, and prominently in the prologue of the *Oedipus: est maius aliquod patre mactato nefas?* (18: "Is there any crime greater than a father slain?"), and, with a compound of *fas* bringing out the etymology: *infanda timeo* (15: "I fear unspeakable things").

[33] See Jacques Taminiaux, *Le théâtre des philosophes: la tragédie, l'être, l'action* (Grenoble: Millon, 1995), 291–96.

committed years before. Indeed, Hölderlin sees Oedipus' sin as his own creation, the effect of his excessive speech. For Hölderlin, *Oedipus* is the depiction of *Geist* losing control of itself, as stable consciousness is overtaken by madness. Oedipus' *nefas* has disrupted the coexistence of god and man, and set in motion a catastrophic process of division. This division takes place first of all in Oedipus' own mind, as he seeks to secure his self-knowledge in "the foolish-wild search for a consciousness [das närrischwilde Nachsuchen nach einem Bewußtsein]," and finally in a "spirit-diseased seeking for a consciousness [das geisteskranke Fragen nach einem Bewußtsein]" (*E&L* 321–22; *SWB* 2, 853–54). Hölderlin sees Oedipus on a collision course with divinity, which causes his mental degeneration. He describes Oedipus' language in this state as demonic: "Because such men stand in violent relations, their speech also speaks, almost in the way of the Furies, in more violent connection [Weil solche Menschen in gewaltsamen Verhältnissen stehn, spricht auch ihre Sprache, beinahe nach Furienart, in gewaltsameren Zusammenhange]" (*E&L* 323; *SWB* 2, 855). Hölderlin grounds the tragic firmly in its mode of representation, seeing the language of tragedy—and particularly the Greek language—as itself a cause of the tragic.[34] Where nearly all previous commentators on *Oedipus* had been interested in the plot or the central character, Hölderlin focuses on speech as constitutive of both. Language is the site of Oedipus' transgression and his tragedy.

The concentration on language in the *Oedipus* "Notes" is importantly developed in the discussion of *Antigone*. Hölderlin had pointed to the way that Oedipus' language creates his tragedy, and in discussing *Antigone* he goes further, to suggest that the process of translation is itself a locus of the tragic. Having described the tragic as a linguistic phenomenon, Hölderlin creates an analogy between tragic *peripeteia* and his own translation. The *Antigone* "Notes" emphasize the difference between ancient and modern modes of representation, and call attention to Hölderlin's interventions in the Greek text. *Antigone* for Hölderlin is a study in the process of epochal change, which is both an element of the tragic within *Antigone*, and a characteristic of the process of translation. In some of his most challenging reflections, Hölderlin describes reversal (*Umkehr*) as immanent both to Sophocles' language and to the process of translation.

The reversal in *Antigone*, as in *Oedipus*, centers on theology. Antigone's adherence to the unwritten laws of the gods appears to herald a new relation to divinity, which stands in contrast to Creon's adherence to the positive, written laws of the state. Hölderlin further emphasizes the contrast in his translations, which have a tendency to make references to divinity more comprehensible in Christian terms. The second section of the "Notes" begins by quoting an exchange between Antigone and Creon:

[34]On the role of language, see Schmidt, *On Germans and other Greeks*: 149.

"How did you dare to break such a law?"
"For this reason: *my* Zeus did not announce it to me." (*E&L* 326)

["Was wagtest du, ein solch Gesetz zu brechen?"
"Darum, *mein* Zeus berichtete mirs nicht."] (*SWB* 2, 914)

Hölderlin has changed Antigone's words, which read οὐ γάρ τι μοι Ζεὺς ἦν κηρύξας τάδε (*Juntina* 451; OCT 450: "For it was not in any way Zeus who announced these things to me"), so that she speaks of "*my* Zeus" (the emphasis is Hölderlin's). This appropriation of divinity is characteristic of Antigone's closer relation to the gods, which suggests something like Christian theology. Hölderlin describes this passage in his commentary as "the boldest moment [der kühnste Moment]" for its juxtaposition of Creon's lawfully mediated understanding of divinity and Antigone's immediate one (*E&L* 326; *SWB* 2, 914). Like Oedipus, Antigone is a theological anomaly, yet she appears in a more favorable light, looking forward to a new understanding of the gods as immediately present in human action. Translation and commentary here reinforce one another in a kind of circularity.[35] Hölderlin's translation has the effect of making Antigone more forward-looking—a characteristic his commentary understands as decisive for the work's content.

The presence of divinity in human action is fundamentally mysterious to Hölderlin, and he accentuates the inscrutability of the divine in the next passage, which again juxtaposes Antigone's and Creon's notions of right and wrong:

CREON: But the bad are not to be considered equal to the good.
ANTIGONE: Who knows, there could be another custom below. (*E&L* 326)

[KREON: Doch, Guten gleich, sind Schlimme nicht zu nehmen.
ANTIGONE: Wer weiß, da kann doch drunt' ein andrer Brauch sein.] (*SWB* 2, 914)

Where Creon assumes a moral equivalence between action and reward, Antigone denies the possibility of secure ethical knowledge, as a result of man's uncertainty concerning divinity. The themes of divine absence and inscrutability may seem unusual for a putatively Christian understanding of theology, but they are again characteristic of Hölderlin's pietist upbringing, and its emphasis on faith over knowledge. Antigone's words appear as "the actual speech of Sophocles" for their depiction of the "human understanding as wandering beneath the unthinkable [eigentliche Sprache des Sophokles [. . .] des Menschen Verstand, als unter Undenkbarem wandelnd]" (*E&L* 326–27; *SWB* 2, 914–15). The incomprehensible nature of divinity seems to

---

[35]Jochen Schmidt, "Tragödie und Tragödientheorie: Hölderlins Sophokles-Deutung," *Hölderlin-Jahrbuch* 29 (1995): 64.

mark Sophocles' works, and makes them particularly pregnant for Hölderlin's theological understanding of tragedy.

The reading of *Antigone* centers on a theological opposition between Creon's positive, law-governed relation to divine knowledge, and Antigone's negative, personal one. Hölderlin suggests that Antigone's personal relation to the gods is spreading to society at large. The relation between Creon and his son Haimon becomes a battleground for the two theologies. Hölderlin quotes from their exchange:

> CREON: If I stand faithfully by my beginning, do I lie?
> HAIMON: You are not that, if *you do not keep holy the name of god.*
> Instead of: you tread on the honors of the gods. It was certainly necessary to change the holy expression here, since it is meaningful in the middle, as seriousness and independent word, on which all else objectifies and transfigures itself.
> (*E&L* 327)

> [KREON: Wenn meinem Uranfang' ich treu beistehe, lüg' ich?
> HÄMON: Das bist du nicht, hältst *du nicht heilig Gottes Nahmen.*
> statt: trittst du der Götter Ehre. Es war wohl nötig, hier den heiligen Ausdruck zu ändern, da er in der Mitte bedeutend ist, als Ernst und selbstständiges Wort, an dem sich alles übrige objektivieret und verklärt.] (*SWB* 2, 915)

The translation loses the text's parallel construction: ἁμαρτάνω γὰρ τὰς ἐμὰς ἀρχὰς σέβων; / οὐ γὰρ σέβεις, τιμάς γε τὰς θεῶν πατῶν (*Juntina* 746–47; *OCT* 744–45: "Do I then err keeping holy my rule?" "You do not keep holy, treading on the honours of the gods."). The notes and typography draw attention to the most significant of Hölderlin's interventions, altering the plural "gods" to a singular "god." By changing Haimon's polytheism to a monotheism, Hölderlin suggests that the two generations are on different sides of a theological divide. Creon's relation to divinity is based on custom and determined by his "Uranfang" (translating ἀρχή as "beginning" rather than "rule," which would make more sense), while Haimon exhibits a forward-looking consciousness of a single god. Hölderlin's comments see theological difference as decisive for the conflicts of the piece, "meaningful in the middle." This authorizes a translation practice that alters "the holy expression" so that the process of change becomes more comprehensible to modern readers.

"The middle" (*die Mitte*) might be understood as a generalization of the concept of the caesura: it is a moment within *transport* at which the process of change can be grasped.[36] Yet here it is not only the middle of the work itself, but also of the transition from Greek to German. The *transport* of tragedy

[36]On the "middle" in Hölderlin's thought, see Rüdiger Görner, *Hölderlins Mitte: zur Ästhetik eines Ideals* (Munich: iudicium, 1993).

and the process of translation coincide in Hölderlin's alteration of the text. He continues, in a passage that is decisive for his understanding of tragedy and translation alike:

> Indeed, the way that time turns itself in the middle is not really changeable, so too the way a character categorically follows the categorical time, and how it moves from Greek to Hesperian [is not changeable]; the opposite is true of the holy name, under which the highest is felt or takes place. (*E&L* 327)

> [Wohl die Art, wie in der Mitte sich die Zeit wendet, ist nicht wohl veränderlich, so auch nicht wohl, wie ein Charakter der kategorischen Zeit kategorisch folget, und wie es vom griechischen zum hesperischen gehet, hingegen der heilige Namen, unter welchem das Höchste gefühlt wird oder geschiehet.] (*SWB* 2, 915)

Hölderlin differentiates between what in Greek tragedy is essential, and therefore unchangeable in translation, and what is contingent, and therefore necessary to change, justifying his practice of altering the names of the gods. Unchangeable are the elements relating to transition: the turning of time, the action of character, and the transition from Greek to Hesperian. Hölderlin suggests that these changes are all somehow coincident in tragedy. This develops the Böhlendorff letter's notion of Greek art striving towards the Hesperian, but now sees the dynamic as internal to tragedy. Greek tragedy's unalterable core consists in a historical transition; its contingent, alterable quality is the linguistic form of expression—the names of the gods, for example. Hölderlin authorizes his modernizing process of translation by what he sees as the incipient modernity of Sophocles' language.

Hölderlin reserves the most extensive comment for two passages taken from lyric exchanges with the chorus in Antigone's final scene on stage. Both center on comparisons, implicit and explicit, between Antigone and other mythological figures who encountered divinity. First, Hölderlin quotes Antigone's words comparing herself to Niobe, a queen of Thebes who was turned into stone for boasting that she had borne more children than the goddess Leto. Hölderlin gives only the first line of her speech, "Ich habe gehört, der Wüste gleich sei worden" ("I have heard that [she] became like a desert"), which he describes as "probably the highest trait in Antigone [wohl der höchste Zug an der Antigonä]" (*SWB* 2, 915; *E&L* 327). The Greek reads ἤκουσα δὴ λυγροτάταν [sic] ὀλέσθαι / τὰν φρυγίαν ξέναν / Ταντάλου, Σιπύλῳ πρὸς ἄκρῳ (*Juntina* 822–4; *OCT* 823–6: "I have heard that the Phrygian guest, child of Tantalus, perished most awfully on the top of Sipylos"). Hölderlin turns a description of destruction ("perished most awfully") into a process of transformation, looking forward to Niobe's petrification, and to Antigone's confinement in a cave. In her final moments, Antigone appears to meet the god of death "with a bold and often even blasphemous word [...] and so retains the holy living possibility of spirit [mit kühnem oft sogar blasphemischem Worte [. . .] und so die heilige lebende Möglichkeit des Geistes erhält]" (*E&L* 328; *SWB* 2, 916). Hölderlin draws out what is only implicit in Sophocles: the analogy between Antigone's transgression and Niobe's hubristic mockery (which lead to similar punishments). Antigone sees her own action and punishment in the most exalted terms possible, as a meeting with the gods. The parallel with Oedipus is implicit in Hölderlin's thought: both establish overly intimate relations to divinity, which lead to a loss of their previous self-consciousness and a new relation to the gods.

The last passage on which Hölderlin comments relates again to Antigone's punishment. The chorus compares her to Danae, the Argive princess confined by her father in response to an oracular utterance. Though inaccessible to men, Danae was impregnated by Zeus in a stream of gold. Hölderlin comments on his intervention in the chorus' description of Danae:

> She counted for the father of time / the strokes of hours, golden.
> Instead of: she maintained for Zeus the gold-streaming becoming. In order to make it closer to our mode of representation. (*E&L* 328)

> [Sie zählete dem Vater der Zeit
> Die Stundenschläge, die goldnen
> statt: verwaltete dem Zeus das goldströmende Werden. Um es unserer Vorstellungsart mehr zu nähern.] (*SWB* 2, 916)

Hölderlin draws attention to his appropriation of the Greek, which reads καὶ Ζηνὸς ταμεύε- / σκε γονὰς χρυσορρύτους (*Juntina* 947–48; *OCT* 950: "and guarded for Zeus the gold-streaming seeds"). The changes Hölderlin introduces all relate to temporality: the name "Zeus" becomes "father of time," and "guarded the seeds" (or in Hölderlin's diplomatic translation "maintained the becoming") is translated "counted the strokes of hours." Hölderlin brings out the temporal nature of Sophocles' text, making the duration of Danae's counting the main feature of comparison with Antigone's confinement. This removes the sexual connotations of the original and makes the lines refer to an infinity of solitary waiting—the punishment to which Antigone is condemned. Hölderlin's translation has the effect of temporalizing Antigone's fate. His understanding of tragedy as the genre of temporality leads him to emphasize the element of duration in the Greek text.

Hölderlin justifies the changes as bringing the lines "closer to our mode of representation." Though the name Zeus was significant for Sophocles' audience, modern audiences require a description of the function of the god in order for his role to be clear. As in the earlier instance of changing plural to singular gods, it is seriousness (*Ernst*) that is at issue. *Ernst* seems to denote a way of reading that grasps the full theological meaning of the ancient divinity, necessitating a translation out of the Greek pantheon. In order to make myth meaningful, Hölderlin demythologizes the names of the gods.[37] This is part of Hölderlin's effort "to present myth everywhere *more demonstrably* [die Mythe nämlich überall *beweisbarer* darstellen]" (*E&L* 328; *SWB* 2, 916). The striking image of Danae counting the hours belongs to modern modes of representation because divinity is experienced in thought, rather than (as in Sophocles' text) in physical presence. As the Böhlendorff letter had suggested, her infinite confinement represents the distinctively modern character of the tragic as a living death. Hölderlin makes the story of Antigone more demonstrable by making her (or her analogue, Danae's) fate more spiritual.

Between the second, interpretive sections of the Sophocles "Notes," there seems to be a process of change already in motion: both works depict closeness to divinity as destructive, yet *Antigone* points to a closer, less hierarchical theology emerging. Though Hölderlin does not explicitly state it, there is a suggestion that the two works represent stages in a single process, begun by Oedipus' *nefas* and carried forward by Antigone's holy blasphemy, and (though this will only be clear in the following section) completed in Creon's downfall.[38] Both "Notes" have emphasized how the language of tragedy is pervaded by theological understanding. *Antigone*'s references to the gods, in Hölderlin's translation, have a distinctly Christian tone. They suggest the personal relation to a single god, who is not known as "Zeus" but rather as "father." This modern or modernizing tinge is not simply Hölderlin's imposition on the work, but is fundamental to how he understands its content: *Antigone* is a tragedy of the transition from one theology to another, from Creon's lawful hierarchy to Antigone's lawless equality. By modernizing the names of Sophocles' gods, Hölderlin brings out the modern characteristics he finds latent in *Antigone*, making the work a depiction of the birth of modern theology out of ancient polytheism.

Vaterländische Umkehr

In the first section of both "Notes," Hölderlin describes the law of the caesura as a means of regulating the formal economy of the work through a break in the action; in the second sections, he interprets *Oedipus* and *Antigone* as representations of *transport*, which are themselves subject to the *transport* of translation. Caesura and *transport*, synchrony and diachrony, are the

---

[37] Schmidt, "Tragödie und Tragödientheorie," 70.
[38] For the continuity between *Oedipus* and *Antigone*, see Meta Corssen, "Die Tragödie als Begegnung zwischen Gott und Mensch," *Hölderlin-Jahrbuch* 3 (1949).

poles that Hölderlin's theory of tragedy mediates. They come together in the third sections of the "Notes," which describe the "presentation of the tragic [Darstellung des Tragischen]" as the appearance of divine infinity in human finitude. Tragedy's meeting of god and man has a "monstrous" quality for Hölderlin. Coming-together and breaking-apart coincide in the moment of catastrophe, which leads to the destruction of the individual but also to the reconstitution of human relation to the divine. In the tragic moment, the extreme of comprehension (the experience of the caesura) is paradoxically coincident with the extreme of forgetting (the process of *transport*). Here is Hölderlin on *Oedipus*:

> The presentation of the tragic relies primarily on this: that the monstrous—how god and man are united, and boundlessly the power of nature and the inmost of man become one in wrath—comprehends itself in that the boundless becoming-one purifies itself through boundless division. *Τῆς φύσεως γραμματεὺς ἦν τὸν κάλαμον ἀποβρέχων εὔνουν* [*He was the writer of nature, dipping his well-thinking pen*]. (*E&L* 323)

> [Die Darstellung des Tragischen beruht vorzüglich darauf, daß das Ungeheure, wie der Gott und Mensch sich paart, und grenzenlos die Naturmacht und des Menschen Innerstes im Zorn Eins wird, dadurch sich begreift, daß das grenzenlose Eineswerden durch grenzenloses Scheiden sich reiniget. *Της φυσεως γραμματευς ην τον καλαμον αποβρεχων ευνουν*.] (*SWB* 2, 856)

And on *Antigone*:

> Tragic presentation relies, as has been indicated in the "Notes" to *Oedipus*, on this: that the immediate god, wholly one with man (since the god of an apostle is more mediate, is the highest understanding in the highest spirit), that the *infinite* inspiration grasps itself *infinitely*, that is to say, in oppositions, in consciousness that sublates consciousness, dividing itself in a holy way, and the god, in the form of death, is present. (*E&L* 329)

> [Die tragische Darstellung beruhet, wie in den Anmerkungen zum Oedipus angedeutet ist, darauf, daß der unmittelbare Gott, ganz Eines mit dem Menschen (denn der Gott eines Apostels ist mittelbarer, ist höchster Verstand in höchstem Geiste), daß die *unendliche* Begeisterung *unendlich*, das heißt in Gegensätzen, im Bewußtsein, welches das Bewußtsein aufhebt, heilig sich scheidend, sich faßt, und der Gott, in der Gestalt des Todes, gegenwärtig ist.] (*SWB* 2, 917)

At the heart of both descriptions is a moment of cognition: the monstrous union of god and man "comprehends itself" or "grasps itself" through a process of division. Hölderlin accents the tragic variously in his notes to *Oedipus* and to *Antigone*: in *Oedipus*, he emphasizes the meeting of god and man in *Zorn* ("anger", a word used repeatedly to characterize Oedipus' disintegrating mind in the section previous), while in *Antigone*, he focuses on the consciousness of this meeting, which is characterized by "infinite inspiration."

Both *Oedipus* and *Antigone* present humans who appropriate divine authority, accessing the consciousness of the divine and initiating a process of union; these impossible unions lead to a catastrophic division that reestablishes a hierarchy of god and man. The tragic protagonist and the divinity both grasp their relation anew through the process of division. Behind this description is an interpretation of *catharsis* ("the boundless becoming-one purifies itself through boundless division"), which Hölderlin understands as the purgation of the previous unstable coexistence. The Greek citation in the *Oedipus* passage refers in its original context to Aristotle, but here seems to relate especially to Sophocles, the "writer of nature" whose "well-thinking pen" captures the destructive course of existence.[39] Tragedy for Hölderlin represents a natural process that leads from unstable coexistence to stable division through a cathartic process of learning.

The process of division in *Oedipus* is manifested in a pervasive atmosphere of opposition: "All is speech against speech, which reciprocally sublates itself [Alles ist Rede gegen Rede, die sich gegenseitig aufhebt]" (*E&L* 323; *SWB* 2, 856). This formal principle of opposition demands a violent mode of representation

> as speech for a world where, among plague and confusion of the senses and a generally enflamed spirit of prophecy, in an idle time, god and man, so that the course of the world has no gap and *the memory of the heavenly ones does not go out, communicate in the all-forgetting form of unfaithfulness*, since divine unfaithfulness is best retained. (*E&L* 324)

> [als Sprache für eine Welt, wo unter Pest und Sinnesverwirrung und allgemein entzündetem Wahrsagergeist, in müßiger Zeit, der Gott und der Mensch, damit der Weltlauf keine Lücke hat und *das Gedächtnis der Himmlischen nicht ausgehet, in der allvergessenden Form der Untreue sich mitteilt*, denn göttliche Untreue ist am besten zu behalten.] (*SWB* 2, 856)

The communication of god and man is unfaithful in that it reverses the false closeness that previously reigned. Those, like Creon, who stand "faithfully by [their] beginning," find themselves out of step with the time. Where Oedipus had believed himself to be favored by the gods, he realizes that he has been cursed. This *Mitteilung* ("communication" but also an echo of *mit-teilen*, "divide with") disrupts the previous coexistence of man and

---

[39]The citation is from the *Suda*, s.v. "Aristotle," but Hölderlin would have seen it (mis-)quoted on the title page of J. B. Robinet's *De la nature* (Amsterdam: Harrevelt 1766). See Rémi Brague, "Ein rätselhaftes Zitat über Aristoteles in Hölderlins 'Anmerkungen über Oedipus,'" in *Idealismus mit Folgen: die Epochenschwelle um 1800 zwischen Kunst und Geisteswissenschaften*, ed. Hans-Jürgen Gawoll and Christoph Jamme (Munich: Fink, 1994).

god, but in doing so, restores human knowledge of the power of divinity as memory.[40] In man's weakness, the strength of the god appears, and the "course of the world" is saved from the interruption threatened by transgression. As divinity is remembered, "man forgets himself and the god, and reverses himself, admittedly in a holy way, like a traitor [vergißt der Mensch sich und den Gott, und kehret, freilich heiliger Weise, wie ein Verräter sich um]" (E&L 324; SWB 2, 856). This process of forgetting is a kind of *catharsis*, which is paradoxically the result of the recognition of divine causality. Hölderlin interprets tragic *anagnorisis* and *peripeteia*, (which, according to Aristotle, coincide in Oedipus) as a cognitive process that alters the relation to the gods and, consequently, the quality of time itself. Oedipus' *Umkehr* (reversal) in *Untreue* (unfaithfulness) restores the presence of the divine in human temporality.

For Hölderlin, time in tragedy is not a simple container of events, any more than language is a neutral medium of expression. Tragic time, like tragic language, has its own violent, ecstatic quality, which demands the sacrifice of the individual (as in *Empedocles*).[41] This temporality is not incidental to Oedipus' *nefas* but might be understood to cause it: his theological excess was a symptom of the idleness of his time, which has led man to forget the prerogatives of divinity (an explanation also of why a general purification of the city was necessary). The cathartic suffering of the individual brings about a reversal of temporality generally:

> In this [extreme limit of suffering], man forgets himself because he is wholly in the moment; god [forgets himself] because he is nothing but time; and both are unfaithful: time, because it turns itself categorically in such a moment, and beginning and end simply cannot be rhymed in it; man, because in this moment of categorical reversal he must follow, therefore in the following simply cannot equal the beginning. (E&L 324)

> [In dieser (äußerste Grenze des Leidens) vergißt sich der Mensch, weil er ganz im Moment ist; der Gott, weil er nichts als Zeit ist; und beides ist untreu, die Zeit, weil sie in solchem Momente sich kategorisch wendet, und Anfang und Ende sich in ihr schlechterdings nicht reimen läßt; der Mensch, weil er in diesem Momente der kategorischen Umkehr folgen muß, hiermit im Folgenden schlechterdings nicht dem Anfänglichen gleichen kann.] (SWB 2, 856–57)

A concept of tragic fate becomes visible, which recalls the assertion of the "Basis for Empedocles" that tragic characters are all "attempts to solve the

---

[40] See the discussion in Hühn, *Mnemosyne: Zeit und Erinnerung in Hölderlins Denken*: 240–43.

[41] On the theme of sacrifice, see Peter-André Alt, "Subjektivierung, Ritual, implizite Theatralität: Hölderlins 'Empedokles'-Projekt und die Diskussion des antiken Opferbegriffs im 18. Jahrhundert," *Hölderlin-Jahrbuch* 37 (2011).

problems of fate." Oedipus' downfall, Hölderlin suggests, was a necessity of his time, the consequence of its "categorical reversal." The change in time is "categorical" in a Kantian sense, unconditional and universally binding (as in the "categorical imperative").[42] The disintegration Hölderlin had pointed to in Oedipus' consciousness appears at once as a symptom of the time's forgetfulness of divinity and as the example that causes the "categorical reversal" that makes both man and god "unfaithful."[43] Oedipus, like Haimon in *Antigone*, is "in the middle" of the work, a figure in whom the changes in consciousness of the divine are played out (in contrast to Antigone, who seems already to have undergone the theological change, to be an agent of the transition rather than an object of it). Oedipus' *nefas* had expressed the fatelessness of his time; his fate restores time itself.

Antigone appears as the work bridging the gap between ancient Greece and the *Vaterland*, making clear their contrast as well as their continuity. There is a form of parallel thought running through the *Antigone* notes, centering on the areas of language and theology, both of which appear to be in transition. Hölderlin contrasts the speech of tragedy in Greece and the *Vaterland*: "*The Greek tragic word is deadly-factic*," he writes (recalling the Latin verb *facere*, "to do" or "make"), "because the body which it seizes really kills [*Das griechischtragische Wort ist tödlichfaktisch*, weil der Leib, den es ergreifet wirklich tötet]" (*E&L* 330; *SWB* 2, 918). This could refer to Oedipus' curse in the *OT* or Creon's death sentence in the *Antigone*, both deadly acts committed under the corrupting influence of monarchical power. The tragic word is itself a force acting on the agents of tragedy, and causing them to destroy. How the word acts, however, distinguishes Greek from *vaterländisch* tragic speech. The Greek word physically compels tragic characters, "becomes *more mediately factic*, in that it seizes the more sensible body [*mittelbarer faktisch* wird, indem es den sinnlicheren Körper ergreift]" (*E&L* 329; *SWB* 2, 918). On the contrary, the tragic word "according to our time and way of representation becomes more immediate, in that it seizes the more spiritual body [nach unserer Zeit und Vorstellungsart unmittelbarer [wird], indem es den geistigeren Körper ergreift]" (*E&L* 330; *SWB* 2, 918). In Greece, speech had the power to instigate physical violence, while in Hölderlin's time, the word contributes to destruction in a more spiritual way:

> A national [form of art] may, as could well be demonstrated, be more a killing-factic than a deadly-factic word; it may not actually end with murder or death, because the tragic must still be grasped in this way, but rather more in the style of *Oedipus at Colonus*, so that *the word* is terrible out of inspired mouth, and kills, though not in a Greek, palpable way, in athletic and plastic spirit, where the word seizes the body, so that the body kills. (*E&L* 330)

[42] Dastur, *Hölderlin: le retournement natal*: 75.
[43] There may be an echo of Schiller's "Concerning the Sublime" and of Hegel's "Spirit of Christianity."

[Eine vaterländische (Kunstform) mag, wie wohl beweislich ist, mehr tötend-faktisches, als tötlichfaktisches Wort sein; nicht eigentlich mit Mord oder Tod endigen, weil doch hieran das Tragische muß gefaßt werden, sondern mehr im Geschmacke des Oedipus auf Kolonos, so daß *das Wort* aus begeistertem Munde schreklich ist, und tötet, nicht griechisch faßlich, in athletischem und plastischem Geiste, wo das Wort den Körper ergreift, daß dieser tötet.] (*SWB* 2, 918–19)

Hölderlin understands the *OC* as a more *vaterländisch* work, perhaps following the chronology of the works' composition (though not the chronology of the story, in which the events of the *OC* take place between the *OT* and *Antigone*). The contrast between the *OT* and *OC* can be understood through the curses of the respective works: in the *OT*, Oedipus' curse of the murderer is undefined but has real consequences within the work (which Hölderlin has pointed out); it "grasps the body" physically and causes destruction (even though Oedipus does not die in the play).[44] In the *OC*, on the other hand, Oedipus curses his son Polyneices, an act that, though terrible, is not the direct cause of the latter's death. Oedipus' curse destroys Polyneices' spirit for battle, and so is "killing" but not itself "deadly." Hölderlin has emphasized this violence of language in his interpretations (especially of the *OT*) and it appears as one of the distinguishing features of ancient as opposed to modern tragedy.

The other aspect of tragedy that Hölderlin contrasts in Greece and the *Vaterland* is the "form of reason" (*Vernunftform*) or, alternatively, the "way of representation" (*Vorstellungsart*). Both seem to result from the difference between ancient polytheism and modern monotheism, and Hölderlin uses the terms to discuss a whole host of concerns external to tragedy (just as his discussion of tragic language seems to subsume both considerations of plot and character). The different notions of theological meaning manifest themselves in opposed tendencies of the individual, and, implicitly, in opposed notions of the tragic:

> For us, since we stand under the more actual Zeus, who not only *remains* between this earth and the wild world of the dead, but *more decisively forces to earth* the eternal course of nature, hostile to man, on its way into the other world; and because this greatly changes the essential and national representations, and our poetry must be national, its materials chosen according to our view of the world and its representations national, the Greek ways of representation transform themselves in so far as their primary tendency is to grasp themselves, because their weakness lay there, while on the contrary the primary tendency in the ways of representation of our time is to be able to achieve something, to have skill, because fatelessness, the δύσμορον, is our weakness. (*E&L* 330)

[Für uns, da wir unter dem eigentlicheren Zevs stehen, der nicht nur zwischen dieser Erde und der wilden Welt der Toten *inne hält*, sondern den ewig menschenfeindlichen Naturgang, auf seinem Wege in die andre Welt, *entschiedener zur Erde*

---

[44] See Billings, "The ends of tragedy," 119–21.

zwinget, und da dies die wesentlichen und vaterländischen Vorstellungen groß
ändert, und unsere Dichtkunst vaterländisch sein muß, so daß ihre Stoffe nach
unserer Weltansicht gewählt sind, und ihre Vorstellungen vaterländisch, verändern
sich die griechischen Vorstellungen in sofern, als ihre Haupttendenz ist, sich fas-
sen zu können, weil darin ihre Schwäche lag, da hingegen die Haupttendenz
in den Vorstellungsarten unserer Zeit ist, etwas treffen zu können, Geschick zu
haben, da das Schicksallose, das δυσμορον, unsere Schwäche ist.] (*SWB* 2, 918)

Hölderlin's repeated use of the comparative suggests that the categories are
not absolute; there is no single moment of theological change, but it is
emergent already in and from the ancient texts. The modern Zeus is "more
actual" (*eigentlicher*, equally "more our own") and so takes a greater interest
in protecting humans from nature's destructive tendencies. Christian divinity
moderates tragic figures' tendency to approach the "other world" by keeping
humanity more decisively grounded on earth.[45] The need of the Greeks "to be
able to grasp themselves" (the Oedipus of the *OT* is surely the best example)
appears as a consequence of their divinity's more direct and dangerous intervention in human affairs as "the eternal course of nature, hostile to man."

The "ill-fated" (δύσμορον) quality of moderns is a result of their "fatelessness" (*Schicksallose*). Hölderlin describes the difference between the two ages
in relation to *Geschick* ("skill" or, less often in Hölderlin, "fate") and *Schicksal*
(fate), both from the root *schicken*, "to send." It is *Schicksal* that seems to
doom the heroes of tragedy, but lacking such destiny, modernity finds itself
without the innate *Geschick* of the Greeks. Hölderlin describes a chiasmus
between ancient and modern tendencies: moderns, though secure in self-
consciousness, are uncertain of the physical world; while ancients, secure
in the physical world, are uncertain in their self-consciousness. Both ages
strive towards what is innate to the other for completion. Thus, the young
Oedipus' search for a consciousness would be typical of ancient fates, while
the old Oedipus' effort to grasp his fate would be typical of modern ones. By
seeking to recover something of the ancient concept of fate, modernity, like
the blinded Oedipus, finds its errancy redeemed in tragedy.[46]

The *Antigone* for Hölderlin takes place in an "upheaval" (*Aufruhr*) and
represents *vaterländische Umkehr*, the change from ancient to modern theology and political organization. In describing the process of transition, his
focus moves away from the protagonists to society as a whole:

> In national reversal [. . .] all that is mere necessity supports the change; there-
> fore, when such a change is possible, the neutral one—not only the one who is

---

[45] See Beda Allemann, *Hölderlin und Heidegger* (Zürich: Atlantis, 1954), 26–29. Allemann
describes the two tendencies as "Empedoclean" (striving out of the world) and "kingly" (being
bound to the world).

[46] The provenance of the term δύσμορον has never been satisfactorily explained. The word
appears occasionally in the *OT* and *Antigone*, but is particularly prominent in the *OC*. Antigone
describes herself as δυσμόρου δύσμορα (*OC* 1109: "ill-fated daughter of an ill-fated one").

seized *against* the national form—can be compelled by a spiritual violence of the time to be patriotic, to be present, in infinite form, in the religious, political, and moral [form] of his nation. (προφάνηθι θεός.) [Appear, god!] (*E&L* 331)

[In vaterländischer Umkehr [. . .] ist alles bloß Notwendige parteiisch für die Veränderung, deswegen kann, in Möglichkeit solcher Veränderung, auch der Neutrale, nicht nur, der *gegen* die vaterländische Form ergriffen ist, von einer Geistesgewalt der Zeit; gezwungen werden, patriotisch, gegenwärtig zu sein, in unendlicher Form, der religiösen, politischen und moralischen seines Vaterlands. (προφανηθι θεος.)] (*SWB* 2, 919–20)

The word "revolution" does not occur, but Hölderlin is describing a situation that could have been inspired by the events in France. The Greek parenthesis refers to the fifth stasimon, the ode to Dionysus, which invokes the god in a time when "von gewaltiger / Krankheit die ganze Stadt ist befangen" (1189: "the whole city is gripped by a powerful sickness"), to aid them as "Chorführer der Gestirn' und geheimer / Reden Bewahrer!" (1196–97: "chorus-leader of the stars and protector of secret words").[47] Dionysus is an appropriate god to preside over *vaterländische Umkehr* as he is consistently associated in Hölderlin's thought with historical process and revolution.[48] Antigone's opposition to Creon now seems to represent only the beginning of a larger transformation, which spreads throughout the citizenry. In the heat of the moment, even those, like Haimon, who were previously neutral are taken up in the overpowering process of *Umkehr*. The whole population is driven by a "spiritual violence of the time" to oppose the old, sclerotic order. The new *Vaterland* develops through destruction of the old—the very process that Hölderlin had treated in the *Empedocles* complex and observed in the French Revolution. Tragedy is essentially about the process of social transition, a transition that takes place, paradoxically, somewhere between the ancient and the modern.

Hölderlin describes the new order in terms that cannot but recall the French Revolution:

The form of reason that here develops tragically is political, and even republican, because between Creon and Antigone, formal and anti-formal, the balance is held too equally. This shows itself particularly at the end, when Creon is almost abused by his servants. (*E&L* 332)

[Die Vernunftform, die hier tragisch sich bildet, ist politisch und zwar republikanisch, weil zwischen Kreon und Antigonä, förmlichem und gegenförmlichen,

---

[47] Translating ὡς βιαίας / ἔχεται πανδήμος πόλις / ἐπὶ νόσου (*Juntina* 1136–38; *OCT* 1140–41: "as the whole city is held in violence by sickness") and χοραγὲ ἄστρων, καὶ νυχίων / φθεγμάτων ἐπισκοπε (*Juntina* 1143–44; *OCT* 1147–48: "chorus-leader of the stars and overseer of night-voices").

[48] See Bernhard Böschenstein, *Frucht des Gewitters: Hölderlins Dionysos als Gott der Revolution* (Frankfurt: Insel, 1989).

das Gleichgewicht zu gleich gehalten ist. Besonders zeigt sich dies am Ende, wo Kreon von seinen Knechten fast gemißhandelt wird.] (*SWB* 2, 920)

Hölderlin recognizes the danger of this political upheaval (the balance is held *too* equally), but does not question its necessity. Its "tragic" character is that an old form has to be destroyed in order for a new one to emerge. Hölderlin reads the *Antigone* as staging the shift in power from Creon's hierarchical order to Antigone's egalitarian one. Though Antigone is dead, her form of reason is in the ascendant, and has spread even to Creon's servants, who speak roughly to their master in his moment of need: "Du mußt nichts wünschen. Vom zuvorgesetzten / Verhängnis hat kein Sterblicher Befreiung" (1388–89: You must wish nothing. No mortal has liberation from predetermined doom).[49] Greek tragedy seems to have a levelling tendency in the human sphere, striking down men who come too close to divine power. There is a parallel between Creon and Oedipus, whose subordination to his servants Hölderlin emphasized earlier: both rulers find themselves destroyed for their excess and reduced to a status below those who previously served them. Yet it appears that the transformation of *Antigone* is far more comprehensive than that of *Oedipus*. The monarchical order has been destroyed in favor of a "republican" constitution. For Hölderlin, who had so ardently desired such a revolution in his own time, tragedy preserves the republican form of reason as yet unrealized in modernity.

Hölderlin's conclusion returns to the beginning of the "Notes" and to the question of antiquity's exemplarity. His focus, though, has shifted, from the technique of ancient poetry to its ways of presentation. Again, Hölderlin's discussion of the content of tragedy is bound up with the question of translation, how ancient modes of thought should be presented to the modern reader. Continuing from the discussion of Creon's abuse, Hölderlin writes:

> Sophocles is right. This is the fate of his time and form of his nation. One can, indeed, idealize, i.e., choose the best moment, but the national ways of representation should not be changed, at least with respect to their subordination, by the poet who presents the world in a reduced scale. (*E&L* 332)

> [Sophokles hat Recht. Es ist dies Schicksal seiner Zeit und Form seines Vaterlandes. Man kann wohl idealisieren, z.B. den besten Moment wählen, aber die vaterländischen Vorstellungsarten dürfen, wenigstens der Unterordnung nach, vom Dichter, der die Welt in verringerten Maßstab darstellt, nicht verändert werden.] (*SWB* 2, 920)

---

[49]Hölderlin's translation here is hardly more emphatic than Sophocles' original: μὴ νῦν προσεύχου μηδέν, ὡς πεπρωμένης / οὐκ ἔστι θνητοῖς συμφορᾶς ἀπαλλαγή (*Juntina* 1329–30; *OCT* 1337–8: Do not pray at all, since there is no release for mortals from destined misfortune).

Hölderlin draws attention to the historical specificity of tragedy's form of political reason, which must be preserved in translation. The republican content emergent in tragedy is appropriate to Sophocles' democratic Athens, even though it is out of place in the modern *Vaterland*. Still, Hölderlin sees the value of Greek tragedy as giving an insight into something that is indeed eternal: "For us, such a form is very useful, because the infinite, like the spirit of states and the world, cannot in any case be *grasped* otherwise than from an awkward point of view [Für uns ist eine solche Form gerade tauglich, weil das Unendliche, wie der Geist der Staaten und der Welt, ohnehin nicht anders, als aus linkischem Gesichtspunkt kann *gefaßt* werden]" (*E&L* 332; *SWB* 2, 920–21). Like Hegel in the simile of the maiden, Hölderlin articulates the place of Greek tragedy *for us*. Its value is not based on any timeless quality, but on the particular timeliness of its form, which—because alien—allows an insight, "from an awkward point of view" into the universal. Greek tragedy for Hölderlin is the depiction of historical process itself, affording a glimpse into the way the individual exists in a changing world. Greek forms, then, ultimately teach what it is to be modern.

Hölderlin can nevertheless prefer modern forms to ancient ones, as offering a fuller grasp of the specificity of his own time:

> The national forms of our poets, where there are such, are still to be preferred because they do not merely exist to learn to understand the spirit of the time, but rather to hold it fast and feel it, when once it has been comprehended and learned. (*E&L* 332)

> [Die vaterländischen Formen unserer Dichter, wo solche sind, sind aber dennoch vorzuziehen, weil solche nicht bloß da sind, um den Geist der Zeit verstehen zu lernen, sondern ihn festuzuhalten und zu fühlen, wenn er einmal begriffen und gelernt ist.] (*SWB* 2, 921)

Hölderlin's notes close here, coming full circle to the question of the relation of ancient and modern forms with which the notes began. Now, though, it is modernity that is to be preferred: having "learn[ed] to understand the spirit of the time" from Greek tragedy, modern poets are able to create in ways the Greeks could not, to "hold it [the spirit of the time] fast and to feel it." Sophocles teaches what it is to exist in time, even as his own time is past, providing the theory that would inform an authentic modern practice. There is for Hölderlin a continuing importance to Greek tragedy, created by its particular historical character as a genre of transition. Yet it is only in translation, out of context, that the full power of Sophocles can be actualized, as modernity discovers its own fate in Greek tragedy. The final paradox of Hölderlin's tragic thought, then, is that the death of Greek tragedy is the birth of the tragic.

Births of the Tragic

THE CONCEPT OF THE TRAGIC emerged from a few small, interconnected circles, centered geographically on the Weimar/Jena area (with a few satellites), over the fifteen years between Schiller's first essay on the tragic sublime in 1792 and Hegel's *Phenomenology* in 1807. During these years, a sense of the "spiritual violence of the time" (Hölderlin's words) extending to political, philosophical, artistic, and religious life seems to have been powerfully and widely felt, and the turn to tragedy is best understood as a response to these forms of upheaval. Though this revolutionary moment has passed, responses to it constitute a central element of intellectual modernity, as defined equally by Reinhart Koselleck and Michel Foucault.[1] In the years around 1800, theories of tragedy and ideas of modernity often coincide and establish a pervasive sense of modernity as itself tragic. Idealism's investment of profound meaningfulness in tragedy remains with the genre, and is visible in scholarship, adaptation, and performance. When we speak of the "relevance" or "timelessness" of the *Antigone* or the *Bacchae*, we are giving voice to a way of meaning that is uniquely modern. The kind of meaning they hold for us is different from the kind they held for Dacier, Steinbrüchel, or even Herder. They are at once more ancient and more modern: more thoroughly situated within an alien culture and more importantly related to our own concerns. This is the paradoxical movement of the concept of the tragic, which finds contemporary meaning in the historical nature of Greek tragedy.

By 1807, the constellations that had produced the turn to tragedy had dispersed—Schiller was dead, Hölderlin mad, Friedrich Schlegel in France, August Wilhelm in Berlin and abroad, Schelling had taken professorships in Würzburg and then in Munich, and Hegel would move from Jena to Bamberg and then Nuremberg following the publication of the *Phenomenology*. The close connections that gave life to the concept were severed, as the major thinkers drifted apart and turned to other concerns. But, in an important sense, the history of the tragic had not yet begun. Hölderlin's largely unread and totally uncomprehended "Notes" to Sophocles was the only substantial publication directly concerned with the tragic to emerge during

---

[1] The essential texts are Koselleck, *Futures past*; Michel Foucault, *The order of things: an archaeology of the human sciences* (London: Routledge, 2002). See also Friedrich A. Kittler, *Discourse networks, 1800/1900* (Stanford: Stanford University Press, 1990).

this period (A.W. Schlegel's and Schelling's lectures were still unpublished), and Schiller remained by far the most prominent theorist of tragedy. To be sure, individuals connected to idealist circles had gone considerably further in thinking systematically about the tragic in lectures and scattered publications (Hermann's *Poetics* being a good example), but these remained only rumblings for the broader public. At the same time, translation of Greek works (as well as of Spanish and English tragedy) accelerated and improved, while productions of Schiller's *Bride* across Germany, as well as of romantic "tragedies of fate" (*Schicksalstragödien*) contributed to a broad interest in high tragedy.[2] The explosion of discourse on the tragic at this time, though, is a function mainly of August Wilhelm Schlegel's *Lectures on Dramatic Art and Literature* (*Vorlesungen über dramatische Kunst und Literatur*).

Delivered in Vienna in 1808 and published beginning the following year, Schlegel's lectures were the dominant theory of tragedy throughout Europe until the publication of Hegel's *Aesthetics* in 1835 (and for substantially longer outside of Germany). Schlegel's lectures brought an idealist viewpoint on tragedy to its widest audience yet, and were quickly translated into many European languages.[3] His viewpoint on Greek tragedy is not radically innovative or distinctive, and represents in large part an expansion of his earlier lectures, which are themselves founded on the thoughts of his brother Friedrich, his friend Schelling, and his sometime antagonist Schiller. Still, the clarity and breadth of these lectures distinguished them from every previous idealist treatment of tragedy, and made them into an important vehicle for the new understanding of the genre.[4] Schlegel assumes no previous knowledge or language skills on the part of his listeners, introducing them to most of the extant Greek tragedies (Euripides predictably gets a bit slighted), before moving on to Greek and Roman comedy, Seneca, and modern works in Italian, French, Spanish, English, and finally, German. He treats an extraordinarily wide range of works, and the catholicity of his taste was a great part of the appeal of the lectures. Schlegel's critical acumen and relatively unobtrusive metaphysics made his reflections on drama particularly attractive to university philologists, and one finds him cited as an

[2]On translation, see Josefine Kitzbichler, "Von 1800 bis zur Mitte des 19. Jahrhunderts," in *Theorie der Übersetzungen antiker Literatur in Deutschland seit 1800* (Berlin: de Gruyter, 2009). *Schicksalstragödien* (or *Schicksalsdramen*), such as Zacharias Werner's *Der vierundzwanzigste Februar* (*The Twenty-fourth of February*, 1810) and Franz Grillparzer's *Die Ahnfrau* (*The Ancestress*, 1817) were quite popular in the early decades of the century. They are often, like Schiller's *Bride*, strange amalgams of classical themes of fate and Gothic settings.

[3]The lectures were translated into French in 1814, English in 1815, and Italian in 1817 (to name a few of many translations).

[4]See Bernard Franco, *Le despotisme du goût: débats sur le modèle tragique allemand en France, 1797–1814* (Göttingen: Wallstein, 2006). There is much more to be said about Schlegel's reception in Germany, especially within classical philology. His importance beyond Germany was probably even greater, given the relatively late reception of Hegel's *Aesthetics* in France and England.

important authority in much German philology of the nineteenth century.[5] Though he is very often dismissed as peripheral to discussions of the tragic, his was by far the most widely discussed theory of tragedy in the 1810s and 1820s, and influential well beyond.[6]

Schlegel articulates some central, though often unspoken, assumptions of idealist thinking on tragedy, which gained a wider currency as a result of his advocacy. Most important is the concept of "the tragic" itself, which he defines in a systematic fashion, in relation to other genres of poetry and drama. Schlegel's discussion proceeds by first developing the principles of the tragic and the comic, and then moving on to their manifestation in individual works. The concept of the tragic is related to the sense of "seriousness [Ernst]" and is born of "the need, inherent to our essence, for the infinite, at the limits of the finite in which we are confined [die unserm Wesen inwohnende Forderung des Unendlichen an den Schranken der Endlichkeit, worin wir befangen sind]" (*Lectures* 45; *KSB* 5, 41). Schlegel's virtuosic and pathos-laden description of the root of the tragic recalls Schiller's account of the sublime:

> All that we create and do is transient and insignificant; death, towards which every moment, well or poorly used, brings us, stands everywhere in the background [. . .] then every mind that is not impervious to pain must be overtaken by an unspeakable sadness, against which there is no other means of protection than the consciousness of a vocation extending beyond the earthly. This is the tragic mood [die tragische Stimmung]. (*Lectures* 45; *KSB* 5, 41–42)

Schlegel describes a version of the tragic sublime, though he does not use the term until later in the lectures.[7] The method of discussion is important: Schlegel affords a priority to discussion of "the tragic" (rather than of tragedies), and so speaks to the increasing reification of the concept, glimpsed also in Schelling's lectures. Previous considerations, whether in the *Encyclopédie* or in Hölderlin's Sophocles "Notes," had largely assumed that the tragic was a quality extracted from tragedies. Schlegel, though, sees the tragic as prior, the quality on which tragedies are built. The tragic appears independent of its particular instances, and works called tragedies may or may not be tragic

---

[5] For example, August Böckh, *Über die Antigone des Sophokles* (Berlin: Abhandlungen der Königlich-Preussische Akademie der Wissenschaften, 1824), 68. Friedrich Gottlieb Welcker, "Über den Ajas des Sophokles," *Rheinisches Museum* 3 (1829): 68. Solger's review of Schlegel's lectures is particularly interesting: Karl Wilhelm Ferdinand Solger, "Beurtheilung der Vorlesungen über dramatische Kunst und Literatur," in *Nachgelassene Schriften und Briefwechsel* (Leipzig: Brockhaus, 1826), vol. 2. Solger is particularly critical of Schlegel's reconciliatory and moralizing tendency, which is diametrically opposed to Solger's more negative concept of the tragic.

[6] He does not, for example, make it into Szondi's *Essay*, let alone the more philosophical treatments of Schmidt or Krell. Scholarship on August Wilhelm and editions of his writings and lectures are still quite spotty, especially in contrast to his brother Friedrich.

[7] Discussing the essence of Greek tragedy, he refers to the Kantian sublime as the explanation for tragic pleasure (*Lectures* 69; *KSB* 5, 64).

(Shakespeare being as ever the example of such hybridity). The guarantor of continuity within the genre is no longer formal qualities of tragedy (as it was for most of the eighteenth century), but a tragic content.

In counterpoint to this abstraction of the tragic, Schlegel demonstrates the idealist conviction that tragedy is essentially Greek. Greek works represent the "concepts of the tragic and comic purely grasped," and so form the beginning of any investigation of drama "not merely because of the ordering of time, but because of the ordering of concepts" (*Lectures* 47; *KSB* 5, 43). The Greeks, for Schlegel, are the logical origin of dramatic forms, and only Greek works can manifest the generic essence of tragedy. This sense had certainly been emerging through the second half of the eighteenth century, but it represents a significant change from discussions of the *Querelle*, which were focused either on Greek poetics as the measure of the tragic or on an ostensibly atemporal standard of taste, which more often than not conflicted with Greek reality. For Schlegel, such a conflict is impossible, though he recognizes that Greek works do not always live up to their own concept. This new focus on Greek plays is ultimately no less normative than the rational Aristotelianism of the eighteenth century, since it inevitably extracts its notion of the tragic from one or two works (in Schlegel's case, primarily the *OT*). Schlegel's lectures make a valiant effort to reconcile breadth of discussion with philosophical consistency, but the result is an idealist canon of tragedy that looks very much like the (neo-)Aristotelian one.

The two points noted in Schlegel's lectures—the hypostasis of the tragic and the essentialization of Greek tragedy—have been present in some idealist approaches, but gain wide acceptance following Schlegel's lectures. The assumptions are easy to discern in Schopenhauer's *World as Will and Representation* (*Die Welt als Wille und Vorstellung*, 1819), in K.W.F. Solger's *Lectures on Aesthetics* (delivered in 1819 and published posthumously in 1829), and of course, in Hegel's own *Aesthetics* lectures, which were reconstructed from auditor notes and published in 1835, four years after Hegel's death.[8] This is not the place for an extensive comparison of the *Aesthetics* with the pages on tragedy in the *Phenomenology*, but hypostasis and essentialization describe much of the transformation from Hegel's reading of Greek culture as a form of spirit to his account of Greek drama as the highest form of art. Hegel's notion of the tragic in the *Aesthetics* generalizes from his reading of the *Antigone* in the *Phenomenology* to create a model of "the original tragic" with broad, normative implications for his understanding of other works.[9] It is impossible to know whether this is due to the increasing rigidity and

[8] Schopenhauer, admittedly, preferred Shakespearean to Greek tragedy, but nevertheless saw Greek tragedy as the origin of the tragic.

[9] See *Aesthetics* 1196; *WZB* 15, 523: "The original tragic consists in the fact that within such collisions both sides of the opposition have *justification* taken in themselves."

monomania of Hegel's own thought or the systematizing efforts of the group that pieced together the text. Whatever the reason, the distorting effects of such a perspective have become increasingly obvious in recent years, as critics have placed greater weight on the historical and political contexts of drama, often disavowing the idealist legacy for its tendency to abstraction and universalism.[10]

The most enduring aspect of the idealist legacy, though, is even more fundamental: it is the assumption that *tragedy presents a form of meaning*, a way of making sense of the world. This is so typical of contemporary critical approaches that it is easy to forget that it is an idealist discovery or invention. The eighteenth century by and large did not believe that art could construct an image of what is valuable in human existence. In so far as tragedy was seen to be intellectually constructive, this was understood in rhetorical terms, as a demonstration of a moral maxim or warning to avoid certain behaviors. The essence of tragedy was usually sought in its emotional effect, which might serve reason (i.e., by instilling admiration for heroic actions) but would not itself bear on questions of ultimate importance. The connection between art and the supersensible, dimly suggested in Kant and elaborated by Schiller, was developed into a full-blown philosophy of art by Idealism. Tragedy became a privileged object of this philosophical development, since it was seen by most thinkers of the period, following the Kantian notion of the sublime, as the negative presentation of the absolute. Obviously, very few readers now would subscribe to this epistemological structure, but most commentators on Greek tragedy do share the assumption that tragedy presents an insight into questions and problems of great importance—whether philosophical, ethical, religious, psychological, social, or political. These very contexts for understanding tragedy are unique to approaches since 1800, and their continuing importance in research today reveals traces of a residual and often unacknowledged idealism.

Even as they exhibit fundaments of recognizably modern approaches to tragedy, idealist theories remain profoundly grounded in the questions and problems that have defined thinking since antiquity. At the heart of post-idealist approaches to tragedy is a concept of *mimesis* that draws more from Plato than Aristotle, understanding art as the presentation of a form

---

[10]The work of Jean-Pierre Vernant and Pierre Vidal-Naquet has been particularly influential: Jean-Pierre Vernant and Pierre Vidal-Naquet, *Myth and tragedy in ancient Greece*, trans. Janet Lloyd (New York: Zone, 1990). Some major collections related to the political turn in studies of tragedy are John J. Winkler and Froma I. Zeitlin, eds., *Nothing to do with Dionysos? Athenian drama in its social context* (Princeton: Princeton University Press, 1990); Simon Goldhill and Robin Osborne, eds., *Performance culture and Athenian democracy* (Cambridge: Cambridge University Press, 1999); D. M. Carter, ed., *Why Athens? A reappraisal of tragic politics* (Oxford: Oxford University Press, 2011). But see Mark Griffith's introduction to the last ("Twelve principles for reading Greek tragedy") for a sensitive balancing of the claims of historicism.

of reality.[11] Tragedy for the idealist era presents an image of truth, yet the artistic image is not a debased reflection of ultimate reality (as for Plato), but the nearest access that humans have to a higher realm. This is true even for Hegel, who holds the most emphatically immanent view of art, in so far as he conceives of tragedy as the height of Greek culture's consciousness of substance. Idealism's confluence of Platonic and Kantian approaches to art reformulates the Aristotelian insight into drama's mimetic form as a sense that tragedy is uniquely able to represent the ground of human freedom. As *mimesis* of serious actions, tragedy presents freedom as it is known and experienced in history.

The particular effect of tragic representation, likewise, emerges from an ancient crux: Aristotle's *catharsis*, understood as a quasi-philosophical moment of cognition.[12] From Schiller's notion of the sublime to Hegel's description of the insight brought about by Greek tragedy, the end of tragedy is conceived as paradox, a loss that is also a gain. This is rendered only more urgent by the new context of *mimesis*: tragedy presents us with a world, and that world must (for idealists) somehow find redemption. The question of tragic pleasure, accordingly, was much more deeply troubling to Idealism—and to us today as well—than it was to Aristotle or Dacier. The notions of *catharsis* suggested by Idealism (often under the name of the sublime) are far more wide-ranging than any previous understanding, because they respond to a far deeper sense of the horror of the tragic. Today, tragedy can seem to indict existence as a whole and must offer a correspondingly sweeping sense of reconciliation.[13] Or alternatively, tragedy can be the genre of nihilism, a representation of horror or the strangeness of existence.[14] Concepts of *mimesis* and *catharsis* remain central to the understanding of tragedy's meaning, even if that meaning is defined in terms that would have been unrecognizable to Aristotle. Idealist thought on tragedy does not replace the Aristotelian tradition of poetics so much as "sublate" it: negating, preserving, and raising it to a new level of meaning.

• • • • •

The echoes of Idealism's tragic thought could be followed further, both synchronically and diachronically. Within the next half-century, they could lead to Kleist, Hugo, and Hebbel as creative artists, to the philosophers Solger, Schopenhauer, and Kierkegaard, and to the scholars August Böckh, Connop

---

[11] On the romantic inheritance of concepts of *mimesis*, see Halliwell, *Aesthetics of mimesis*: 358–69. As Halliwell argues, against common conceptions of the period, Romanticism does not bring about the end of mimetic theory, but reformulates it.

[12] See Lacoue-Labarthe, "The caesura of the speculative," 213–19.

[13] As in A. D. Nuttall, *Why does tragedy give pleasure?* (Oxford: Clarendon, 1996).

[14] As in Karl Heinz Bohrer, *Das Tragische: Erscheinung, Pathos, Klage* (Munich: Hanser, 2009); Paul Hammond, *The strangeness of tragedy* (Oxford: Oxford University Press, 2009).

Thirlwall, and Karl Otfried Müller. Particularly important was the collaboration of Felix Mendelssohn and Ludwig Tieck in setting and staging Johann Jakob Donner's translation of *Antigone* in Potsdam in 1841, creating an instant sensation that traveled through the major cities of Europe and was widely recognized as the first successful modern staging of a Greek tragedy.[15] Through these years, Greek tragedy was widely understood through idealist thought, which formed common ground between quite disparate scholarly positions.[16] Very often, this does not take the form of explicit citation of idealist thinkers, but of the simple sense that tragedy, and especially Aristotelian *catharsis*, must be understood in a speculative context.[17]

Tracing these lines of dissemination, and the interplay of philology and philosophy in the nineteenth-century research university, is the work of another book. The major figures and moments are well known: Friedrich August Wolf's founding of the philological seminar in Halle in 1787, the establishment of the Berlin University in 1810 by a group led by Wilhelm von Humboldt, and the professorships there of F. A. Wolf and Böckh in philology and rhetoric, respectively, and of Hegel and Schelling, successively, in philosophy. There is need both for synthesis and for comparison. The question of the relation between philology and philosophy, though, is less urgent looking forward from Idealism (for which philology was still in its institutional infancy) than it is looking backward from the most important post-idealist thinker on tragedy: Friedrich Nietzsche.

Nietzsche's "impossible book," *The Birth of Tragedy out of the Spirit of Music* (*Die Geburt der Tragödie aus dem Geiste der Musik*, 1872), has been extensively researched in various disciplines, and is by now familiar to classicists.[18] Its approach to tragedy is unthinkable without the precedent of German Idealism, which Nietzsche largely received at second hand, through

[15] See Jason Geary, "Reinventing the past: Mendelssohn's *Antigone* and the creation of an ancient Greek musical language," *The Journal of Musicology* 23 (2006); Flashar, *Inszenierung der Antike*: 58–79.

[16] See Porter, "Tragedy and the catharsis of modernity"; Constanze Güthenke, "The middle voice: German classical scholarship and the tragic Greek chorus," in *Choruses, ancient and modern*, ed. Joshua Billings, Felix Budelmann, and Fiona Macintosh (Oxford: Oxford University Press, 2013).

[17] For example, Karl Otfried Müller's 1833 edition of the *Eumenides*: K. O. Müller, *Aeschylos Eumeniden: griechisch und deutsch mit erläuternden Abhandlungen über die äussere Darstellung, und über den Inhalt und die Composition dieser Tragödie* (Göttingen: Dieterich, 1833), 197. On the edition, see Glenn W. Most, "Karl Otfried Müller's edition of Aeschylus' *Eumenides*," in *Zwischen Rationalismus und Romantik: Karl Otfried Müller und die antike Kultur*, ed. William M. Calder and Renate Schlesier (Hildesheim: Weidmann, 1998).

[18] Most important for classicists are M. S. Silk and J. P. Stern, *Nietzsche on tragedy* (Cambridge: Cambridge University Press, 1981); James I. Porter, *The invention of Dionysus: an essay on The birth of tragedy* (Stanford: Stanford University Press, 2000).

Schopenhauer and Wagner.[19] The importance of Nietzsche to the present context, though, lies less in the specifics of his account of tragedy than in his investigation of the relation between historical, "scientific" method on the one hand, and present meaning on the other. The question of how Greek tragedy—and antiquity broadly—can be meaningful to the present has been the central focus of this book, and Nietzsche provides an answer as profound and challenging as any. His perspective, moreover, is importantly close to our own in that he writes after the institutionalization of classical learning in the academic discipline of philology, which was only nascent in the idealist period. Idealism's engagement with tragedy was enabled in part by the relative fluidity of the boundaries between philosophy and philology, and between academic and popular discourse—all of which hardened shortly after. Nietzsche's writings crystallize the possibility of finding meaning in the study of ancient literature in modern, academic context.

Introducing a new (though barely revised) edition of *Birth* in 1886, Nietzsche's *Attempt at Self-Criticism* (*Versuch einer Selbstkritik*) recognizes many failures in the book, but points to one major achievement:

> What I was able to grasp then, something terrible and dangerous, a problem with horns, not necessarily a bull, but nevertheless a *new* problem: today I would say that it was the *problem of science* itself—science grasped for the first time as problematic, as questionable [das *Problem der Wissenschaft* selbst war—Wissenschaft zum ersten Male als problematisch, als fragwürdig gefasst]. (*BT* 4; *KSA* 1, 14)

Wissenschaft (science) for Nietzsche has a dual valence: most immediately, it is the "Socratic" culture that in his mind killed tragedy and still rules western culture. But it is also *Wissenschaft* as a method of knowledge, which he himself practiced during his career as a classical philologist, and which he invokes in the opening words of *Birth* (*BT* 14; *KSA* 1, 25: "We will have gained much for the aesthetic *Wissenschaft* . . ."). From Nietzsche's later standpoint, the two forms of *Wissenschaft* seem entwined, and *Birth* appears as an incomplete effort to break out of the mode of scientific presentation. "It should have *sung*, this 'new soul'—and not spoken!" Nietzsche laments (*BT* 6; *KSA* 1, 15). The possibilities of song and speech, art and science, appear incommensurable, and a mediation of the two discourses impossible. Such, certainly, was the lesson Nietzsche gleaned from the fallout from the book, which left him even more isolated within his discipline than he had been, and contributed to his decision to resign his chair in 1879. In

---

[19] See Silk and Stern, *Nietzsche on tragedy*: 301–31; Stephen Houlgate, *Hegel, Nietzsche, and the criticism of metaphysics* (Cambridge: Cambridge University Press, 1986), 182–220; Martin, *Nietzsche and Schiller*; Paul Bishop and R. H. Stephenson, *Friedrich Nietzsche and Weimar classicism* (Rochester: Camden House, 2005).

the *Attempt*, he seems almost to have accepted the ironic suggestion of the young Ulrich von Wilamowitz-Möllendorff's response to *Birth*: "Let Herr N. keep his word, let him seize the thyrsus, let him move from India to Greece, but let him stand down from the *cathedra* on which he should teach science [Wissenschaft]."[20] To Nietzsche as to his antagonist, *Birth* could not be a work of science, and was written from a perspective already far removed from the concerns of *Wissenschaft*.

Yet the image of dry, prosaic science is more complex and equivocal than one might expect. Despite Nietzsche's by-then total alienation from the academic establishment, he still retains a kind of faith in the task of the philologist: "How sad that what I had to say then I did not dare to say as a poet [Dichter]. I might perhaps have been able to! Or at least as a philologist [Philologe]—for today nearly everything in this area still remains for the philologist to discover and dig out!" (*Birth* 6; *KSA* 1, 15). Philology—if practiced correctly—might elude the criticisms of *Wissenschaft* leveled at it in *Birth*.[21] A hint at what this entails comes in the 1887 preface to *Daybreak* (*Morgenröthe*), in which Nietzsche writes, "it is not for nothing that one has been a philologist, one is perhaps still, that is to say, a teacher of slow reading [ein Lehrer des langsamen Lesens]" (*KSA* 3, 17). As a practice of slow reading, philology opens possibilities of meaning beyond those discovered by *Wissenschaft*—becoming a discourse that would sing and not speak.

On the face of it, nothing could seem further from the *Wissenschaft* practiced by Wilamowitz. Wilamowitz's 1889 edition of Euripides' *Hercules* is prefaced with an *Introduction to Attic Tragedy* (*Einleitung in die attische Tragödie*, published separately in 1907) that remains one of the most acute and rigorous historicist discussions of Greek tragedy. It contains Wilamowitz's famous definition, "An Attic tragedy is a self-enclosed piece of heroic legend [Heldensage], poetically adapted in elevated style [in erhabenem Stile] for presentation by an Attic citizen chorus and two or three actors, and intended to be performed as part of public worship in the sanctuary of Dionysus."[22] Anything further from the "metaphysical consolation" and "aesthetic justification" of *Birth* is hard to imagine, and the definition is striking for leaving out entirely the question of tragic emotions and of *catharsis*—indeed, of

[20] Ulrich von Wilamowitz-Möllendorff, *Zukunftsphilologie! Eine Erwidrung auf Friedrich Nietzsches "Geburt der Tragödie"* (Berlin: Borntraeger, 1872), 32.

[21] The best treatment of Nietzsche's earlier understanding of philology—which can only be touched on very superficially here—is James I. Porter, *Nietzsche and the philology of the future* (Stanford: Stanford University Press, 2000).

[22] Ulrich von Wilamowitz-Möllendorff, *Euripides Herakles* I: *Einleitung in die attische Tragödie* (Berlin: Weidmann, 1889), 107. On Wilamowitz and Greek tragedy generally, see Herwig Görgemanns, "Wilamowitz und die griechische Tragödie," in *Wilamowitz nach 50 Jahren*, ed. William M. Calder, Hellmut Flashar, and Theodor Lindken (Darmstadt: Wissenschaftliche Buchgesellschaft, 1985).

tragic content altogether.[23] Wilamowitz explicitly rejects "aesthetic theory" as ulterior to philology: where aesthetics seeks to define tragedy *tout court*, "philology however has to do with Attic tragedy" and must avoid any discussion of tragic effect as being inessential to the constitution of the form in fifth-century Athens.[24] The essence of tragedy lies not in an invariant content, but in a relation to *Sage* (legend), which determines all the characteristics of the form, and which can only be uncovered through careful historical research. Against poetic and philosophical approaches, Wilamowitz asserts the right of the philologist, who "alone bears the keys to Attic tragedy."[25]

One cannot deny the force of Wilamowitz's warnings; for all their dogmatism and occasional chauvinism, they are consistent with an understanding of the task of philology as a science. At the end of his survey of modern approaches to criticism of tragedy in the *Hercules* volume, Wilamowitz turns to "the specifically philological task"—that is, what differentiates the philologist from the historian, and what makes the careful reading of texts essential:

> It is necessary to immerse oneself in an alien soul, be it that of an individual, be it that of a people. In the sacrifice of our own individuality lies our strength. We philologists as such have nothing of the poet nor the prophet, both of which the historian to a certain extent must be. On the contrary we must bear something of the actor in us, not of the virtuoso, who shapes his role by his own lights, but of the true artist, who gives the dead word life through his own heart's blood.[26]

Philology, for Wilamowitz, is the revival of an alien moment through language. Bringing the words of a distant culture to life requires a study that mortifies the individuality of the philologist. While the historian tells stories of the past and makes predictions for the future, the philologist's work is directed to a single moment of comprehension in the present. These are not mutually exclusive roles for Wilamowitz, but distinct aspects of a single program. The metaphor of the actor is obviously appropriate to a commentary on tragedy, but also suggests a deeper sense of philology as a performance—absorbing, enlightening, but perhaps evanescent.[27] The ultimate aim is pedagogical, "to

[23] There must be a hint in the phrase "in erhabenem Stile," as Wilamowitz was obviously aware of the association of tragedy with *das Erhabene*—but it is a faint one.

[24] Wilamowitz-Möllendorff, *Einleitung in die attische Tragödie*: 107–109. Further, see Markus C. Dubischar, "Wilamowitz and Sophocles: a classicist idol from the perspective of an anti-classicist admirer," in *Wilamowitz und kein Ende*, ed. Markus Mülke (Hildesheim: Olms, 2003), 69–75.

[25] Wilamowitz-Möllendorff, *Einleitung in die attische Tragödie*: 119.

[26] Ibid., 257. I am indebted to the discussion and translation of this passage in Güthenke, "The middle voice."

[27] Compare Nietzsche's description of an "artistic element" (*KGW* 2.1, 249) and comparison of the philologist to a virtuoso (268).

allow the modern reader the pleasure of the ancient auditor."[28] Philology as such, then, may be as much an art as a science.[29]

Classicists today are much more the descendants of Wilamowitz than of Nietzsche—and could not be otherwise. A conception of *Wissenschaft* is at the heart of the modern understanding of research in the humanities (though it is worth remembering that this conception is only two hundred years old). The particularity of philology is that it is not only a historical science, which sifts evidence, debates theories, and reaches conclusions, but also a way of approaching texts as if their significance can be reconstituted across temporal and spatial difference—as if they can be meaningful *for us*.[30] This possibility of meaning, even in the fairly minimal form propounded by Wilamowitz, is at the heart of the modernity of ancient literature, and differs from the kinds of meanings found in the eighteenth century and before. Reading in this way is anachronistic, as it involves types of attention that no ancient critic or audience seems to have thought worthwhile, and is connected to a notion of "literature" that is itself a recent invention. *Wissenschaft* and slow reading are distinct practices, with incompatible relations to history: "scientific" research tends to the goal of perspective-free knowledge of the past, while "literary" study tends towards an experience of meaningfulness in the present. Their coexistence in classical studies is rooted in a founding antinomy of the discipline, which defines its method historically and its object ahistorically (through the concept of the "classical," which draws arbitrary boundaries around cultures thought to be uniquely educative).[31] We can deplore the notion of a "classical" antiquity (as both Wilamowitz and Nietzsche do), but we cannot escape it when we find meaning in readings or performances of Greek tragedy. It is not, then, a question of whether we follow the path of Nietzsche or Wilamowitz, but of whether we recognize that the path we are already following is complex. As readers of classical literature, we are both historians and philologists. We can no more do without science than we can do without slow reading.

Wilamowitz's statement of the "specific philological task" helps also to frame a role for philosophy in reading Greek tragedy. Philosophy, like philology (in Wilamowitz's sense), is basically ahistorical; it can be conditioned

[28] Wilamowitz-Möllendorff, *Einleitung in die attische Tragödie*: 257.

[29] See Ingo Gildenhard, "*Philologia perennis*? Classical scholarship and functional differentiation," in *Out of Arcadia: classics and politics in Germany in the age of Burckhardt, Nietzsche and Wilamowitz*, ed. Ingo Gildenhard and Martin Ruehl (London: Institute of Classical Studies, 2003), 166–69. Gildenhard also notes how "Nietzschean" Wilamowitz can seem (187).

[30] On the tension between historicist and philological perspectives, see Goldhill, *Sophocles and the language of tragedy*: 259–63. I am using the terms somewhat differently, but to express a related antinomy—not that between "historical self-consciousness" and philological "value" (Goldhill's epistemological focus), but that between the practices of historical investigation and philological interpretation (my own methodological focus).

[31] See Porter, *Nietzsche and the philology of the future*: 265–73.

by history, but its assertions relate to meaning that is actualized in the present. Both philology and philosophy are ways of reading that seek a common space where ancient and modern might meet. This meeting can be more or less historically informed, but it is at heart inimical to history's effort to increase the real specificity of its image of antiquity. The young Nietzsche, in his 1869 inaugural lecture "Homer and Classical Philology" ("Homer und die klassische Philologie"), diagnosed precisely this tension:

> The entire scientific-artistic movement of this strange centaur [classical philology] strives with monstrous force, though with cyclopic slowness, at bridging the gulf between the ideal antiquity—which is perhaps only the most beautiful flower of the German love-longing for the south—and the real antiquity; and thus classical philology pursues nothing other than the final perfection of its ownmost being, the complete growing-together and becoming-one of the originally hostile basic drives that have only violently been brought together [und damit erstrebt die klassische Philologie nichts als die endliche Vollendung ihres eigensten Wesens, völliges Verwachsen und Einswerden der anfänglich feindseligen und nur gewaltsam zusammengebrachten Grundtriebe]. (*KGW* 2.1, 253)

The "centaur" of classical studies remains as strange as it was in 1869, even if we have become still less comfortable with notions of an "ideal antiquity" (which is not merely a creation of Teutonic, but of all modern longing). My suggestion—and where the philosophical perspective is necessary—is that we embrace this centauric (or paradoxical) quality of classical studies to think dialectically about the relation between the real and ideal antiquity. The pedagogical force of classical studies has always come from its duality of aims. It is the ideal antiquity that authorizes the care we spend in discovering the real antiquity, and the real antiquity that in turn shapes the ideal. This ideal is necessarily philosophical—not in the sense of proving any theory, idealist or otherwise, but in offering a vision of what is valuable in our own existence. Idealism has demonstrated ways of grasping the interrelation of philological and philosophical antiquities, and suggests approaches that mediate between tragedy's past and present meaning. Nietzsche's "confession of faith" (*Glaubensbekenntnis*) at the end of his lecture might describe the reality and the possibility of reading Greek tragedy today: *philosophia facta est quae philologia fuit.*

Bibliography

Acton, H. B. "Introduction." In *G.W.F. Hegel, Natural law: the scientific ways of treating natural law, its place in moral philosophy, and its relation to the positive sciences of law*, 9–47. Philadelphia: University of Pennsylvania Press, 1975.

Adler, Jeremy. "On tragedy: 'Notes on the Oedipus' and 'Notes on the Antigone.'" *Comparative Criticism* 5 (1983): 205–44.

Adorno, Theodor. "On the classicism of Goethe's Iphigenie." Translated by Shierry Weber Nicholsen. In *Notes to literature*, vol. 2, 153–70. New York: Columbia University Press, 1992.

Allemann, Beda. *Hölderlin und Heidegger*. Zürich: Atlantis, 1954.

Allen, William S. *Ellipsis: of poetry and the experience of language after Heidegger, Hölderlin, and Blanchot*. Albany: State University of New York Press, 2007.

Alt, Peter-André. *Tragödie der Aufklärung: eine Einführung*. Tübingen: Francke, 1994.

Alt, Peter-André. *Schiller: Leben—Werk—Zeit*. 2 vols. Munich: Beck, 2000.

———. "Subjektivierung, Ritual, implizite Theatralität: Hölderlins 'Empedokles'— Projekt und die Diskussion des antiken Opferbegriffs im 18. Jahhundert." *Hölderlin-Jahrbuch* 37 (2011): 30–67.

Ammon, Christoph Friederich. *Hekabe und Andromache: zwei Trauerspiele des Euripides*. Erlangen: Palm, 1789.

Barone, Paul. *Schiller und die Tradition des Erhabenen*. Berlin: Erich Schmidt, 2004.

Barret-Kriegel, Blandine. *La défaite de l'érudition*. Paris: Presses Universitaires de France, 1988.

Barth, Bernhard. *Schellings Philosophie der Kunst: göttliche Imagination und ästhetische Einbildungskraft*. Freiburg: Alber, 1991.

Batteux, Charles. "Observations sur l'Hippolyte d'Euripide et sur la Phèdre de Racine." *Mémoires de la littérature, tirez des registres de l'Académie Royale des inscriptions et belles lettres* 42 (1786): 452–72.

———. "Second mémoire sur la tragédie." *Mémoires de la littérature, tirez des registres de l'Académie Royale des inscriptions et belles lettres* 39 (1777): 71–90.

Bäuerle, Martin. *Kommunikation mit Texten: Studien zu Friedrich Schlegels Philologie*. Würzburg: Königshausen & Neumann, 2008.

Baumgarten, Alexander. *Meditationes philosophicae de nonnullis ad poema pertinentibus*. Halle: Grunert, 1735.

Behler, Ernst. "Einleitung: Friedrich Schlegels Studium-Aufsatz und der Ursprung der romantischen Literaturtheorie." In *Friedrich Schlegel, Über das Studium der griechischen Poesie: 1795–1797*, 13–128. Paderborn: Schöningh, 1981.

———. "A. W. Schlegel and the nineteenth-century *damnatio* of Euripides." *Greek, Roman, and Byzantine Studies* 27 (1986): 335–67.

Beiser, Frederick C. *Diotima's children: German aesthetic rationalism from Leibniz to Lessing*. Oxford: Oxford University Press, 2009.

———. *Enlightenment, revolution and romanticism: the genesis of modern German political thought, 1790–1800*. Cambridge, MA: Harvard University Press, 1992.

Beiser, Frederick C. *The fate of reason: German philosophy from Kant to Fichte.* Cambridge, MA: Harvard University Press, 1987.

——. *German Idealism: the struggle against subjectivism, 1781–1801.* Cambridge, MA: Harvard University Press, 2002.

——. *Schiller as philosopher: a re-examination.* Oxford: Oxford University Press, 2005.

Beissner, Friedrich. *Hölderlins Übersetzungen aus dem Griechischen.* Stuttgart: Metzler, 1961.

Belhalfaoui, Barbara. "Johann Gottfried Herder: Shakespeare—ein Vergleich der alten und der modernen Tragödie." *Deutsche Vierteljahrsschrift für Literaturwissenschaft und Geistesgeschichte* 61 (1987): 89–124.

Benjamin, Walter. *Ursprung des deutschen Trauerspiels.* In *Gesammelte Schriften* 1.1, edited by Rolf Tiedemann and Hermann Schweppenhäuser, 203–430. Frankfurt: Suhrkamp, 1974.

Bennholdt-Thomsen, Anke, and Alfredo Guzzoni. *Analecta Hölderliniana* 2: *Die Aufgabe des Vaterlands.* Würzburg: Königshausen & Neumann, 2004.

Berghahn, Klaus L. "'Das Pathetischerhabene'—Schillers Dramentheorie." In *Schiller: Ansichten eines Idealisten*, 27–58. Frankfurt: Athenäum, 1986.

Bertrand, Pierre. "Le sens du tragique et du destin dans la dialectique hégélienne." *Revue de Métaphysique et de Morale* 47 (1940): 165–86.

Betzwieser, Thomas. "Musical setting and scenic movement: chorus and 'chœur dansé' in eighteenth-century Parisian Opéra." *Cambridge Opera Journal* 12 (2000): 1–28.

Biet, Christian. *Œdipe en monarchie: tragédie et théorie juridique à l'âge classique.* Paris: Klincksieck, 1994.

Biet, Christian, and Susanne Saïd. "L'enjeu des notes: les traductions de l'Antigone de Sophocle au XVIIIe siècle." *Poétique* 58 (1984): 155–69.

Billings, Joshua. "'An alien body?' Choral autonomy around 1800." In *Choruses, ancient and modern*, edited by Joshua Billings, Felix Budelmann and Fiona Macintosh, 133–49. Oxford: Oxford University Press, 2013.

——. "Choral dialectics: Hölderlin and Hegel." In *Choral mediations in Greek tragedy*, edited by Renaud Gagné and Marianne Hopman, 317–38. Cambridge: Cambridge University Press, 2013.

——. "The ends of tragedy: *Oedipus at Colonus* and German Idealism." *Arion* 21 (2013): 111–29.

——. "Greek tragedy and *vaterländische Dichtkunst*." In *"Das Fremde im Eigensten": die Funktion von Übersetzungen im Prozess der deutschen Nationenbildung*, edited by Bernd Kortländer and Sikander Singh, 1–14. Tübingen: Narr, 2011.

——. "Hyperion's symposium: an erotics of reception." *Classical Receptions Journal* 2 (2010): 4–24.

Binder, Wolfgang. "Hölderlin und Sophokles." *Hölderlin-Jahrbuch* 16 (1972): 19–37.

Bishop, Paul, and R. H. Stephenson. *Friedrich Nietzsche and Weimar Classicism.* Rochester: Camden House, 2005.

Blumenberg, Hans. *Shipwreck with spectator: paradigm of a metaphor for existence.* Translated by Steven Rendall. Cambridge, MA: MIT Press, 1997.

Böckh, August. *Über die Antigone des Sophokles.* Berlin: Abhandlungen der Königlich Preussische Akademie der Wissenschaften, 1824.

Bodmer, Johann Jakob. *Kritische Betrachtungen über die poetischen Germälde der Dichter*. Zürich: Orell, 1741.

Böhler, Michael. "Die Zuschauerrolle in Schillers Dramaturgie: Zwischen Aussendruck und Innenlenkung." In *Friedrich Schiller: Kunst, Humanität und Politik in der späten Aufklärung*, edited by Wolfgang Wittkowski, 273–93. Tübingen: Niemeyer, 1982.

Bohrer, Karl Heinz. *Das absolute Präsens: die Semantik ästhetischer Zeit*. Frankfurt: Suhrkamp, 1994.

———. *Das Tragische: Erscheinung, Pathos, Klage*. Munich: Hanser, 2009.

Boileau Despréaux, Nicolas. *Oeuvres diverses du Sr Boileau Despreaux*. 2 vols. Paris: Thierry, 1701.

Böschenstein, Bernhard. *Frucht des Gewitters: Hölderlins Dionysos als Gott der Revolution*. Frankfurt: Insel, 1989.

Bourgeois, Bernard. *Hegel à Francfort, ou Judaïsme—Christianisme—Hegelianisme*. Paris: Vrin, 1970.

———. *Le droit naturel de Hegel (1802–1803): commentaire*. Paris: Vrin, 1986.

Bowie, Andrew. *Aesthetics and subjectivity: from Kant to Nietzsche*. 2nd ed. Manchester: Manchester University Press, 2003.

———. *Schelling and modern European philosophy: an introduction*. London: Routledge, 1993.

Boyle, Nicholas. *Goethe: the poet and the age*. Vol. 1: *The poetry of desire*. Oxford: Oxford University Press, 1992.

———. "Goethe's theory of tragedy." *Modern Language Review* 105 (2010): 1072–86.

Bradley, A.C. *Oxford lectures on poetry*. London: Macmillan, 1909.

Brague, Rémi. "Ein rätselhaftes Zitat über Aristoteles in Hölderlins 'Anmerkungen über Oedipus.'" In *Idealismus mit Folgen: die Epochenschwelle um 1800 zwischen Kunst und Geisteswissenschaften*, 69–74, edited by Hans-Jürgen Gawoll and Christoph Jamme. Munich: Fink, 1994.

Breitinger, Johann Jakob. *Critische Dichtkunst*. 2 vols. Zürich: Orell, 1740.

Brown, John. *A dissertation on the rise, union, and power, the progressions, separations, and corruptions, of poetry and music*. London: Davis and Reymers, 1763.

Brumoy, Pierre. *Le théâtre des Grecs*. 3 vols. Paris: Rollin, 1730.

Brumoy, Pierre, et al., ed. *Le théâtre des Grecs*. 13 vols. Paris: Cussac, 1785–89.

Brunck, Richard. *Sophoclis quae exstant omnia, cum veterum grammaticorum scholiis*. 2 vols. Strassburg: Treuttel, 1786.

Bubner, Rüdiger. "The 'religion of art.'" In *Hegel and the arts*, edited by Stephen Houlgate, 296–309. Evanston: Northwestern University Press, 2007.

Budelmann, Felix. "The reception of Sophocles' representation of physical pain." *American Journal of Philology* 128 (2007): 443–67.

Burian, Peter. "Gender and the city: *Antigone* from Hegel to Butler and back." In *When worlds elide: classics, politics, culture*, edited by Karen Bassi and J. Peter Euben, 255–99. Lexington: Lanham, 2010.

Burke, Edmund. *Reflections on the Revolution in France, and on the proceedings in certain societies in London relative to that event*. London: Dodsley, 1790.

Butler, Judith. *Antigone's claim: kinship between life and death*. New York: Columbia University Press, 2000.

Carter, D. M., ed. *Why Athens? A reappraisal of tragic politics.* Oxford: Oxford University Press, 2011.

Cave, Terence. *Recognitions: a study in poetics.* Oxford: Clarendon, 1988.

Clarke, M. L. *Greek studies in England, 1700–1830.* Cambridge: Cambridge University Press, 1945.

Commagre, Geneviève. "De l'avenir des Anciens: la polemique entre Mme Dacier et Houdar de La Motte." *Littératures classiques* 72 (2010): 145–56.

Constantine, David. *Hölderlin.* Oxford: Clarendon, 1988.

Corssen, Meta. "Die Tragödie als Begegnung zwischen Gott und Mensch." *Hölderlin-Jahrbuch* 3 (1949): 139–97.

Courtine, Jean François. "Tragedy and sublimity: the speculative interpretation of *Oedipus Rex* on the threshold of German Idealism." Translated by Jeffrey S. Librett. In *Of the sublime: presence in question*, 157–74. Albany: SUNY Press, 1993.

Couturier-Heinrich, Clémence. "Gottfried Hermann, un philologue kantien." *Revue germanique internationale* 14 (2011): 73–90.

Curtius, Michael Conrad. *Aristoteles Dichtkunst.* Hanover: Richter, 1753.

Dacier, André. *L'Oedipe et l'Electre de Sophocle: tragédies grecques.* Paris: Barbin, 1692.

———. *La Poëtique d'Aristote.* Paris: Barbin, 1692.

Daskarolis, Anastasia. *Die Wiedergeburt des Sophokles aus dem Geist des Humanismus: Studien zur Sophokles-Rezeption in Deutschland vom Beginn des 16. bis zur Mitte des 17. Jahrhunderts.* Tübingen: Niemeyer, 2000.

Dastur, Françoise. *Hölderlin: le retournement natal.* La Versanne: Encre Marine, 1997.

Dawe, Roger D. "Hermann and tragedy." In *Gottfried Hermann (1772–1848): internationales Symposium in Leipzig, 11.–13. Oktober 2007*, edited by Kurt Sier and Eva Wöckener-Gade, 255–64. Tübingen: Narr, 2010.

de Beistegui, Miguel. "Hegel: or the tragedy of thinking." In *Philosophy and tragedy*, edited by Miguel de Beistegui and Simon Sparks, 11–37. London: Routledge, 2000.

de Beistegui, Miguel, and Simon Sparks, eds. *Philosophy and tragedy.* London: Routledge, 2000.

DeJean, Joan E. *Ancients against moderns: culture wars and the making of a fin de siècle.* Chicago: University of Chicago Press, 1997.

Dickey, Laurence. *Hegel: religion, economics, and the politics of spirit, 1770–1807.* Cambridge: Cambridge University Press, 1987.

Diderot, Denis. *Le fils naturel, ou les epreuves de la vertu.* Amsterdam 1757.

Dubischar, Markus C. "Wilamowitz and Sophocles: a classicist idol from the perspective of an anti-classicist admirer." In *Wilamowitz und kein Ende*, edited by Markus Mülke, 51–86. Hildesheim: Olms, 2003.

Düsing, Klaus. "Ästhetischer Platonismus bei Hölderlin und Hegel." In *Homburg von der Höhe in der deutschen Geistesgeschichte: Studien zum Freundeskreis um Hegel und Hölderlin*, edited by Christoph Jamme and Otto Pöggeler, 101–17. Stuttgart: Klett-Cotta, 1981.

Düsing, Wolfgang. "Die Tragödientheorie des späten Herder." In *Johann Gottfried Herder, 1744–1803*, edited by Gerhard Sauder, 238–50. Hamburg: Meiner, 1987.

Eagleton, Terry. *Sweet violence: the idea of the tragic.* Oxford: Blackwell, 2003.

Edelstein, Dan. *The Enlightenment: a genealogy.* Chicago: University of Chicago Press, 2010.

Feger, Hans. *Poetische Vernunft: Moral und Ästhetik im Deutschen Idealismus*. Stuttgart: Metzler, 2007.

Ferris, David S. *Silent urns: Romanticism, Hellenism, modernity*. Stanford: Stanford University Press, 2000.

Flashar, Hellmut. *Inszenierung der Antike: das griechische Drama auf der Bühne*, 2nd ed. Munich: Beck, 2009.

Ford, Andrew. *The origins of criticism: literary culture and poetic theory in classical Greece*. Princeton: Princeton University Press, 2002.

Förster, Eckart. "'To lend wings to physics once again': Hölderlin and the 'Oldest System-Programme of German Idealism.'" *European Journal of Philosophy* 3 (1995): 174–98.

Forster, Michael N. *Hegel's idea of a phenomenology of spirit*. Chicago: University of Chicago Press, 1998.

———. "Herder and Spinoza." In *Spinoza and German Idealism*, edited by Eckart Förster and Yitzhak Y. Melamed, 59–84. Cambridge: Cambridge University Press, 2012.

Fóti, Véronique M. *Epochal discordance: Hölderlin's philosophy of tragedy*. Albany: State University of New York Press, 2006.

Foucault, Michel. "Nietzsche, genealogy, history." In *Essential works of Michel Foucault, 1954–84*. Vol. 2: *Aesthetics, method, and epistemology*, edited by James D. Faubion, 369–91. New York: New Press, 1998.

———. *The order of things: an archaeology of the human sciences*. London: Routledge, 2002.

Franco, Bernard. *Le despotisme du goût: débats sur le modèle tragique allemand en France, 1797–1814*. Göttingen: Wallstein, 2006.

Frank, Manfred. *Der kommende Gott: Vorlesungen über die neue Mythologie*. Frankfurt: Suhrkamp, 1982.

Fumaroli, Marc. "Les abeilles et les araignées." In *La querelle des anciens et des modernes: XVIIe–XVIIIe siècles*, edited by Anne-Marie Lecoq, 7–218. Paris: Gallimard, 2001.

Furth, Peter. "Antigone—oder zur tragischen Vorgeschichte der bürgerlichen Gesellschaft." *Hegel-Jahrbuch* 1984/5 (1988): 15–29.

Gadamer, Hans-Georg. *Wahrheit und Methode: Grundzüge einer philosophischen Hermeneutik. Gesammelte Werke* 1. Tübingen: Mohr Siebeck, 2010.

Gaier, Ulrich. "Hölderlins vaterländische Sangart." *Hölderlin-Jahrbuch* 25 (1987): 12–59.

———. "Volkspoesie, Nationalliteratur, Weltliteratur bei Herder." In *Die Europäische République des Lettres in der Zeit der Weimarer Klassik*, edited by Michael Knoche and Lea Ritter-Santini, 101–16. Göttingen: Wallstein, 2007.

Galle, Roland. "The disjunction of the tragic." In *Tragedy and philosophy*, edited by N. Georgopoulos, 39–56. Basingstoke: Macmillan, 1993.

Geary, Jason. "Reinventing the past: Mendelssohn's *Antigone* and the creation of an ancient Greek musical language." *Journal of Musicology* 23 (2006): 187–226.

Gedike, Friedrich. *Sophoclis Philoctetes graece*. Berlin: Mylius, 1781.

Gellrich, Michelle. *Tragedy and theory: the problem of conflict since Aristotle*. Princeton: Princeton University Press, 1988.

George, Theodore G. *Tragedies of spirit: tracing finitude in Hegel's Phenomenology*. Albany: State University of New York Press, 2006.

Gerstenberg, Heinrich Wilhelm von. *Briefe über Merkwürdigkeiten der Litteratur*. Reprint ed. Hildesheim: Olms, 1971.

Gethmann-Siefert, Annemarie. *Die Funktion der Kunst in der Geschichte: Untersuchungen zu Hegels Ästhetik*. Bonn: Bouvier, 1984.

———. *Einführung in Hegels Ästhetik*. Munich: Fink, 2005.

Gildenhard, Ingo. "*Philologia perennis?* Classical scholarship and functional differentiation." In *Out of Arcadia: classics and politics in Germany in the age of Burckhardt, Nietzsche and Wilamowitz*, edited by Ingo Gildenhard and Martin Ruehl, 161–203. London: Institute of Classical Studies, 2003.

Giuliani, Luca. "Naturalisierung der Kunst versus Historisierung der Kunst." In *Historicization-Historisierung*, edited by Glenn W. Most, 129–48. Göttingen: Vandenhoeck & Ruprecht, 2001.

Goessler, Lisette. "Zu Goethes *Iphigenie*." *Antike und Abendland* 18 (1973): 161–72.

Goldhagen, Eustachius Moritz. *Des Sophokles Trauerspiele*. Mitau: Hinz, 1777.

Goldhill, Simon. *Sophocles and the language of tragedy*. New York: Oxford University Press, 2012.

———. *Victorian culture and classical antiquity: art, opera, fiction, and the proclamation of modernity*. Princeton: Princeton University Press, 2011.

Goldhill, Simon, and Robin Osborne, eds. *Performance culture and Athenian democracy*. Cambridge: Cambridge University Press, 1999.

Görgemanns, Herwig. "Wilamowitz und die griechische Tragödie." In *Wilamowitz nach 50 Jahren*, edited by William M. Calder, Hellmut Flashar and Theodor Lindken, 130–50. Darmstadt: Wissenschaftliche Buchgesellschaft, 1985.

Görner, Rüdiger. *Hölderlins Mitte: zur Ästhetik eines Ideals*. Munich: iudicium, 1993.

Gottsched, Johann Christoph. *Versuch einer critischen Dichtkunst*. 4th ed. Leipzig: Breitkopf, 1751.

Grell, Chantal. *Le dix-huitième siècle et l'antiquité en France, 1680–1789*. Oxford: Voltaire Foundation, 1995.

Griffith, Mark. "Twelve principles for reading Greek tragedy." In *Why Athens? A reappraisal of tragic politics*, edited by D. M. Carter, 1–7. Oxford: Oxford University Press, 2011.

Grimm, Sieglinde. "Von der 'sentimentalischen Dichtung' zur 'Universalpoesie': Schiller, Friedrich Schlegel und die 'Wechselwirkung' Fichtes." *Jahrbuch der deutschen Schillergesellschaft* 43 (1999): 159–87.

Güthenke, Constanze. "The middle voice: German classical scholarship and the tragic Greek chorus." In *Choruses, ancient and modern*, edited by Joshua Billings, Felix Budelmann and Fiona Macintosh, 53–66. Oxford: Oxford University Press, 2013.

———. *Placing modern Greece: the dynamics of romantic Hellenism, 1770–1840*. Oxford: Oxford University Press, 2008.

———. "The potter's daughter's sons: German classical scholarship and the language of love circa 1800." *Representations* 109 (2010): 122–47.

Habermas, Jürgen. *Das Absolute und die Geschichte: von der Zwiespältigkeit in Schellings Denken*. Bonn: Bouvier, 1954.

Hall, Edith. *Adventures with Iphigenia in Tauris*. Oxford: Oxford University Press, 2013.

Hall, Edith, and Fiona Macintosh. *Greek tragedy and the British theatre, 1660–1914*. Oxford: Oxford University Press, 2005.

Halliwell, Stephen. *The aesthetics of mimesis: ancient texts and modern problems*. Princeton: Princeton University Press, 2002.

Hamacher, Werner. "(The end of art with the mask)." Translated by Kelly Barry. In *Hegel after Derrida*, edited by Stuart Barnett, 105–30. London: Routledge, 1998.

———. *Pleroma—reading in Hegel: the genesis and structure of a dialectical hermeneutics in Hegel*. Translated by Nicholas Walker and Simon Jarvis. London: Athlone, 1998.

Hammond, Paul. *The strangeness of tragedy*. Oxford: Oxford University Press, 2009.

Hansen, Frank-Peter. *"Das älteste Systemprogramm des deutschen Idealismus": Rezeptionsgeschichte und Interpretation*. Berlin: de Gruyter, 1989.

Hardimon, Michael O. *Hegel's social philosophy: the project of reconciliation*. Cambridge: Cambridge University Press, 1994.

Harloe, Katherine. "Pausanias as historian in Winckelmann's *History*." *Classical Receptions Journal* 2 (2010): 174–96.

———. *Winckelmann and the invention of antiquity*. Oxford: Oxford University Press, 2013.

Harris, H. S. *Hegel's development: night thoughts (Jena 1801–1806)*. Oxford: Clarendon, 1983.

———. *Hegel's development: toward the sunlight, 1770–1801*. Oxford: Clarendon, 1972.

Harrison, R. B. *Hölderlin and Greek literature*. Oxford: Clarendon, 1975.

Hartog, François. *Anciens, modernes, sauvages*. Paris: Galaade, 2005.

Häublein, Renata. *Die Entdeckung Shakespeares auf der deutschen Bühne des 18. Jahrhunderts*. Tübingen: Niemeyer, 2005.

Haugen, Kristine Louise. *Richard Bentley: poetry and enlightenment*. Cambridge, MA: Harvard University Press, 2011.

Heller, Erich. "Goethe and the avoidance of tragedy." In *The disinherited mind*, 37–63. New York: Harcourt Brace Jovanovich, 1975.

Hempel, Dirk. *Friedrich Leopold Graf zu Stolberg (1750–1819): Staatsmann und politischer Schriftsteller*. Weimar: Böhlau, 1997.

Henrich, Dieter. *Hegel im Kontext*. Rev. ed. Frankfurt: Suhrkamp, 2010.

———. "Philosophisch-theologische Problemlagen im Tübinger Stift zur Studienzeit Hegels, Hölderlins und Schellings." *Hölderlin-Jahrbuch* 25 (1987): 60–92.

Henrichs, Albert. "The last of the detractors: Friedrich Nietzsche's condemnation of Euripides." *Greek, Roman, and Byzantine Studies* 27 (1986): 369–97.

Hepp, Noémi. *Homère en France au XVIIe siècle*. Paris: Klincksieck, 1968.

Hermann, Gottfried. *Aristotelis de arte poetica liber cum commentariis*. Leipzig: Fleischer, 1802.

———. "De poeseos generibus." In *Opuscula* 1, 20–43. Leipzig: Fleischer, 1827.

———. *Handbuch der Metrik*. Leipzig: Fleischer, 1799.

Heydemann, Klaus. "Literarische Fingerübungen—oder mehr? Zur Geschichte der Sophokles-Übersetzungen im deutschen Sprachraum im 18. Jahrhundert." In *Übersetzung als Vermittlerin antiker Literatur*, edited by Wolfgang Kofler, Florian Schaffenrath, and Karlheinz Töchterle, 120–37. Innsbruck: StudienVerlag, 2009.

Hofmann, Michael. "Die unaufhebbare Ambivalenz historischer Praxis und die Poetik des Erhabenen in Friedrich Schillers *Wallenstein*-Trilogie." *Jahrbuch der deutschen Schillergesellschaft* 43 (1999): 241–65.

Holmes, Susanne. *Synthesis der Vielheit: die Begründung der Gattungstheorie bei August Wilhelm Schlegel.* Paderborn: Schöningh, 2006.

Hölscher, Uvo. *Empedokles und Hölderlin.* Frankfurt: Insel, 1965.

———. "Selbstgespräch über den Humanismus." In *Das nächste Fremde: von Texten der griechischen Frühzeit und ihrem Reflex in der Moderne,* 257–81. Munich: Beck, 1994.

Homann, Renate. *Erhabenes und Satirisches: zur Grundlegung einer Theorie ästhetischer Literatur bei Kant und Schiller.* Munich: Fink, 1977.

Honig, Bonnie. *Antigone, interrupted.* Cambridge: Cambridge University Press, 2013.

Houlgate, Stephen. *Hegel, Nietzsche, and the criticism of metaphysics.* Cambridge: Cambridge University Press, 1986.

Howard, Patricia. *Gluck: an eighteenth-century portrait in letters and documents.* Oxford: Clarendon, 1995.

Hühn, Helmut. *Mnemosyne: Zeit und Erinnerung in Hölderlins Denken.* Stuttgart: Metzler, 1997.

Hühn, Lore. "Die Philosophie des Tragischen: Schellings *Philosophische Briefe über Dogmatismus und Kriticismus.*" In *Die Realität des Wissens und das wirkliche Dasein: Erkenntnisbegründung und Philosophie des Tragischen beim frühen Schelling,* edited by Jörg Jantzen, 95–128. Stuttgart: frommann-holzboog, 1988.

Hyppolite, Jean. "Le tragique et le rationnel dans la philosophie de Hegel." *Hegel-Jahrbuch* (1964): 9–15.

Jacobs, Wilhelm G. *Zwischen Revolution und Orthodoxie? Schelling und seine Freunde im Stift und an der Universität Tübingen.* Stuttgart: frommann-holzboog, 1989.

Jacobshagen, Arnold. *Der Chor in der französischen Oper des späten Ancien Régime.* Frankfurt: Lang, 1997.

Jacquet, Louis. *Parallèle des tragiques Grecs et François.* Lyon: Duplain, 1760.

Jähnig, Dieter. *Schelling: die Kunst in der Philosophie.* 2 vols. Pfullingen: Neske, 1966/99.

Jamme, Christoph. *"Ein ungelehrtes Buch": die philosophische Gemeinschaft zwischen Hölderlin und Hegel in Frankfurt, 1797–1800.* Bouvier: Bonn, 1983.

Jamme, Christoph, and Helmut Schneider, eds. *Mythologie der Vernunft: Hegels "Ältestes Systemprogramm des deutschen Idealismus."* Frankfurt: Suhrkamp, 1984.

Jamme, Christoph, and Frank Völkel, eds. *Hölderlin und der deutsche Idealismus: Dokumente und Kommentare zu Hölderlins philosophischer Entwicklung und den philosophisch-kulturellen Kontexten seiner Zeit.* 4 vols. Stuttgart: frommann-holzboog 2003.

Janz, Rolf-Peter. "Antike und Moderne in Schillers *Braut von Messina.*" In *Unser commercium: Goethes und Schillers Literaturpolitik,* edited by Wilfried Barner, Eberhard Lämmert, and Norbert Oellers, 329–49. Stuttgart: Cotta, 1984.

Jaucourt, Louis. "Tragique." In *Encyclopédie ou dictionnaire raisonné des sciences, des arts et des métiers,* vol. 16, edited by Denis Diderot and Jean le Rond d'Alembert, 521. Paris: Briasson, 1765.

Jauß, Hans Robert. "Ästhetische Normen und geschichtliche Reflexion in der 'Querelle des anciens et des modernes.'" In *Charles Perrault, Parallèle des anciens et des modernes en ce qui regarde les arts et les sciences,* 8–64. Munich: Eidos, 1964.

———. "Schlegels und Schillers Replik auf die 'Querelle des anciens et des modernes.'" In *Literaturgeschichte als Provokation,* 67–106. Frankfurt: Suhrkamp, 1970.

Jenisch, Daniel. *Agamemnon, ein Trauerspiel.* Berlin, 1786.

Jessing, Benedikt. "Schillers Rezeption von Goethes *Iphigenie*." *Goethe-Jahrbuch* 122 (2005): 147–61.

Judet de la Combe, Pierre. *Les tragédies grecques sont-elles tragiques? Théâtre et théorie.* Montrouge: Bayard, 2010.

Julliard, Catherine. *Gottsched et l'esthétique théâtrale française: la réception allemande des théories françaises.* Bern: Lang, 1998.

Jurist, Eliot L. *Beyond Hegel and Nietzsche: philosophy, culture, and agency.* Cambridge, MA: MIT Press, 2000.

Kasper, Monika. *"Das Gesez von allen der König": Hölderlins Anmerkungen zum Oedipus und zur Antigonä.* Würzburg: Königshausen & Neumann, 2000.

Kittler, Friedrich A. *Discourse networks, 1800/1900.* Translated by Michael Metteer, with Chris Cullens. Stanford: Stanford University Press, 1990.

Kitzbichler, Josefine. "Von 1800 bis zur Mitte des 19. Jahrhunderts." In *Theorie der Übersetzungen antiker Literatur in Deutschland seit 1800*, 13–235. Berlin: de Gruyter, 2009.

Kivy, Peter. "What *really* happened in the eighteenth century: The 'modern system' re-examined (again)." *British Journal of Aesthetics* 52 (2012): 61–74.

Köhler, Johann Bernhard. *Iphigenia in Aulis: ein Trauerspiel des Euripides.* Berlin: Nicolai, 1778.

Kommerell, Max. *Lessing und Aristoteles: Untersuchung über die Theorie der Tragödie.* Frankfurt: Klostermann, 1957.

Korzeniewski, Uta. *"Sophokles! Die Alten! Philoktet!" Lessing und die antiken Dramatiker.* Konstanz: Universitätsverlag Konstanz, 2003.

Koselleck, Reinhart. *Futures past: on the semantics of historical time.* Translated by Keith Tribe. New York: Columbia University Press, 2004.

Krämer, Jörg. *Deutschsprachiges Musiktheater im späten 18. Jahrhundert: Typologie, Dramaturgie und Anthropologie einer populären Gattung.* Tübingen: Niemeyer, 1998.

Krell, David Farrell, ed. *Friedrich Hölderlin: The death of Empedocles, a mourning-play.* Albany: State University of New York Press, 2008.

———. *The tragic absolute: German Idealism and the languishing of God.* Bloomington: Indiana University Press, 2005.

Kreuzer, Johann. *Erinnerung: zum Zusammenhang von Hölderlins theoretischen Fragmenten "Das untergehende Vaterland . . ." und "Wenn der Dichter einmal des Geistes mächtig ist . . . ."* Königstein: Hain, 1981.

Kristeller, Paul Oskar. "The modern system of the arts: a study in the history of aesthetics." *Journal of the History of Ideas* 12–13 (1951–52): 496–527, 17–46.

La Harpe, Jean-François. *Philoctète.* Paris: Lambert and Baudouin, 1781.

Lacoue-Labarthe, Philippe. "The caesura of the speculative." In *Typography: mimesis, philosophy, politics* edited by Christopher Fynsk, 208–35. Cambridge, MA: Harvard University Press, 1989.

———. *Métaphrasis, suivi de le théâtre de Hölderlin.* Paris: Presses universitaires de France, 1998.

Lambropoulos, Vassilis. *The tragic idea.* London: Duckworth, 2006.

Lancaster, H Carrington. *French tragedy in the reign of Louis XVI and the early years of the French Revolution, 1774–1792.* Baltimore: Johns Hopkins Press, 1953.

Latacz, Joachim. "Schiller und die griechische Tragödie." In *Tragödie: Idee und Transformation* edited by Hellmut Flashar, 235–57. Stuttgart: Teubner, 1997.

Lear, Jonathan. *Open minded: working out the logic of the soul*. Cambridge, MA: Harvard University Press, 1999.

Lechevalier, Claire. "L'imaginaire de la représentation dans *Le Théâtre des Grecs* de Brumoy (1730)." *Anabases* 14 (2011): 75–86.

———. *L'invention d'une origine: traduire Eschyle en France de Lefranc de Pompignan à Mazon: le Prométhée enchaîné*. Paris: Champion, 2007.

Lennox, Charlotte. *The Greek theatre of Father Brumoy*. 3 vols London: Millar et al., 1759.

Leonard, Miriam. *Athens in Paris: ancient Greece and the political in postwar French thought*. Oxford: Oxford University Press, 2005.

———. *Socrates and the Jews: Hellenism and Hebraism from Moses Mendelssohn to Sigmund Freud*. Chicago: University of Chicago Press, 2012.

———. "Tragedy and the seductions of philosophy." *The Cambridge Classical Journal* 58 (2012): 145–64.

Lesure, François, ed. *Querelle des gluckistes et des piccinnistes: texte des pamphlets*. 2 vols. Geneva: Minkoff, 1984.

Leventhal, Robert S. *The disciplines of interpretation: Lessing, Herder, Schlegel and hermeneutics in Germany, 1750–1800*. Berlin: de Gruyter, 1994.

Lewis, Thomas A. *Religion, modernity, and politics in Hegel*. Oxford: Oxford University Press, 2011.

Loock, Reinhard. *Schwebende Einbildungskraft: Konzeptionen theoretischer Freiheit in der Philosophie Kants, Fichtes, und Schellings*. Würzburg: Königshausen & Neumann, 2007.

Louth, Charlie. *Hölderlin and the dynamics of translation*. Oxford: Legenda, 1998.

Lukács, Georg. *Der junge Hegel: ueber die Beziehungen von Dialektik und Oekonomie*. Zürich: Europa, 1948.

Lurie, Michael. "Facing up to tragedy: toward an intellectual history of Sophocles in Europe from Camerarius to Nietzsche." In *A companion to Sophocles* edited by Kirk Ormand, 440–61. Chichester: Blackwell, 2012.

Lurje, Michael. *Die Suche nach der Schuld: Sophokles' Oedipus Rex, Aristoteles' Poetik und das Tragödienverständnis der Neuzeit*. Munich: Saur, 2004.

Lypp, Bernhard. *Ästhetischer Absolutismus und politische Vernunft: zum Widerstreit von Reflexion und Sittlichkeit im deutschen Idealismus*. Frankfurt: Suhrkamp, 1972.

Magne, Bernard. *Crise de la littérature française sous Louis XIV: humanisme et nationalisme*. Toulouse: Université de Toulouse Le Mirail, 1976.

Maligne, Thierry. "La Harpe et la tragédie politique." *Littératures* 62 (2010): 45–58.

Marchand, Suzanne L. *Down from Olympus: archaeology and philhellenism in Germany, 1750–1970*. Princeton: Princeton University Press, 1996.

Martin, Nicholas. *Nietzsche and Schiller: untimely aesthetics*. Oxford: Clarendon, 1996.

Martindale, Charles, and Richard F. Thomas, eds. *Classics and the uses of reception*. Malden: Blackwell, 2006.

Martinec, Thomas. "Von der Tragödientheorie zur Philosophie des Tragischen: poetikgeschichtliche Skizze eines Umschwungs." *Jahrbuch der deutschen Schillergesellschaft* 49 (2005): 105–28.

Matuschek, Stefan. "Winckelmänner der Poesie: Herders und Friedrich Schlegels Anknüpfung an die *Geschichte der Kunst des Altertums*." *Deutsche Vierteljahrsschrift für Literaturwissenschaft und Geistesgeschichte* 77 (2003): 548–63.

Mee, Erin B., and Helene P. Foley, eds. *Antigone on the contemporary world stage*. Oxford: Oxford University Press, 2011.

Meid, Christopher. *Die griechische Tragödie im Drama der Aufklärung: "Bei den Alten in die Schule gehen."* Tübingen: Narr, 2008.

Menke, Christoph. *Tragic play: irony and theater from Sophocles to Beckett*. Translated by James Phillips. New York: Columbia University Press, 2009.

———. *Tragödie im Sittlichen: Gerechtigkeit und Freiheit nach Hegel*. Frankfurt: Suhrkamp, 1996.

Michel, Wilhelm. *Hölderlins abendländische Wendung*. Weimar: Feuerverlag, 1922.

Millán-Zaibert, Elizabeth. *Friedrich Schlegel and the emergence of romantic philosophy*. Albany: State University of New York Press, 2007.

Most, Glenn W. "Classical scholarship and literary criticism." In *The Cambridge history of literary criticism*. Vol. 4: *The eighteenth century*, edited by H. B. Nisbet and Claude Rawson, 742–57. Cambridge: Cambridge University Press, 1997.

———. "Generating genres: the idea of the tragic." In *Matrices of genre: authors, canons, and society*, edited by Mary Depew and Dirk Obbink, 15–36. Cambridge, MA: Harvard University Press, 2000.

———, ed. *Historicization-Historisierung*. Göttingen: Vandenhoeck & Ruprecht, 2001.

———. "Karl Otfried Müller's edition of Aeschylus' *Eumenides*." In *Zwischen Rationalismus und Romantik: Karl Otfried Müller und die antike Kultur*, edited by William M. Calder and Renate Schlesier, 349–73. Hildesheim: Weidmann, 1998.

———. "Schlegel, Schlegel und die Geburt eines Tragödienparadigmas." *Poetica* 25 (1993): 155–75.

———. "The second Homeric Renaissance: allegoresis and genius in early modern poetics." In *Genius: the history of an idea*, edited by Penelope Murray, 54–75. Oxford: Blackwell, 1989.

Mueller, Martin. *Children of Oedipus, and other essays on the imitation of Greek tragedy, 1550–1800*. Toronto: University of Toronto Press, 1980.

Müller, Joachim. "Choreographische Strategie: zur Funktion der Chöre in Schillers Tragödie *Die Braut von Messina*." In *Friedrich Schiller, Angebot und Diskurs: Zugänge—Dichtung—Zeitgenossenschaft*, edited by Helmut Brandt, 431–48. Berlin: Aufbau, 1987.

Müller, K. O. *Aeschylos Eumeniden: griechisch und deutsch mit erläuternden Abhandlungen über die äussere Darstellung, und über den Inhalt und die Composition dieser Tragödie*. Göttingen: Dieterich, 1833.

Müller, Urs. *Feldkontakte, Kulturtransfer, kulturelle Teilhabe: Winckelmanns Beitrag zur Etablierung des deutschen intellektuellen Felds durch den Transfer der "Querelle des anciens et des modernes."* Leipzig: Leipziger Universitätsverlag, 2005.

Mulsow, Martin, and Marcelo Stamm, eds. *Konstellationsforschung*. Frankfurt: Suhrkamp, 2005.

Norman, Larry F. *The shock of the ancient: literature & history in early modern France*. Chicago: University of Chicago Press, 2011.

Northeast, Catherine M. *The Parisian Jesuits and the Enlightenment, 1700–1762*. Oxford: Voltaire Foundation, 1991.

Norton, Robert E. *Herder's aesthetics and the European Enlightenment*. Ithaca: Cornell University Press, 1991.

Nussbaum, Martha C. *The fragility of goodness: luck and ethics in Greek tragedy and philosophy*. Rev. ed. Cambridge: Cambridge University Press, 2001.

Nuttall, A. D. *Why does tragedy give pleasure?* Oxford: Clarendon, 1996.

Oergel, Maike. *Culture and identity: historicity in German literature and thought, 1770–1815*. Berlin: de Gruyter, 2006.

Orfanos, Charalampos. "La critique suspendue: le P. Brumoy et l'histoire." *Anabases* 14 (2011): 43–59.

Pascal, Jean-Noël. "De la somme à l'encyclopédie: parcours à travers un siècle d'éditions du *Théâtre des Grecs* (1730–1826)." *Anabases* 14 (2011): 113–31.

Paulin, Roger. *The critical reception of Shakespeare in Germany, 1682–1914: native literature and foreign genius*. Hildesheim: Olms, 2003.

Perrault, Charles. "Critique de l'Opera, ou Examen de la tragédie intitulée Alceste." In *Alceste, suivi de La querelle d'Alceste: anciens et modernes avant 1680*, edited by William Brooks, Buford Norman, and Jeanne Morgan Zarucchi, 77–102. Genève: Droz, 1994.

———. *Parallèle des anciens et des modernes en ce qui régarde les arts et les sciences*. 4 vols. Paris: Coignard, 1688–97. Reprint ed. Munich: Eidos, 1964.

Petersen, Uwe. *Goethe und Euripides: Untersuchungen zur Euripides-Rezeption in der Goethezeit*. Heidelberg: Winter, 1974.

Pinkard, Terry. *German philosophy, 1750–1860: the legacy of Idealism*. Cambridge: Cambridge University Press, 2002.

———. *Hegel: a biography*. Cambridge: Cambridge University Press, 2000.

———. *Hegel's Phenomenology: the sociality of reason*. Cambridge: Cambridge University Press, 1994.

Pippin, Robert B. *Hegel's idealism: the satisfactions of self-consciousness*. Cambridge: Cambridge University Press, 1988.

———. *Idealism as modernism: Hegelian variations*. Cambridge: Cambridge University Press, 1997.

———. *Modernism as a philosophical problem: on the dissatisfactions of European high culture*. 2nd ed. Malden: Blackwell, 1999.

Plumpe, Gerhard. *Ästhetische Kommunikation der Moderne I: Von Kant bis Hegel*. Opladen: Westdeutscher Verlag, 1993.

Pöggeler, Otto. *Hegels Idee einer Phänomenologie des Geistes*. Freiburg: Alber, 1973.

Porter, James I. *The invention of Dionysus: an essay on The birth of tragedy*. Stanford: Stanford University Press, 2000.

———. "Is art modern? Kristeller's 'modern system of the arts' reconsidered." *British Journal of Aesthetics* 49 (2009): 1–24.

———. *Nietzsche and the philology of the future*. Stanford: Stanford University Press, 2000.

———. "Tragedy and the catharsis of modernity." In *Tragedy and the idea of modernity*, edited by Joshua Billings and Miriam Leonard. Oxford: Oxford University Press, forthcoming.

Potts, Alex. *Flesh and the ideal: Winckelmann and the origins of art history*. New Haven: Yale University Press, 1994.

Prévost, Pierre. *Les tragédies d'Euripide*. 3 vols. Paris: Pissot, 1782.

Prignitz, Christoph. *Hölderlins Empedokles: die Vision einer erneuerten Gesellschaft und ihre zeitgeschichtlichen Hintergründe*. Hamburg: Buske, 1985.

Primoratz, Igor. *Banquos Geist: Hegels Theorie der Strafe*. Bonn: Bouvier, 1986.

Pugh, David. *Dialectic of love: Platonism in Schiller's aesthetics*. Montreal & Kingston: McGill-Queen's University Press, 1996.

Racine, Louis. "Comparaison de l'Iphigénie d'Euripide avec l'Iphigénie de Racine." *Mémoires de la littérature, tirez des registres de l'Académie Royale des inscriptions et belles lettres* 8 (1733): 288–99.

———. "Reflexions sur l'Andromaque d'Euripide et sur l'Andromaque de Racine." *Mémoires de la littérature, tirez des registres de l'Académie Royale des inscriptions et belles lettres* 10 (1736): 311–22.

Rapin, René. *Reflexions sur la Poetique d'Aristote, et sur les ouvrages des Poetes anciens & modernes*. Paris: Muguet, 1674.

Reichard, Georg. *August Wilhelm Schlegels "Ion": das Schauspiel und die Aufführungen unter der Leitung von Goethe und Iffland*. Bonn: Bouvier, 1987.

Reinhardt, Hartmut. "Schillers *Wallenstein* und Aristoteles." *Jahrbuch der deutschen Schillergesellschaft* 20 (1976): 278–337.

Riedel, Wolfgang. "'Weltgeschichte ein erhabenes Objekt': zur Modernität von Schillers Geschichtsdenken." In *Prägnanter Moment: Studien zur deutschen Literatur der Aufklärung und Klassik*, edited by Peter-André Alt, Alexander Kosenina, Hartmut Reinhardt and Wolfgang Riedel, 193–214. Würzburg: Königshausen & Neumann, 2002.

Ritzer, Monika. "Not und Schuld: zur Funktion 'antiken' Schicksalsbegriffs in Schillers *Braut von Messina*." In *Schiller heute*, edited by Hans-Jörg Knobloch and Helmut Koopmann, 131–50. Tübingen: Stauffenburg, 1996.

Roche, Mark William. *Tragedy and comedy: a systematic study and a critique of Hegel*. Albany: State University of New York Press, 1998.

Rochefort, Guillaume Dubois de. "Discours sur l'objet et l'art de la tragédie grecque." In *Le théâtre des Grecs*, edited by Pierre Brumoy et al., 1, 215–68. Paris: Cussac, 1785.

———. "Mémoires sur les moeurs des siècles heroïques." *Mémoires de la littérature, tirez des registres de l'Académie Royale des inscriptions et belles lettres* 36 (1774): 396–481.

———. "Premier mémoire sur l'objet de la tragédie chez les Grecs." *Mémoires de la littérature, tirez des registres de l'Académie Royale des inscriptions et belles lettres* 39 (1777): 125–58.

———. *Théatre de Sophocle*. 2 vols. Paris: Nyon, 1788.

Schadewaldt, Wolfgang. "Antikes und modernes in Schillers *Braut von Messina*." *Jahrbuch der deutschen Schillergesellschaft* 13 (1969): 286–307.

———. "Hölderlins Übersetzung des Sophokles." In *Hellas und Hesperien*, vol. 2, 275–332. Zürich: Artemis, 1970.

Schäfer, Gerhard. "Der spekulative württembergische Pietismus des 18. Jahrhunderts —Systeme und Ausstrahlung." In *Hölderlin und Nürtingen*, edited by Peter Härtling and Gerhard Kurz, 48–78. Stuttgart: Metzler, 1994.

Scheier, Claus-Artur. "Kants dritte antinomie und die Genese des tragischen Gedankens: Schelling 1795–1809." *Philosophisches Jahrbuch* 103 (1996): 76–89.

Schings, Hans-Jürgen. *Der mitleidigste Mensch ist der beste Mensch: Poetik des Mitleids von Lessing bis Büchner*. Munich: Beck, 1980.

Schlegel, Johann Elias. *Werke*, edited by J. H. Schlegel. 5 vols. Leipzig: Mumm, 1764–73.

Schlosser, Johann Georg. *Prometheus in Fesseln, aus dem Griechischen des Aeschylus.* Basel: Thurneysen, 1784.

Schmidt, Dennis J. *On Germans and other Greeks: tragedy and ethical life.* Bloomington: Indiana University Press, 2001.

Schmidt, Jochen. *Die Geschichte des Genie-Gedankens in der deutschen Literatur, Philosophie und Politik, 1750–1945.* 3rd ed. Heidelberg: Winter, 2004.

———. "Tragödie und Tragödientheorie: Hölderlins Sophokles-Deutung." *Hölderlin-Jahrbuch* 29 (1995): 64–81.

Schmitt, Arbogast. "Zur Aristoteles-Rezeption in Schillers Theorie des Tragischen." In *Antike Dramentheorien und ihre Rezeption,* edited by Bernhard Zimmermann, 191–212. Stuttgart: M & P Verlag für Wissenschaft und Forschung, 1992.

Schramm, Michael. "Hermann und Kant: Philologie als (Kantische) Wissenschaft." In *Gottfried Hermann (1772–1848): internationales Symposium in Leipzig, 11.–13. Oktober 2007,* edited by Kurt Sier and Eva Wöckener-Gade, 83–121. Tübingen: Narr, 2010.

Schulte, Michael. *Die "Tragödie im Sittlichen": zur Dramentheorie Hegels.* Munich: Fink, 1992.

Schwinge, Ernst-Richard. *"Ich bin nicht Goethe": Johann Gottfried Herder und die Antike.* Hamburg: Joachim Jungius-Gesellschaft der Wissenschaften, 1999.

———. "Schiller und die griechische Tragödie." In *Schiller und die Antike,* edited by Paolo Chiarini and Walter Hinderer, 15–48. Würzburg: Königshausen & Neumann, 2008.

Senarclens, Vanessa de. "Éditer le théâtre antique grec au siècle des Lumières: *Le Théatre des Grecs* de Pierre Brumoy (1730) et ses nombreuses rééditions au cours du dix-huitième siècle." In *Die Antike in der Moderne: vom Umgang mit der Antike im Europa des 18. Jahrhunders,* edited by Veit Elm, Günther Lottes, and Vanessa de Senarclens, 243–58. Hanover: Wehrhahn, 2009.

Shapiro, Gary. "An ancient quarrel in Hegel's *Phenomenology.*" *The Owl of Minerva* 17 (1986): 165–80.

Sharpe, Lesley. "Schiller and Goethe's *Iphigenie.*" *Proceedings of the English Goethe Society* 54 (1985): 101–22.

Shaw, Devin Zane. *Freedom and nature in Schelling's philosophy of art.* London: Continuum, 2010.

Silk, M. S., ed. *Tragedy and the tragic: Greek theatre and beyond.* Oxford: Oxford University Press, 1996.

Silk, M. S., and J. P. Stern. *Nietzsche on tragedy.* Cambridge: Cambridge University Press, 1981.

Simonsuuri, Kirsti. *Homer's original genius: eighteenth-century notions of the early Greek epic (1688–1798).* Cambridge: Cambridge University Press, 1979.

Solger, Karl Wilhelm Ferdinand. "Beurtheilung der Vorlesungen über dramatische Kunst und Literatur." In *Nachgelassene Schriften und Briefwechsel,* Vol. 2, 493–628. Leipzig: Brockhaus, 1826.

———. *Des Sophokles Tragödien.* 2 vols. Berlin: Realschulbuchhandlung, 1808.

Sonenscher, Michael. *Sans-culottes: an eighteenth-century emblem in the French Revolution.* Princeton: Princeton University Press, 2008.

Speight, Allen. *Hegel, literature, and the problem of agency.* Cambridge: Cambridge University Press, 2001.

————. "Tragedy and the human image: German Idealism's legacy for theory and practice." In *The impact of Idealism: the legacy of post-Kantian German thought*, vol. 3, edited by Nicholas Boyle, Liz Disley, Christoph Jamme, and Ian Cooper. Cambridge: Cambridge University Press, 2013.

Steffens, Johann Heinrich. *Oedipus: ein Trauerspiel in Versen nach den Sophocles eingerichtet.* Zelle: Gsellius, 1746.

Steinbrüchel, Johann Jacob. *Das tragische Theater der Griechen.* 2 vols. Zürich: Gessner, 1763.

Steiner, George. *Antigones.* Oxford: Clarendon, 1984.

————. *The death of tragedy.* London: Faber and Faber, 1961.

Stolberg, Christian zu. *Sofokles.* 2 vols. Leipzig: Göschen, 1787.

Stolberg, Friedrich Leopold zu. *Vier Tragödien des Aeschylos.* Hamburg: Perthes and Besser, 1802.

Stoneman, Richard. "'A crazy enterprise': German translators of Sophocles, from Opitz to Boeckh." In *Sophocles revisited: essays presented to Sir Hugh Lloyd-Jones,* edited by Jasper Griffin, 307–29. Oxford: Oxford University Press, 1999.

Süvern, W. *Über Schillers Wallenstein in Hinsicht auf griechische Tragödie.* Berlin: Königliche Realschule, 1800.

Szondi, Peter. "Antike und Moderne in der Ästhetik der Goethezeit." In *Poetik und Geschichtsphilosophie I,* edited by Senta Metz and Hans-Hagen Hildebrandt, 11–265. Frankfurt: Suhrkamp, 1974.

————. *An essay on the tragic.* Translated by Paul Fleming. Stanford: Stanford University Press, 2002.

————. "Schellings Gattungspoetik." In *Poetik und Geschichtsphilosophie II,* edited by Wolfgang Fietkau, 185–307. Frankfurt: Suhrkamp, 1974.

————. "Überwindung des Klassizismus: der Brief an Böhlendorff vom 4. Dezember 1801." In *Schriften I,* 345–66. Frankfurt: Suhrkamp, 1978.

Taminiaux, Jacques. *Le théâtre des philosophes: la tragédie, l'être, l'action.* Grenoble: Millon, 1995.

Torbruegge, Marilyn K. "Bodmer and Longinus." *Monatshefte* 63 (1971): 341–57.

Trousson, Raymond. "Le Théâtre tragique grec au siècle des Lumières." *Studies on Voltaire and the Eighteenth Century* 155 (1976): 2033–47.

Verene, Donald Phillip. *Hegel's recollection: a study of images in the Phenomenology of Spirit.* Albany: State University of New York Press, 1985.

Vernant, Jean-Pierre, and Pierre Vidal-Naquet. *Myth and tragedy in ancient Greece.* Translated by Janet Lloyd. New York: Zone, 1990.

Völher, Martin. *Pindarrezeptionen: sechs Studien zum Wandel des Pindarverständnisses von Erasmus bis Herder.* Heidelberg: Winter, 2005.

Voltaire, François Marie Arouet de. *Le siècle de Louis XIV.* 2 vols. Leipzig: Francheville, 1754.

Wanning, Berbeli. *Konstruktion und Geschichte: das Identitätssytem als Grundlage der Kunstphilosophie bei F.W.J. Schelling.* Frankfurt: Haag + Herchen, 1988.

Weilenmann, Anton. *Das aufgeklärte Zürich in seinem Verhältnis zur Antike.* Winterthur: Keller, 1961.

Weissberg, Liliane. "Language's wound: Herder, Philoctetes, and the origin of speech." *Modern Language Notes* 104 (1989): 548–79.

Welcker, Friedrich Gottlieb. "Über den Ajas des Sophokles." *Rheinisches Museum* 3 (1829): 43–92.

Wieland, Christoph Martin. "Versuch über das Teutsche Singspiel und einige dahin einschlagende Gegenstände." *Teutsche Merkur* (1775): 3, 63–87 and 4, 156–73.

Wilamowitz-Möllendorff, Ulrich von. *Euripides Herakles I: Einleitung in die attische Tragödie*. Berlin: Weidmann, 1889.

———. *Zukunftsphilologie! Eine Erwiderung auf Friedrich Nietzsches "Geburt der Tragödie."* Berlin: Borntraeger, 1872.

Wild, Christopher. "Geburt der Theaterreform aus dem Geist der Theaterfeindlichkeit: Der Fall Gottsched." *Lessing Yearbook / Jahrbuch* 34 (2002): 57–77.

Williamson, George S. *The longing for myth in Germany: religion and aesthetic culture from Romanticism to Nietzsche*. Chicago: University of Chicago Press, 2004.

Wilm, Marie-Christin. "Die 'Construction der Tragödie': zum Bedingungsverhältnis von Tragischem und Ästhetischem in Goethes Tragödientheorie." *Goethe-Jahrbuch* 123 (2006): 39–53.

———. "Ultima Katharsis: zur Transformation des aristotelischen Tragödiensatzes nach 1800." In *Die Tragödie der Moderne: Gattungsgeschichte—Kulturtheorie—Epochendiagnose*, edited by Daniel Fulda and Thorsten Valk, 85–105. Berlin: de Gruyter, 2010.

Wilmer, S. E., and Audronė Žukauskaitė, eds. *Interrogating Antigone in postmodern philosophy and criticism*. Oxford: Oxford University Press, 2010.

Winckelmann, Johann Joachim. *Gedanken über die Nachahmung der Griechischen Werke in der Malerey und Bildhauerkunst*, 2nd ed. Dresden: Walther, 1756.

———. *History of the art of antiquity*. Translated by Harry Francis Mallgrave. Los Angeles: Getty Publications, 2006.

Winkler, John J., and Froma I. Zeitlin, eds. *Nothing to do with Dionysos? Athenian drama in its social context*. Princeton: Princeton University Press, 1990.

Wolff, Eugen. *Johann Elias Schlegel*. Berlin: Oppenheim, 1889.

Yilmaz, Levent. *Le temps moderne: variations sur les Anciens et les contemporains*. Paris: Gallimard, 2004.

Young, Edward. *Conjectures on original composition: in a letter to the author of Sir Charles Grandison*. London: Millar and Dodsley, 1759.

Young, Julian. *The philosophy of tragedy: from Plato to Žižek*. Cambridge: Cambridge University Press, 2013.

Zammito, John H. *Kant, Herder, and the birth of anthropology*. Chicago: University of Chicago Press, 2002.

Zanucchi, Mario. "Die 'Inokulation des unvermeidlichen Schicksals': Schicksal und Tragik in Schillers *Wallenstein*." *Jahrbuch der deutschen Schillergesellschaft* 50 (2006): 150–75.

Zelle, Carsten. *Die doppelte Ästhetik der Moderne: Revisionen des Schönen von Boileau bis Nietzsche*. Stuttgart: Metzler, 1995.

———. "Erhabene Weltuntergänge im Kleinen: Über Schiffbrüche und Schlachten vor Zuschauer." In *Il gesto, il bello, il sublime: Arte e letteratura in Germania '700 e '800*, edited by Emilio Bonfatti, 77–111. Rome: Artemide, 1997.

Zimmermann, Bernhard. "Teoria e utilizzo del coro in Friedrich Schiller." In *". . . un enorme individuo, dotato di polmoni soprannaturali": Funzioni, interpretazioni, e rinascite del coro drammatico greco*, edited by Andrea Rodighiero and Paolo Scattolin, 291–305. Verona: Edizioni Fiorini, 2011.

Index

Made in the USA
Monee, IL
29 April 2020